AF479272

MACHINE
INTELLIGENCE 14

MACHINE INTELLIGENCE

Machine Intelligence 1 (1967) (eds N. Collins and D. Michie) Oliver & Boyd, Edinburgh

Machine Intelligence 2 (1968) (eds E. Dale and D. Michie) Oliver & Boyd, Edinburgh

(1 and 2 published as one volume in 1971 by Edinburgh University Press) (eds N. Collins, E. Dale and D. Michie)

Machine Intelligence 3 (1968) (ed D. Michie) Edinburgh University Press, Edinburgh

Machine Intelligence 4 (1969) (eds B. Meltzer and D. Michie) Edinburgh University Press, Edinburgh

Machine Intelligence 5 (1970) (eds B. Meltzer and D. Michie) Edinburgh University Press, Edinburgh

Machine Intelligence 6 (1971) (eds B. Meltzer and D. Michie) Edinburgh University Press, Edinburgh

Machine Intelligence 7 (1972) (eds B. Meltzer and D. Michie) Edinburgh University Press, Edinburgh

Machine Intelligence 8 (1977) (eds E. W. Elcock and D. Michie) Ellis Horwood, Chichester/Halsted, New York

Machine Intelligence 9 (1979) (eds J. E. Hayes, D. Michie and L. Mikulich) Ellis Horwood, Chichester/Halsted, New York

Machine Intelligence 10 (1982) (eds J. E. Hayes, D. Michie and Y.-H. Pao) Ellis Horwood, Chichester/Halsted, New York

Machine Intelligence 11 (1988) (eds J. E. Hayes, D. Michie and J. Richards) Oxford University Press, Oxford

Machine Intelligence 12 (1991) (eds J. E. Hayes, D. Michie and E. Tyugu) Oxford University Press, Oxford

Machine Intelligence 13 (1994) (eds K. Furukawa, D. Michie and S. Muggleton) Oxford University Press, Oxford

Machine Intelligence 14 (1995) (eds K. Furukawa, D. Michie and S. Muggleton) Oxford University Press, Oxford

Donald Michie

MACHINE INTELLIGENCE 14

Applied Machine Intelligence

edited by

K. FURUKAWA

Keio University, Tokyo

D. MICHIE

Emeritus Professor, Edinburgh University

and

S. MUGGLETON

Oxford University Computing Laboratory

CLARENDON PRESS · OXFORD
1995

Oxford University Press, Walton Street, Oxford OX2 6DP

Oxford   New York
Athens   Auckland   Bangkok   Bombay
Calcutta   Cape Town   Dar es Salaam   Delhi
Florence   Hong Kong   Istanbul   Karachi
Kuala Lumpur   Madras   Madrid   Melbourne
Mexico City   Nairobi   Paris   Singapore
Taipei   Tokyo   Toronto
and associated companies in
Berlin   Ibadan

Oxford is a trade mark of Oxford University Press

Published in the United States
by Oxford University Press Inc., New York

© *K. Furukawa, D. Michie, and S. Muggleton and individual contributors, 1995*

All rights reserved. No part of this publication may be
reproduced, stored in a retrieval system, or transmitted, in any
form or by any means, without the prior permission in writing of Oxford
University Press. Within the UK, exceptions are allowed in respect of any
fair dealing for the purpose of research or private study, or criticism or
review, as permitted under the Copyright, Designs and Patents Act, 1988, or
in the case of reprographic reproduction in accordance with the terms of
licences issued by the Copyright Licensing Agency. Enquiries concerning
reproduction outside those terms and in other countries should be sent to
the Rights Department, Oxford University Press, at the address above.

This book is sold subject to the condition that it shall not,
by way of trade or otherwise, be lent, re-sold, hired out, or otherwise
circulated without the publisher's prior consent in any form of binding
or cover other than that in which it is published and without a similar
condition including this condition being imposed
on the subsequent purchaser.

A catalogue record for this book is available from the British Library

Library of Congress Cataloging in Publication Data
(Data applied for)

ISBN 0 19 853860 X

Typeset by the authors using LaTeX
Printed in Great Britain by
Biddles Ltd., Guildford, Surrey

PREFACE

The 14th Machine Intelligence workshop has special significance since it commenced on Donald Michie's 70th birthday (11th November, 1993). Michie has had a distinguished scientific career of the highest order. During the Second World War he worked on machine-oriented cryptography at Bletchley Park, where his friends and associates included I.J. Good and Alan Turing. As is well known, Turing not only laid the theoretical grounds for modern digital computing but was also one of the most influential forefathers of research into Machine Intelligence. Turing's discussions with Donald Michie and Jack Good concerning the possibility of Machine Intelligence inspired Michie's later involvement in the subject.

After the war, Michie trained as a geneticist and during the 1950's carried out award-winning work that led to today's medical and agricultural uses of intra-uterine embryo transfer. In the early 1960's Michie founded the first University department and teaching course in Machine Intelligence. Its lineal successor, the Department of Artificial Intelligence, is still the strongest in this area within the UK. At Edinburgh Michie headed the team that built, programmed and demonstrated the world's first non-trivial assembly robot. Michie has also made substantial contributions to graph search and statistically-based machine learning.

Donald Michie has been editor-in-chief of the Machine Intelligence series since the 1960's. The series contains many of the classic papers of the Artificial Intelligence literature. To mark the practical orientation of Michie's scientific contributions, the theme of this volume is 'Applied Machine Intelligence'. Many of the papers reflect Donald Michie's continuing interests in Machine Learning, Biology, Robotics and Control.

August 1994

Stephen Muggleton
Executive Editor

ACKNOWLEDGEMENTS

The Machine Intelligence 14 workshop was generously supported by the Daiwa Anglo-Japanese Foundation under an agreement concluded in 1991 between the Turing Institute, UK and the Japan Society for Artificial Intelligence, Tokyo. The Foundation provided funding, covering Workshops 13 and 14, to defray travel and attendance costs for six Japanese and six British scientists nominated by the respective parties. The Daiwa Anglo-Japanese Foundation has recently announced its intention to extend its support to Workshop 15, which will be held in July 1995 at St. Catherine's College Oxford. Hitachi kindly provided support and facilities by allowing the Machine Intelligence 14 workshop to be held at its spacious Advanced Research Laboratory near Tokyo. Like its predecessor, Machine Intelligence 13, this volume reflects the vigour with which the subject is being advanced in Japan.

Thanks are also due to the Oxford University Computing Laboratory for kindly allowing use of printing and document preparation facilities in the production of this volume, and to David Page for his work in producing the final camera-ready pages.

CONTENTS

COMPLEX DECISION TAKING

1

Game Mastery and Intelligence

Donald Michie

University of Edinburgh, UK

Abstract

'Brute force' programs unable to understand or explain what they are doing have begun to hold their own with world-class human players in chess, checkers ('draughts'), backgammon, Go-Moku and Othello. AI workers have been obliged to ponder the separability of three phases of problem-solving behaviour:

1. prior research and plan-formation;
2. runtime performance, including planning on the fly;
3. rationalizing the actions taken and the solutions found.

This paper's usage of the term 'intelligence' pivots on a solver's demonstrable understanding of the problem-domain—that is to say on possession and use of stored knowledge. Three subcategories are distinguished, according to the stage in the solving cycle at which the knowledge is used, whether (1) in developing the solving procedure (develop-time intelligence), (2) in guiding, monitoring and re-directing its execution (runtime intelligence), or (3) in commenting on the solution and the means for obtaining it (report-time intelligence).

1 INTRODUCTION

The evidence from brute force in game-playing systems suggests that, for the *second* of the above three phases, until a certain task-complexity threshold is reached, intelligence is scarcely even a marginal requirement. Embedded intelligence *would* be at a premium were points allotted not only for a program's won–drawn–lost outcome but also for the level of concepts expressed in an after–the–game annotation, i.e. phase 3. Of course, to generate and display purely tactical analyses is probably within reach of today's search-oriented capabilities. Indeed, the International Computer Chess Association has this year initiated an event in which chess computers compete in their ability to make such comments (*see* Editors *ICCA Journal* 1994). But to show that the higher level of the commentator's art lies well beyond simple extensions of today's chess programming, it is sufficient to choose almost any sentence from a modern Grandmaster commentary, e.g. 'A poor move. In view of Black's pressure on the g-file and along the b7-h1 diagonal, White's king is hardly going to the kingside, so at some stage White will have to play 0-0-0.' Here implicit reasoning is conducted in a space of descriptive concepts (pressure, file, diagonal, kingside, etc), rather than of individual positions, and hence qualifies for the use of the term 'intelligent' adopted in this review.

A commercial requirement for at least low-level commenting is now surfacing in the design of portable chess machines. Attainable levels of machine play already outstrip those of their users. Accordingly tutorially organized commentary and advice is displacing sheer playing skill as a selling point. Manufacturers' responses are preliminary. Techniques however in the public domain already extend beyond the pure tactical level, using conceptual position-descriptions and models of a fallible opponent (e.g. Michie 1986; Shapiro and Michie 1986; *also see* Carmel and Markowitch 1993, and recent papers in the *ICCA Journal* by Peter Jansen). Opponent-models are necessary for handling psychologically rooted notions such as 'traps,' or the meaning of the comment '!?' (conventionally interpreted as 'brilliant but probably unsound').

Complementary to the machine phenomenon of game-mastery by subintelligent programs is the following case of game-mastery by a human patient tragically rendered subintelligent by injury. This severely brain-damaged patient is referred to as Boswell (I am indebted to Patricia Smith Churchland for the following account, based on a study by A. Damasio, Idaho University, USA).

> In addition to losing the hippocampal structures, he has massive damage to frontal cortex. He can identify a house, or a car, but he cannot identify his house or his car; he cannot remember that he was married, that he has children, and so forth. He seems to have no retrograde episodic memory, as well as no anterograde episodic, ... Boswell can still play a fine game of checkers, though when asked he says it is bingo. He cannot learn new faces and does not remember 'pre-morbid' faces such as that of his wife and his children ... Boswell can play checkers, tie his shoes, carry on a conversation, etc.

Here 'retrograde' refers to recollection of events that occurred before the damage occurred and 'anterograde' to subsequent occurrences.

The survival of Boswell's checkers skill is in keeping with the earlier-remarked observation that procedural skills are invariably found to have been spared after damage to the brain's cortex. The assumption here is that sufficient practice can fully proceduralize, indeed automatize, even 'intellectual' tasks such as this, and that the sites of procedural memory are subcortical. The absurdity of any attempt to subject Boswell's checkers expertise to 'dialogue elicitation' must be evident. A.L. Samuel's (1959, 1968) pioneering studies on machine learning using the game of checkers attempted dialogue-elicitation, not with brain-damaged subjects but with checkers masters. He reported (personal communication) that he had never had such frustrating experiences in his life. The elicited material proved to be unusable operationally, and in contradiction with the recorded practice of the same masters in the tournament room.

So even for a game traditionally associated with mental excellence, expert performance can be purely procedural, with declarative models seemingly maintained as an epiphenomenon. Whether in the days before his accident the declarative apparatus of intelligence had to be intact for Boswell to *acquire* the intuitive expertise remains open. It is well established (*see* Squire, 1987) that *some* new procedural skills can be learned even after damage such as that sustained by Boswell. But direct evidence is lacking for this high level of task-complexity.

2 COMPUTER CHESS

Chess is by almost thirty orders of magnitude a larger combinatorial domain than checkers. The role of detailed move-by-move lookahead is also considered more important. The manner in which mental searches are conducted by players of various playing strengths was studied by Adriaan de Groot (1965). His strongest group of subjects were international grand-masters. In considering their moves, these players mentally examined a smaller lookahead tree of possibilities on average than that characteristic of weaker players. Fewer continuations tended to be considered at each potential branch point, and the total number of positions considered in forward analysis rarely exceeded about thirty.

Lookahead analysis of this type is at the heart of the game's tactics, which on occasion require forward analysis to probe ahead to depths spanning many moves by each side. The number of legal moves per position generally lies in the 30–35 range. Hence in human play forward analysis cannot be exhaustive. For three moves on each side the corresponding tree of possibilities would have a billion positions. De Groot found that the capacity to cut search down from these humanly intractable numbers to two or three dozen lies in the master's large mental store of descriptive patterns in which his or her past experience of chess positions has been encoded. In this way, only 'interesting' continuations are selected for further exploration. Many of the features of a position that a master takes in 'at a glance' correspond to explicitly named concepts, grouped in such categories as mobility, king-safety, pawn structure, open files etc. Whether or not these are processed in consciousness during actual play, some are certainly introspectable as intermediate goals in long-range plans and in retrospective commentary. But of an estimated total of 70 000 – 100 000 patterns stored in memory (Simon and Gilmartin 1973; Nievergelt 1977) the majority are not explicitly identified, and presumptively reside in procedural memory. There may be parallels here with the 'understanding at a glance' of geometrical figures and musical scores.

3 PATTERNS SUBSTITUTE FOR SEARCH

Strong masters can sustain reasonable standards of play under 'lightning' conditions (roughly five seconds per move). Their strong pattern-orientation supports the view that nuances of position-evaluation are for the most part transacted intuitively below the articulable level. Every master develops a concept of 'king safety,' for example. Yet the relatively bald versions that chess programmers can extract from them do not measure up to the subtle complex of considerations that must be postulated to explain the accuracy with which a Grandmaster assesses this property, and the poor job made of it by even the strongest chess computers.

Figure 1.1 shows a position concocted by International Grandmaster David Norwood and International Master William Hartston for an experiment on chess cognition. Is the white king safe? As Norwood (1993) remarks, human players '... tend to see that if they just move the white king around, Black cannot break through and win.' Norwood further states that 'even Deep Thought,...' (an early version of DT2) 'the world's strongest chess computer at the time of testing, could not resist the gain in material' from 'pawn takes rook.' After this, is the white king still safe? Any loss of king-safety points, which 'at a glance' should be large since the move opens up the position, was less than the 5-point gain (a rook is ordinarily reckoned as worth about 5 pawns) DT2 saw in the capture. The same holds for the many millions of positions that Deep Thought must have examined in lookahead. So far in the future lies the eventual nemesis that in this particular case Norwood has calculated that DT2 would have required a 50-move search to spot it.

A point made to me by International Master David Levy emphasizes the need for more precise definition of 'pattern'. The term 'pattern' is here used to denote a class of which the membership predicate is expressed in such a way as to be evaluable 'at a glance' by an experienced observer (what is a pattern to

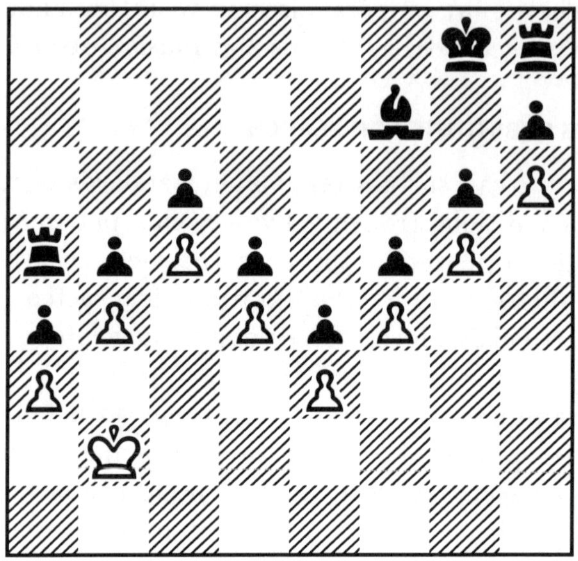

Figure 1.1. An illustrative chess position, with White to move, from Hartson and Norwood (*see* text). Totally resistant to the brute force powers of analysis of today's strongest chess computers, it nevertheless succumbs 'at a glance' to the human player's perception that for White to capture Black's rook with the knight's pawn would be a fatal act of short-term greed. With White's otherwise impregnable pawn fortress thus breached, Black brings his remaining two-piece advantage to bear for an easy, if protracted, win.

one observer may not be to another). 'Pattern' is thus a subset of 'concept-expression.' The latter has no bound set to its time-complexity. Contrast the concept 'prime integer' with that of 'odd integer.' For large integers expressed in the decimal system, only the latter class presents an instantly recognizable pattern ('string terminating in one of {1, 3, 5, 7, 9}'). In a similar sense the class of 'totally pawn-blocked' chess positions constitutes an instantly recognizable pattern.

4 GRANDMASTER-LEVEL PROGRAMS

The modern era of computer play can conveniently be dated from the defeat of International Grandmaster (IGM) Bent Larsen by the first version of this same program, Deep Thought

(DT1). Written by three graduate students at Carnegie Mellon University, DT1 ran on a Unix workstation extended with special-purpose chess hardware. In common with the hundreds of DT1's predecessors developed around the world since the 1960's, DT1 lacked significant intelligence. An analysis of the game, with a discussion of DT1's structure and features, is available elsewhere (Michie 1990).

The program subsequently consolidated its ranking in master tournament play at an International rating in the 2450–2500 range, corresponding to weak Grandmaster level. Meanwhile two of the program's authors, Feng Hsu and Murray Campbell, moved to IBM's T. J. Watson Laboratories, at Yorktown Heights, USA, where with resources from their new employer they completed the development of its successor, Deep Thought 2. This system is seen as an experimental prototype for 'Deep Blue,' to be ready for a challenge match against the World Champion in 1996. DT2's assets of brute force in both hardware and software have been considerably strengthened, and also its rather modest knowledge endowment, which centres on the position-evaluation function. Table 1.1 shows comparative facts about DT2 for which I am indebted to Dr. Campbell.

5 BRUTE-FORCE MENTALITY

The mental profile of DT2 differs radically from that of a human Grandmaster, in three ways in particular:

1. From de Groot's (1965) and other studies, we know that the average number of positions mentally evaluated in lookahead by a Grandmaster is of the order of 30 positions in three minutes, or about one every six seconds. In assessing the element of brute force in machine play, the leading comparison is between this figure and DT2's several million per second.

2. DT2's openings book now contains a few million positions, at least an order of magnitude larger than the feasible limit to human memorization. In consequence it is now the rule rather than the exception for the human player to be the

first to leave the protective shelter of rote memory (i.e. the stored 'book' of openings).

3. Exhaustive computation can solve endgames that are not fully understood by Grandmasters, nor by life-time students of the endgame. DT2 has installed over a hundred optimal-move databases, mostly from Ken Thompson (*see*, for example, Thompson 1986). They cover virtually all the nontrivial four-piece endgames, together with 56 (almost all) the nontrivial five-piece endgames. Endgames in which just one of the pieces is a pawn are included, but not those with two or more.

Should play happen to find its way to any position covered by any of the stored tables, the advantage to the machine is self-evident. But there is a more important payoff, which follows from a principle of rote-memory management first established in A.L. Samuel's (1959) study with checkers. The principle states that automatic storage of past calculative outcomes simplifies future calculations not only in rare recurrences of the same problems, but also in the far commoner case of their recurrence in planning space. The principle was demonstrated in the software 'memo function' utility (*see* Michie 1968; van Emden 1974) as applied to the evaluation of recursive functions. With DT2's search capabilities of 3–4 million positions per second, a move that is pondered for a few minutes allows the growth of a tree of possibilities containing over a billion positions in its search horizon. Thanks to DT2's selective extension algorithms a small but important minority of these horizon nodes lie twenty or more ply deep (ten moves by each side). If just one of these terminal nodes finds a match with a 'favourable' position belonging to any of the stored endgame databases, remaining play becomes a foregone conclusion.

As to the interpretation of the epithet 'favourable,' positions in such databases are routinely tagged with their game-theoretic values, won, drawn or lost. Where the recorded value constitutes a nontrivial improvement on the machine's estimate of its current position on the board, then transition to the database position is 'favourable' in a fairly obvious sense. Less obviously,

Table 1.1. Main features of the Deep Thought 2 (DT2) chess program. The 'Thompson endgame databases' are Kenneth Thompson's (e.g. 1986) exhaustive tabulations of optimal moves from all legal positions of 4-piece and 5-piece endgames. They include positions with just one pawn.

- Processors and lookahead search capacity:
  DT1—2 processors, 700 000 positions per second per processor. DT2—up to 24 processors, 7 000 000 positions per second.

- Evaluation hardware:
  DT2 included a number of additional features in the hardware evaluation. These included connected and protected passed pawns, blockading of pawns, improved king shelter, and improved evaluation of rooks on open/semi-open files.

- Evaluation software:
  DT2 included software calculation of a number of additional features, including mobility, rooks on seventh rank, and bishops of opposite colour.

- Endgames:
  All the Thompson endgame databases have been incorporated into DT2. DT1 had a small collection of endgame databases, confined to 4-piece endings. The new library includes virtually all the nontrivial 5-piece endgames, and occupies altogether four megabytes of store.

- Search:
  Significant improvements were made in DT2 in the extension algorithm, allowing much better control of the search and improved performance.

- Opening book:
  DT1 had only a few tens of thousands of positions. DT2 has a much larger book, with several million positions.

it has been found that optimal (i.e. maximally delaying) machine defence of a lost position is not infrequently rewarded with sufficient Grandmaster inaccuracy to present the machine with a draw. Such theoretically lost positions can also be regarded as 'favourable' from the operational point of view. The argument applies *a fortiori* to the swelling list of humanly impenetrable five-piece and six-piece endgames that have been reduced to database form by exhaustive retrograde analysis (*see* various issues of the *ICCA Journal*; also *Scientific American*, November 1991, for a summary of Lewis Stiller's ground-breaking analysis of KRBKBN comprising about 100-billion positions).

6 MACHINES (AND THEIR OPPONENTS) STRENGTHEN

The upward step in computational and chess-knowledge parameters from DT1 to DT2 was accompanied by a step up in the program's respective International chess ratings. DT2 has not participated in regular tournament play, so that it is not easy to calculate a firm numerical rating. The program has participated in two matches. One of the matches, in response to a 'revenge' challenge to a four-game match from IGM Bent Larsen, was lost $1\frac{1}{2} - 2\frac{1}{2}$. The other was a $3 - 1$ victory over the Danish National team of two IGM's and two IM's. These results, combined with less direct evidence, indicate a rating for DT2 in the 2550–2600 range, about 100 International rating points above DT1's. Because ratings are calculated from results of games against human masters, the 100-point increase may understate the real gain, since master play against machines has been improving during the period in question. An era in which chess computers were not regarded as serious by chess professionals has been yielding to one in which they are taken very seriously. A program's recorded games are now studied in advance of an encounter just as are the games of human opponents. Similarly, machine play in the evolving species of commercial chess machines has continued to increase as measured against standardized machine opposition. But International ratings of chess machines, where available, have tended to stagnate in consequence of losses to increasingly machine-savvy Masters.

7 'BLITZ' CHESS

An exception to the above-mentioned stagnation is the speeded up version of the game commonly known as 'Blitz.' Here the use of deliberative human thought is effectively disabled by the requirement to select moves at a rate of approximately one per five seconds. Human players are thrown back on the procedural pattern-stores underlying purely reactive skills. A substantial advantage is thereby conferred upon high-speed machine opponents. Thus in the Final of the Intel World Chess Express Challenge (Munich, May 1994) the 90 MHz running speed of the sole computer entrant, Fritz3, allowed the evaluation of over half a million positions in lookahead within the five-second average move-selection time.

Organized by the Professional Chess Association, the event started with a qualifier with 64 participants, from which eight emerged for the Final. These contestants, all Grandmasters, were joined by nine top-seeded Grandmasters plus Fritz3, making 18. Of the 17 human contestants ten rated over 2600 on the Elo scale. In the ensuing play Fritz3 defeated all but two of the nine top seeds including the world champion Kasparov, with whom the program tied for first place. In a best-of-six play-off, Kasparov won with three wins and two draws.

Fritz3 ran on a 90 MHz Olivetti Pentium Plus IBM-compatible personal computer and was developed by Chessbase in Hamburg and subsequently released commercially in July 1994. The program was rewritten by Frans Morsch from its predecessor, Fritz2, incorporating improved search techniques and other speed-ups. Three significant innovations distinguish Fritz3 from previous chess programs. The following is based on a report from Frederic Friedel, technical manager and co-founder of the Chessbase company.

1. A special openings book was written by C. de Gorter optimized for play against humans. It is very broad and includes openings which are normally excluded from tournament books because they are considered 'too dangerous.' In general Fritz3's 'book' strives for open, unclear and exciting positions (see 2 below), rather than blocked,

strategic ones requiring long-term planning.

2. Fritz3 is the first tournament program explicitly to incorporate the 'hunger for complexity' elaborated theoretically in the late 1970's (*see* Michie 1986). Friedel writes 'We didn't try to implement sound strategic play, at which the top players are superior anyway. Fritz3 was tuned to strive for unbalanced positions and seek tension. Attack a piece and it should counterattack rather than exchange, try to block the position and it should unblock it with aggressive thrusts.'

3. Other chess programs employ various elementary forms of storing the fruits of their own experience. In the endgame in particular the use of 'transposition tables' is widespread, a form of rote learning similar to that pioneered in checkers by Samuel. The latest version of Fritz3, developed since the Munich tournament, has a new learning feature that automates an experience-based selective pruning of the openings book's horizon of positions. Those positions whose continuations are found by the machine to be punished in short order are automatically marked for future avoidance.

8 DISCRIMINABILITY OF HUMAN AND MACHINE

It is sometimes asserted that chessmasters presented with computer-versus-human games can spot which player is the computer and which the human. Positions can indeed be concocted in which human and machine responses are easy to discriminate, as in the Norwood–Hartston position illustrated in Figure 1. But where positions and moves are generated by human–machine contests, published evidence is inconclusive. A possible conclusion is that discriminability is at best weak, reflecting a low incidence in master play of positions that evoke recognizably *unintelligent* responses from the machine side. It is an open question whether human players at World Championship level will be able to learn to steer towards such positions sufficiently to motivate chess programmers to incorporate long term planning (runtime intelligence).

The question has recently been sharpened by the unexpected elimination in September 1994 of Gary Kasparov from the London leg of the Intel Grand Prix by the Pentium Genius program running on a 100 MHz personal computer. The tournament was played to a 30-minute time limit within which all moves had to be completed. The program was defeated in the semi-final by Grandmaster Anand, a player rated 3rd or 4th in the world.

9 COMPUTER CHECKERS

Samuel's pioneering studies of the 1950's advanced AI by demonstrating and analysing the gains obtainable from rote-learning and parameter-learning. His program attained the level of a county player but not that of a Master. Master play at the very highest level was finally attained by the program Chinook developed at the University of Alberta, Canada, by a group led by Jonathan Schaeffer (Schaeffer *et al.* 1992). In August 1992 the World Checkers Champion, Dr. Marion Tinsley, defended his title against Chinook, gaining 4 wins to Chinook's 2 in a 40-game match. Prior to this, Tinsley had lost a game only five times in 40 years. A re-match was set for late 1994, from which Tinsley was forced to retire by illness. Chinook has subsequently consolidated its position as the acknowledged World Champion.

The following summary description of Chinook is from Schaeffer *et al.* (1993).

Chinook's strength comes from deep searches (deciding which positions to examine), a good evaluation function (deciding how favourable a position is), an openings book (knowledge of the first few moves of the game) and endgame databases (perfect information on all positions with 7 pieces or less and the important 8-piece positions). ... During the World Championship match, the program searched to an average *minimum* depth of 17-, 19-, and 21-ply (one ply is one move by one player) in the opening, middlegame and endgame respectively, under the condition of having to play 20 moves per hour. The program's evaluation function has

25 heuristic components, each of which is weighted and summed to give a position evaluation... The game is divided into 4 phases, each with its own set of weights.

10   FUTILITY OF YET DEEPER LOOKAHEAD

The authors report that as performance has improved, the returns to be gained from additional search depth have declined, reaching a virtual plateau. A systematic experiment using self-play, with one side set to search 2 ply deeper than the other, gave convincing support to this conclusion, as summarized in Table 1.2.

For the first time, then, it would seem that an 'intelligence' boundary has been reached in computer mastery of a board game, not penetrable by adding further brute force. There are two dimensions to brute force, namely processor-intensive (as in search) and store-intensive (as in Chinook's 'book' and endgame databases). It might seem premature to announce arrival also at this second barrier were it not for the following facts.

Table 1.2. Self-play experiment with Chinook. The cost of searching an additional two ply (one move by each side) is roughly a factor of four in computing time. Return on the additional search investment declines to near-zero when depths of 17 or more are reached. Each side scores one point for a win and 1/2 point for a draw. Hence a margin of 14 to 6 could mean that the deeper-searching side won 14 wins and lost 6, or won 8 and lost none with 12 draws, etc.

Search depths of the two sides	Margin of victory for the deeper-searching side in self-play in a twenty-game match
depth 7 v. depth 5	14 to 6
depth 9 v. depth 7	15 to 5
depth 11 v. depth 9	12 1/2 to 7 1/2
depth 13 v. depth 11	11 1/2 to 8 1/2
depth 15 v. depth 13	10 1/2 to 9 1/2
depth 17 v. depth 15	11 to 9
depth 19 v. depth 17	9 1/2 to 10 1/2

11   INFEASIBILITY OF DATABASE EXPANSION

Chinook's endgame databases altogether comprise 150 billion positions, occupying 5.5 gigabytes of store and covering all the balanced (i.e. equal number of men on each side) 8-piece endings, plus all positions with fewer pieces. Empirically 90% of the contribution to play is made by less than 10% of the stored positions, the remainder hardly ever being encountered in the course of Chinook's lookahead searches. To compute the contents of these databases by retrograde analysis occupied $1\frac{1}{2}$ years during which there were at no time less than 30 workstations in round-the-clock operation, augmented by supercomputer computations contributed by the Lawrence Livermore Laboratory.

Addition of a database covering the 9-piece endings is estimated as requiring a ten-fold increase of storage and a more than ten-fold increase of computation. On a conservative estimation the same multipliers again apply to the step from 9-piece to 10-piece. A 9-piece database has little playing value, since almost all such unbalanced positions are uninteresting foregone conclusions, but it must be constructed as a step towards the 10-piece. The latter, as we have seen, incurs expenditures of database-manufacturing resources that are unlikely to be brought within reach by any foreseeable advances in hardware technology. So just at the very pinnacle of task complexity that the game of checkers is capable of offering (namely defeat of the game's greatest human player), Chinook is brushing a boundary at which machine acquisition of *runtime intelligence* may be needed. It is not known whether, and at what depth, signs of similar 'plateauing' of brute force can be expected to appear in chess.

12   STORE-TIME TRADEOFF

The only part of Chinook's structure on which state-of-the-art techniques of computing and AI have not been pushed to the limit concerns the program's scoring function for evaluating positions. It is here that the system's currently still modest endowment of checkers knowledge resides. It is, of course, precisely Marion Tinsley's enormous knowledge resource that enabled him for so long to remain ahead.

Chinook's scoring function has been subjected to extensive optimization procedures. But these have been conducted exclusively within the scoring polynomial format introduced into the game by Samuel in 1959. In problems where *logical patterns* of input attributes rather than simple arithmetic combinations dominate outcome values, the limitation may be severe. In statistical terms, the question concerns the degree to which the independent variables (Chinook's 25 'heuristic components') satisfy the conditional independence required by a linear model, e.g. by a multiple regression equation of which the independent variables represent the heuristic features and the dependent variable the estimated position value. This question applies equally to the chess program DT2. Samuel (1968) eventually concluded that for the position-evaluation problem in checkers, linear models are not good enough. In a remedial attempt he proposed his 'signature tables' representation, but with the techniques then available was not able to obtain satisfactory gains in evaluation accuracy.

13   SUITABLE CASE FOR MACHINE LEARNING

Thirty years of developments in machine learning have since passed. Various well tried and well honed advances beyond the linear forms of numerical predictors and classifiers have been made for problems in which conditional dependencies are severe (for recent reviews *see* Ripley 1994; Michie *et al.* 1994). Schaeffer's group has made trials of genetic algorithms for the evaluator-tuning requirement. They did not confer the desired improvement. No trials have yet been made of other learning formalisms.

14   COMPUTER BACKGAMMON

Backgammon is a board game combining deterministic and stochastic features. The latest version of Gerald Tesauro's (1993) TD–Gammon plays at a strong master level comparable to that of some of the world's leading players. It owes its steady rise over the last few years to unremitting application of multilayer neural-net learning to tune the the weights of a nonlinear evaluation function of a mixed set of primitive and hand-crafted features. The first phase used supervised learning on human expert examples, leading to a program, Neurogammon, that convincingly won the 1989 machine-against-machine International Computer Olympiad.

The second phase used reinforcement learning and started with raw board information only (zero initial knowledge). Subsequently the same hand-crafted feature set as used by Neurogammon was added to these primitive features for further tuning of weights. The program applied Sutton's $TD(\lambda)$ reinforcement algorithm to training data generated not by experts but (in a manner reminiscent of Samuel's early learning experiments) by self-play. At every stage both sides of self-play were guided by the current state of the evaluation function. Hence at the start, before anything at all had been learned, play was random and games could last for hundreds or even thousands of steps. In normal human play games last about 50–60 steps.

The neural network observes a sequence of board positions leading to a final reward-or-punishment signal determined by the outcome of the game. Its task is to build an outcome-predictor, and successive forms of this are used for evaluating potential positions, and hence for choosing the next move. As increasing amounts of non-random know-how accumulate, game-lengths shorten and the relation between positions and outcomes becomes less remote, endowing further learning cycles with more leverage. Tesauro writes:

> The rather surprising result, after tens of thousands of training games, was that a significant amount of learning actually took place, even in the zero initial knowledge experiments. These networks achieved a strong intermediate level of play approximately equal to Neurogammon. The networks with handcrafted features have greatly surpassed Neurogammon and all other previous computer programs, and have continued to improve with more and more games of training experience.

After a total of 1.5 million self-play games as training experience TD-Gammon 2.1 using a 2-ply lookahead achieved near-parity with Bill Robertie, a highly respected former World Champion. In a 40-game match: '... after trailing the entire session, Robertie managed to eke out a narrow one-point victory by the score of 40 to 39. Robertie's overall assessment is that, due to the program's steadiness (it never gets tired or careless, as even the best of humans inevitably do), TD-Gammon would actually be the favourite against any human player in a long money-game session or in a gruelling tournament format such as the World Cup competition.'

In backgammon Tesauro has evidently been able to exploit ideal conditions for neural-net learning, namely

1. training-time investment on a vast scale (neural nets learn slowly);
2. user indifference to the opacity of the learning process and of its fruits;
3. pervasive nonlinearities of the domain's logical and statistical structure.

In Tesauro's case, brute force is more conspicuous at develop time than at run time. In the work of Schaeffer and colleagues on Chinook, brute force has been conspicuous during both these phases, as also in the DT2 chess system.

15 CHANCE PERTURBATIONS DURING LEARNING

Tesauro also makes an important point in relation to the 'brittleness' phenomenon treated in Section 2: 'One possibly very important effect of the stochastic dice rolls in backgammon is that during learning, they enforce a certain minimum amount of exploration of the state space. By stochastically forcing the system into regions of state space that the current evaluation function tries to avoid, it is possible that improved evaluations and new strategies can be discovered.'

16 COMPUTER GO-MOKU

Allis *et al.* (1993) describe Go-Moku as

played on the 225 intersections of 15 horizontal and 15 vertical lines... Two players, Black and White, move in turn by placing a stone of their own color on an empty intersection... Black starts the game. The player who first makes a line of five consecutive stones of his color (horizontally, vertically or diagonally) wins the game. The stones once placed on the board during the game never move again nor can they be captured. If the board is completely filled and no-one has five-in-a-row, the game is drawn... An overline is a line of six or more consecutive stones of the same color. In the variant of Go-Moku played most often today, an overline does not win (this restriction applies to both players). Only a line of exactly five stones is considered a winning pattern.

In the 1960's, E.W. Elcock, J.M. Foster and others at the University of Aberdeen, Scotland, chose Go-Moku as a suitable domain for developing an important complex of ideas on declarative programming. Their studies are reported in early volumes of the *Machine Intelligence* series.

Recently Allis and colleagues developed the world's strongest tournament program, Victoria. Unique among high-performance programs, its lookahead search, when applied to the opening position and run in distributed style on 10 workstations, found a complete winning strategy-tree for Black (the opening player) at a total cost of about 1 million seconds of CPU time (approximately 2 weeks). With this, Black always wins against any defence. The strategy is not optimal. It forces a win but not in the fewest possible moves. When used by White it produces play that is strong, but not sufficient to stand up to the world's top players. These almost always win as Black against their peers. The result of a match between Victoria and such a player is therefore predictable. Each game will be won by whichever player's turn it is to be Black, until the first human slip.

The strategy was discovered and proved by use of Victoria's combination of 'threat-space search' and 'proof-number search.' The latter is a domain-independent 'best first' search method, described in detail by Allis *et al.* (1994), that substantially improves on previous game-tree search algorithms. Threat-space search uses domain-specific heuristics to constrain the initial phase of a search for a winning threat sequence. If successful, it returns the value of the current position as 'win' with a strategy for forcing it as a side-product. To conduct this 'reconnaissance' and report back takes no more than a tenth of a second of CPU time. If the report is negative then the proof-number search module takes over, using iterated calls of threat-space search as the position-evaluation function of its 'best first' minimax lookahead.

17 GRADATIONS OF 'SOLVING'

In a sense the authors can claim to have *solved* this variant of Go-Moku. There are, however, different gradations of what is meant by 'solution.'

1. A *strong solution* takes the form of a feasibly computable function that provably maps every legal position to a labelled outcome value, where the label of each non-drawn position is an integer denoting the minimax-optimal least number of moves required to force that outcome. For drawn positions it is usual to allow the empty label (an agreed definition of 'minimax-optimal' would otherwise have to be developed for this context). The function may be partly or wholly in tabular form (as Lewis Stiller's solution of the KRBKBN endgame of chess, *see* earlier). Such a function, used in conjunction with a legal move generator, can be used to develop *optimal* strategy-trees for both sides over all non-drawn positions.

2. A *weak solution* (applicable only if the game-value is not drawn) is a strategy with a proof that it always wins, not necessarily optimally, for one of the players. If in addition a strategy for the other player is supplied and if the properties described below are proved for it, then we designate it (2a), and otherwise (2b). On these definitions, Go-Moku has been solved in the sense of (2b).

3. An *ultra-weak solution* is the determination and non-constructive proof of the outcome value of the game. For example, the game of Hex has been shown to be a win for

the opening player without, however, any winning strategy being shown.

Victoria's threat-space search, used by the main proof-number search as a position-evaluator, simulates the way that human expert Go-Moku players find winning threat sequences. Combination with the highly efficient brute force of proof-number search is critical. Without it, Victoria falls far short of top human play. The proof-number search algorithm has been used also to solve (in sense (2b)) the games Connect-Four and Qubic. Related ideas have also been successfully applied to theorem-proving (Elkan 1989), and the proof number algorithm is now being tried in the more complex game of Awari (Allis *et al.* 1994).

18 CONCLUSIONS FROM GAME-PLAYING

In his autobiographical 'Life of a Philosopher' Charles Babbage wrote:

> I endeavoured to ascertain the opinions of persons of every class of life and of all ages, whether they thought it required human reason to play games of skill. The almost constant answer was in the affirmative. Some supported this view of the case by observing, that if it were otherwise, then an automaton could play such games.

Today automata can play such games. Human reason is thus not *required* for games of skill. But could particular components of intelligence, although not *necessary* for machine play at master level, nevertheless raise the level further, or allow the same level to be reached at less computational expense?

Consider chess, the most complex of the four games reviewed. Some positions totally resist computational brute force and yet succumb, sometimes rather easily, to human intelligence, as in the example of Figure 1. Perhaps these booby traps are so sparsely distributed that even massive incorporation of runtime intelligence would not noticeably improve a machine's tournament statistics? Yet however apparently sparse, to ignore their existence invites machine-savvy Masters to learn to make them operationally less sparse—by steering play towards them.

Pending empirical demonstration, possible gains from runtime intelligence in machine play of games remains debatable. But the power of symbolic learning to find significant patterns in data has meanwhile been amply proved in the industrial arena (for recent reviews *see* Michie 1991, 1992; Michie *et al.* 1994). These learning tools could now be used to enrich DT2's or Chinook's position-evaluation functions with explicit target patterns. A modicum of runtime intelligence could thus further empower brute-force, rather as air-borne target-spotters guide brute-force ground artillery.

To recapitulate, below a certain task-complexity threshold, runtime intelligence is not a requirement. Intelligence's dispensable role is to invoke, monitor, guide, and where appropriate to abort, the execution of solving procedures. Once 'automatized,' as in the trained expert, these procedures are opaque to inspection and become capable if necessary of running without higher-level supervision. The latter may monitor attainment of procedural goals and (where time allows) may selectively re-set them. But intelligence is only mandatory after the success or failure of each given solving attempt. Then from memories of runtime goal-settings, sometimes confabulated, a socially-oriented report on 'how and why I did it' is prepared. In humans, the main task of intelligence is social, demanding more of the team's press officer (report-time intelligence) than of its non-playing captain (runtime intelligence) or of its coach (develop-time intelligence). Indeed, with coach, captain and press officer all inactivated the team can still play on. This was illustrated earlier with the retention of checkers skill by the neurological patient Boswell. Today's users, however, demand something more insightful and communicative than the Boswell model of interactive computing.

When generalized to real-world and real-time decision-taking, this discussion appears to undermine certain fundamental assumptions of main-stream AI. Undermining, indeed demolition, may be needed to clear this road. At the end of it lies a new methodology for generating symbolic models of the subsymbolic players themselves. Michie and Camacho (1994) have sketched some first steps in this direction.

Acknowledgements

In completing this paper I was assisted by facilities of the Programming Research Group of the Oxford University Computing Laboratory during the tenure of a Visiting Fellowship awarded to Dr. Stephen Muggleton's Machine Learning group in support of my stay. I am additionally indebted to V. Allis, J.R. Quinlan, and Jonathan Schaeffer for valuable comments and suggestions.

REFERENCES

Allis, L.V., van den Herik, H.J. and Huntjens, M.P.H. (1993). Go-Moku solved by new search techniques. In *Games: Planning and Learning (papers from the 1993 AAAI Fall Symposium)*, Technical Report FS 9302, Menlo Park, CA: AAAI Press.

Allis, L.V. van der Meulen, M. and van den Herik, H.J. (1994). Proof number search. *Artif. Intell.*, **66** (1), 91–124.

Carmel, D. and Markowitch, S. (1993). Learning models of opponent's strategy in game playing. In *Games: Planning and Learning* (papers from the 1993 AAAI Fall Symposium), Technical Report FS 9302, Menlo Park, CA: AAAI Press.

de Groot, A. (1965). *Thought and Choice in Chess* (ed. G. W. Baylor), The Hague: Mouton [English translation, with additions, of the Dutch 1946 version].

Editors (1994). The best annotation award. *ICCA Journal*, **17** (1), 39–40.

Elkan, C. (1989). Conspiracy numbers and caching for searching and/or trees and theorem-proving. In *Proc. Iint. Joint Conf on AI*, Detroit, MI, pp. 341–346 [cited by Allis *et al.* 1994].

Michie, D. (1968). Memo functions and machine learning. *Nature*, **218**, 19–22.

Michie, D. (1986). A theory of evaluative comments in chess. In *On Machine Intelligence* (2nd ed.) Chichester: Ellis Horwood (first published in *The Computer J.*, 1981).

Michie, D. (1990). Brute force in chess and science. In *Chess, Computers and Cognition* (eds. T.A. Marsland and J. Schaeffer), pp. 82–111.

Michie, D. (1991). Methodologies from machine learning in software and data analysis. *Computer Journal*, **34** (6), 559–565. (1991).

Michie, D. (1992). Directions in machine intelligence. *Computer Bulletin*, Sept/Oct, 9–11.

Michie, D. and Camacho, R. (1994). Building symbolic representations of intuitive real-time skills from performance data. In *Machine Intelligence 13* (eds. K. Furukawa, D. Michie and S. Muggleton), Oxford: Oxford University Press, 385–418.

Michie, D., Spiegelhalter, D.S. and Taylor, C.C. (1994, eds.). *Machine Learning, Neural and Statistical Classification.* Hemel Hempstead: Ellis Horwood (Simon and Schuster).

Nievergelt, J. (1977). The information content of a chess position and its implication for the chess-specific knowledge of chess players. *SIGART Newsletter*, **62**, 13–15. A revised and expanded version appears in *Machine Intelligence 12* (Hayes, Michie and Tyugu, eds., 1991).

Norwood, David (1993). Cited in the *New Scientist*, 4th September, 1993. A full account is available in *Norwood's Chess and Education*, an academic publication of Gresham College, London, UK, 1993 (55 pp.)

Ripley, B.D. (1994). Neural networks and related methods for classification. *J. Roy. Statist. Soc. B*, **56** (3), 409–456.

Samuel, A.L. (1959). Some studies in machine learning using the game of checkers. *IBM J. Res. and Dev.*, **3**, 210–229.

Samuel, A.L. (1968). Some studies in machine learning using the game of checkers. II Recent progress. *IBM J. Res. and Dev.*, **11**, 601–617.

Schaeffer, J., Treloar, N., Knight, B. Lu, P. and Szafron, D. (1992). A world championship caliber checkers program. *Artificial Intelligence* **53** (2–3), 273–290.

Schaeffer, J., Lu, P. Szafron, D. and Lake, R. (1993). A re-examination of brute force search. In *Games: Planning and Learning* (papers from the 1993 AAAI Fall Symposium), Technical Report FS 9302, Menlo Park: AAAI Press.

Shapiro, A.D. and Michie, D. (1986). A self-commenting facility for inductively synthesized end-game expertise. In *Advances in Computer Chess 5* (ed. D.F. Beal), Oxford: Pergamon.

Simon, H.A. and Gilmartin, K. (1973). A simulation of memory for chess positions. *Cog. Psych.*, 29–46. Reprinted as chapter 6.3 of Models of Thought by H.A.Simon (1979), Yale University Press.

Squire, L.R. (1987). *Memory and Brain*, Oxford: Oxford University Press.

Tesauro, G. (1993). TD-Gammon: a self-teaching backgammon program achieves master-level play. In *Games: Planning and Learning (papers from the 1993 AAAI Fall Symposium)*, Technical Report FS 9302, Menlo Park: AAAI Press.

Thompson, K. (1986). Retrograde analysis of certain endgames. *ICCA Journal*, **9** (3), 131–139.

van Emden, M.H. (1974). Lib Memo Functions. *Pop-2 Program Library: Program Specification*. University of Edinburgh, Department of Machine Intelligence.

2

Reacting, Planning, and Learning in an Autonomous Agent

Scott Benson and Nils J. Nilsson

Robotics Laboratory, Department of Computer Science, Stanford University, Stanford, CA 94305

Abstract

We present an autonomous agent architecture and its component subsystems that integrate important abilities needed for robust, flexible performance in dynamic environments. These abilities involve appropriate reaction to environmental situations given the agent's goals; selective attention to multiple, competing goals; planning new action routines when innovation beyond designer-provided routines is necessary; and learning the effects of actions so that the planner can use them to build ever more reliable plans. The teleo-reactive format allows actions to be closely coupled to continuous environmental feedback and is also especially compatible with conventional AI planning and learning mechanisms. The workings of the proposed architecture and its subsystems are illustrated in a simulated robot domain. We conclude by noting areas where future work is needed.

1 INTRODUCTION

This work introduces and integrates a number of techniques that we think will be important in the development of autonomous agents. By *autonomous*, we mean ones that can operate with only minimal supervision by a human. Such agents would be *managed* by humans, but their actions would not need to be controlled step-by-step by humans. By *agents* we mean computer systems that perceive and model their environments and take actions in those environments to achieve and maintain goals. Autonomous agents can exist and function in either physical or computational environments. Robots, for example, are physical agents. They sense and act in the physical world. Agents confined to a computational world are sometimes called *knowbots* or *softbots*. These might be simulations of physical robots, information-gathering assistants, or actors in an interactive, virtual reality program. Of course, combinations of both types of agents are possible. Our emphasis here is on robots and simulated robots.

Mobile robots have several important societal applications. Some of these involve manufacturing and warehouse jobs, delivery, transportation, construction, maintenance, janitorial and household tasks, military and space applications, and work in dangerous environments. Such robots must be robust under a wide variety of environmental conditions and be able to survive without human help for long periods of time. The environments in which these robots must operate are dynamic and somewhat unpredictable, containing humans, machines, and other robots.

Here, we focus on four sets of general abilities that we think will be necessary for robots in these applications:

- **Teleo-Reactive Behaviour**. We want robots that can react appropriately and rapidly to commonly occurring situations that require stereotypical programs of actions. They must avoid crashing into things, get out of the way of other robots, and refuel themselves, to name just a few examples. But we also want their actions to be influenced by their goals (hence 'teleo'). Teleo-reactivity in dynamic, uncertain environments implies a short sense-act cycle of the sort common in feedback control systems. The *teleo-reactive (TR) program* formalism proposed earlier in Nilsson (1994) seems well suited to these needs.

- **Attention to Multiple Goals**. Our robots will typically have several goals of different and time-varying urgencies. The robots should take actions which, in so far as possible, work simultaneously toward many of their goals—taking into account the current urgency of each goal and the estimated effort required to achieve it. We have developed an attention-focusing mechanism that is able to adjudicate efficiently among competing goals.

- **Planning**. It will not be possible to store stereotypical action programs matched to all possible situation–goal pairs. Occasional innovation of new action programs and modifications of existing ones will be required. Our agent architecture incorporates a planning system to augment the teleo-reactive programs as needed.

- **Learning**. Constructing a robot control program will require, to be sure, initial human design and coding as well as automatic synthesis by a planning system. Success in complex environments may even require some human recoding of the TR programs. Yet, recoding will be expensive and impractical in many applications, so we seek to incorporate learning and adaptation methods that enable the robot to change its program automatically according to a variety of protocols including declarative instructions from humans, successful and unsuccessful experiences, and supervised and unsupervised training methods.

(In robotics, providing these abilities is usually overshadowed by work on perception and effectors. We have not addressed these critical two components in our research since they depend heavily on the specific application.)

Most of our experimental work on autonomous agents has been carried out using simulated robots and a simulated environment called *Botworld* (Teo 1992). Botworld is a two-dimensional space of robots, obstacles, bars, and assemblies of bars. Each robot can pick up bars, move them around the environment, and connect them to other bars and structures. Robots can move over bars lying on the 'floor' but cannot move through other robots or obstacles.

Each Botworld robot senses the environment at a rapid sampling rate, receiving information about its own position and orientation and whether or not it is holding a bar. It also senses the locations and orientations of nearby bars, obstacles, and robots. We can simulate imperfect sensors by adding noise to these measurements. A sample scene from Botworld is shown in Fig. 2.1.

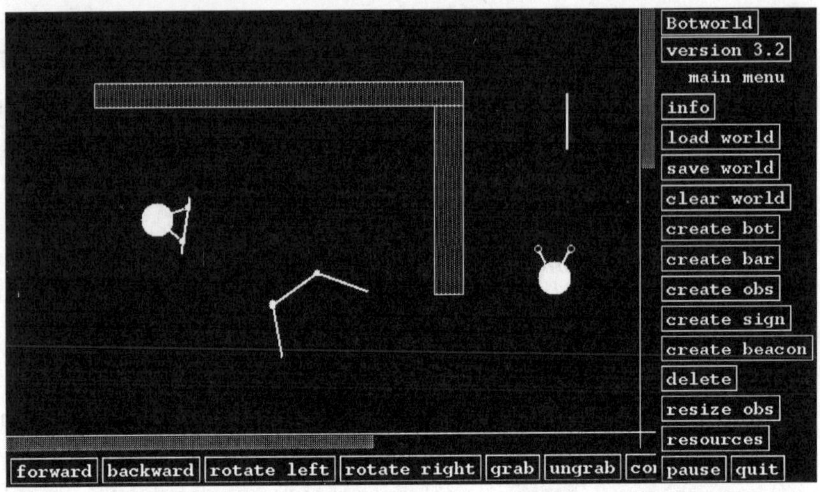

Figure 2.1. Botworld

The next four sections describe the results of preliminary efforts on a coherent architecture and its component subsystems addressing the four abilities listed above. We first summarize the TR program formalism and describe some recent augmentations to it. Next, we describe our architecture for arbitrating among multiple goals within the TR program framework. Then, we present a straightforward, STRIPS-style planning system that is able to create and modify TR programs. Next, we present a learning system that creates models of actions that can be used by the planning system. Along the way, we relate our work to research of others. In the final section, we conclude by noting areas where future work is needed.

2 TELEO-REACTIVE BEHAVIOUR

2.1 Summary of TR programs

A *teleo-reactive (TR)* program is an agent control program that directs the agent toward a goal in a manner that continuously takes into account changing environmental circumstances. The formalism is described in detail in Nilsson (1994). In its simplest form, a TR program consists of an ordered list of production rules:

$$
\begin{aligned}
K_1 &\rightarrow a_1 \\
K_2 &\rightarrow a_2 \\
&\cdots \\
K_i &\rightarrow a_i \\
&\cdots \\
K_m &\rightarrow a_m
\end{aligned}
$$

The K_i are conditions (on perceptual inputs and on a stored model of the world), and the a_i are actions (on the world or which change the model). An action may be primitive or it may itself be a TR program (thus recursive TR programs are also possible). In typical usage, the condition K_1 is a goal condition, which is what the program is designed to achieve, and the action a_1 is the null action. The conditions K_i may have free variables which are bound when the TR program is called to achieve a particular ground instance of K_1. These bindings are then applied to all the free variables in the other conditions and actions in the program. A TR program is interpreted in a manner roughly similar to the way in which ordered production systems are interpreted: The list of rules is scanned from the top for the first rule whose condition part is satisfied, and the corresponding action is then executed. A TR program is designed so that for each rule $K_i \rightarrow a_i$, K_i is the regression, through action a_i, of some particular condition higher in the list. That is, K_i is the weakest condition such that the execution of action a_i (under ordinary circumstances)[1] achieves some particular condition, say K_j, higher in the list (with $j < i$). Thus, executing the actions prescribed by a TR program ultimately achieves the goal. Additionally, TR programs are robust in that should an action have an unexpected effect, the program will nevertheless continue working toward the goal.

---

[1] We assume that an action achieves its expected effects unless some unusual execution error occurs or unless some other agent interferes.

TR programs differ substantively from conventional production systems, however, in that their actions can be *durative* rather than discrete. A durative action is one that can continue indefinitely. For example, a mobile robot is capable of executing the durative action *move*, which propels the robot ahead (say at constant speed) indefinitely. Such an action contrasts with a discrete one, such as *move forward one metre*. In a TR program, a durative action continues so long as its corresponding condition remains the highest true condition in the list. When the highest true condition changes, the action changes correspondingly. Thus, unlike ordinary production systems, the conditions must be *continuously* evaluated; the action associated with the *currently* highest true condition is always the one being executed. An action terminates only when its associated condition ceases to be the highest true condition. The regression condition for TR programs must therefore be rephrased for durative actions: For each rule $K_i \rightarrow a_i$, K_i is the weakest condition such that continuous execution of the action a_i (under ordinary circumstances) eventually achieves some particular condition, say K_j, with $j < i$. (The fact that K_i is the *weakest* such condition implies that, under ordinary circumstances, it remains true until K_j is achieved.)

In thinking about the semantics of TR programs, it is important to imagine that the conditions, K_i, and all of their parameters, are being *continuously* computed. However, in computational implementations of TR programs, we compute the conditions (and the parameters upon which they depend) at discrete time steps, and then execute small increments of durative actions. A sufficiently high sampling rate is chosen—depending on the domain—to approximate continuous computation and execution.

One way to approximate continuous computation is to evaluate at every time step a Lisp version of a TR program: `(cond (K1 a1) (K2 a2) ... (Kn an))`. When actions themselves are TR programs, the top-level `cond` statement embeds nested `cond` statements. The program is evaluated at every time step down to a primitive action, an increment of that primitive action is executed, and program evaluation starts over from the top on the next time step.

This sort of approximation to continuous computation opens the possibility that a condition might be achieved between time steps without being noticed. For instance, if a condition in a TR program is satisfied if and only if the agent is facing within 0.1 degrees of a specific desired direction, the agent might turn sufficiently fast that this condition would hold only *between* two sampling points—leading the agent to turn past the desired direction rather than switching to the appropriate next action. There are at least two obvious solutions to this problem. First, the condition can be relaxed so that at least one sampling point must fall within it, given the agent's execution speed and sampling rate. Second, some measure of the time needed to satisfy the expected next condition can be used to insure that the agent slows down as that condition is approached. This solution has the effect of decreasing the distance between sampling points when necessary so that again, at least one sampling point will necessarily fall within the condition region. Both methods have been implemented successfully for various agent tasks, although the first method occasionally results in activation conditions so weak that the recommended action is no longer always appropriate.

In our work, we have found it convenient to represent a TR program as a tree, called a *TR tree*. Suppose two rules in a TR program are $K_i \rightarrow a_i$ and $K_j \rightarrow a_j$ with $j < i$ and with K_i the regression of K_j through action a_i. Then we have nodes in the TR tree corresponding to K_i and K_j and an arc labelled by a_i directed from K_i to K_j. That is, when K_i is the shallowest true node in the tree, execution of its corresponding action, a_i, will achieve K_j. The root node is labelled with the goal condition and is called the *goal node*. When two or more nodes have the same parent, there are correspondingly two or more ways in which to achieve the parent's condition. Continuous execution of a TR tree would be achieved by a continuous computation of the shallowest true node and by execution of its corresponding action.[2] We call the shallowest true node in a TR tree the *active*

---

[2] We assume that ties among equally shallow true nodes are broken by

node.

We now have had a great deal of experience in writing TR programs for the control of actual physical robots (Galles 1993), the simulated robots of Botworld, and for the control of a Silicon Graphics Flight Simulator aircraft. In the hierarchy of robot control, we have found TR programs to be most appropriate for what might be called *mid-level* robot control. At the lowest level, classical control theory is required for the feedback control of motors and other effectors. Since there is less demand for continuous feedback at the highest levels, conventional program control structures suffice there.

The TR formalism is related to a number of other 'circuit-based' agent control methods such as the subsumption architecture (Brooks 1986), universal plans (Schoppers 1987), and situated automata (Rosenschein and Kaelbling 1986). Comparisons are discussed in Nilsson (1994). We prefer the TR formalism because, as we shall see, it is more readily incorporated in an architecture that accommodates planning and learning.

2.2 Extensions to the TR formalism

The basic TR tree formalism has been extended to deal more efficiently with rules having certain kinds of conjunctive conditions. The extension permits subprograms to be executed in arbitrary order depending on circumstances at execution time. It also avoids the necessity of explicit coding of all possible orderings of the subprograms. Consider a condition, K, in a TR rule that is composed of a conjunction of subconditions: $K \equiv C_1 \wedge C_2 \wedge \cdots \wedge C_m$. Suppose, also, that there are TR programs for achieving each of these subconditions such that if any one of them, say C_i, is satisfied, the achievement of any other of them (by their corresponding TR programs) will not cause C_i to become false. That is, the TR programs for achieving the C_i can be executed in any order. In this special case, the TR node labelled by the conjunction is called a *conjunctive node* and is

---

some fixed tie-breaking rule. Also, instead of selecting the shallowest true node, the interpreter might select that true node corresponding to a least-costly path to the goal, if estimates of the relative costs of actions along that path are available.

given m successor nodes, called *AND nodes*, in the tree—each labelled by one of the conjuncts, C_i. (By convention, we do not label the arcs between the AND nodes and their parent conjunctive node.) Each AND node is the root of a TR subtree that achieves its condition without interacting with the other conditions in the conjunction, and thus the TR subtrees can be executed in whatever order circumstances dictate. A TR tree containing AND nodes can be executed by the usual TR execution mechanism: we execute that action corresponding to the shallowest true node, ignoring the AND nodes since they have no action labels on the arcs exiting them. When this special case does not obtain (that is, when programs that achieve the separate conjuncts in a conjunction interact), the entire conjunction must be regressed through all of the actions that achieve the separate conjuncts—resulting in a much larger tree.

An example of a TR tree with AND nodes is shown in Fig. 2.2. This tree will cause a Botworld robot to place two bars at specific locations and orientations in the world and then return to a 'home base'. Since the acts of placing the two bars can successfully be done in either order, the program for positioning each bar becomes an independent subtree. (Note that the goal node in Fig. 2.2 cannot itself be split into non-interacting conjuncts.)

2.3 Simulating continuous execution

Approximating continuous computation by searching the entire TR tree at each time step becomes impractical for sufficiently large TR programs. Therefore, we have developed a heuristic method of action selection which usually produces the same result and runs in constant time in nearly all cases regardless of the size of the tree.

In this heuristic method, the agent remembers which node K_i (with associated action a_i) was active during the previous time step. It expects that in the absence of surprises, K_i will remain active until its parent node K_j (with associated action a_j) becomes active. Therefore, so long as K_i remains true while K_j remains false, a_i is selected as the default action. When and if K_j becomes true, a_j will be selected as the default action.

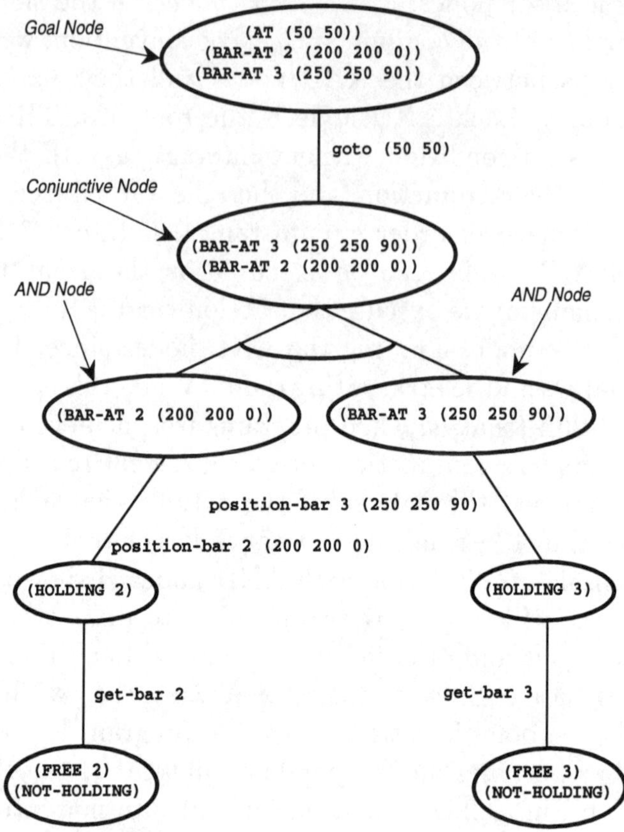

Figure 2.2. A TR tree with AND nodes.

Only when neither K_i nor K_j holds will the agent fail to have a default action to fall back on.[3]

This default action computation is supplemented by a separate process that scans through the rest of the tree examining a few nodes on each cycle (only nodes higher than the default node need be examined). If this separate process ever finds a true node that is higher than the default node, this higher node will be selected as the active node and the new default.

---

[3]Note that only in this case can we not guarantee constant time execution. Since this case arises only due to execution failures, it seems reasonable then to expect a reaction delay. Naturally, we would be forced to provide explicit error-handling routines to handle those execution failures in which such reaction delays could not be tolerated.

In summary, the agent will execute a normal sequence of goal-achieving actions (so long as they have their expected effects) while searching for serendipitous situations with whatever extra time it has.

3 ATTENTION TO MULTIPLE GOALS

In many applications, a robot will have several goals—each presumably achievable by a TR tree. Some goals relate to the maintenance of the robot itself (e.g., when the battery is low, get it recharged), some correspond to low-priority background tasks (e.g., routine mail delivery to offices), and some are given from time to time by humans (e.g., deliver this package immediately to room 14). All of these goals must be attended to, although some will be more important than others. The problem of attending to all of them is different than the classical AI problem of conjunctive goals; not all active goals need be satisfied simultaneously. We describe our technique for dealing with multiple goals in the context of our overall agent architecture, illustrated in Fig. 2.3.

Each goal that is being attended to is pursued by a TR program in the TR memory. These are instantiated from the Plan Library at the time the goal is given to the agent by the user. TR programs corresponding to goals that are to be achieved just once are expunged from the TR memory once their goals are achieved; programs corresponding to goals of maintenance are kept in the TR memory as long as those goals should be maintained. (Later, we describe the Planner and the Learning System which are used to create new TR programs and to modify existing ones.)

The agent's inputs are such that they allow the computation of conditions needed by its TR programs and by its planning and learning subsystems. The immediate sensory data required for these computations are provided more-or-less continuously by a separate perceptual module—not shown in Fig. 2.3—and are stored in the World Model along with other information about the environment that cannot be immediately sensed but that can be remembered. (The perceptual module is an independent

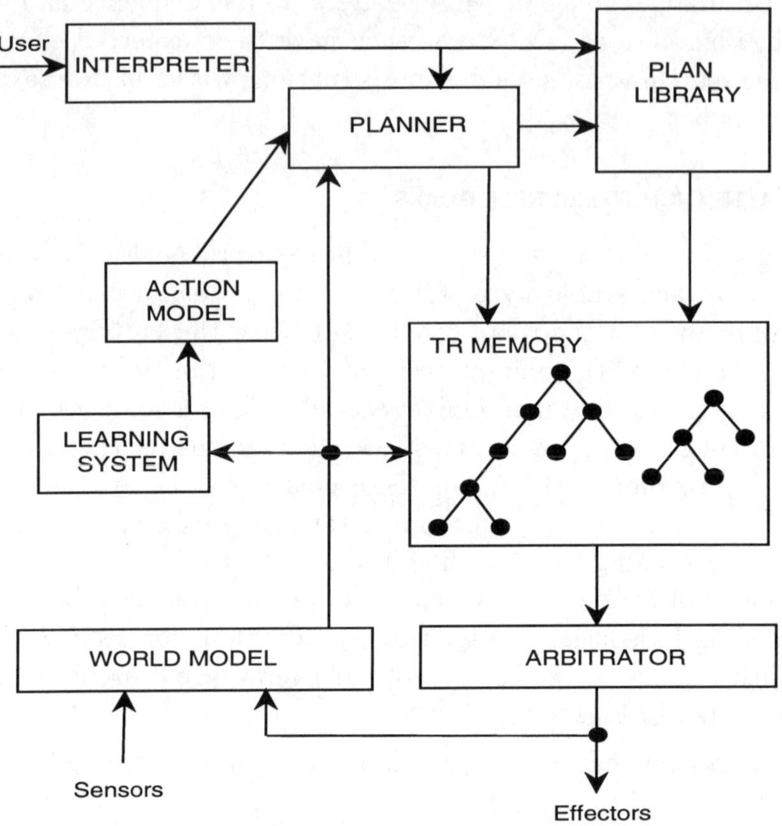

Figure 2.3. Agent architecture.

component of the architecture and will not be further discussed here.) Besides having effects on the world, TR programs can change the World Model. (Such a change might be appropriate, for example, if a TR program is known to achieve reliably a certain condition that cannot immediately be perceived.)

The Arbitrator decides which of the actions recommended by the separate TR programs in the TR memory should be selected for execution. For that computation, we have adopted a generalization of the concept of a goal that is similar to that used by researchers in delayed-reinforcement learning (Sutton 1990). Achieving goal conditions produces *rewards*. Reward amounts can vary according to user priorities and internal and external conditions. Reward possibilities can also evaporate (if the user retracts an assigned task), and therefore the Arbitrator should prefer to work first for high rewards that can be achieved with little effort as soon as possible. This preference is realized by ordering the m goals in the TR memory in a way that minimizes $\sum_{i=1}^{m} R_i T_i$, where R_i is the reward for goal i and T_i is the earliest time at which i is expected to be achieved.[4] Note that this formula, as desired, favours orderings which achieve goals with large R_i values as early as possible.

A first attempt at optimizing rewards based on this formula might be to consider each goal independently and to select the one which is expected to provide the highest reward per unit time, based on an estimate, t_i, of the time that it would take to reach each goal from the *current* situation. At worst, the estimate for t_i can be simply the number of nodes on the path to the root of the TR tree for that goal, but ordinarily the agent will have some better heuristic estimate of the time required by each action.[5] The goal, i, which maximizes R_i/t_i then provides the maximum average reward during its completion, and the Arbitrator would select the action corresponding to the shallowest node in the TR tree for goal i.

We can state certain conditions under which this greedy strategy is guaranteed to achieve one of the goals in the TR memory (so long as there are goals to be achieved in the TR memory):

1. There is an active node in at least one TR tree in the TR memory,

2. The execution of any action in a TR tree always has its expected effect (i.e., the parent node of the previously shallowest true node eventually becomes true),

3. In every TR tree in the TR memory, the time estimate, t_i, of a node is always greater than the time estimate of its parent, and the time estimates for all nodes are fixed,

---

[4] Minimizing this sum is a rough approximation to the more difficult problem of maximizing discounted future reward. It is also an instance of a 'cable-routing' problem—a special case of which has been studied by Blum *et al.* (1994).

[5] For instance, the duration of a **MOVE** action can generally be approximated as a function of the distance to be travelled.

4. The reward values R_i are constant over time.

However, like most greedy algorithms, it is too focused in its behaviour and will prefer one isolated high-reward goal to a set of medium-reward goals even though the medium-reward goals might be much easier to achieve now than they would be after achieving the isolated goal. Also, it is unable to take advantage of serendipitous situations which do not involve goal completion. For instance, if one of the agent's lesser goals is to deliver a certain library book to a far-away office, it will not realize that it can save time by picking up the book while it happens to be in the library for some other reason.

A modification that handles these problems uses the concept of a *stable node*. A condition is stable relative to a set of TR trees if once it holds, it will continue to hold while any of the TR trees in the set are executed. For example, the condition that the agent has a certain book is stable with respect to most TR programs (assuming that the agent has an unlimited carrying capacity), whereas the condition that the agent is in the library is not stable with respect to any TR program that might require the agent to leave the library. By extension, we call a node in a TR tree stable, relative to a set of TR trees, if its associated condition is stable, relative to those TR trees.

Stable nodes can easily be detected using **STRIPS**-style delete lists. If the condition at a node is not deleted by any of the actions used by a set of TR trees, then that node is stable with respect to those TR trees. We use this process to determine all of the stable nodes in the trees in the TR memory (with respect to those trees). Since a node is stable or unstable with respect to some context of other TR programs, this process needs to be repeated only when a tree is added to or deleted from the TR memory.

The Arbitrator uses stable nodes as milestones along the way toward achieving the root node of a TR tree. Instead of computing R_i/t_i for each TR tree in the TR memory (recall that t_i is the estimate of the time required to achieve the root node of the tree), we compute R_i/t_i^{sn} for each tree, where t_i^{sn} is the estimated time required to achieve the closest stable node in the tree. The Arbitrator selects the action recommended by the TR tree yielding the largest of these quantities. (If a tree has no stable nodes other than the root, we simply compute R_i/t_i for the tree.) Acting to achieve the best stable-node milestones (as measured by R_i/t_i^{sn}) helps to ensure that progress already made toward goals is not lost by subsequent actions.

Let us return to consider the situation in which an agent is in the library and has two goals. One is very urgent but involves leaving the library. The other involves delivering a library book to a far-away office. We see that if having the book is a stable node in the program for delivering the book, that delivery task may well have a high value of R_i/t_i^{sn} because t_i^{sn} is small when the agent is in the library. The agent will then pick up the book before working on the other more urgent goal.

Our arbitration method interacts nicely with the TR formalism to select opportunistic actions. For example, suppose the robot always had in its TR memory the goal of having its battery fully charged. We can assume that the reward value for achieving this goal varies in some manner inversely with the current charge level. Although this goal might not be pursued in a situation in which the battery was reasonably well charged relative to the distance to the charging station, it might happen that on the way to achieving some more important goal the robot happened to pass by the charging station. In this case, depending on its charge level at the time, the Arbitrator might decide to make a small detour for a recharge.

We have integrated this ability to pursue multiple goals into our agent architecture and have verified that it chooses intuitively reasonable actions in a variety of Botworld situations.

Many researchers have proposed architectures for a reactive intelligent agent based on various control schemes. We mention briefly a few representative examples:

- Maes uses spreading activation in behaviour networks (Maes 1989; Maes 1990) to select an appropriate action based on the agent's goals and percepts. However, behaviour networks do not provide any form of hierarchy, allow only discrete actions, and provide no guarantee against looping even in benign situations.

- The BB1 architecture has been used to arbitrate among modules which do planning, goal selection, and execution (Hayes-Roth *et al.* 1993) for Nomad^{TM} robots. These robots have more high-level capabilities, including meta-planning and motion planning, than is currently supported by our architecture. However, the BB1 decision cycle does not provide the real-time responses of TR trees, and the present BB1-based architecture can only handle interactions among goals by first merging them and then generating a single plan.

- The subsumption architecture (Brooks 1986) has been used to control a variety of mobile robots that act effectively in the world. However, it is primarily concerned with lower-level issues than those addressed by our architecture; it does not presently have the capability to arbitrate among multiple varying goals or to plan for novel goals.

- Mitchell has proposed a system called the Theo-Agent (Mitchell 1990) which combines planning, learning, and re-action through gradual compilation of stimulus–response rules. The Theo-Agent's performance improvement through speedup learning is beyond the current capabilities of our TR agent. However, the Theo-Agent does not perform inductive learning, or goal-arbitration.

- A variety of agents have been created in **SOAR** (Laird and Rosenbloom 1990; Jones *et al.* 1993), including a mobile robot and a flight simulator pilot. The **SOAR** architecture (Laird *et al.* 1987) provides a unified framework for an agent architecture, as well as speed-up learning and planning systems. However, none of the **SOAR** agents appear to handle multiple, time-varying goals.

- Gat has implemented a control architecture called **AT-LANTIS** which integrates reactive behaviour with a motion planning system (Gat 1992). The system does not yet have a learning component nor a goal-arbitrator.

- The **PRS** system (Georgeff and Lansky 1987) achieves both reactivity and goal-directedness by combining a reasoning system and a library of plans covering commonly occurring tasks. PRS is probably the most similar architecture to ours, but it does not incorporate learning.

4 PLANNING

We turn now to the matter of creating new TR programs and modifying existing ones by an automatic planning system. TR programs resemble the search trees constructed by backward-chaining AI planning systems. The overall goal is the root of the tree; any non-root node i is the regression of its parent node, j, through the action, a_i, connecting them. We have exploited this similarity by developing an automatic planning system that regresses conditions through durative actions to build a search tree. The search tree is then converted in a straightforward manner to a TR program.

Our planner uses STRIPS-like operators (Fikes *et al.* 1972) to model the effects of durative or atomic actions. A durative action itself does not have a STRIPS-like model, though, because a durative action has several effects depending on how long it is executed. STRIPS operators assume that actions are discrete with definite effects.

The representation we use, which we call a *teleo operator (TOP)*, is based on the backward regression of a literal through an action. The literals that we use are all those that we might want as components of TR conditions. For any literal λ_i and any action a_j, we can define a TOP, τ_{ij}, that describes the process of continuously executing a_j until λ_i becomes true. (If executing a_j never makes λ_i true, there is no such TOP.) The planner can treat a TOP model of a durative action as if the action were discrete. When the planner calls for the execution of an action corresponding to a TOP, it intends that that action be executed just exactly as long (no longer, no shorter) as is needed to achieve its intended effect. Thus a TOP describes a discrete action and can be used exactly like a STRIPS operator.

Following work on directional preimages in robot motion planning (Lozano-P'erez *et al.* 1984) we define the *preimage*, π, of a literal, λ, through durative action, α, as the weakest condition under which continuous execution of α will eventually satisfy λ while maintaining π until λ does becomes true. In analogy with STRIPS operators, π is the precondition for the TOP that models α when used to achieve λ.

Since we are defining TOPs only for each literal action pair, when the planner regresses a more complex condition through a TOP, it will need the equivalent of STRIPS to add and delete lists, so our TOPs will have these also. In our system, a TOP, then, has four components. These are:

1. the name of the action, a

2. a *postcondition* literal, λ, that is the intended effect of the TOP

3. a *preimage*, π, of the TOP

4. the set of *side effects*, S, of the TOP

Components of the side effects are analogous to add and delete lists. For a TOP with action a, postcondition λ, and preimage π, a side effect is a literal, σ, which is not necessarily true at the time action a was begun but (usually) becomes true by the time λ becomes true. Positive-literal side effects correspond roughly to elements of a STRIPS add list, and negative-literal side effects correspond to elements of a STRIPS delete list. Given the set of side effects, the planner can now do regression on a condition of any form using the standard STRIPS regression methods—treating the positive and negative side effects as the add and delete lists of the TOP, respectively.

Our planner can generate hierarchical and nonlinear plans, and can extend an existing plan to handle unexpected circumstances. Given any goal and a current situation, the planner does breadth-first backward-chaining until one or more subgoals are produced that hold in the current situation. The paths from all currently satisfied nodes to the goal are included in a TR tree for this goal, while the unsuccessful branches of the search may either be retained, potentially increasing the coverage of the tree, or pruned as likely to be irrelevant. Currently, unsuccessful branches are pruned to prevent overly large trees.

Hierarchical planning is implemented by having the planner develop TR programs for achieving a set of designer-specified goals, such as (HOLDING ?x). These programs are given names, such as (pickup-bar), generalized (by replacing constants by variables as appropriate (Fikes *et al.* 1972)), and stored as macro-operators (with their effects described by TOPs). The planner can then utilize these macro-operators as actions when constructing trees for other goals. An example of a hierarchical Botworld plan constructed by the system is shown in Fig. 2.4.

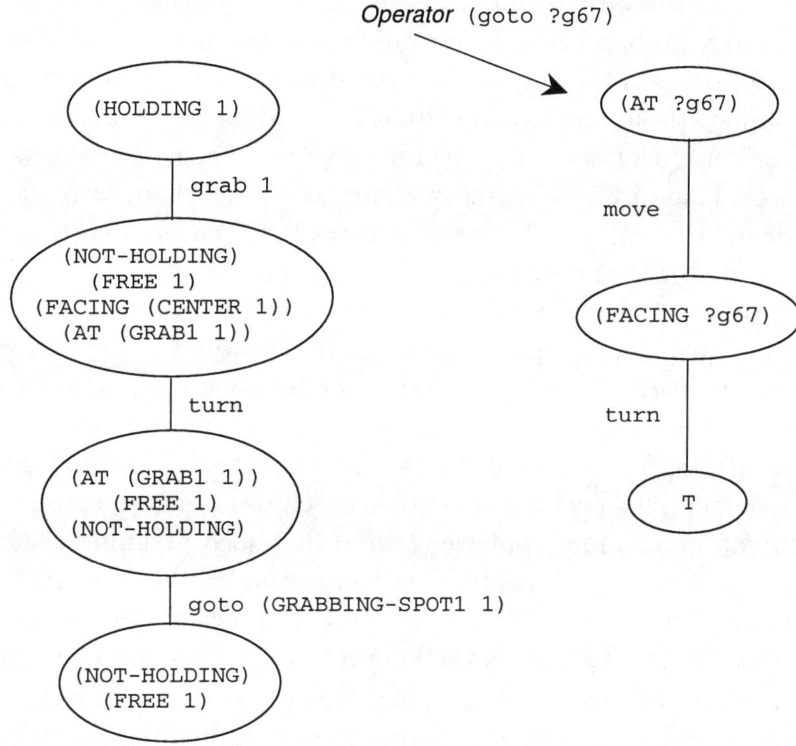

Figure 2.4. A hierarchy of TR trees produced by the planner.

Only a simplified form of nonlinear planning is implemented at present. (See (McAllister and Rosenblitt 1991) for a thorough discussion of nonlinear planning.)

When faced with any conjunctive goal or subgoal, our planner first attempts to treat each conjunct as an independent subgoal, creating AND node successors for each of them. If a conjunctive goal cannot be split in this way (because achieving one of its conjuncts would render an already achieved one false), the conjunction is treated instead as a single goal that must be regressed in its entirety through TOPs to produce successors.

A key advantage of the TR tree formalism over other reactive formalisms is the ease of replanning during execution (Nilsson 1994). Since the initial trees generated by the planner do not usually represent universal plans, situations will arise during execution that are not covered by any node in the current tree. (Such a circumstance can occur for a variety of reasons, including probabilistic action outcomes, execution errors, and the actions of other agents.) Instead of requiring complete replanning, these unexpected situations will usually require only an extension of the existing TR program. Such an extension can be made by having the planner backward chain from each node in the current TR program until the novel condition is reached. Since the existing nodes in a TR tree are retained in this process, the coverage of the tree increases monotonically as the agent gains more experience in the world. The revised trees are kept in the Plan Library for future use, and thus the agent's TR programs cover an increasing variety of situations that are representative of the situations actually encountered. Of course, pausing for plan extension causes a delay before action can be resumed, but we assume that such planning occurs asynchronously with continuous monitoring of the trees in the TR memory. If situations requiring action occur (recognizable by the existing TR trees), the appropriate actions will be taken.

We have incorporated this planning system into our agent architecture, and have demonstrated smooth interactions between the execution of existing TR programs and their modifications by the planner.

5 LEARNING

5.1 A method for learning TOPs

The ability to learn from experience and from instruction is a necessary component of useful robots. We are exploring a number of learning mechanisms in our research. Perhaps the simplest of these is the ability to learn categories of physical locations from sensor data. In Galles (1993), we endowed a mobile Nomad^{TM} robot with a neural-net-like structure with sonar inputs to learn how to distinguish between different locations (such as corridors, T-junctions, and corners) which it encountered in a simple office environment. The system represents these locations in a topological map that it makes of this environment. In other work, John has proposed and implemented a method for direct supervised learning of TR programs (John 1993).

Several authors have used reinforcement learning techniques to learn action policies that lead to rewards (Mahadevan and Connell 1992; Sutton 1990). One of the problems with reinforcement learning methods is that the policies learned depend too much on the reward structure used during learning. We would like what is learned while pursuing one set of goals to transfer easily to another set whenever possible. Therefore, we have concentrated on learning TOP models of the effects of actions and then using these models in a planner to produce TR programs.

We have developed a technique for learning and updating TOPs from both directed and random exploration of an environment by a robot. We have integrated this style of learning into our architecture and have demonstrated that it does indeed produce TOPs that can be used by our planning system.

To learn a TOP, we first decide on a set, Γ, of predicates thought to be needed to describe adequately the state of the environment and the effects of actions (postconditions, preimages, and side effects). These predicates must be ones that are continuously computable from perceptual and stored information. Learning is based on experiences recorded during one or more training runs. Each run consists of a series of actions taken in the world, whether guided by a teacher, resulting from random exploration, or produced during problem-solving. While the agent is acting and perceiving during training, the values of all predicates in Γ are collected at every time step. At the i-th time step, these values are represented by a *state formula*, ξ_i. (For example, if the predicates in Γ are x_1, x_2, and x_3 with values at time step i of T, T, and F, respectively, the corresponding

ξ_i would be $x_1 \wedge x_2 \wedge \neg x_3$.) We first describe how these state formulas are used to learn the preimages of TOPs.

Recall from our earlier description of TOPs that if a preimage, π, of a TOP, τ_{ij}, is entailed by a formula, ξ, then the durative execution of action a_j starting in an environmental state characterized by ξ is predicted eventually to lead to a state characterized by a formula that entails the postcondition λ_i. Thus, learning a preimage is a concept learning problem in which we seek to induce a formula π that is entailed by all of the 'positive' state formulas and is not entailed by any of the 'negative' state formulas. Positive examples for the TOP, τ_{ij}, are provided by those training instances in which the durative execution of a_j actually did lead to λ_i, and negative ones are provided by those instances that did not lead to λ_i. For the moment, let's postpone the details of how we partition the state formulas collected during the training runs into positive and negative sets. For now, we assume we have a set Ξ^+ of positive formulas and a set Ξ^- of negative formulas for each TOP to be learned. From these, we use a simple concept learning method that finds a disjunctive-normal-form formula that is entailed by all of the formulas in Ξ^+ and is not entailed by any of the formulas in Ξ^-.

We now describe the method for learning a particular TOP, τ_{ij}. (TOPs are learned for each action a_j and each literal, λ_i composed of predicates in Γ.)

- Set the initial preimage condition, π, of the TOP to F (*False*).

- Iterate over each (positive) $\xi_i \in \Xi^+$ (this outer loop creates disjunctions):

    * If π subsumes ξ_i (i.e., if $\xi_i \models \pi$), go on to the next example in Ξ^+.

    * Otherwise, create a new concept $\phi_i \leftarrow \xi_i$.

    * Iterate through the other positive examples $\{\xi_j \mid j \neq i\}$ (this inner loop creates conjunctions of literals):

        o compute $C(\phi_i, \xi_j)$, where $C(\alpha, \beta)$ is the *consensus* of α and β. (The *consensus* of two conjunctions, α and β, is the conjunction of all and only those literals appearing in either α or β that do not appear positively in one and negatively in the other. For example, the consensus of $x_1 \wedge \neg x_2 \wedge x_3$ and $x_2 \wedge x_3$ is $x_1 \wedge x_3$. The consensus of α and F is α. The consensus of α and T is T.)

     o If $C(\phi_i, \xi_j)$ does not subsume any (negative) $\xi \in \Xi^-$, set $\phi_i \leftarrow C(\phi_i, \xi_j)$. (This operation generalizes ϕ to subsume other members of Ξ^+ when such a generalization doesn't include any negative examples. That is, ϕ_i is the most specific conjunction that includes ξ_i and as many of the other ξ in Ξ^+ as possible without including any negative examples.)

     o Set $\pi \leftarrow \pi \vee \phi_i$.

We next describe how we obtain positive and negative state formulas for learning the preimage of τ_{ij}. We first find a trial preimage from the positive examples, and then use the trial preimage to identify negative examples.

- All state formulas, ξ_i (with i now an index over time steps), collected during a training run are assembled in a *sequence trace*, Σ.

- We first collect positive state formulas for learning the preimage of τ_{ij} by isolating all subsequences of Σ during which action a_j is being continuously executed and for which λ_i is false during the entire subsequence but then becomes true at the end of the subsequence. For example, suppose one such subsequence, Σ_{ij}, is $\{\xi_1, \xi_2, \ldots, \xi_i, \ldots, \xi_k\}$, where λ_i is true only in the last formula, ξ_k. Each of $\xi_1, \ldots \xi_{k-1}$ is a positive instance of the preimage π_{ij}.

- Next, we apply the above concept learning algorithm using the positive instances only. (This application will typically result in an overly general preimage.)

- We use this possibly over-general preimage, π, to identify a set of negative examples by isolating all subsequences of Σ during which action a_j is being continuously executed and during which π holds of the formulas in the subsequence. For each such subsequence $\{\xi_1, \xi_2, \ldots, \xi_i, \ldots, \xi_k\}$, in which λ_i never holds, the ξ_i are all negative examples if either:

* π no longer holds in ξ_{k+1} while a_j is still being executed, or
* λ_i is not achieved during the entire time a_j is being executed, and if the total length of time for which a_j was executed without achieving λ_i is significantly greater than the average time τ_{ij} takes to achieve λ_i. Currently, 'significantly greater' means greater than the average by a factor of at least 3.

Now that we have a set of positive and negative examples, we reapply the learning algorithm to produce a more specialized preimage that excludes the negative examples. Since the addition of negative examples can only make the preimage more specific, there is no need to repeat the process of finding more negative examples.

We compute the side effects of τ_{ij} by examining the 'positive' subsequences, Σ_{ij}. The side effects of τ_{ij} are all of those literals that have values in ξ_k (the 'final' state formula that entails λ_i) that are opposite from their values in at least one of ξ_i for $i < k$ in Σ_{ij}. It is, of course, possible that a literal determined to be a side effect in one subsequence might not be a side effect in another. We attach to each side effect, σ, a conditional probability estimate, p, which measures the proportion of those subsequences for τ_{ij} in which σ is true in ξ_k, given that σ was false at some earlier ξ_i. When using learned TOPs for planning, the planner will consider only side effects with probabilities above some threshold; other side effects correspond to superstitions that arise by chance coincidence. If a side effect σ is a positive literal, it is called a positive side effect; otherwise it is called a negative side effect.

This learning procedure may be repeated an arbitrary number of times as the agent gains experience. Each time the agent takes some series of actions in the world, it provides the action model learner an opportunity to refine its models. Thus, the TOPs become increasingly close approximations of the true effects of the actions.

5.2 Sample run

We illustrate our learning method by showing how it learns the effects of the actions used in grabbing a bar in Botworld. The learned TOPs are then used by the planner to construct a TR program for bar grabbing. We assume that the agent's perceptual system computes whether or not:

- it is holding a bar
- it is facing the bar midline
- it is aligned with the bar midline
- it is at the correct distance from the bar in order to grab it
- it is parallel to the long axis of the bar
- it is facing the centre of the bar

These predicates comprise the elements of Γ for this illustrative example. Most of the relevant terms used in these predicates are shown in Fig. 2.5.

Using these predicates, we had the agent collect several series of experimental traces, 16 traces in each series. In each series, half of the traces represented successful bar-grabbing runs guided by a human-coded TR program, while half represented random exploration of the world. The learning system then produced TOPs from each series of traces. Between 19 and 21 TOPs were learned from each series, of which 7 are essential for the bar grabbing task. The other TOPs represented reasonable but unnecessary operators such as turning to face away from the bar.

The learned TOPs were then given to our TR planner which planned a TR tree to accomplish the bar-grabbing task. This learned/planned tree was successful in completing the task in all of the examples we gave it.

Three of the TOPs learned by the system are shown in Fig. 2.6. A '+' sign in front of a side effect expression indicates it is used as an add-list item; a '−' sign indicates it is used as a

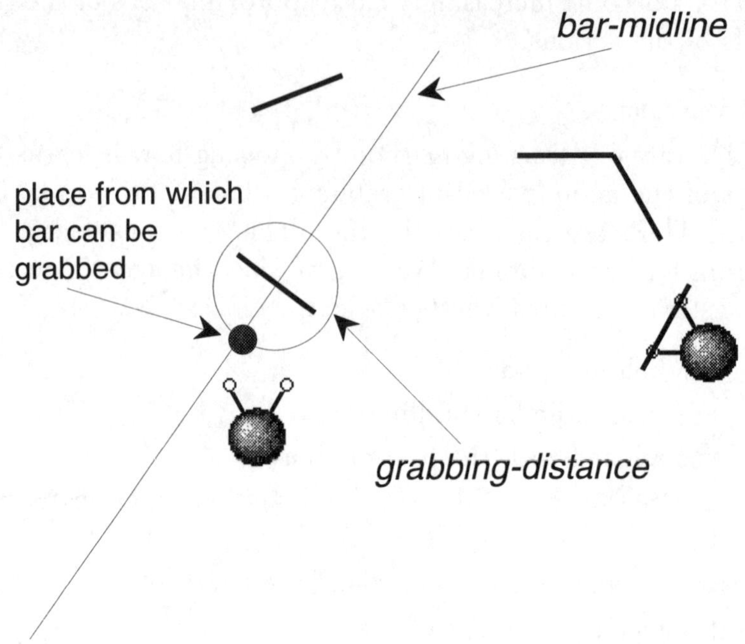

Figure 2.5. Terms used in Botworld predicates.

delete-list item. Generalization was done by a simple constant-to-variable conversion similar to that done for storing plans in the Plan Library.

All three of the TOPs shown in the figure represent correct and useful operations, but there are several details worth mentioning. First, there are two different situations in which the agent can move forward to achieve AT-GRABBING-DISTANCE for a bar, either by being too close to the bar to start with, or by facing the bar directly from any distance. Both situations are represented in the preimage of the TOP <(AT-GRABBING-DISTANCE ?x), forward>. Second, the predicate (PARALLEL-TO ?x) has an interesting relationship to the predicate (FACING-BAR ?x) in that they can be simultaneously true only in the rare circumstance in which the robot is on the long axis of the bar bound to ?x. This relationship is reflected in the side effects of the TOP <(PARALLEL-TO ?x), turn> in that (FACING-BAR ?x) has a very high, but not certain, probability of being deleted when turn is executed, and a small but non-zero chance of be-

```
<(HOLDING ?x), grab>
```
Preimage condition: (AT-GRABBING-DISTANCE ?x) ∧
                         (FACING-BAR ?x) ∧ (ON-MIDLINE ?x)
Average timing: 1.0
Side effects: none


```
<(AT-GRABBING-DISTANCE ?x), forward>
```
Preimage condition: (NOT (TOO-FAR ?x)) ∨ (FACING-BAR ?x)
Average timing: 17.0
Side effects: −(TOO-FAR ?x) [100%]
                    −(ON-MIDLINE ?x) [55%]
                    −(TOWARD-MIDLINE ?x) [63%]


```
<(PARALLEL-TO ?x), turn>
```
Preimage condition: TRUE
Average timing: 25.5
Side effects: −(FACING-BAR ?x) [99%]
                    +(FACING-BAR ?x) [3%]
                    +(TOWARD-MIDLINE ?x) [58%]
                    −(TOWARD-MIDLINE ?x) [45%]

Figure 2.6. Three TOPs learned during some training runs.

ing added when (PARALLEL-TO ?x) is achieved.

5.3 Related work on learning

The TOP model of actions and the method of learning from positive experiences derive from Vere's relational predicate learning algorithm (Vere 1980). However, all of Vere's learning occurred in deterministic and discrete domains. Our TOP models are similar to the low-level goal achievement rules used by the compiler in GAPPS (Kaelbling and Rosenschein 1990). The GAPPS rules do not include side effects, and are explicitly programmed rather than learned. TOPs are quite similar to the empirical backprojections in Christiansen (1991). Christiansen's work is the only work we have seen that learns action models on a real physical robot. However, Christiansen's algorithm used only discrete actions and operated in a very simple environment.

The problem of learning action models from experience has been studied extensively by Gil (1992) and by Shen (1989). Both of them assumed deterministic domains, and assumed primarily discrete worlds. One of Shen's experiments did involve learning action models in a continuous robot arm domain and had a somewhat more quantitative emphasis than does the work described here.

Mahadevan learns action models for a robot in a continuous domain sensed through a 12 by 12 certainty grid (Mahadevan 1992). These models are learned for one step actions only and provide no method of focusing on a specific aspect of the environment. Grefenstette and Ramsey view the process of learning action models for a robot as learning parameters of user-defined operators, using an algorithm they call *case-based anytime learning* (Grefenstette and Ramsey 1992). Their work is a promising approach to robot control, but relies heavily on the user-defined parameterized operators and is more quantitative than our approach.

6 CONCLUSIONS AND FUTURE WORK

We have presented an agent architecture that integrates the ability to react appropriately in dynamic worlds with the abilities to plan and to learn. Although the work reported here is preliminary and has been tested only on simulated robots, we think the ideas embodied in this work exemplify what will be required for robust, adaptive, and flexible autonomous agents. Our research has also given us some perspective about the extensive work that remains to be done.

We now mention some areas that we intend to pursue and cite some preliminary work by others in each of these. First, we have assumed that the perceptual system is able to compute the values of a set of predicates on which the agent bases its actions and its planning and learning. Providing an adequate perceptual system for a robot requires advances in computer vision and other sensory modalities. In this connection, we will be looking closely at the sort of work being done by Horswill (1993) and by

Ballard (1991) on 'active vision' in which processing is matched to the particular task at hand rather than on complete analyses of scenes.

We have assumed that the agent's designer specifies the sensors and the perceptual predicates that will be needed. But in many applications the designer will not be able to predict all of the predicates that the agent will need—even though the set of sensors on which all perceptual predicates are based will necessarily be fixed by the designer. It will be important for the agent to be able to extend its set of predicates automatically to cover aspects of its world that turn out to be important. Some initial work in this area has been done by Shen (1989) and by Drescher (1991).

On the other side of the perception–action spectrum, we have provided a few primitive actions and some higher level routines constructed from these primitives. Because of insurmountable combinatorial problems, both planning and learning require hierarchies of actions. Planning must operate first at high levels of the hierarchy and then articulate these plans in increasing detail. We imagine that the learning system will first construct low level TOPs and then gradually learn the effects of higher level actions. Some work has already been done on learning hierarchies of actions in domains unfamiliar to the learner. Drescher's schema mechanism develops complex actions (Drescher 1991), while Ring combines actions to create operators using reinforcement learning (Ring 1991).

Several other automated planning techniques could be effectively used in conjunction with our architecture. Two promising directions involve 'anytime planning' (Boddy and Dean 1989) and temporal reasoning (Dean and Wellman 1991). Anytime planning would allow the agent to react as best it can in critical situations where there is insufficient time to plan a complete TR tree before acting. Reasoning about time is necessary if the agent must deal with goals that have real-time deadlines.

There are several directions in which the learning component of the architecture could be extended. One problem with the current method is that the total number of TOPs that might be created is the product of twice the number of predicates times the number of actions. While this product was not excessive in the Botworld domain, in more complex environments a large number of TOPs would severely slow any planner trying to use them. Discarding seldom-used TOPs might keep the number of TOPs manageable.

Another clear limitation of the present learning system is its dependence on a teacher to generate useful experiences. The TOP learning algorithm does not itself depend on the experiences being goal-directed, but (just as in reinforcement learning) random exploration does not provide sufficient coverage of the state space to learn all of the operators the planner might need. (For example, in Botworld, the likelihood that the robot would ever successfully execute a GRAB action during random exploration is extremely remote.) Exploration and experimentation have been studied in other work on learning action models (Gil 1992; Shen 1989), and these studies will provide a starting point for our future work.

We also intend to try more sophisticated concept learning algorithms (e.g., C4.5 (Quinlan 1992) or FOIL (Quinlan 1990)) to approximate the preimage of a TOP. This will also allow us to state computational properties of our learning algorithm, which we have not yet developed for the present system. However, the more difficult problem of proving convergence properties of learning agents in complex environments will likely remain unresolved for some time.

Constructing a useful World Model can also be considered a problem in machine learning. A key problem here for mobile robots involves building some kind of map of the environment and then using this map first to avoid getting lost and (when needed) to re-orient. Kuipers has worked extensively on map-making (Kuipers 1991), and we have done some preliminary work (Galles 1993), which we plan to extend.

Finally, our ideas and their planned extensions must be tested in other, more complex domains. The Botworld tasks have provided useful preliminary tests, and we are now considering other application domains. Among these are: more work with the Silicon Graphics flight simulator, control of a physical mobile robot in office domains, and the interactive system of 'Woggleworld' cartoon characters (Bates 1992).

Acknowledgements

This work was partially supported by the National Science Foundation under grant number IRI-9116399 and by the Advanced Research Projects Agency under grant number F49620-94-1-0090 (monitored by the Air Force Office of Scientific Research). Mr. Benson was partially supported by a National Defense Science and Engineering Graduate Fellowship. The authors are grateful for the useful comments made by Andrew Kosoresow.

REFERENCES

Ballard, D. (1991). Animate vision. *Artificial Intelligence*, 48, pp. 57–86.

Bates, J. (1992). Virtual reality, art, and entertainment. *PRESENCE: Teleoperators and Virtual Environments*, **1**(1), 133–138.

Blum, A., Chalasani, P., Coppersmith, D., Pulleyblank, B., Raghavan, P., and Sudan, M. (1994). The minimum latency problem. *Proc. of STOC-94*, pp. 163–171. Association for Computing Machinery.

Boddy, M. and Dean, T. (1989). Solving time-dependent planning problems. *Proc. IJCAI-89*, pp 979–984. San Francisco, CA: Morgan Kaufmann.

Brooks, R. (1986). A robust layered control system for a mobile robot. *IEEE Journal of Robotics and Automation*, March 1986.

Christiansen, A. (1991). Manipulation planning from empirical back-projection. *Proc. IEEE Conference on Robotics and Automation.*

Dean, T. and Wellman, M. (1991). *Planning and Control*, Chapter 3. San Francisco, CA: Morgan Kaufmann.

Drescher, G. (1991). *Made Up Minds: A Constructivist Approach to Artificial Intelligence*. Cambridge, MA: MIT Press.

Fikes, R., Hart, P. and Nilsson, N.J. (1972). Learning and executing generalized robot plans. *Artificial Intelligence*, **3**, 251–288.

Galles, D. (1993). Map building and following using teleo-reactive trees. In F.C.A. Groen, S. Hirose and C.E. Thorpe (Eds.) *Intelligent Autonomous Systems: IAS-3*, 390–398. Washington: IOS

Press.

Gat, E. (1992). Integrating planning and reacting in a heterogeneous asynchronous architecture for controlling real-world mobile robots. *Proc. of AAAI-92*, 809–815. Cambridge, MA: MIT Press.

Gil, Y. (1992). *Acquiring Domain Knowledge for Planning by Experimentation*. PhD Thesis, Carnegie Mellon University.

Georgeff, M. and Lansky, A. (1987). Reactive Reasoning and Planning. *Proc. of AAAI-87*, 677–682. San Francisco, CA: Morgan Kaufmann.

Grefenstette, J.J. and Ramsey, C.L. (1992). An approach to anytime learning. *Machine Learning: Proceedings of the Ninth International Workshop*, 189–195. San Francisco, CA: Morgan Kaufmann.

Hayes-Roth, B., Lalanda, P., Morignot, P., Pfleger, K. and Balabanovic, M. (1993). Plans and Behavior in Intelligent Agents. KSL Report No. KSL 93–43, Stanford University, May.

Horswill, I. (1993). Polly: a vision-based artificial agent. *Proc. of AAAI-93*, 824–829. Cambridge, MA: MIT Press.

John, G. (1993). SQUISH: A Preprocessing Method for Supervised Learning of T-R Trees from Solution Paths. (Unpublished) Robotics Laboratory, Stanford University.

Jones, R.M., Tambe, M., Laird, E. and Rosenbloom, P. (1993). Intelligent automated agents for flight training simulators. *Proceedings of the Third Conference on Computer Generated Forces and Behavioral Representations*, March.

Kaelbling, L.P. and Rosenschein, S.J. (1990). Action and planning in embedded agents. *Robotics and Autonomous Systems*, **6**(1 and 2), 35–48.

Kuipers, B. (1991). A robot exploration and mapping strategy based on a semantic hierarchy of spatial representations. *Robotics and Autonomous Systems*, 8(1–2), 47–63.

Laird, J. and Rosenbloom, P. (1990). Integrating execution, planning, and learning in soar for external environments. *Proc. of AAAI-90*. Cambridge, MA: MIT Press.

Laird, J., Newell, A. and Rosenbloom, P. (1987). SOAR : an architecture for general intelligence. *Artificial Intelligence*, **33**(1), 1–64, September 1987.

Lozano-Pérez, T., Mason, M.T., and Taylor, R.H. (1984). Automatic synthesis of fine-motion strategies for robots. *International Journal of Robotics Research*, **3**(1), 3–24.

McAllister, D. and Rosenblitt, D. (1991). Systematic nonlinear planning. *Proc. of AAAI-91*. Cambridge, MA: MIT Press.

Maes, P. (1989). How to do the right thing. *Connection Science Journal*, **1**(3), 291–323.

Maes, P. (1990). Situated agents can have goals. *Robotics and Autonomous Systems*, 6(1–2), 49–70.

Mahadevan, S. (1992). Enhancing transfer in reinforcement learning by building stochastic models of robot actions. *Machine Learning: Proceedings of the Ninth International Workshop*. San Francisco, CA: Morgan Kaufmann.

Mahadevan, S. and Connell, J. (1992). Automatic programming of behaviour-based robots using reinforcement learning. *Artificial Intelligence*, **56**(2–3), 311–365.

Mitchell, T. (1990). Becoming increasingly reactive. *Proc. of AAAI-90*. Cambridge, MA: MIT Press.

Nilsson, N. J. (1994). Teleo-reactive programs for agent control. *Journal of Artificial Intelligence Research*, **1**, 139–158, January 1994.

Quinlan, J. R. (1990). Learning logical definitions from relations. *Machine Learning*, **5**(3), 239–266.

Quinlan, J. R. (1992). *C4.5: Programs for Machine Learning*. San Francisco, CA: Morgan Kaufmann.

Ring, M. (1991). Incremental development of complex behaviours through automatic construction of sensory-motor hierarchies. In L. Birnbaum and G. Collins (Eds.), *Machine Learning: Proceedings of the Eighth International Workshop*, 343–347. San Francisco, CA: Morgan Kaufmann.

Rosenschein, S. J. and Kaelbling, L. P. (1986). The synthesis of machines with provable epistemic properties. In J. Halpern (Ed.), *Proceedings of the 1986 Conference on Theoretical Aspects of Reasoning about Knowledge*, pp. 83–98. San Francisco, CA: Morgan Kaufmann. (Updated version: Technical Note 412, Artificial Intelligence Center, SRI International, Menlo Park, CA, 1986.)

Schoppers, M. J. (1987). Universal plans for reactive robots in unpredictable domains. In *Proceedings of IJCAI-87*. San Francisco, CA: Morgan Kaufmann.

Shen, W.M. (1989). *Learning from the Environment Based on Actions and Percepts*. PhD Thesis, Carnegie Mellon University.

Sutton, R. (1990). Integrated architectures for learning, planning, and reacting based on approximating dynamic programming. *Machine Learning: the Proceedings of the Seventh International Workshop*, pp. 216–224. San Francisco: Morgan Kaufmann.

Teo, P. (1992). Botworld. (Unpublished) Robotics Laboratory, Computer Science Dept., Stanford University, December 1992.

Vere, S. A. (1980). Multilevel counterfactuals for generalizations of relational concepts and productions. *Artificial Intelligence*, **14**, 139–164.

3

Multi-entity Models

Yoram Moses

Department of Applied Mathematics and Computer Science, Weizmann Institute of Science, Rehovot, 76100 Israel

Moshe Tennenholtz

Faculty of Industrial Engineering and Management, Technion—Israel Institute of Technology, Haifa 32000, Israel

Abstract

In a seminal paper, McCarthy and Hayes (1969) suggested first-order logic as a basis for knowledge representation and reasoning about action. They considered, and rejected, a model of *interacting automata* as being epistemologically inadequate. This chapter suggests *multi-entity models*, a framework closely related to the interacting automata of McCarthy and Hayes, as a tool for knowledge representation and reasoning. Multi-entity models are designed so as to overcome some of the main criticisms of interacting automata. A number of basic issues in multi-agent activity are investigated in the framework of these models, illustrating both the expressiveness and the computational tractability of multi-entity models.

1 INTRODUCTION

In an extremely influential paper, McCarthy and Hayes (1969) laid the foundations for much of the research carried out since then on knowledge representation and reasoning about action. In that paper, the authors suggested (first-order) logic as a basic framework for knowledge representation and for reasoning about action. The only other model considered in McCarthy and Hayes (1969) is the *interacting automata* model. In this model, a relevant part of the world is represented as an automaton consisting of a collection of subautomatons that interact via a predetermined topology of communication links. These links make the output of one automaton become the input of another. The actions of an automaton are assumed to be a deterministic function of its current state, and its next state is assumed to be a deterministic function of its current state and its current inputs. One way in which McCarthy and Hayes envisioned using this model is by representing every agent in the world by an automaton, while the environment is represented by one or more automatons as well. McCarthy and Hayes view the interacting automata model as being a *metaphysically adequate* representation, which means that the actual world represented by the model 'could have the form depicted in the model without contradicting the facts of the aspects of reality that interest us'. They argue in favour of representations that are also *epistemologically adequate*, which means that '...it [the representation] can be used practically to express the facts that one actually has about the aspect of the world'. While McCarthy and Hayes find the interacting automata model useful for defining relevant notions (such as *can*), they reject it as a general representation framework. The two main arguments they give for this are:

- The number of states required in a subautomaton that represents an agent's knowledge may be very large, and
- the representation is epistemologically inadequate, since we never know a person well enough to list his internal states.

They add two secondary arguments for its inappropriateness. One is that geometric information is hard to represent in such a model, and the other is that assuming fixed interconnections between automata is inadequate.

In this chapter, we introduce the *multi-entity* model, which is closely related to the interacting automata model. We argue that, with a slightly modified interpretation, our model has a number of distinct advantages for use in multi-agent systems. Moreover, this model will, at least to some extent, overcome (or avoid) many of the faults that McCarthy and Hayes found in the interacting automata model. After introducing multi-entity models, we shall investigate a number of basic issues in multi-agent activity in the framework of these models. In particular, we aim to show that multi-entity models expose a relatively good tradeoff between expressiveness (of the representation) and complexity (of computing various relevant properties in the context of this representation). In our opinion, it is not an accident that McCarthy and Hayes use an automata-structured model as their first attempt to supply a general scheme of knowledge representation and reasoning. Indeed, automata-based models have been found to be useful abstractions in many areas of science and engineering. One purpose of this work is to suggest the possibility of carrying out research on knowledge representation and reasoning in the framework of automata-based models.

Interestingly, a number of automata-based models discussed in the AI literature resemble the interacting automata model of McCarthy and Hayes. An example of useful automata-based models are the architectures discussed by Brooks (1986) and his colleagues. While the approach set forth by McCarthy and Hayes (1969) can be thought of as having rejected the use of automata-based models, other approaches such as that of Brooks (1986) can be considered as having rejected the use of the knowledge representation and reasoning paradigm. In this chapter, we argue that there exists a middle ground, where automata-based models serve as a useful, powerful, and natural setting for knowledge representation and reasoning.

This chapter is organized as follows. Section 2 is a discussion of the basic features that motivate the design of multi-entity models as knowledge representation and reasoning mechanisms. It presents a sketch of multi-entity models and relates them to the criticism that McCarthy and Hayes had for interacting automata. In Section 3 a further discussion of these models is provided, as well as basic formal definitions. Section 4 demonstrates the expressiveness of multi-entity models. In particular, we show how to encode both STRIPS-like representations and reactive sensor–effector architectures in a multi-entity model setting. In Section 5 it is shown how uncertainty can be handled by multi-entity models. The general *cooperative goal achievement* problem in the framework of multi-entity models is introduced and investigated. In particular, it is shown to be decidable. In Section 6 we look further into the cooperative goal achievement problem, and study it in multi-agent settings with complete information. We show that the corresponding cooperative goal achievement problem is relatively tractable. In Section 7 we investigate the case where some agents might fail during the execution of a cooperative plan. We show that that the decision problem corresponding to cooperative goal achievement in this case is not harder than in the complete information case. Section 8 concludes with a short summary and discussion of some related work. Proofs appear in Section 9.

2 MOTIVATING OUR APPROACH

A collection of interacting automata *à la* McCarthy and Hayes can be viewed as a finite-state machine. Clearly, it is not realistic to present a detailed model of many practical systems and scenarios in terms of a finite-state machine. Nevertheless, we argue that it may often be sensible to design artificial agents using finite-state representations of their environment. The representation an agent uses simply need not present the world in sufficient detail to require more expressive description languages. Intuitively, let us distinguish between the physical state of agents, say robots, and between their computational (or 'mental') state at a given point. In many cases, a finite-state description can serve very well as a metaphysically adequate representation of the physical state. It is the computational state that we have a difficulty adequately modelling by finite-state machines. The computational state of other agents, however, will generally not be accessible to a given agent of interest. As a result, this agent may very well get by with a description of the physical state of other agents and, perhaps, a limited amount of information regarding their mental state.

Let us consider a simple-minded example. You are driving a car, and see another person driving a car in the other direction. While the other driver's mental state may be very rich and complex, as far as you are concerned in the given application, the other driver's behaviour can be classified into one of a small number of states. The other driver may have a number of potential actions to take, and you have only a rough idea of how she will behave. You plan your actions according to this rough idea, as well as according to the physical state of the other car: where it is, how fast it is going and in what direction, whether it is signalling, etc. Your model of the other driver need not be very detailed for you to function safely and effectively on the road.

As illustrated by this example, we believe that by allowing the model to abstract away some of the complexity of the world, it is possible to revive finite-state automata as a useful framework for knowledge representation and reasoning. In particular, since the computational state of other agents is mostly inaccessible to an agent, we argue that it is often reasonable for our agent, when planning her own actions, to consider other agents as if they behave in a nondeterministic fashion. By modelling agents as nondeterministic machines, we are allowing their actions to be generated by a mechanism that is not necessarily fully represented in the model. As far as the model is concerned, in a given (coarse) state the agent may perform any of a number of actions. In fact, the agent's actual state may be more detailed than is represented, and the action it performs may be the result of a sophisticated computation. Recall that the interacting automata of McCarthy and Hayes were assumed to be *deterministic* state machines, and hence did not allow this type of interpretation. (Notice that while deterministic and nondeterministic finite-state machines have equal expressive power in defining formal languages, they are not equivalent for the purposes of representation for which we are considering them.)

Another issue that needs to be addressed in going to finite-state descriptions is that even when we abstract away various aspects of an agent's state, it may still have a large number of possible states. It is often possible to take advantage of the structure of an agent in order to derive useful and concise descriptions of its state. For example, an agent may be viewed as being composed of a number of fairly independent components, each with its own state. Consider, for example, describing the state of the wheels of a robot, its arms, and its motor as separate components of the robot's state. We shall, in fact, define an agent, or entity, to correspond to a set of finite-state components.

A final point to be considered is that the transition function of the automata comprising the model needs to be described in a concise fashion. Clearly, if the states of agents and entities are decomposed to a fairly orthogonal collection of components, then the transition function can often be described by specifying how it acts on each component, thereby obtaining considerable savings in the size of the representation. We shall choose a particular language for describing transition functions which, while slightly arbitrary, can help reduce the size of the description of the transition function.

In our model, there will be quite a bit of freedom in choosing what an 'agent' or 'entity' should be. An agent can actually be a physical entity in the world (such as a hand, a door, etc); it can also be composed of finite-state components whose states describe locations of certain items, the truth of an assertion, etc. Agents are often composed of subparts that are fairly independent. By representing each such part (e.g., arms, legs, fingers) as a separate component of the agent's state, we obtain a natural way of describing local change in an efficient manner.

3 THE FORMAL MODEL

We now turn to formally define the multi-entity model based on the informal discussion of the previous section. A multi-entity model is a tuple $\langle E_1, \ldots, E_n, \mathcal{A}, T \rangle$, where $E_1, \ldots, E_n$ are *agents* (or *entities*), $\mathcal{A}$ is a set of *actions* and T is a *state transition function*. Each agent E_i is a non-deterministic finite-state machine (L_i, A_i), where L_i is its set of (local) states, and $A_i : L_i \to 2^{\mathcal{A}}$ determines its possible actions in every local state.

A *system configuration* is the tuple $(s_1, \ldots, s_n)$ of the states of the different agents. We denote the set of system configurations by C. We assume that a distinguished action denoted by Λ, which we shall think of as the *null* action, can always be generated by each agent. We consider an agent to be passive if it can generate only the Λ action. The sequence $(a_1, \ldots, a_n)$ of actions generated by all agents at a particular point constitute a *joint action*. The effects of joint actions are determined by a state transition function $T : C \times \mathcal{A}^n \longrightarrow C$. (This is in the spirit of Shapley (1953) and Halpern and Fagin (1989).)

The above description captures the essential aspects of a basic multi-entity model. However, in order to have a succinct representation some care has to be taken regarding the representation of the agents' states, of the joint actions, the state transition function, and of the action functions A_i. In the sequel we will suggest a succinct representation of these elements of the model. The representation we suggest seems natural to us, and can facilitate considerable succinctness in many cases. Nevertheless, there is nothing that should force this representation, and other succinct representations of a similar spirit can also be used.

We think of an agent's actions as depending in general on the agent's complete state. In many cases, however, it is possible to think of an agent E_i as being composed of components $\{M_{i_1}, \ldots, M_{i_{f(i)}}\}$. These may correspond to a robot's arms, its wheels, its motor, etc. While these components are interdependent to some degree, much of the activity concerning a single component may be independent of the rest. Thus, the local state s_i of agent E_i may very well be represented as a sequence $(\ell_{i_1}, \ldots, \ell_{i_{f(i)}})$ of the states of its components, and its actions may also be represented in a similar fashion. We shall denote the state space of a component M_{i_j} by L_{i_j}, and we assume for ease of exposition that the sets L_{i_j} are pairwise disjoint.

The state transition function determines how the state of each component of every agent changes, given a particular joint action and certain conditions on the states of other agents and components. Hence, we can achieve a succinct representation by taking the restriction of T to states of component M_{i_j} to be defined as $T_{i_j} : L_{i_j} \times \mathcal{A}^n \times \mathcal{L} \longrightarrow L_{i_j}$ where $\mathcal{L}$ is a set of conditions on the configurations of the system. Formally, $\mathcal{L}$ is a propositional language closed under the Boolean operators conjunction $\wedge$ and negation $\neg$, whose primitive propositions are elements of the form $in(s)$ for all the states s such that $s \in L_{i_j}$ for some component M_{i_j}. A proposition of the form $in(s)$ will be satisfied if the corresponding machine is in state s, and the satisfaction of more complex propositions is defined in the standard way. Hence, T_{i_j} will determine the effects of joint actions on the state of the component M_{i_j} given different conditions on the configuration of the system. As a default, if $T_{i_j}(s, \bar{a}, \psi) = s$ for all ψ and s, so that the joint action $\bar{a}$ does not affect the state of component M_{i_j}, we can have a convention that $T_{i_j}(s, \bar{a}, \psi)$ need not be explicitly defined. We also assume that the T_{i_j}'s are deterministic.

Naturally, the function T_{i_j} will be defined using only a small number of formulas of $\mathcal{L}$. In addition, in a case that the action of a particular agent is irrelevant to the effects of a transition, we can have the convention that this action need not explicitly appear in the joint action. In order to have a succinct representation of A_i, we assume that A_i is a function of the form $A_i : \mathcal{A} \to \mathcal{L}_i$, where $\mathcal{L}_i$ is a restriction of $\mathcal{L}$ to formulas whose primitive propositions are of the form $in(s)$ where s is a state of a component of agent i only. Hence, each A_i associates with each action a, a condition on agent i states under which action a can be generated.

An instance of a multi-entity model will consist of a description of the entities, their transition functions, their action functions, and a set $\mathcal{C}_0$ of possible initial configurations. For every entity i, it specifies the set L_i of states of i, the sets L_{i_j} of component states for $1 \le j \le f(i)$, the function A_i, and the transition functions T_{i_j} for $1 \le j \le f(i)$. Each such transition function is a set of tuples of the form (from-state, joint action, condition, to-state), where the conditions are formulas of $\mathcal{L}$. It is assumed that the number of conditions that appear for every from-state is polynomially bounded in the total number of entity components. The size of the formulas constituting the conditions in the T_{i_j}'s and in A_i is similarly bounded. The size of such an instance, which will be relevant when we consider the computational complexity of solving various problems in the context of a given multi-entity model, is the total size of the representations of these agents.

4 THE USE OF MULTI-ENTITY MODELS

We feel that multi-entity models present a reasonably succinct operational framework for settings involving multiple agents. To support this claim, we consider the expressiveness of these models in this section. We now discuss how they can be used to represent natural situations, and show how they capture known representations and architectures of different flavours.

Let us start by considering an example of how a simple situation can be represented in this framework. Assume that Alice, Bob, and Chris are three people who are standing in location O on one side of a lake. There are two islands in the middle of our lake, denoted by X and Y. There is a boat with a pair of oars nearby. This boat can carry up to four people, and two people are needed in order to operate the boat (each handling one of the oars). The boat will move in a certain direction only if both operators row in that direction. Clearly, many details are still missing in order to have a complete description of the situation, but we can already consider how it can be represented in the framework of a multi-entity model. We will have three active agents: Alice, Bob, and Chris, and two passive agents: the boat and the oars. Examples of components that correspond to an active agent can be: a component that corresponds to the location of an agent (either X, Y, or O), a component that corresponds to the situation of an agent (in the boat, out of the boat, etc), and a component that corresponds to the hand of an agent (whether it holds an oar or not, etc). Similarly, the boat's location will be handled by one of the boat's components. Examples of actions that an agent can perform include: enter/exit the boat, row in a certain direction, pick an oar. The ability of generating such actions and the effects of joint actions will depend on the agent state and the system configuration respectively (e.g., the boat will move in a certain direction only if both agents that operate it happen to row in that direction and the boat is in the water). This gives a fairly direct and succinct representation of the situation described, as well as allowing us to represent the operational aspects of this context in a straightforward fashion. Had we represented the whole system as one component or each of the agents as one component, then the resulting representations could have been exponentially larger (at least if this was done in a naive fashion). Once the situation is just a little bit more complicated, this last fact will become crucial.

It is very natural to use multi-entity models to model situations at the sensor–effector level (in the spirit of (Brooks 1986)). In particular, we can treat an agent's component as a sensor, whose states correspond to a condition about that sensor (e.g, whether it observes a 'close object' in its current direction). The effectors are associated with the actions an agent may generate. A crucial factor, however, is that the multi-entity model does not necessarily model (in difference to the interacting automata discussed in McCarthy and Hayes (1969) and simple sensor–effector mechanisms) the exact program the agents follow. If we would like to explicitly represent (part of) an agent's computational state (or program), then this can be achieved by allowing only the actions selected by the computational mechanism to be executed in the corresponding computational states. In other words, we can have some components that succinctly represent the computational state (as in (Brooks 1986)) and generate actions based on this computational state; this turns out to be a special case of our model where in the corresponding (computational) states the agent can generate only one action. Formally, this is achieved by adjusting the corresponding A_i's. This simple representation allows interesting deterministic finite-state architectures such as the ones discussed in (Brooks 1986) to be represented efficiently as multi-entity models. Notice that multi-entity models support also situations where only part of the computational states is explicitly represented, allowing us to combine reactive approaches such as those of Agre and Chapman (1987), Agre (1991), Brooks (1986) and Schoppers (1987), with the more standard knowledge representation and reasoning paradigm (Levesque 1986) in one joint framework.

As another example of the expressiveness of multi-entity models, consider a STRIPS-like (Fikes and Nilsson 1971) representation in which the preconditions are propositional formulas and the postconditions (add-list/delete-list) are subsets of a set of atomic propositions and their negations. Formally, it is defined as follows. We have a set of primitive propositions $p_1, \ldots, p_n$ which describe an environment. Each truth assignment to the primitive propositions defines a state of the environment. In addition, we have a set of operators, $o_1, \ldots o_m$, which might change the environment. At each point in time at most one operator is applied. Each operator o_i is associated with a pair: a *precondition* pre$_i$ and a *postcondition* post$_i$. A precondition pre$_i$ is a propositional formula in the propositional logic whose primitive propositions are $p_1, \ldots, p_n$. An operator o_i can be executed in a particular environment state, if the corresponding precondition pre$_i$ is satisfied in that state. A postcondition post$_i$ consists of two elements: an *add-list a_i* and a *delete-list d_i*. Each such element consists of a set of primitive propositions. The add-list a_i and the delete-list d_i of an operator o_i should be disjoint. The postcondition q_i describes which primitive propositions needs to be true, as determined by the add-list a_i, and which primitive propositions needs to be false, as determined by the delete-list d_i, after the execution of the corresponding operator o_i.

We now show a linear reduction of the above STRIPS-like representation into a simple multi-entity model with only one agent. With each primitive proposition we associate a component with two states—*true* and *false* (this describes whether the appropriate proposition is true or false). The planner's possible operators are represented by actions of the agent in the multi-entity model. The agent can generate for any possible operator o_i in the STRIPS-like representation a unique action of the multi-entity model. The preconditions of the possible operators become propositions in $\mathcal{L}$ that are conditions for the generation of the corresponding actions. The postconditions (add list, delete list) are represented by adding appropriate transitions that affect the state of the components according to the delete-list/add-list in the STRIPS-like representation. The reader should notice that we did not use in this representation the ability to represent multi-agent situations and options such as that the effects of joint actions may depend on propositions in $\mathcal{L}$. Notice also that the above simulation is efficient. The size of the multi-entity model generated is linear in the size of the original STRIPS-like representation. This is an immediate result of the fact that the total number of states in the multi-entity model is $2n$, the number of actions in the multi-entity model equals the number of operators in the STRIPS-like representation, the number of propositions in $\mathcal{L}$ in the multi-entity model equals the number of preconditions in the STRIPS-like representation, and the size of the representation of the transition function in the multi-entity model equals the total size of the add-lists and delete-lists in the STRIPS-like representation.

STRIPS is usually considered a declarative form of knowledge representation. The fact that we have a direct way of encoding STRIPS-style representations in multi-entity models illustrates the fact that used appropriately, these models may provide some of the features of standard declarative approaches. Specifically, for any fixed finite collection of primitive propositions, it is straightforward to add entities to the model that represent the truth of these propositions. Recall that even statements that are most easily described using first-order or higher-order logic can often be considered as primitive propositions. Doing so, however, we commit to a small fixed set of relevant formulas. What is lost, of course, is the flexibility of generating new nonpropositional formulas of interest in the course of the reasoning. Nevertheless, we believe that the declarative aspects made available through multi-entity models can be appropriate for many practical applications. Whether there are extensions that will allow multi-entity models to enjoy more of the declarative and reasoning aspects of representations based on first-order logic is beyond the scope of this chapter, and is left as a question for further research.

The above examples demonstrate that multi-entity models are natural in a reasonably large class of applications, as well as being fairly expressive and succinct. Notice, however, that these examples did not use much of the power of multi-entity models. We will consider some uses of this power of representation to handle uncertainty and interactions between agents in later sections.

5 COOPERATIVE GOAL ACHIEVEMENT IN UNCERTAIN TERRITORY

Multi-entity models allow rigorous definitions and study of various aspects of multi-agent planning. We shall now describe and study one version of multi-agent planning in this framework. It is natural to think of a plan of an agent as being a function determining the actions that an agent should take, as a function of its current state. Since, however, we often interpret a multi-entity model as abstracting away various aspects of the agents' mental states, the agent's plan need not depend only on its state as described by the multi-entity model. Rather, we think of the agent's current state as describing its current observation of the world, and its 'mental' state for the purpose of carrying out its plans will consist of the sequence of observations it has made from the start up to the current point. We therefore take a plan to be a function from state histories to actions. A *multi-agent plan* is a tuple of such plans, consisting of a unique plan for each agent. We remark that by treating multi-entity models in this way, we are allowing the knowledge that agents have to be implicit in their history, and we do not require it all to be explicitly represented in their current state. This is another place where succinctness of representation is facilitated by this approach.

A *goal* for an active agent i is a formula of $\mathcal{L}$. We will say that a goal g_i of agent i is achieved if the system reaches a configuration that satisfies g_i. A multi-agent plan is called *satisfactory* with respect to a joint goal $(g_1, \ldots, g_m)$ consisting of a goal for each active agent, an instance $\mathcal{S}$ of a multi-entity model, and a list $(\ell_1, \ldots, \ell_m)$ of the active agent's local states in an initial configuration of $\mathcal{C}_0$, if for each i the system will reach a configuration satisfying g_i starting from any possible initial configuration in $\mathcal{C}_0$ in which the active agents have the states $(\ell_1, \ldots, \ell_m)$, respectively. We define the (general) *Cooperative Goal Achievement* (CGA) problem as follows:

Definition 3.1 (CGA) Given a multi-entity model $\mathcal{S}$ with m active agents, a list $(\ell_1, \ldots, \ell_m)$ of agent states, and a joint goal $(g_1, \ldots, g_m)$ for these agents, find a satisfactory multi-agent plan for the active agents if one exists, and otherwise announce that no such plan exists.

The name *cooperative goal achievement* is due to the fact that the multi-agent plan involves all of the agents, cooperating to try to satisfy all goals. Even after the goal g_i of agent i is attained, this agent may need to continue to help others attain their goals. CGA is a computational problem, in which the complete structure of the multi-entity model is assumed to be given. Moreover, the planning stage involves a centralized computation that has access to the initial states of all of the agents. This essentially corresponds to all of the agents starting out having common knowledge of their joint state. Nevertheless, since the desired plan is required to succeed starting from every initial configuration in C_0 in which the agents have this joint state, we still allow for a considerable degree of uncertainty. Many aspects of the configuration may depend on entities other than the agents for which the plan is being designed. These may describe properties of the environment that the agents do not initially know about. As a result, the agents in a CGA will typically be uncertain about the state of the environment in which they operate (which in our case may be represented by passive entities). Moreover, during the execution of the plans the agents may individually learn various things about the environment. Their joint state will typically not be common knowledge during the execution of their multi-agent plans.

The CGA problem, in its current formulation, is sufficiently general to apply in many contexts and might therefore be very complex. Fortunately, we are able to show:

Theorem 3.2 The general CGA problem is decidable.

Theorem 3.2 shows that multi-entity models offer a relatively good tradeoff between expressiveness and complexity. As we saw, the multi-entity model is powerful and can efficiently encode many natural (although nontrivial) agent interactions and uncertainty. In spite of this, the general problem is still decidable. As we mentioned at the beginning of this article, our aim is both to show the usefulness of multi-entity models and to initiate research on automata-based representation and reasoning in the AI context. Theorem 3.2 is an initial result in this study. An example of a further study is the study of the corresponding planning problem when agents have complete information about the initial configuration they are starting in. Such studies will be the topic of the following sections.

6   COMPLETE INFORMATION

The previous section discussed the general case of multi-agent planning with incomplete information in the framework of the multi-entity model. However, much more has to be done in addition to studying the general problem. As with work on 'logical representations' one can study the issue of (multi-agent) planning with complete information in the framework of multi-entity models. This will be the automata-based alternative to classical (multi-agent) planning.

Given the machinery of the previous section, one can define (multi-agent) planning with complete information in the context of the multi-entity model. The assumption of complete information is captured in the framework of the multi-entity model by a requirement that $C_0 = \{c_0\}$ where c_0 is the actual initial configuration. This is straightforward from the discussion of the previous section. We denote the CGA problem where the agents have complete information by C-CGA.

Let us return to the example of Section 4. Assume that Alice and Bob want to go to place X, while Chris wants to go to Y which is distant from X. The agents' goals are to be in their respective desired locations. It is easy to see that the C-CGA problem is solvable in this case: All agents row to Y, Chris gets off, and Alice and Bob continue to X. If there were two boats, one of which is 'good' and one broken, and the agents will drown if they operate the wrong boat, then the C-CGA is still solvable, but the CGA problem where the identity of the 'good' boat is not initially known is not solvable.

We can show:

Theorem 3.3 The C-CGA problem is PSPACE-complete.

Theorem 3.3 points again to the fact that the multi-entity models offer a relatively good tradeoff between expressiveness and complexity in the context of multi-agent activity. The reader should notice that since plans might in general be of exponential length (in the number of agents or the size of the description of the model), planning in nontrivial models is in general beyond NP (NP-hard but not in NP), and hence we cannot hope for a much better result. A multi-entity model is not a simple syntactic restriction of first-order logic. It is a semantic model that treats the world in a specific way. The fact that such semantic models allow this good tradeoff points to the potential use of such models in multi-agent activity. In other words, multi-entity models remove much of the complexity of first-order logic while keeping us in a framework that is tailored for handling multi-agent activity.

Although the aim of this chapter is mainly to initiate research on succinct automata-based knowledge representation and reasoning, one can easily notice that the structure of multi-entity models suggest useful assumptions one can make in order to have tractable planning. For example, in the multi-entity model there are many components, but usually the number of components that will be involved in a specific plan is small. If we identify 'small' with a certain *a priori* given constant, then we can get polynomial solutions for the C-CGA. Assumptions about the amount of interaction among components might be also useful. We believe such a study to be a useful direction for further research.

7 COOPERATION WITH CRASH FAILURES

The previous sections introduced multi-entity models and investigated them in two general settings. In one setting the agents were assumed to act in an arbitrary (perhaps uncertain) territory and in the other one they were assumed to act with complete information. An interesting complementary study is concerned with a study of a situation where the agents basically have complete information, but uncertainty may arise since some of the active agents may suddenly crash. As an example one may think about the multi-entity model as controlled by a 'master' agent that specifies the behaviour of agents at all points in order to enable them to achieve their goals (this is the classical complete information scenario), but some of the agents might crash during execution, and the master would like to guarantee that failures of some of the agents will not prevent the rest of the agents from achieving their goals. This is an interesting case that is important for practical applications. The notion of crash failures is central in distributed computing, see Pease *et al.* (1980), Dwork and Moses (1990, 1992). Our computational study of the corresponding problem will lead to an interesting and somewhat surprising result.

We capture 'faultiness' in our model by allowing an active agent to fail at any step of an execution. We assume that the failures are crash failures (an agent that fails ceases to operate and is never revived), and that the number of agents that may fail in any execution is bounded above by f, where f is given and may depend on the number of active agents, m. With each active agent we associate a distinguished 'state' which we call *failure*. The failure of active agent i given that the system is in configuration c occurs as follows:[1] Active agent number i generates one of its possible actions in configuration c, and then agent i moves into its *failure* state. When the agent is in its *failure* state it becomes passive, and no transition can change the agent's state at any later point in time. We assume that the failure of an agent is observable (as the other changes in the world) by the other active agents (e.g., by the above-mentioned master agent).

The appropriate analogue to C-CGA will be the question: is there a multi-agent plan for the active agents that, against any pattern of up to f failures, ensures that all the non-faulty agents achieve their goals? Identifying whether the agents' goals can be achieved in this framework can be thought to be harder than before (the plan in this case consists of a strategy to be used against an adversary determining who fails, as opposed to its being a single 'good execution' that needs to be guessed). The reader may notice, however, that there are cases where this problem becomes very easy (if it is known that achieving a certain goal requires the cooperation of at least $m - f + 1$ active agents, for example). We denote the corresponding decision

---

[1]Other abstractions of crash failures can be treated similarly.

problem by F-CGA, and we are able to show that (perhaps surprisingly) the complexity of this problem is the same as the complexity of the C-CGA problem.

Theorem 3.4 Let f be an upper bound on the number of possible failures.

1. If f is taken as input, then the complexity of F-CGA is PSPACE-complete.

2. For a fixed $f = \frac{m}{2}$ (or in general $f = \alpha \cdot m$ for some constant $0 < \alpha < 1$), the F-CGA problem is PSPACE-complete.

The reader might notice that even when we are interested in plans whose length (i.e., the number of actions that are actually executed in a course of a plan) is polynomially bounded, we might need exponential space for encoding the appropriate plan (strategy) when failures might occur. However, our result shows that a planner does not need to represent the exponential size plan. In addition, since the general CGA problem is also PSPACE-hard, our result implies the existence of an efficient reduction from multi-agent planning with possible crash failures to multi-agent planning with complete information, which is a better studied problem.

8   SUMMARY AND RELATED WORK

This chapter suggests that we reconsider the use of automata-based knowledge representation and reasoning. We modified the basic interacting automata model discussed in McCarthy and Hayes's seminal paper in order to yield a natural, succinct, and efficient type of models. We introduced automata-based models, which we call multi-entity models, that are powerful and expressive. We introduced and investigated multi-agent activity in uncertain territory in the framework of these models. We showed that the corresponding computational problem, the cooperative goal achievement problem, is decidable. We also presented and investigated the related problem in the context of complete information. In addition, we showed how we can treat crash failures of agents in the framework of multi-entity models, and pointed to illuminating properties of the corresponding computational problem.

Since this chapter concentrates on an automata-based framework, there is a strict difference between our work and most work in AI. Nevertheless, researchers in the area of multi-agent planning have concentrated on problems that resemble the problems we have investigated, but in the framework of different models. This includes work on knowledge and action such as Moore (1980), Morgenstern (1987), Halpern and Moses (1990) and Rosenschein (1985), work on the representation of joint actions such as Georgeff (1986), and on the generation of multi-agent plans such as Lansky (1988), Stuart (1985) and Pnueli and Rosner (1990). Although the main aspect that distinguishes our work from these works is the type of models considered, our work can also be considered as having the unique feature of combining the various aspects of these works (i.e. reasoning about knowledge and action, the succinct representation of actions, and the study of plan generation) in a simple unified framework. Work in theoretical computer science on interacting processes (Ladner 1979) can be also considered to be of some relevance. Nevertheless, these works do not supply the necessary syntax and semantics needed for succinct knowledge representation in multi-agent domains, and do not address issues in multi-agent planning.

Automata-based frameworks are common in many areas. For example, they are the major study of Discrete Event Systems (DES) in control theory (Ramadge 1988), (Ramadge and Wonham 1989).[2] Moreover, automata-based settings were shown to be useful by researchers in the AI community that concentrate on specific architectures for intelligence that are different from the knowledge representation and reasoning paradigm (Brooks 1986). Our work reconsiders the use of automata-based models, and shows how some of the problems exposed in the use of such models for knowledge representation and reasoning can be addressed. We conclude that there is a point to a systematic study of AI related questions in the context of such models; this work initiates such a study, and provides several basic results.

---

[2]The possibility of interaction between AI related research and control theory is well known; see Dean and Wellman (1991).

9 PROOF OUTLINES

Proof of Theorem 3.2 First, observe that since the plans of the agents are common knowledge, then every fact that is learned by an agent can be translated to a fact that is learned about the initial configuration. Hence, each agent can learn only finitely many facts.

A plan for an agent can be associated without loss of generality with a decision tree, where whenever there is a branching in the tree, then a new fact is learned. Hence, a plan is executed in stages, where at each stage a decision may be made based on new observations. If starting at stage k and until stage m of the multi-agent plan, no branching occurs along any branch of any of the plans, where $m - k > size(C)$, and where $size(C)$ is the (finite) number of possible system configurations, then there exists a shorter multi-agent plan that achieves the desired goal. The reason for the latter is that in such a case the plans must visit the same configurations twice without learning anything.

Combining the above we get that it is enough to consider only plans with finitely many branches, where the number of actions executed between any pair of branch is finite. Hence, we can limit ourselves to multi-agent plans of finite size, and the problem is decidable. $\qquad\square$

Proof of Theorem 3.3 We will show that the problem is NPSPACE, and use the fact that NPSPACE=PSPACE. First, observe that we have exponentially many configurations and hence we can consider only plans whose length is exponentially bounded. In addition, notice that each configuration can be encoded in a polynomial amount of space. The NPSPACE algorithm will start from the initial configuration and will guess the next joint action, and then compute the next configuration and so on. Since the multi-agent plan in the C-CGA problem is a sequence of joint actions, we get that the problem is in PSPACE.

The hardness result is achieved by reduction from 'Finite State Automata Intersection', denoted by FSAI in Garey and Johnson (1979). One of the representations that can be simulated in our model is a system of n finite automata. In this representation an input $a \in A$ changes the state of all the machines (where A is a set of possible inputs). We associate each automaton with an active agent which includes a unique component. The states of every such component are associated with the states of the appropriate automaton. We decompose each $a \in A$ into $a_1, ..., a_n$, where a_i becomes a basic action of agent number i. The transitions in our system correspond to the changes that are caused by the input in the automata model. We denote by $\bar{a} = (a_1, ..., a_n)$ the transition that is generated by the previous a_i's. The changes that $\bar{a}$ causes to our agents are defined as the changes that a causes in the corresponding automata. Now, we take an instance of the FSAI and reduce it to our model as was done above. Note that this reduction is polynomial. Assume that the number of automata is m. Therefore, we will have m active agents that correspond to these automata, and no passive agents. Each active agent contains just one component. For each i ($1 \le i \le m$), we add to the component of agent number i a new state, denoted s_{g_i}. This state will be the goal of agent i. We add m new actions— $e_1, \ldots, e_m$. For each i ($1 \le i \le m$), e_i can be generated by agent i in the states that correspond to accepting states of the appropriate automaton, and cannot be generated by any other agent or in any other state. There will also be a new transition $E = (e_1, ..., e_m)$, which will change the state of the component of agent number i ($1 \le i \le m$) into s_{g_i}. Our result can be easily verified now. $\qquad\square$

Proof of Theorem 3.4

1. PSPACE-hardness follows from assigning $f = 0$ and using the result regarding C-CGA. To show that the problem is in PSPACE we have to notice that we have here a game between the joint actions the agents perform and the failures. The joint actions will correspond to an existential quantifier in the description of a strategy in this game, while the failures will correspond to a universal quantifier in this description. However, instead of using the universal quantifier we can in each stage enumerate the possible failures and keep just the configurations where there

were failures. We can then supply an NPSPACE algorithm which at each stage 'guesses' the next joint action to be executed. In our enumeration of possible failures at each stage we will put the 'no failures in this stage' as the last option in our enumeration. We will keep on 'guessing' along each 'path', and after getting to the 'goal' we have to make a backtracking and continue to 'guess' (for the next element in the enumeration.) It is easy to see that we have to remember at each point only polynomially many configurations since there can be only polynomially many failures along a 'path'. We will add to the configuration of the system signs for agents' failures. The number of such configurations will be exponential (which is needed in order to show that the number of guesses is bounded). Because of the fact that in each stage we have to remember just a polynomial number of configurations we can decide in NPSPACE=PSPACE.

2. The fact that the problem is in PSPACE is achieved in 1. For the hardness result we will make a reduction from C-CGA. Note first that the theorem regarding C-CGA is valid even if our system is the system of automata described in the proof of that theorem. We will make use of the states s_{g_i} $(1 \leq i \leq m)$ and the actions described in that proof. Therefore, we can assume that we have m agents, each one of them corresponding to one automaton (and therefore we can assume that each agent is active and includes just one component). We will add to these m agents, m new active agents, each one of them containing only one component with one state. New active agent number i can generate m new actions, $a_{i,j}$ $(1 \leq j \leq m)$, and nothing else. For each $1 \leq j \leq m$, the actions $a_{i,j}$ $(1 \leq i \leq m)$ can also be generated by old agent number j in its initial state, and in no other state, and by no other agent. For each i $(1 \leq i \leq m)$ there is a set of new actions $b_{i,j}$ $(1 \leq j \leq m \; ; \; i \neq j)$ that can be generated in state s_{g_i} of old agent number i. The actions $b_{i,j}$ $(1 \leq i \leq m \; ; \; i \neq j)$ can also be generated by old agent number j where it is

in its initial state (and cannot be generated in any other state or machine). The new transitions in the system will be pairs of $a_{i,j}$'s and pairs of $b_{i,j}$'s (where the two members in the pair are identical). A pair of $a_{i,j}$'s and a pair of $b_{i,j}$'s will change the state of old active agent number j from its initial state to s_{g_j}. The goals of the old active agents are as in the C-CGA case, and the goals of the new agents are to stay in their states (which is always satisfied). It is easy to see that we can decide positively if and only if all of the old agents can achieve their goals (in the case where there are no 'failures'). $\qquad\square$

Acknowledgements

This chapter is based on results presented in Tennenholtz and Moses (1989), Moses and Tennenholtz (1991) and Tennenholtz (1991). This work was supported in part by a grant from the US–Israel Binational Science Foundation. The first author was supported in part by a Helen and Milton A. Kimmelman Career Development Chair. The second author was supported in part by an Eshkol fellowship of the Israeli Ministry of Science and Technology, and later by the Air Force Office of Scientific Research. Part of the research was carried out while the second author was in the department of Applied Mathematics and Computer Science at the Weizmann Institute of Science, and part while he was in the Computer Science department at Stanford University.

REFERENCES

Agre, P. (1991). *The Dynamic Structure of Everyday Life*. Cambridge University Press, Cambridge, UK.

Agre, P. and Chapman, D. (1987). Pengi: an implementation of a theory of activity, *Proceedings of of AAAI-87*, pp. 268–272.

Brooks, R. A. (1986). A robust layered control system for a mobile robot. *IEEE Journal of Robotics and Automation* **2**, 14–23.

Dean, T. L. and Wellman, M. P. (1991). *Planning and Control*. Morgan Kaufmann, San Francisco, CA.

Dwork, C. and Moses, Y. (1990). Knowledge and common knowledge in a Byzantine environment: crash failures. *Information and Computation* **88**(2), 156–186.

Fikes, R. E. and Nilsson, N. J. (1971). STRIPS: A new approach to the application of theorem proving to problem solving. *Artificial Intelligence* **2**, 189–208.

Garey, M. and Johnson, D. (1979). *Computers and Intractability—A Guide to the Theory of NP-completeness.* Freeman, San Francisco, CA.

Georgeff, M. P. (1986). The representation of events in multi-agent domains. *Proceedings of of AAAI-86*, pp. 70–75.

Halpern, J. Y. and Fagin, R. (1989). Modelling knowledge and action in distributed systems. *Distributed Computing* **3**(4), 159–179. A preliminary version appeared in *Proceedings of 4th ACM Symposium on Principles of Distributed Computing*, 1985, with the title 'A formal model of knowledge, action, and communication in distributed systems: Preliminary report'.

Halpern, J. Y. and Moses, Y. (1990). Knowledge and common knowledge in a distributed environment. *Journal of the ACM 37*(3), 549–587. A preliminary version appeared in *Proceedings of 3rd ACM Symposium on Principles of Distributed Computing*, 1984.

Ladner, R. E. (1979). The complexity of problems in systems of communicating sequential processes. *Proceedings of 11th ACM Symposium on Theory of Computing*, pp. 214–223.

Lansky, A. L. (1988). Localized event-based reasoning for multiagent Domains, Technical Report 423, SRI International.

Levesque, H. (1986). Knowledge representation and reasoning. *Annual Reviews in Computer Science* **1**, 255–287.

McCarthy, J. and Hayes, P. (1969). Some philosophical problems from the standpoint of artificial intelligence. *Machine Intelligence* **6**.

Moore, R. C. (1980). Reasoning about knowledge and action. Technical Report 191, SRI International.

Morgenstern, L. (1987). Knowledge preconditions for actions and plans. *Proceedings of 10th International Joint Conference on Artificial Intelligence*, pp. 867–874.

Moses, Y. and Tennenholtz, M. (1991). Cooperation in uncertain territory using a multi-entity model. *Artificial Intelligence and*

Computer Vision, Elsevier Science Publishers.

Pease, M., Shostak, R. and Lamport, L. (1980). Reaching agreement in the presence of faults. *Journal of the ACM* **27**(2), pp. 228–234.

Pnueli, A. and Rosner, R. (1990). Distributed reactive systems are hard to synthesize. *Proceedings of 31th IEEE Symp. on Foundations of Computer Science.*

Ramadge, P. (1988). Supervisory control of discrete event systems: a survey and some new results. P. Varaiya and A. Kurzhanski, eds, *Lecture Notes in Control Theory and Information Systems.* Berlin: Springer-Verlag.

Ramadge, P. and Wonham, W. (1989). The control of discrete event systems. *Proceedings of the IEEE* **77**(1), 81–98.

Rosenschein, S. J. (1985). Formal theories of knowledge in AI and robotics. *New Generation Computing* **3**(3), 345–357.

Schoppers, M. (1987). Universal plans for reactive robots in unpredictable environments. *Proceedings of of AAAI-87*, pp. 1039–1046.

Shapley, L. S. (1953). Stochastic games. *Proceedings of the National Academy of Sciences* **39**, 1095–1100.

Stuart, C. (1985). An implementation of a multi-agent plan synchronizer. *Proceedings of 9th International Joint Conference on Artificial Intelligence*, pp. 1031–1033.

Tennenholtz, M. (1991). Efficient representation and reasoning in multi-agent systems. PhD thesis, the Weizmann Institute of Science, Israel.

Tennenholtz, M. and Moses, Y. (1989). On cooperation in a multi-entity model. *Proceedings of the 11th International Joint Conference on Artificial Intelligence*, pp. 918–923.

4

Putting knowledge-rich plan representations to use

Austin Tate

Artificial Intelligence Applications Institute

The University of Edinburgh

80 South Bridge, Edinburgh EH1 1HN, UK

Abstract

AI planning research is now maturing and finding practical application in the commercial, industrial, engineering and defence sectors. This has led to a rapid expansion in the last couple of years of investment in this area. The plan representations which have emerged from the research have been found to be of benefit in a number of areas—even when the *generation* of a plan is not the primary concern. One way in which the research is being exploited is via the use of knowledge-based plan *representations* to underpin systems which can use 'knowledge-rich' plans to improve their monitoring, analysis and advisory capabilities.

Two applications using knowledge-based plan representations will be described and the paper will introduce a further area in which plan representations may find productive use.

First, PLANIT was an application in a company producing fuel tanker trucks and shows how the linking of knowledge-rich representations of product process plans, project plans and shop floor job shop schedules in a single framework can improve coordination and open up new enterprise wide analysis and decision support. Second, OPTIMUM-AIV shows how the use of plan representations from AI research has been used within a system for assembly, integration and verification of spacecraft to improve upon the traditional sources of project management information in use for such tasks. Edinburgh work on the Nonlin and O-Plan plan representations has been used in these two applications. This work and its relevance will be described.

Another way in which knowledge-based plan representations are now finding use is in the area of process modelling—in particular for business process modelling. Enriched process model representations can lead to enhancement of the analysis and critiquing of business processes and can open up a variety of ways to improve the re-engineering of processes, planning aids and intelligent work-flow management systems.

1   THE USE OF AI PLAN REPRESENTATIONS

There is an increasing use of artificial intelligence and knowledge based systems techniques for the generation of plans and schedules. However, whether using traditional computer support in these areas or whether using some of the early AI systems which can support these tasks, there are problems in making use of *predictive* plans and schedules which are difficult to alter and keep up to date as requirements or circumstances change. There is a demand for improved models of processes, plans and schedules in which intentions and alternatives can be captured and which can provide support to *react* to changing circumstances. There is growing interest in the use of such knowledge-rich plan representations to augment the capabilities of project management, process planning and job shop scheduling systems.

Plan representations have been developed over several decades of AI planning research (Allen *et al.* 1990). They can support a rich model of processes, tasks, plans, resources and agents. These representations can be used for purposes other than plan generation.

Knowledge-rich plan representations such as those in the Edinburgh O-Plan (Currie and Tate 1991) and O-Plan2 (Tate *et al.* 1994) planners were used as the basis for the design of an Interactive Planning Assistant (Alvey Directorate 1987), (Drummond and Tate 1992) for the UK Alvey Programme PLANIT Club. This allowed for browsing, explaining and monitoring of plans represented in a more useful form than that provided in conventional computer-based planning support tools. More recently, O-Plan style plan representations were used within the OPTIMUM-AIV system (Aarup *et al.* 1994; Arentoft *et al.* 1991) for spacecraft assembly, integration and verification. These two systems explicitly represent the causal structure or teleology of a plan, which we call it's goal structure (Tate 1977), to hold the dependencies between the preconditions and effects of activities involved in the plan—therefore showing the rationale for the plan. Such rationale and dependencies are useful for describing the internal structure of a plan and for monitoring its execution (Fikes *et al.* 1972; Tate 1984). Dependencies of the same kind may be useful in all aspects of plan generation, execution monitoring and plan repair.

The PLANIT work (Alvey Directorate 1987; Drummond and Tate 1992) is a prototype system in which rich plan representations were *used* without plans being actually generated. In PLANIT, flexible plan representations provided assistance for project management (interfaced to the Metier ARTEMIS system), process planning (interfaced to a Jaguar Cars' process planner) and job shop scheduling (interfaced to the UK Atomic Energy Authority's WASP scheduler). PLANIT could help the user to browse on a plan, monitor its execution and make single-step modifications to it as necessary, taking into account knowledge of resources, agent capabilities, how the original plan was constructed and what the aims of the plan were.

OPTIMUM-AIV (Aarup *et al.* 1994; Arentoft *et al.* 1991) is a more recent example of the use of flexible plan representations in a project management domain alongside Metier's ARTEMIS project support tools. The plan causal structure is represented to give support to replanning when problems occur.

The paper will first describe the PLANIT and OPTIMUM-AIV systems. They used plan representations based on that used within the Edinburgh O-Plan (Currie and Tate 1991) and O-Plan2 (Tate *et al.* 1994) systems. This includes some key concepts of hierarchical plans, rich activity and resource models, the use of goal structure to capture the intentions behind plan steps, and a language in which to express the activity and process models.

The paper will then go on to describe the contributions to knowledge-rich plan representations from the O-Plan research. Edinburgh research on planning and control architectures has been aimed at building a practical prototype system which can generate plans to meet given task requirements and can reliably execute the plans in the face of simple plan failures. We are now using our experience of knowledge-rich plan representations to augment the plan modelling and analysis capabilities that can be provided and which can work alongside a range of existing systems and tools (such as used today for project management, process enactment, etc).

The final part of the paper gives emphasis to the relevance of the work on AI plan prepresentations for modelling business processes and for supporting business process analysis and re-engineering.

2 PLANIT—INTERACTIVE PLANNER'S AID

The UK Alvey Programme's PLANIT Community Club produced a prototype planners' aid called the Interactive Planners' Assistant (IPA) during 1986-7 (Drummond and Tate 1992; PLANIT Club 1987). It could perform 'single-step plan modifications' to allow a user to monitor the actual execution of a plan and to investigate options and the consequences of changes or decisions. Active support to providing valid options for user choice was given by the system. The IPA made use of AI plan representations which could capture intentions, rich resource models, dependencies between tasks, plan alternatives, domain capabilities and task descriptions. The plan representation used was based on Edinburgh work on the AI planners Nonlin (Tate 1977) and O-Plan (Currie and Tate 1991).

The PLANIT Club involved 29 organisations in the UK who worked with support from the government's Alvey Programme of research into intelligent knowledge-based systems during 1986 and 1987. AIAI provided the core rationale and design for the IPA—the main prototype tool produced during the Club programme. A paper (Tate 1987) gives details of our experience of participation in the PLANIT Club.

2.1 Application—an enterprise for oil tanker truck production

The PLANIT IPA was applied to show how an enterprise could use knowledge-based plans to coordinate the production of an oil tanker truck. This showed the relationship between:

- *process plans* for the production of parts of a tanker. In the IPA demonstration several alternative available methods of producing the tanker oil vessel 'end cap' were included (by spinning, by pressing or by rolling and welding).
- *project plans* to show the various steps involved in configuring and making the truck including resource needs and time scales.
- *job shop schedules* for the part of the enterprise concerned with producing the end caps.

This demonstration application showed how the IPA could be used to monitor the execution of the project plan for a specific truck. During the building of the truck, shop floor production difficulties with the chosen end cap production method led to an alternative process being proposed which allowed the project plan to be altered to avoid a bottleneck in the job shop. This went beyond the typical support in project management and job shop scheduling tools, which would have focused on altering times or resources to avoid problems rather than questioning the plan logic or the actual process alternatives currently built into the plan.

2.2 Use of knowledge-based plan features

PLANIT made use of a number of features found in AI-based plan representations.

1. **Separation of domain, task and plan knowledge.**
   Figure 4.1 illustrates the dependencies between domain, task and plan knowledge. Tasks and plans are both based upon the entities in the domain model. Plans also are elaborations of a specific Task.

   - *domain* knowledge describes 'fixed' things like facilities, organizational relationships, procedures, systems, products and the types of resource available.

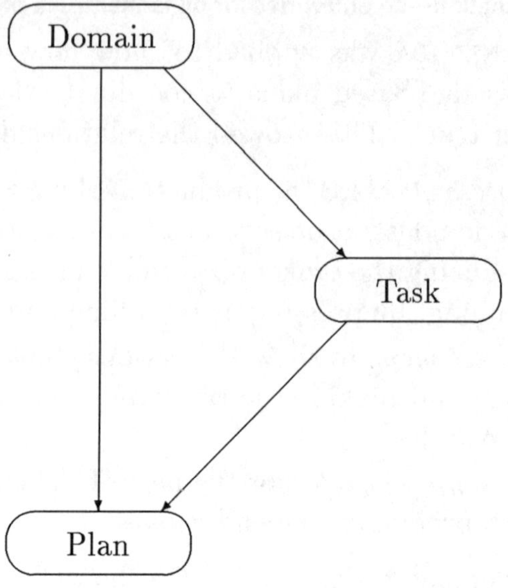

Figure 4.1. Dependencies between domain, task and plan knowledge partitions.

> This knowledge is likely to be highly reusable for many different requirements.
> - *task* knowledge, describes the objectives such as the goal or goals which the plan is designed to achieve, the activity to be carried out, the *actual* resources available, the time available, etc.
> - *plan* knowledge, describes a particular way (currently under exploration) in which the specified task objectives can be achieved in the current domain.

2. **Separation of plan constraint management into specialist activity, resource and product managers.**
In the PLANIT IPA, any change of plan had to meet constraints on activities, resources and products. A number of specialized managers ensured that their own set of constraints were met.

3. **Use of goal structure to explain the functions and intentions of a plan.**

   The IPA could inform the user of the intention of steps in a plan and of their relationship with other steps in the plan and with resource usage.

4. **Description of planning and re-planning capabilities.**

   Knowledge of how to manipulate plans was held as a number of *Plan Modification Operators* (PMOs) through which plan state changes could be made. These PMOs were of two types:

   - *Analysis and planning* knowledge, describing ways of critiquing, optimising or changing the current plan.
   - *Execution* knowledge, describing ways in which the current plan can be translated into action in the current domain with the current task objectives.

5. **Ability to do single-step plan modification.**

   Since the IPA had plan analysis and plan modification capabilities, it was able to suggest valid changes to the plan and inform the user of the consequences of proposed changes to the plan, thus allowing what-if questions to be answered. Valid plan modification operators could be used to 'single-step' through proposed plan changes.

6. **Ability to browse plan states.**

   The IPA provided the ability to browse temporal or logical states in a simulation of the plan. This is useful for critiquing and optimising plans and can provide useful communication back to the person responsible for the task or plan at an appropriate level.

These features combined to allow the PLANIT IPA to act as a flexible tool to support a user who needed to monitor processes, plans and schedules in actual use and to support a user in making changes to a plan during its use. This type of active support to *using* plans is an area where many existing computer-based tools are weak.

3 OPTIMUM-AIV

OPTIMUM-AIV (Aarup *et al.* 1994; Arentoft *et al.* 1991) is able to support the generation and execution of plans for spacecraft assembly, integration and verification. The system was built by a consortium including AIAI for the European Space Agency (ESA). The project followed on from earlier work for ESA on the PlanERS-1 planning system (Fuchs *et al.* 1990) to support mission planning and operations for the ERS-1 Earth resources spacecraft.

The system shows how plan representations from AI research have been used to link to and improve upon the traditional sources of project management information in use for such tasks. OPTIMUM-AIV could be used alongside Metier's ARTEMIS project management tool which is already in use within ESA for space-craft assembly, integration and verification work.

3.1 Application—assembly, integration and verification of spacecraft

The assembly, integration and testing of complex spacecraft is a demanding activity, requiring careful project management. It involves the coordination of many resources, facilities, equipment, test capabilities, etc. Spacecraft components are brought together from suppliers and scientific establishments for environmental, electrical, communications and other tests. The results of the tests conducted will establish whether corrective actions need to be taken to remedy any problems found during the process. Careful records must be kept of the tests and the actions taken. Deadlines, e.g. for meeting launch windows for the spacecraft or for use of expensive testing facilities, must be respected.

It is therefore essential that a flexible plan is maintained which is responsive to the outcomes of tests and to changing delivery or resource availability dates. AI-based plan representations were used to augment the existing project management aids at ESA for spacecraft AIV during the OPTIMUM-AIV project.

3.2 Use of knowledge-based plan features

OPTIMUM-AIV made use of a number of features found in AI-based plan representations.

1. **Hierarchical description of activities and plans.**
   Activities that may be performed in the domain being modelled could be described in a hierarchical fashion. Also plans were hierarchically described. This allowed information to be presented at an appropriate level of detail for the use to which it was to be put.

2. **Search for and re-use of plans.**
   AI-uriented plan generation and search methods were employed. Plan libraries storing generic plans could be maintained to allow previous experience to be recalled and tailored to new situations.

3. **Plan critiquing.**
   Changes made to plans could be criticized or critiqued to ensure that constraints and intentions were not compromised as changes were made to them.

4. **Constraint management.**
   Time feasibility windows were maintained for activities in the plan and for resource usage.

5. **Capture of intentions in plans.**
   The capture of intentions within plans using goal structure was an aid to explanation or justification of parts of the plan and to facilitate flexible re-planning proposals.

6. **Test recovery plan patches.**
   Test recovery plan patches (called 'test failures solutions') were provided to enable a plan to be brought back on track after spacecraft component test failures occurred. The test recovery plan fragments were represented in the same form as activity descriptions and overall plans.

These features combined to allow OPTIMUM-AIV to support a project engineer in initially creating and then monitoring the execution of an AIV plan. The system provided active and flexible support to the consideration of options when tests failed to ensure the plan was brought back on track.

The OPTIMUM-AIV system is now in use on pilot projects within the European space industry (Parrod and Valera 1993).

4 SOME KEY CONCEPTS IN THE O-PLAN KNOWLEDGE-BASED PLAN REPRESENTATION

This section describes in more detail the contributions from work on the O-Plan plan representation used as a basis for systems like PLANIT and OPTIMUM-AIV.

4.1 Three levels—strategic, tactical and operational

This section describes O-Plan's approach to modelling command (task assignment), planning and control (plan execution) activities. We are interested in three levels at which plans are represented. We have deliberately simplified our consideration to three levels with different roles and with possible differences of requirements for skilled user availability, processing capacity and real-time reaction to clarify the presentation of our work. However, the three levels will relate to corresponding organisational or functional boundaries in many organisations involved in planning and control. The levels considered are:

1. A user analyses the problem being faced and sets direction by specifying an objective or set of objectives using some suitable interface. We call this process *task assignment.*
2. A *planner* creates a plan to perform the task specified. The planner reasons about time and resources involved in specific instances of generic plans. The planner has knowledge of the general capabilities of an execution system and its enactment capabilities but does not need to know about the detail of how the activities will actually be performed.
3. The *execution system* seeks to carry out the plan as specified by the planner (using that plan as a set of constraints on how it can behave) while working with a more detailed model of the execution environment than is available to the task assigner and to the planner.

The three levels can communicate to respond to changing requirements, changes in the environment or plan failure. In the O-Plan2 system, the three levels are reflected in separate computational *agents* – the task assignment agent, the planner agent and the execution agent.

We are exploring a common representation for the input/output requirements and capabilities of the planner and plan execution agents. This supports the communication between a user assigning a task or tasks, a planner and an execution system situated in the environment in which the plan is being executed. The common representation includes knowledge about the capabilities of the planning and execution agents, the requirements of the plan and the plan itself (see Figure 4.2).

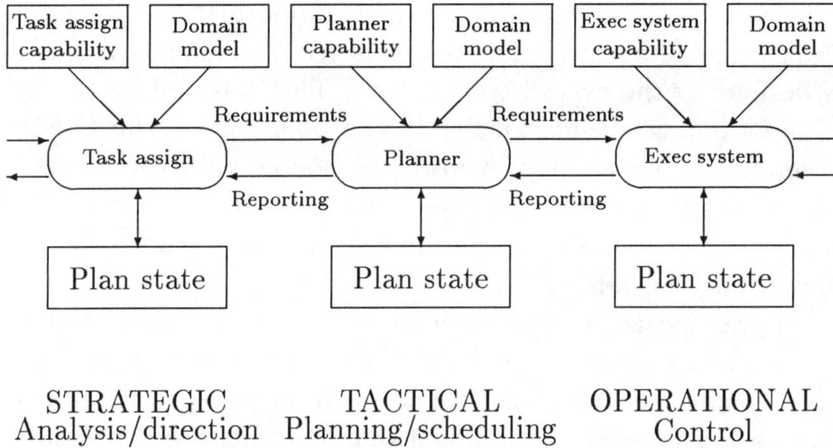

Figure 4.2. Communication between task assignment, planning and execution levels.

4.2 Plan state with agenda

An O-Plan *plan state* represents an abstract view of a set of actual plan elaborations that exist within the constraints it contains. Alternative lower level activities, alternative activity orderings, alternative object selections, and so on are aggregated within a high-level plan state description. Lower levels can use the flexibility allowed within a plan state while carrying out their own role.

The plan state also contains a list of the current *flaws* or *pending processing requirements* in the plan. These are kept on an *agenda*. Such agenda items could relate to abstract activities that still must be expanded before the plan is considered valid for passing on for execution, unsatisfied conditions, unresolved interactions, overcommitments of resources, time constraint violations, etc. The plan state can thus stand alone from the control structure of the planning and execution agents in that it can be saved and restored, passed to another agent, etc.

The plan state cannot contain arbitrary data elements. An O-Plan agent is made up of code that can interpret the plan state data structure and interpret the lists of flaws in such a way that it can select from amongst its computational capabilities and its library of domain-specific information to seek to transform the current plan state it is given into something that is desired by the overall architecture. This is to reduce the list of outstanding agenda entries in the plan state. The O-Plan architecture associates a Knowledge Source with each agenda entry type that can be processed (Currie and Tate 1985). The processing capabilities in the knowledge sources are called to handle each agenda entry.

In practice, the O-Plan architecture is designed for operation in an environment where the ultimate aim of termination will not be achieved. There will be new command requests arriving and earlier ones being modified, parts of plans will be under execution as other parts are being elaborated, execution faults are being handled, etc.

4.3 Plan patches

The requirement for asynchronously operating planners and execution agents (and indeed users and the real world) means that it is not appropriate to consider that a plan requirement is set, passed on for elaboration to the planner and then communicated to a waiting execution agent which will seek to perform the activities involved. Instead, all components must be considered to be operating already and maintaining themselves in some stable mode where they are responsive to requests for activity from the other components. For example, the execution agent may have quite elaborate local mechanisms and instructions to enable it to maintain a device (say a spacecraft or a manufacturing cell) in a safe, healthy, responsive state. The task then is to communicate some change that is requested from one component to another and to insert an appropriate alteration in the receiver such that the tasks required are carried out.

In effect a *delegation* of part of a plan must take place from some superior to some subordinate agent.

We define a *plan patch* as a modified version of the type of plan state used in O-Plan. Communication between the task assigner, planner and execution system is via *plan patches* which share the same representation to plans (Tate 1989). A plan patch is an abstracted or high-level representation of a part of the task that is required of the receiver and contains items relevant to the receiver's capabilities. This provides a simplified or black-box view of possibly quite detailed instructions needed to actually perform the activity (possibly involving iterators and conditionals, etc). Complex execution agent representational and programming languages (Georgeff and Lansky 1986; Nilsson 1988) could be handled by using this abstracted view. For example, reliable task-achieving *behaviours* which included contingencies and safe state paths to deal with unforeseen events could be hidden from the planner by communication in terms of a simplified and more robust model of the execution operations (Malcolm and Smithers 1988).

Outstanding flaws in the plan patch would be communicated along with the patch itself. However, these flaws must be those that can be handled by the receiver. Plan patches also allow execution errors to be passed back to the planner or information to be passed back to the user.

4.4 Triangle model of activity

O-Plan uses a hierarchical model of activity which gives emphasis to an owner's perspective of how an activity is performed and the environment in which it can be sanctioned, resourced and used. This is reflected in the 'triangle' model of an activity (see Figure 4.3). The vertical dimension reflects activity (or plan or task) decomposition, the horizontal dimension reflects time. Inputs and outputs are split into three principal categories (authority, conditions/effects and resources). Arbitrarily complex modelling is possible in all dimensions. 'Types' are used to further differentiate the inputs and outputs and their semantics.

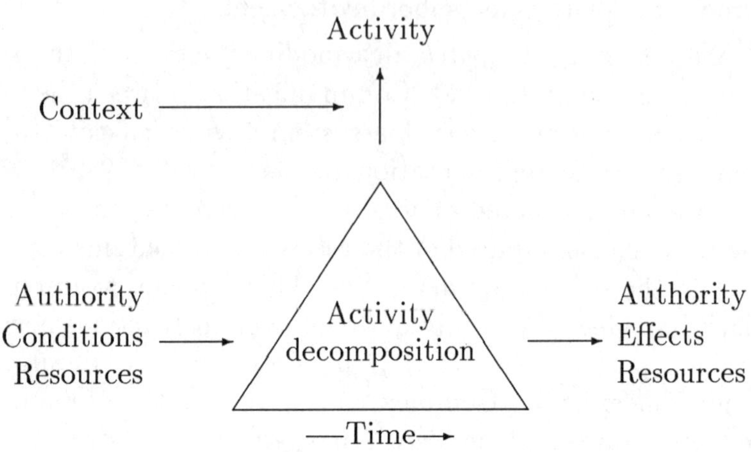

Figure 4.3. Triangle model of activity.

'Entry' to the model can be from any of three points in the triangle model. A 'context' gates use of this particular expansion or decomposition of an activity by ensuring it is relevant in the context of use within the current plan. From the top vertex it is possible to ask for activity (or plan or task) expansions or decompositions (the use of a specific decomposition being filtered by the context of use). From the right side of the triangle, it is possible to ask for activities (or plans or tasks) satisfying or providing the output requirement (a desired effect or 'goal', a required resource, or a needed authority). These two sides are used mostly by our planners to date. The third side on the left can reflect triggering conditions for an activity (or plan or task) and will be needed when improved models of independent processes are used as in the Excalibur (Drabble 1993) system prototype.

4.5 Intentions within plans

The 'intentions' or 'rationale' behind the use of a particular activity in a process or plan can be related to the features of this triangle model. For some time, plan causality or teleology represented in the conditions/effects of activities has been used in AI planners to record plan rationale (or goal structure as we call it at Edinburgh). But in the richer model now in use in O-Plan2, for example, it is also possible to differentiate the purpose of the inclusion of an activity in a plan as being to provide resources (i.e. this activity has been included in a plan only to provide a resource, its post conditions may be a side effect for this *particular* use). The same applies to authority provision.

4.6 Constraint management within plans

Time constraints, resource usage, object selection and condition/effect causal constraints are handled as an integral part of the overall O-Plan2 system structure by treating specialized constraint management as supporting the core decision making components in the architecture. Specialized (and separable) representations and handlers for the various types of constraint can therefore be employed to deal with time, resources, object and causal constraints within a plan state.

Minimum/maximum bound pairs and preference information is maintained for constrained numerical items such as time windows on activities, resource levels, etc.

4.7 Task Formalism

Domain representation for planning attempts to capture the detailed description of permissible activities or operations within an application area, including information about how conditions imposed on the use of these activities should be satisfied, and their effects on the domain if the activities are used. This richness of required information has led to the specification and development of a high-level domain-description language called Task Formalism, or more conveniently TF. TF originated in the Nonlin planning system (Tate 1977) but has been refined and extended for domain descriptions within the O-Plan and O-Plan2 planning systems developed at AIAI.

TF is *not* intended as the normal mode of interaction with the user describing a domain. It is an *intermediate language* which fits between a supportive (graphical) user interface and the planner. TF can be considered to be the target language for a helpful domain writer's support tool. TF has also been designed to allow a useful level of compile time checking to be performed.

TF is used to give an overall hierarchical description of an application area by specifying the activities within the domain and in particular their more detailed representation as a set of sub-activities with ordering constraints imposed. Plans are generated by choosing suitable 'expansions' for activities (by refining it to a more detailed level) in the plan and including the relevant set of more detailed sub-activities described therein. Ordering constraints are then satisfied to ensure that asserted effects of some activities satisfy, and continue to satisfy, conditions on the use of other activities. Other constraints, such as a time window for the activity or resource usage required, are also included in the description. These descriptions of activities form the main structure within TF - the *schema*. Schemas are also used in a completely uniform manner to describe *tasks*, set to the planning system, in the same formalism. Other TF structures hold global information and heuristic information about preferences of choices to be made during planning.

The O-Plan2 design allows for different plan state representations in the different agents. TF is particularly suited to the representation of a plan state within the planner agent and, hence, to act as a basis for communication to the planner's superior (task assignment) and subordinate (execution system) agents. The actual plan state inside the task assignment and execution system agents is likely to differ from that within the planner. For example, the execution system may be based on more procedural representations as are found in languages like PRS (the Procedural Reasoning System (Georgeff and Lansky 1986)) and may allow iteration, conditionals, etc. The execution or enactment level could be based on PML (Bruynooghe *et al.* 1992) or similar process description languages in a process modelling, planning and enactment application of the concepts.

5   USING AI PLAN REPRESENTATIONS FOR PROCESS MODELLING

Knowledge-based approaches are acknowledged as a key component in facilitating the integration of 'islands of automation' in today's enterprises. The First Conference on Enterprise Integration Modelling (Petrie 1992) identified progress on support to change management in business as an important area for the success of enterprise integration efforts. The working groups of the conference also believed that a combination of AI and OR methods as explored by the knowledge-based planning community could be a good basis for this work.

Means to connect executive strategic decision making, analysis and direction with tactical planning and scheduling capabilities and on to effective operations management within an organization may be facilitated by using AI-based plan representation approaches. The three level modelling approach adopted in O-Plan2 can readily be related to a number of existing conventional methodologies (such as IDEF, CORE, etc)[1] in use for modelling aspects of organizations.

One area in which O-Plan2 knowledge-rich plan representations may be used is to support the modelling, analysis and re-engineering of business processes. Our approach is to offer an overall vision of an *executive communication and control* environment in which an enriched corporate model (knowledge and databases) is utilized to offer an 'add-on' to existing tools used in companies (tools for option analysis, risk analysis, business case analysis, project management, work-flow management, etc). In this framework, we are seeking to improve the types of process models that can be captured and to enrich these models in ways that may be done informally in today's requirements capture and modelling tools. The enriched representations allow for improved analyses and open the way to a new generation of tools

---

[1]What is being done is to *augment* or *enrich* these earlier methods, rather than starting afresh and replacing or reinventing what has already been achieved.

for business process engineering that will provide enhanced aids to:

- reliably capture and maintain process knowledge and models
- make decisions using knowledge-based simulation and analysis
- synthesize plans and schedules
- re-engineer parts of a process or plan
- reliably execute processes and plans
- simulate, animate, explain and justify processes and plans.

The approach uses *open* and *inspectable* AI-based representations of processes, tasks, plans and schedules in which dependencies, constraints and preferences are maintained. Experimental methods and tools support the capture and enhanced representation of processes, allow for the synthesis of new processes, support the re-engineering of existing processes, allow for dependency-based justification and explanation, support intelligent work-flow management and support the management of change in a business. This work in process management draws on experience with Nonlin, O-Plan, O-Plan2, PLANIT and OPTIMUM-AIV as follows:

- 3-level view (strategic, tactical, operational) with command or task assignment, planning and control roles, distribution and communication (O-Plan2).
- Knowledge-based plan representations based on a hierarchical activity model supported by representation of time, resources, authority, conditions and effects—summarized in the *triangle* model of activity (Nonlin, O-Plan and O-Plan2).
- Process and plan impact assessment/critiquing (Nonlin, PLANIT).
- Constrained plan editing and single-step plan modification options presentation (O-Plan and PLANIT).
- Plan generation technology (O-Plan).

- Plan question answering, state generation, simulation and animation (Nonlin and O-Plan2).

With enriched process representations and using knowledge-based approaches, it is possible to go beyond *what if?* option analysis and to generate *how to?* option proposals. Higher-level component processes can be selected, combined and tailored to specific requirements. Intentions and dependencies captured in process models allow for the enhancement of the capabilities which can be provided to the executive and operational staff.

6 SUMMARY

AI-based plan representations have found productive use in systems which do not necessarily involve only plan generation. The flexible representation of information about activities, tasks and plans allows dependency and intention knowledge to be captured such that intelligent support can be provided for plan analysis, use, monitoring and change.

The support of process modelling for businesses is an emerging area in which AI-based plan representations are finding use.

Acknowledgements

O-Plan and O-Plan2 are on-going projects at Edinburgh. I am grateful to Brian Drabble and Jeff Dalton on the O-Plan2 project for their input to the work described here. Current O-Plan2 work is supported by the US Advanced Research Projects Agency (ARPA) and the US Air Force Rome Laboratory acting through the Air Force Office of Scientific Research (AFSC) under contract F49620-92-C-0042. The United States Government is authorized to reproduce and distribute reprints for government purposes notwithstanding any copyright notation hereon.
PLANIT concepts were developed by a team at Edinburgh including Mark Drummond and John Fraser. OPTIMUM-AIV was a project for the European Space Agency involving a consortium with AIAI (Jussi Stader in particular), CRI, Matra Espace and Progrespace.
The use of knowledge-rich plan representations as one basis for work in process modelling is a theme that has been developed by

all technical groups at AIAI and through the Enterprise project under the Intelligent Systems Integration Programme funded by the UK DTI. Thanks to Mike Uschold at AIAI for valuable comments on an early version of this paper.

REFERENCES

Aarup, M., Arentoft, M.M., Parrod, Y., Stader, J., Stokes, I. and Vadon, H. (1994). OPTIMUM-AIV: A knowledge based planning and scheduling system for spacecraft AIV. In *Knowledge Based Scheduling* (eds. Fox, M. and Zweben, M.), Morgan Kaufmann, Los Altos, CA.

Allen, J., Hendler, J. and Tate, A. (1990). *Readings in Planning*, Morgan Kaufmann, Los Altos, CA.

Alvey Directorate. (1987). *Alvey Grand Meeting of Community Clubs*, available through IEEE, Savoy Place, London.

Arentoft, M.M., Parrod, Y., Stader, J., Stokes, I. and Vadon, H. (1991). OPTIMUM-AIV: A planning and scheduling system for spacecraft AIV, *Telematics and Informatics*, **8**(4), 239–252, Pergamon Press, Oxford.

Bruynooghe, R.F., Parker, J.M. and Rowles, J.S. (1992). PSS: A System for Process Enactment, published paper from ICL, Kidsgrove, Staffs ST7 1TL, UK.

Currie, K.W. and Tate, A. (1985). O-plan: control in the open planning architecture, *Proceedings of the BCS Expert Systems 85 Conference*, Warwick, UK, Cambridge University Press, Cambridge.

Currie, K.W. and Tate, A. (1991). O-plan: the open planning architecture, *Artificial Intelligence*, **51**(1), 49–86.

Drabble, B. (1993). Excalibur: a program for planning and reasoning with processes, *Artificial Intelligence*, **62**(1), 1–40.

Drummond, M.E., and Tate, A. (1992). *PLANIT Interactive Planners' Assistant - Rationale and Future Directions*, AIAI-TR-108, AIAI, University of Edinburgh.

Fikes, R.E., Hart, P.E. and Nilsson, N.J. (1972). Learning and executing generalized robot plans, *Artificial Intelligence*, **3**, 251–288.

Fuchs, J.J., Gasquet, B., Olalainty, B., and Currie, K.W. (1990). Plan-ERS1: an expert system for generating spacecraft mission plans, *Proceedings of the First International Conference on Expert Planning Systems*, Brighton, UK. Available from IEE, London.

Georgeff, M.P. and Lansky, A.L. (1986). Procedural knowledge. *Proceedings of the IEEE*, Special Issue on Knowledge Representation, Vol. 74, pp. 1383–1398.

Malcolm, C. and Smithers, T. (1988). Programming assembly robots in terms of task achieving behavioural modules: first experimental results. *Proceedings of the Second Workshop on Manipulators, Sensors and Steps towards Mobility as part of the International Advanced Robotics Programme*, Salford, UK.

Nilsson, N.J. (1988). Action networks. *Proceedings of the Rochester Planning Workshop*, October.

Parrod, Y. and Valera, S. (1993). OPTIMUM-AIV: a planning tool for spacecraft AIV. *Preparing for the Future*, ESA's Technology Programme Quarterly, Vol. 3 No. 3, European Space Agency, September.

Petrie, C.J. (ed.) (1992). *Enterprise Integration Modelling, Proceedings of the First International Conference*, MIT Press, Cambridge, MA.

PLANIT Club. (1987). *PLANIT Club Final Report*, published on behalf of the PLANIT Club by Systems Designers plc, Fleet, Hampshire, UK, document ref. C03209.

Tate, A. (1977). Generating project networks. *Proceedings of the International Joint Conference on Artificial Intelligence (IJCAI-77)*, Cambridge, MA.

Tate, A. (1984). Planning and condition monitoring in a FMS. *Proceedings of the International Conference on Flexible Automation Systems*, Institute of Electrical Engineers, London, UK.

Tate, A. (1987). Research to product - the community club experience, invited keynote paper to Artificial Intelligence '87, Sydney, Australia. In *Artificial Intelligence Developments and Applications*, (eds. J.S.Gero and R.Stanton), pp. 5–16, North-Holland, Amsterdam.

Tate, A. (1989). Coordinating the activities of a planner and an execution agent. *Proceedings of the Second NASA Conference on Space Telerobotics*, (eds. G.Rodriguez and H.Seraji), JPL Publication 89-7 Vol. 1 pp. 385–393, Jet Propulsion Laboratory,

February.

Tate, A., Drabble, B. and Kirby, R. (1994). O-Plan2: an open architecture for command, planning and control. In *Knowledge Based Scheduling*, (eds. M.Fox, M. and M.Zweben), Morgan Kaufmann, Los Altos, CA.

5

On dealing with dynamic utility of learned knowledge

Masaki Suwa and Hiroshi Motoda

Advanced Research Laboratory, Hitachi Ltd.,

2520, Hatoyama, Saitama, 350-03, Japan

Abstract

Cost-effective utility of learned knowledge consists of two parts; the cumulative matching costs of testing to apply the knowledge in problems and the cumulative speed-up effects its application has on problem-solving time. To evaluate these two factors correctly, measuring dynamic utility of learned knowledge when it is *actually applied* to problems is required. In that scheme, however, since the utility value of knowledge is in general negative before its application brings about speed-up effects in some problems, we encounter a new issue. What kind of strategy should be taken to retain and/or discard knowledge with currently negative utility value during a training session? This is important because it determines the available set of knowledge to be provided for the subsequent problem in each stage within a training session. The strategy taken greatly affects not only the problem-solving costs incurred in a training session but also the kind of knowledge that gains a positive estimation at the end of the training session and thus will be provided for a test session. This issue is crucial especially in situations where there are strong *interactions* of co-existing knowledge during a training session. Five strategies are presented in the domain of geometry problem-solving and evaluated from the following criterion; a desirable strategy is one that allows really useful knowledge to gain a positive estimation at the end of a training session, while minimizing the problem-solving costs during the session.

1 INTRODUCTION

Measuring the cost-effective utility of learned knowledge, i.e. matching costs needed for applying the knowledge[1] and speed-up effects its application has on problem-solving time, is essential to avoid the learning paradox. The learning paradox is that learning may degrade problem-solving performance (Gratch and DeJong 1991a; Minton 1985; Subramanian and Feldman 1990).

Various techniques of measuring utility value have been proposed so far. In the PRODIGY/EBL system (Minton 1990), speed-up effect is approximately estimated by *initial observation* when the knowledge is learned from a problem, since it is difficult to measure it when the knowledge is actually applied. This simplification was criticized because approximation only by a single instance from which the knowledge is learned does not reflect fluctuating factors of speed-up effects by various problem contexts, i.e. *interactions* from other co-existing knowledge and the kinds of currently existing problem statements (Gratch and DeJong 1991b). Gratch and DeJong proposed a method in which the incremental utility is measured every time a piece of knowledge is learned, and if it is statistically assured as positive after several measurements then it will be adopted as control strategy (Gratch and DeJong 1992). However, this technique neglects the cost that will be spent in testing to apply knowledge in vain after it is adopted as part of the available control knowledge. Actually we have encountered in the domain of geometry knowledge that exhibits big speed-up effects in its application but does not pay as a whole because the cost of testing to apply it in vain to problems is extremely large. These disadvantages are attributed to *statically* measuring utility when knowledge is learned. From these concerns, our view in this paper is that *dynamic*[2] analysis of cost-effective utility of learned

---

[1]This includes the cost taken in testing to apply the knowledge but in vain.

[2]Due to dynamic measurement of cost-effective utility, the utility value

knowledge is required when it is actually applied, *not* when it is first learned.[3]

In the scheme of dynamic measurement of utility values, however, we encounter a new technical issue about how to deal with gathered utility data. Utility value of knowledge is in general negative at first due to the cumulative cost of testing to apply the knowledge, before its application brings about speed-up effects in some problems. This means that we cannot discard a piece of knowledge because it has a negative utility value at present, i.e. it may be useful knowledge which will have positive speed-up effects in the near future.[4] Therefore, in this paper we examine what kind of strategies should be taken to retain and/or discard knowledge of currently negative utility value during a training session. This is important because it determines the available set of knowledge to be provided for the subsequent problem in each stage within a training session. The strategy taken greatly affects not only the problem-solving costs during the training session but also the kinds of knowledge that gains a high utility value at the end of the training session. Under an undesirable strategy, some pieces of really useful knowledge which should have high utility value may not be found in the list of available knowledge when a training session ends, and this will degrade performance in the subsequent test session.

2 STRATEGIES FOR DEALING WITH UTILITY VALUES

Some variations of the following two strategies will be evaluated in this paper.

1. To arrange the pieces of learned knowledge in a descending order of utility value every time a problem is solved and utility values are measured, and then to retain the best N

---

of knowledge is inevitably influenced by interactions of currently available knowledge. We will mention it in Section 5.

[3]As many researchers pointed out, dynamic measurement of speed-up effect is difficult and time-consuming. We show later a simplified technique of measuring it when knowledge is applied, but discussing the technique itself is not the main issue of this paper, as we say in this introduction.

[4]Things would be simpler in static analysis because initial estimation of speed-up effects may give a positive value.

    pieces of knowledge in terms of utility value in the list of available knowledge for the next problem.

2. To discard as soon as possible during a training session, knowledge whose utility has been assessed as 'bad'. For judging the 'badness' of knowledge, we use the technique of *statistical range estimation* of the true population mean of utility values.

Dynamic utility values are dealt with under each variation of the above strategies during the training session, and after that a test problem is solved by use of only the knowledge which has scored a positive utility as a total. And we evaluate the feasibility of those strategies according to the following standard:

1. whether or not the strategy can reduce the problem-solving costs during the training session as much as possible,

2. whether or not the strategy can estimate knowledge of really high utility as positive and available for the test session.

Before going into the detail of the experiments done in the geometry problem-solving domain, we will characterize the domain itself, the learning system and the kind of learned knowledge in the next section. Further we will describe briefly the technique of dynamic analysis of utility value.

3 CHARACTERIZATION OF THE LEARNING SYSTEM

3.1 Domain

Geometry problem-solving involves proving a goal statement deductively by use of domain knowledge when some problem statements are given. The characteristics of this domain are

- that a huge variety of instantiations are produced by preconditions and/or consequent parts of domain knowledge in applying it, and this may potentially impose a heavy burden of matching costs on problem-solving performance,

- and that not only goal-oriented backward reasoning but also bottom-up forward reasoning is essential to constructing a successful proof-tree efficiently especially in complicated problems (Sweller 1988),

- and therefore that search control knowledge suggesting which domain knowledge should be used in a forward manner to an already asserted problem statement plays a significant role in avoiding irrelevant paths of inference.

The first point suggests that in the geometry domain there could be potentially heavy interactions from other co-existing knowledge and/or other factors that will greatly affect dynamic cost-effective utility data. This requires us to provide a feasible strategy of dealing with dynamic utility values.

3.2 Search control knowledge

We do experiments in this paper on the learning system PC-LEARN (Suwa and Motoda 1994a,b). The PCLEARN system acquires some diagram configurations from a solved problem. The acquired configurations will work as search control knowledge in future problems; they help a problem solver select appropriate domain knowledge to be applied.

The diagram configurations which the PCLEARN system learns are called 'perceptual-chunks', or 'schemas' (Greeno 1983), and their significant role in controlling a problem solver's search has been extensively studied in the domain of geometry problem-solving (Koedinger and Anderson 1990; McDougal and Hammond 1992,1993). The characteristic of a perceptual-chunk is that it is acquired from a problem as *a chunk of diagram elements which are meaningful and grouped together with each other* (Suwa and Motoda 1994a,b). In this sense, a perceptual chunk can be regarded as a local chunk frequently found in the diagrams of many problems. Therefore, it does not contribute to directly accomplishing the goal statement, unlike search control knowledge learned by goal-oriented learning techniques, such as explanation-based learning (Minton *et al.* 1989). Rather, a perceptual-chunk only helps problem solvers do *local search* at a local control decision node during problem-solving traces.

The 'freedom' of perceptual-chunks from the goal structure of the problem from which they are learned is advantageous in assuring higher applicability to many future problems (Suwa and Motoda 1994a). But its 'locality' is a major weak point at the same time because it may not always control search in a correct direction globally. Therefore we need to justify whether the learned perceptual-chunks are worth being retained as available knowledge. Only empirical evaluation of their utility values gives us this justification by actually applying them in future problems with different problem situations (Suwa and Motoda 1993).

3.3 Measuring cost-effective data of applied knowledge

We briefly describe the method of measuring cost-effective utility of perceptual chunks. The utility value of a perceptual-chunk is calculated throughout its use over many problems according to the following formula:

$$Utility = TotalEffects - TotalMatchCosts, \qquad (5.1)$$

where *TotalEffects* is the cumulative speed-up effect that results from applying the perceptual-chunk frequently, and *TotalMatchCosts* is the cumulative time cost spent in testing to apply the perceptual-chunk in vain over frequent testings during many problems. Every time a problem is solved, the matching costs are measured for each perceptual-chunk, and if a perceptual-chunk has been applied in solving the problem, speed-up effect by its use is also calculated. In recording both values, we normalize them by the complexity of the current problem in question.[5] This is intended to prevent costs and/or effects measured in larger problems from preferably governing the utility of knowledge.[6]

---

[5] We approximate problem complexity by the problem-solving time spent in solving the problem without using any learned knowledge.

[6] Some readers may not see why cpu-time costs should be normalized in the way they are, thinking that if some effects are larger because they occur in larger problems, these should preferably govern utility. If our objective in addressing the utility problem were to come up with a problem-solving system which solves problems, learns and ends up with saving of as much overall problem-solving cost as possible, larger effects in larger problems should govern utility. But our current objective is to search for a nice way of dealing with utility values that can correctly estimate the utility value of each perceptual-chunk. It may be sometimes the case where the utility of a perceptual-chunk is by chance estimated as extremely bad due

If we intend to correctly make a dynamic analysis of the speed-up effect a piece of knowledge brings about, running the system with and without the piece of knowledge on each problem is required, and this has to be done for each piece of knowledge in question. Doing so requires solving the same problem multiple times and costs too much, as many researchers have pointed out (Minton 1990; Gratch and DeJong 1991b). In this paper, in order to measure the speed-up effect of each perceptual-chunk, we simply compare the current solution trace obtained by applying chunks with the solution trace constructed when the same problem is solved without any chunks,[7] according to the procedure described below:

$$Effect = NoMacroModeCosts - MacroModeCosts. \qquad (5.2)$$

$MacroModeCosts$ is the summation of the matching costs taken at the following nodes of the current solution trace: (a) the node (N_{apl}) to which the perceptual-chunk has been applied, (b) all the other nodes that had to be verified for applying the chunk, and (c) all the nodes newly produced by its application. No-$MacroModeCosts$ is the summation of the matching costs taken at the following nodes of the solution trace constructed without using any perceptual-chunks: (a) the ones that correspond to the above three kinds of nodes and (b) the ones along irrelevant paths that are invoked from the node corresponding to N_{apl}, if any. Note that applying a perceptual chunk to a node N_{apl} may save the costs in the irrelevant paths from N_{apl} and it is a major positive source of speed-up effect. On the other hand, $Macro$-$ModeCost$ will be potentially added up at every relevant node as the number of other co-existing perceptual-chunks increases.

---

to an unfortunate interaction with other co-applied perceptual-chunks. In particular, supposing that it happens in a relatively larger problem, it tends to underestimate the utility of the involved chunks. In the light of our objective, this should not happen. This sort of normalization is intended to alleviate that undesirable happening.

[7]Doing so requires solving the same problem in advance without any search control knowledge. The issue about the cost spent in learning has been a controversy in utility analysis. Refer to the section of related work for further discussion.

This is interaction from other knowledge and may be a negative source of speed-up effect.

After calculating speed-up effect for each of all the perceptual-chunks applied to a problem, we sum up the effects of all the perceptual-chunks. Ideally the total should be equal to the problem-solving time savings obtained by applying those percept-ual-chunks, i.e. the difference of the problem-solving cpu-time currently measured and the cpu-time spent in solving the same problem without using any perceptual-chunks. But in many cases both will not be equal. Therefore, we assume that the dis-crepancy of both values is attributed to interactions among the applied perceptual-chunks and add up/subtract the value of the discrepancy divided by the number of applied chunks to/from the evaluated speed-up effect of each perceptual-chunk.

4 HOW TO DEAL WITH UTILITY DATA

4.1 Experimental setting

We provided twenty geometry problems selected from junior high school reference books. The categories of problems se-lected are restricted to 'features of triangles' and 'parallel lines and angles'. Since problems of the same category would share some common perceptual-chunks, they can be good examples as an experimental platform to address the utility problem. The givens and goals of the problems are shown in Fig. 5.1.

Out of the 20 problems, we assigned 19 problems to a train-ing session and after repeating the training session twice[8] the remaining one problem is to be solved as a test session. In a training session, 19 problems are arranged in the descending or-der of problem complexity, and each of them is solved by use of the currently available set of perceptual-chunks. In a test session, the remaining one problem is solved using only those perceptual-chunks which have scored positive utility values at the end of the training session. Since the number of the ways

---

[8]We repeat this twice because the training session of 19 problems is too short to allow some pieces of really useful knowledge to gain positive estimation. Positive estimation can be obtained only after the knowledge has been applied to problems several times.

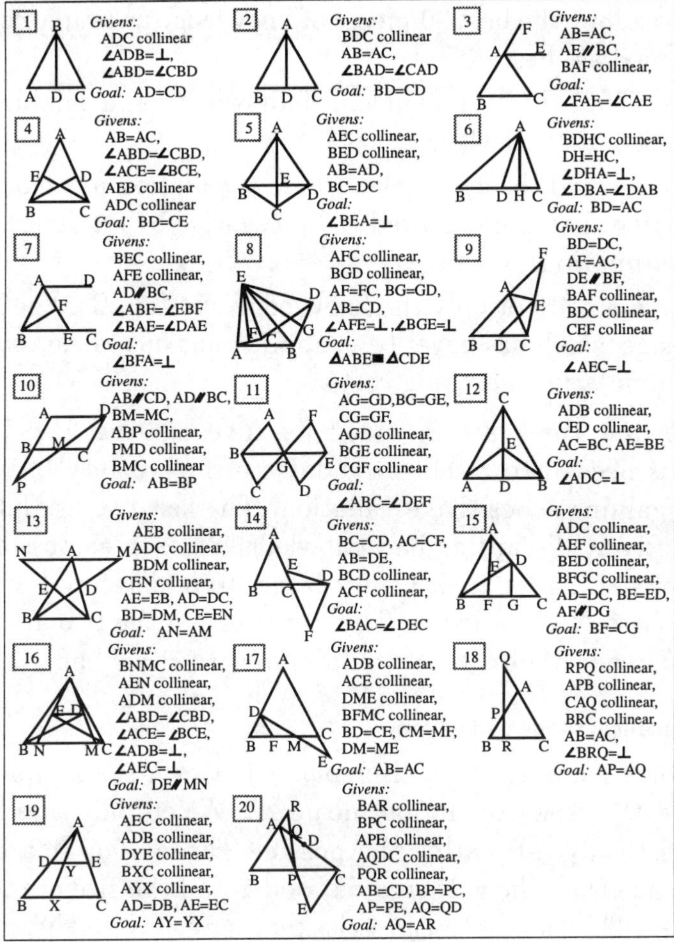

Figure 5.1. The geometry problems used for experiments.

of leaving one out for a test session is twenty, we did the above experiments for all the 20 cases. So we got $19 \times 2 \times 20$ problem-solving data for training sessions and 20 data for test sessions.

We provided the following five strategies of dealing with cost-effective utility data, out of which the first three are variations of the best-N strategy mentioned in Section 1, and the last two are variations of judging the 'badness' of knowledge. We carry out the above experiments for each of these five. They are

1. to adopt the best 20 pieces of knowledge as available (identified as 'best-20'),

2. to adopt the best 40 pieces of knowledge as available (identified as 'best-40'),

3. to adopt the best 60 pieces of knowledge as available (identified as 'best-60'),

4. to discard the knowledge whose population mean of utility values has been assured to be negative by statistical range estimation,

5. to discard not only the knowledge of 4 but also the knowledge which has never been applied but has taken too much cumulative matching costs.[9]

The first three are intended for investigating how large a buffer is needed to retain candidates of high-utility knowledge before gaining a positive estimation. The last two are intended for positively discarding bad knowledge as soon as possible, instead of waiting for their utility values to underscore the lowest in the 'best-N' knowledge. The variations in the two are due to the difference about what would be regarded as 'bad'.

4.2 Statistical range estimation

In general there will be a discrepancy between the sample mean $(\overline{x})$ and the true population mean(μ). We employ a technique of statistically estimating the possible range of μ at a certain confidence from the gathered data on $\overline{x}$ and the size of the sample (n). The sample mean $\overline{x}$ is known to have a distribution around μ according to the sample variance (s^2) and the degree of freedom $(n-1)$. So, if we set

$$t = \frac{\overline{x} - \mu}{s/\sqrt{n-1}}, \tag{5.3}$$

we already have a table of the distribution of t-values. According to this table, we can say at a confidence δ that the t-value lies between $-f(\delta)$ and $f(\delta)$, where $f(\delta)$ is a function of δ. Thus, we can estimate the range of μ at a confidence δ as follows:

$$\overline{x} - f(\delta) \cdot \frac{s}{\sqrt{n-1}} \leq \mu \leq \overline{x} + f(\delta) \cdot \frac{s}{\sqrt{n-1}} \tag{5.4}$$

---

[9]In this experiment, the knowledge whose cumulative costs exceed 0.2 in terms of the value normalized by problem complexity is judged to be 'bad'.

The true utility is calculated from the true population mean of both matching costs and speed-up effects by the following formula:

$$utility = n_{benefit} \cdot \mu_{benefit} - n_{cost} \cdot \mu_{cost} \qquad (5.5)$$

For each of the matching costs and speed-up effects, we can statistically estimate their range of existence. In order to assure the utility of a piece of knowledge as negative, we have only to prove the maximum of *utility* is less than zero by calculating it from the maximum of speed-up effects and the minimum of matching costs. We can assure this at a confidence of $\delta_b \times \delta_c$, where δ_b is the confidence in estimating the range of speed-up effects and δ_c is the confidence in estimating the range of matching costs. In the experiment we made estimation at the confidence of 60 %. [10]

4.3 Experimental results

For each of the five strategies of dealing with utility data, Table 5.1 shows the following; (1) the average of cpu-time costs over 20 test problems, (2) the average of cpu-time costs over 760 training problems, (3) the number of problems out of 20 test problems, in which positive speed-up effects by use of learned knowledge, negative effects and no applications of knowledge are observed respectively. Cpu-time costs are normalized by problem complexity. Below we wrap up the observations about the characteristics of the employed strategies.

1. In using the 'best-20' strategy, the number of problems in which no knowledge was applied is the largest and the number of problems in which positive speed-up effects were observed is the smallest. Consequently, the average cost in the test sessions becomes larger than 1.0. The

---

[10]Some readers may think that that 60% confidence is fairly low. But a higher confidence is actually impractical because it would result in being too tolerant in retaining even bad-looking knowledge until obtaining a large enough sample of evidence to give high confidence; removing bad knowledge as soon as possible is critically important for maintaining sound estimation of utility value, as will be discussed in the subsequent section.

Table 5.1. Problem-solving performance in training and test sessions for each strategy of dealing with utility values.

	The 20 test problems			Average costs	
	positive effects	no application	negative effects	test sessions	training sessions
best-20	4	14	2	1.12	1.22
best-40	8	11	1	0.95	1.45
best-60	8	10	2	0.92	2.94
neg.assure *	7	11	2	0.90	2.22
never-applied **	12	6	2	0.77	1.28

*neg. assure: the strategy of discarding the knowlede which has been statistically assured as negative

** never-applied: the strategy of discarding the knowledge which has never been applied and costs too much

reason is as follows; since the volume of the list of available knowledge during training sessions, i.e. in this case 20, is too small, some pieces of knowledge which should have scored a positive value at the end of a training session have dropped out of the list before gaining positive utility in the training session. This result suggests that **in order to estimate good knowledge as positive at the end of a training session, we need a certain volume of buffer of knowledge that allows currently negative knowledge to be retained during the session.**

2. Retaining too much knowledge during training sessions, however, brings about a rather undesirable outcome. **As the amount of knowledge retained increases, the average training costs tend to become extremely large.** Especially, the use of 'best-60' strategy costs about three times more problem-solving cpu-time than using problems without any learned knowledge, while the average cost of test sessions scores less than 1.0 (as we would like). This is mainly because the solver uses knowledge that is bad but has been retained nevertheless. The situation is aggravated by a snowball effect; bad knowledge degrades the quality of the proof-trees generated in the training sessions, and such proof trees lead to the generation of additional bad knowledge.

3. The strategies of **removing bad knowledge as soon as possible** when it is assured to be bad are effective in **allowing really good knowledge to be estimated as positive** at the end of training sessions, while adequately **containing the training costs.** In particular, in using the fifth strategy, the number of problems in which positive speed-up effects are observed is the largest, and the number of problems in which no knowledge is applied is the least. Consequently, the average cost in test sessions is 0.77, while the average cost in training sessions is 1.28.

Table 5.2 shows the following for each case of using the five strategies: (1) the average of the number of pieces of knowledge that is retained in the list of available knowledge when a training session ends,[11] over the 20 cases, and (2) the average of the number of pieces of knowledge that has obtained positive utility estimation out of the pieces of knowledge of (1), over the 20 cases.

Table 5.2. The characteristics of the knowledge retained at the end of training session.

	All the knowledge*	Positively-estimated knowledge**
best-20	20.0	3.5
best-40	40.0	6.2
best-60	60.0	3.8
neg.assure *	62.8	5.9
never-applied **	45.1	9.3

* the average number of all the retained knowledge at the end of a training session, over the 20 cases

** the average number of pieces of positively estimated knowledge at the end of a training session, over the 20 cases

1. The number of the positively estimated knowledge in case of 'best-20' strategy is the smallest. This observation also tells that the volume of the retained knowledge is too small.

---

[11]This includes not only knowledge of positive utility but also knowledge of negative utility.

2. It is surprising that the number of pieces of positively estimated knowledge in the'best-60' strategy is fewer than that in the 'best-40' strategy. This is mainly caused by **interactions with other bad knowledge**; remember that, as we mention the method of measuring cost-effective utility value, $MacroModeCost$ includes the matching costs at the nodes that have been produced by applying the knowledge itself. This means that, when a piece of knowledge has been applied, if bad knowledge requiring too much cost co-exists, it will potentially degrade the utility value of that applied knowledge. Consequently this will make it difficult for the knowledge to obtain positive estimation. In other words, **the presence of bad knowledge will ruin the estimation of good knowledge.**

3. Table 5.2 shows, in the first column, the average number of the pieces of knowledge that are retained at the end of a training session for each of the fourth and fifth strategies. Each value approximately represents how large a buffer of retaining knowledge has been provided under each strategy. According to these values, the fourth strategy is compatible with the 'best-60' and the fifth one is compatible with the 'best-40'. If we compare (1) the fifth strategy with the 'best-40', and (2) the fourth with the 'best-60', in terms of the average number of positively estimated pieces of knowledge, we can say that the last two (statistical) strategies contribute much to preventing knowledge from being affected by interactions with bad knowledge. It is justified by the fact that much more knowledge is positively estimated in the statistical strategies (the fifth and fourth) than the non-statistical ones ('best-40' and 'best-60') , while the sizes of the buffer are about the same in each case of the compatible strategies.

4. According to the above discussions, the fifth strategy of removing both (1) the knowledge that has been statistically assured as negative and (2) the knowledge that has never been applied but has taken too much matching costs is the most desirable to avoid interactions with bad knowl-

edge and to obtain good performance in test sessions while keeping training costs not so expensive.

4.4 Current limitations and discussions

In the experiments shown in this paper, the best result of the test costs was 0.77 in the fifth strategy. This is worse than we expected first. We mention the reason for this although this paper does *not* aim at implementing a system that exhibits as much learning effect as possible. The main reason is that problems that do not inherently share perceptual-chunks as partial problem structures with other problems are included in the twenty problems. This is obviously found, as shown in Table 5.1, from the observation that under all the five strategies some common problems did not allow for any applications of learned knowledge when they were solved in test sessions. Although we noticed it by observing problem-solving performances during all the training sessions, we didn't change the experimental conditions, thinking that we should not artificially design an ideal environment of training sessions. Those problems are in a way unrelated factors that may potentially degrade learning effects. We rather have to note, however, that under these tough conditions some learning effects as well as the differences of the employed strategies are clearly observed.

The technique of range estimation employed for judging the badness of knowledge could be employed for judging the 'goodness' of knowledge as well. We may seek an alternative strategy to use only the knowledge that has been *statistically assured* to have positive utility[12] for test sessions. Although the feasibility of this strategy is an open question at present, we currently have a negative view against it. The set of knowledge that has scored a positive value in the current version consists of three types; (1) knowledge which is applied frequently and exhibits some speed-up effects whenever it is applied, (2) knowledge which frequently exhibits small negative effects (or is rarely applied) but sometimes big positive speed-up effects, and (3) knowledge which

---

[12]Notice that this is different from the knowledge that has scored a positive utility value at the end of a training session. In this paper the latter strategy has been taken.

sometimes exhibits big negative effects but frequently some positive effects (resulting in positive estimation as a total). If we assure the goodness of knowledge as mentioned above, only the knowledge of the first class would be selected as available for test sessions. That may be problematic because it may potentially cause the situation again that no knowledge is applied in many problems of test sessions. We have to examine it in the near future.

We repeated each training session twice to make the most of the statistical strategies under a restricted source of geometry problems. Ideally we should have collected greater numbers of different problems. Repeating a training session twice, however, might suffice because when the same problem is solved for the second time the utility of the knowledge learned from the problem for the first time can be testified in the different contexts of interactions with co-existing knowledge from the first situation.

The order of problems in a training session may potentially influence the set of learned knowledge. In this paper, we fixed it in the descending order of problem complexity. This may have been one of the factors governing the costs in training sessions and test sessions. We have to examine this factor in the future.

5 RELATED WORK

Most studies on learning systems have so far evaluated cost-effective utility in a *static* way, i.e. it is measured simultaneously when knowledge is learned, because it is the simplest way. They don't have to solve the same problem many times. On the other hand, dynamic analysis in this paper requires solving the same problem without using any learned knowledge in advance. This is obviously more time-consuming than static analysis. But our view is that this is a sort of inevitable cost because dynamic analysis of learned knowledge can be carried out only when it is actually applied in problems. Our simplified technique is still less time-consuming than the ideal method of solving the same problem with and without the knowledge for each piece of knowledge in question. Due to this simplification, however, our technique would yield rather rough estimation of utility values. But we assume that we can compensate for this roughness by doing statistical estimation.

We do not address the *interaction problem* in the same sense as Gratch and DeJong do so in their paper (Gratch and DeJong 1992). They address it in the following way: in general the measured utility values inherently include some interactions from the current available set of control knowledge. They propose a framework where only the knowledge which gains good interaction from the current available set will be adopted as new control knowledge. This was possible only by gathering static utility values of knowledge simultaneously in learning. In this respect, they make the most of interactions among knowledge toward the goal of improving the planner's performance in a hill-climbing way. On the other hand, we view the interaction problem differently; we understand that interactions between knowledge are one of the fluctuating factors like other factors,[13] and also that deterioration of training costs due to applying learned knowledge before knowing its utility is inevitable as a cost of learning. In other words, this matches well the human way of learning; when actually using knowledge in real problems causes fatal failure, we humans learn to avoid using it.

This attitude toward interaction problem originates from the following notion. We think that we do not necessarily have to improve the system's performance in a hill-climbing way. Rather, if there should be a set of perceptual-chunks that have high utility as a whole in any contexts including interactions from other knowledge and/or other fluctuating factors, we want to obtain such an organized set of perceptual-chunks in the domain in question. It may be a success if we can finally come up with satisfactory performance by doing so, even if we pay some costs to reach the final state.

6 CONCLUSION

We address the issue of how to deal with dynamic utility values of knowledge during a training session, the main factor deter-

---

[13]An example of other factors is high dependence of utility values on what kinds of problem statements exist in the problem space when a piece of knowledge is applied.

mining the available set of knowledge to be provided for the subsequent problem in each stage within the session. The strategy taken has a great impact on problem-solving costs in the training session. But perhaps more importantly, it determines whether or not truly useful knowledge can gain positive estimation by the end of the training session. The extent to which useful knowledge can gain positive estimation determines problem-solving performance in the subsequent test session.

Five strategies were examined in this paper. They are (1) using the best 20 pieces of knowledge in terms of cost-effective utility values, out of all the learned knowledge, (2) using the best 40 pieces of knowledge, (3) using the best 60 pieces of knowledge, (4) discarding as soon as possible any piece of knowledge whose utility has been statistically assured as negative, and (5) discarding not only knowledge as defined in (4) but also knowledge which has never been applied but has cost too much.

We have come up with the following insights.

- Some buffer to retain knowledge of currently negative utility values in the list of available knowledge is needed to enable some such knowledge to eventually obtain positive estimation in the subsequent training session.

- Too large a buffer, however, will undesirably cause *interactions from bad knowledge* and *snowballing effects* during training sessions. If the two effects coincide, the problem-solving costs in training sessions will pile up and, what is worse, the utility value of even useful knowledge will be improperly underestimated due to interactions and discarded from the list of available knowledge. The latter phenomenon badly affects problem-solving performance in test sessions.

- The strategies of discarding 'bad' knowledge as soon as possible are effective in allowing really useful knowledge to gain positive estimation at the end of training sessions, while restricting the training costs to a certain degree.

Although this is sort of a pilot study which is carried out in the geometry problem-solving domain, the insights obtained about how to deal with dynamic utility are general enough to be applied to such a class of problems in which the matching cost in applying knowledge imposes a heavy burden on problem-solving performance.

REFERENCES

Gratch, J. and DeJong, G. (1991a). A hybrid approach to guaranteed effective control strategies, *Proceedings of ML-91.*

Gratch, J. and DeJong, G. (1991b). On Comparing Operationality and Utility, Tech. Report, UIUCDCS-R-91-1713, University of Illinois at Urbana–Champaign.

Gratch, J. and DeJong, G. (1992). COMPOSER: a probabilistic solution to the utility problem in speed-up learning, *Proceedings of AAAI-92,* 235–240.

Greeno, J. G. (1983). Forms of understanding in mathematical problem-solving, Paris, S.G *et al.* (eds.), *Learning and Motivation in the Classroom.* Lawrence Erlbaum Associates.

Koedinger, K. R. and Anderson, J. R. (1990). Abstract planning and perceptual chunks: elements of expertise in geometry, *Cognitive Science* **14**, 511–550.

McDougal, T. and Hammond, K. (1992). A recognition model of geometry theorem-proving, *Proc. of the 14th Annual Conference of the Cognitive Science Society,* 106–111.

McDougal, T. and Hammond, K. (1993). Representing and using procedural knowledge to build geometry proofs, *Proc. of AAAI-93,* 60–65.

Minton, S. (1985). Selectively generalizing plans for problem solving, *Proceedings IJCAI-85,* 596–602.

Minton, S. (1990). Quantitative results concerning the utility of explanation-based learning, *Artificial Intelligence* **42**, 363–391.

Minton, S., Carbonell, J. G., Knoblock, C. A., Kuokka, D. R., Etzioni, O. and Gil, Y., (1989). Explanation-based learning: a problem solving perspective, *Artificial Intelligence* **40**, 63–118.

Subramanian, D. and Feldman, R. (1990). The utility of EBL in recursive domain theories, *Proceedings of AAAI-90,* 942–949.

Suwa, M. and Motoda, H. (1993). A perceptual criterion for visually controlling learning, *Proceedings of 4th International Workshop on Algorithmic Learning Theory, Lecture Notes in AI 744,* 356–

369, Springer-Verlag, Berlin.

Suwa, M. and Motoda, H. (1994a). Learning perceptually-chunked macro-operators, *Machine Intelligence* **13**, 419–440, Oxford University Press, Oxford.

Suwa, M. and Motoda, H. (1994b). PCLEARN: A model for learning perceptual-chunks, In *Proceedings of the 16th Annual Meetings of the Cognitive Science Society*, Atlanta, Georgia.

Sweller, J. (1988). Cognitive load during problem-solving: effects on learning, *Cognitive Science* **12**, 257–285.

INDUCTIVE LOGIC PROGRAMMING

6

Inverting Entailment and Progol

Stephen Muggleton

Oxford University Computing Laboratory

Abstract

This paper firstly provides a re-appraisal of the development of techniques for inverting deduction, secondly introduces Mode-Directed Inverse Entailment (MDIE) as a generalisation and enhancement of previous approaches and thirdly describes an implementation of MDIE in the Progol system. Progol is implemented in C and available by anonymous ftp. The re-assessment of previous techniques in terms of inverse entailment leads to new results for learning from positive data and inverting implication between pairs of clauses.

1 INTRODUCTION

Since its inception in Muggleton (1991a) Inductive Logic Programming (ILP) has grown to become a substantial sub-area of both Machine Learning and Logic Programming (see Muggleton and De Raedt (1994)). The success of the subject lies partly in the choice of the core representation language of logic programs. Least Herbrand models of logic programs (Lloyd 1984) fit neatly with the distinction between examples and conjectured theories in inductive inference. The syntax of logic programs provides modular blocks which, when added or removed, generalize or specialize the program. Depth-bounded Prolog interpreters, used for theorem-proving, allow efficient testing of hypothesized Horn clause theories. Most importantly, Turing-equivalence of logic programs is allowing a broader range of Machine Learning applications in ILP than was possible with more restrictive representations.

Recent research in ILP has spawned a variety of new theoretical topics. These include the problem of inverting resolution (Muggleton and Buntine 1988; Wirth 1989; Rouveirol 1992), inversion of clausal implication (Lapointe and Matwin 1992; Idestam-Almquist 1993; Muggleton and Page 1994a), predicate invention (Muggleton 1994c), closed-world specialization (Bain and Muggleton 1991) and U-learnability (Muggleton and Page 1994c). As with any subject, the diversity of sub-topics can be better understood by following the development of a particular line of ideas. The aims of this paper are firstly to provide a re-appraisal of the development of techniques for inverting deduction, secondly to introduce Mode-Directed Inverse Entailment (MDIE) as a generalization and enhancement of previous approaches and thirdly to describe an implementation of MDIE in the Progol[1] system.

At each stage in the development of ILP there has been an attempt to solve existing technical restrictions of implemented systems. The five main approaches described in this paper are as follows:

1. inverse resolution (IR) in propositional logic,
2. IR in first-order definite clause logic,
3. determinate relative least general generalization,
4. inverse implication and
5. mode-directed inverse entailment.

The paper is structured as follows. First the logical and statistical setting for ILP are introduced (Section 2). This is followed by a synopsis of the results and restrictions for approaches 1 to 4 (Sections 3 to 6). The remainder of the paper (Sections 7 to 12) deals with theoretical and practical aspects of mode-directed inverse entailment. Instructions for obtaining Progol by anonymous ftp are given in Section 11. The paper closes with a discussion of research issues related to inverse entailment. Standard definitions taken from Logic Programming and ILP are given

---

[1]Prolog inverted in the middle.

in Appendix 14. In Appendix 15 a statistical setting for ILP is described. Properties of the subsumption lattice are described in Appendix 16. The algorithms used in Progol are given in Appendix 17. A table of Progol's runtimes on various data sets is presented in Appendix 18.

2 LOGICAL AND STATISTICAL SETTING FOR ILP

Deductive inference derives consequences E from a prior theory T. Thus if T says that all swans are white, E might state that a particular swan is white. Inductive inference derives a general belief T from specific beliefs E. After observing one or more white swans T might be the conjecture that all swans are white. In both deduction and induction T and E must be consistent and

$$T \models E. \tag{6.1}$$

The requirement of consistency means that the observation of a black swan rules out conjecture T. Inductive inference is, in a sense, the inverse of deduction. However, deductive inference proceeds by application of sound rules of inference, while inductive inference typically involves unsound conjecture. Such conjectures have at best statistical support from observed data. However, the association of probability values with hypotheses requires the assumption of a prior probability distribution over the hypothesis language. Occam's razor can be taken as an instance of a distribution which assigns higher prior probability to simpler hypotheses. It has been shown (Cohen 1993) that without such distributional assumptions the class of all logic programs is not even PAC-predictable. On the other hand, it has recently been demonstrated (Muggleton and Page 1994c) that the class of all time-bounded logic programs is polynomial-time learnable (U-learnable) under fairly broad families of prior probability distributions. Appendix 15 gives more details of the relationship between data, posterior probabilities and U-learnability.

Within ILP it is usual to separate the elements of (6.1) into examples (E), background knowledge (B), and hypotheses (H).

These have the relationship

$$B \wedge H \models E. \tag{6.2}$$

B, H and E are each logic programs. E usually consists of ground unit clauses of a single target predicate. E can be separated into E^+, ground unit definite clauses and E^-, ground unit headless Horn clauses. However, the separation into B, H and E is a matter of convenience, as the following example shows.

Example 6.1 White swans. The swan example might be represented using the following logic program.

$$E^+ = \left\{ \begin{array}{l} white(swan1) \leftarrow \\ swan(swan1) \leftarrow \end{array} \right.$$

$$E^- = \left\{ \begin{array}{l} black(swan2) \leftarrow \\ swan(swan2) \leftarrow \end{array} \right.$$

$$B = \left\{ \; \leftarrow black(X), white(X) \right.$$

$$H = \left\{ \; white(X) \leftarrow swan(X) \right.$$

Relationship (6.2) does not hold since $swan(swan1)$ is not entailed by $B \wedge H$. It does not help to argue that $swan(swan1)$ is background knowledge, since this is an observation about swan1. E^- does not contain headless Horn clauses, although together with B it refutes H. These problems can most simply be avoided by dropping all but the restriction that B, H and E are arbitrary logic programs.

3   INVERSE RESOLUTION IN PROPOSITIONAL LOGIC

The idea of carrying out induction by inverting deduction was first investigated in depth mathematically by the 19th century political economist and philosopher of science Stanley Jevons (Jevons 1874).[2] Jevons solved by tabulation the 'Inverse or Inductive Problem' involving two propositional symbols. The following quote from Jevons' book on inductive inference (Jevons

---

[2] George Boole's algebraic approach to deduction inspired Jevons to use truth-functional tabulations to design and build a logical calculator (Jevons 1870). Jevons' mechanical *Organon* is complete for deciding satisfiability of propositional clauses in 4 variables, and can be found in the Museum of Scientific Instruments in Oxford.

1874) is both modern-sounding and relevant to the problems addressed in this paper.

> Induction is, in fact, the inverse operation of deduction, and cannot be conceived to exist without the corresponding operation, so that the question of relative importance cannot arise. Who thinks of asking whether addition or subtraction is the more important process in arithmetic? But at the same time much difference in difficulty may exist between a direct and inverse operation; the integral calculus, for instance, is infinitely more difficult than the differential calculus of which it is the inverse. Similarly, it must be allowed that inductive investigations are of a far higher degree of difficulty and complexity than any questions of deduction;
>
> ...

At the time of Jevons logicians, not yet persuaded of Boole's algebraic approach to logic, employed an array of inference rules derived from Aristotelian syllogisms. Robinson (Robinson 1965) was later to show that deductive inference in first-order predicate calculus could be effected by a single rule of inference, that of resolution. Inductive inference based on inverting resolution in propositional logic was first discussed in Muggleton (1991b) (originally a technical report from 1987) as an analysis of the inductive inference rules within the Duce system (Muggleton 1987).

3.1 Inductive inference rules

Duce had six inductive inference rules. Four of these were concerned with definite clause propositional logic. In the following description of the inference rules lower-case letters represent propositional variables and upper-case letters represent conjunctions of propositional variables.

$$\textbf{Absorption:}\quad \frac{p \leftarrow A, B \qquad q \leftarrow A}{p \leftarrow q, B \qquad q \leftarrow A}$$

$$\textbf{Identification:}\quad \frac{p \leftarrow A, B \qquad p \leftarrow A, q}{q \leftarrow B \qquad p \leftarrow A, q}$$

$$\textbf{Intra-construction:}\quad \frac{p \leftarrow A, B \qquad\qquad p \leftarrow A, C}{q \leftarrow B \qquad p \leftarrow A, q \quad q \leftarrow C}$$

Inter-construction:
$$\frac{p \leftarrow A, B \qquad\qquad q \leftarrow A, C}{p \leftarrow r, B \quad r \leftarrow A \quad q \leftarrow r, C}$$

Each of Duce's rules is superficially similar to that of a deductive rule of inference of the form

$$\frac{X}{Y}$$

Such a deductive inference rule would be called sound if and only if X entailed Y. We will call a rule of inference *inductively sound* if and only if Y logically entails X, or equivalently $\overline{X}$ entails $\overline{Y}$. A set of inductive inference rules will be written with an overline as $\overline{I}$. Each clause above the line is either a resolvent of two clauses below the line or is itself found below the line. Duce's inference rules invert single-depth applications of resolution. Using the rules a set of resolution-based trees for deriving the examples can be constructed backwards from their roots. The set of leaves of the trees represent a theory from which the examples can be derived. In the process new proposition symbols, not found in the examples, can be 'invented' by the intra- and inter-construction rules.

3.2 Completeness

Continuing the analogy with deduction we might write

$$\overline{X} \vdash_{\overline{I}} \overline{Y}$$

to say that theory Y is derivable using inductive inference rules $\overline{I}$ from examples X. There are two senses in which a set of inference rules $\overline{I}$ may be said to be complete.

Definition 6.2 Weak completeness. Let the example language $\mathcal{E}$ and hypothesis language $\mathcal{H}$ both be subsets of the first-order predicate calculus and let $\overline{I}$ be a set of inductive inference rules. $\overline{I}$ is said to be *weak complete* for $\mathcal{E}$ and $\mathcal{H}$ if and only if for each $H \subseteq \mathcal{H}$ there exists $E \subseteq \mathcal{E}$ such that $\overline{E} \vdash_{\overline{I}} \overline{H}$.

In Muggleton (1991b) it was shown that $\overline{I}$ consisting of only *absorption* and *intra-construction* is weak complete under particular hypothesis and example language restrictions.

Definition 6.3 Strong completeness. Let the example language $\mathcal{E}$ and hypothesis language $\mathcal{H}$ both be subsets of the first-order predicate calculus and let $\overline{I}$ be a set of inductive inference rules. $\overline{I}$ is said to be *strong complete* for $\mathcal{E}$ and $\mathcal{H}$ if and only if for each $H \subseteq \mathcal{H}$ and $E \subseteq \mathcal{E}$ $H \models E$ implies $\overline{E} \vdash_{\overline{I}} \overline{H}$.

The four Duce inference rules in Section 3.1 are not strong complete for definite clause propositional calculus.

3.3 Occam compression

In Duce every application of an inductive inference rule $\frac{X}{Y}$ was chosen to maximize information compression.

Definition 6.4 Occam compression. Let X, Y be wffs for which $Y \models X$ and $X \wedge Y \not\models \square$. Let $|X|$ and $|Y|$ be the number of bits required to encode X and Y. The Occam compression of X relative to Y is $|X| - |Y|$.

Suppose $|P| = b.symbols(P)$ where $symbols(P)$ is the number of propositional symbol occurrences in P and b is the number of bits to encode each such occurrence. With reference to Appendix 15, an encoding is the expression of a prior distribution. $F(P)$ expresses the relative frequency with which the teacher chooses P as target concept. Assume the learner knows $F(P)$ and uses it as a prior distribution on $\mathcal{H}$. Then according to Shannon and Weaver (Shannon and Weaver 1963) $|P|$ is $-\log_2 F(P)$ and

$$F(P) = 2^{-|P|}$$

Note that since this is an exponential-decay distribution, in the situation in which the learner knows $F(P)$, the results in Muggleton and Page (1994c) show that the class of all time-bounded logic programs is polynomial-time learnable (U-learnable). However, note also that if the teacher's prior is known to the learner then on average theories chosen by the teacher have extremely low information content. Alternatively this might be viewed as the expectation that only a small augmentation of an existing theory is expected from any short presentation of the teacher's examples.

Remark 6.5 Let E be a wff and $\mathcal{H}$ be a set of wffs containing E such that for each $H \in \mathcal{H}$ it is the case that $H \models E$ and

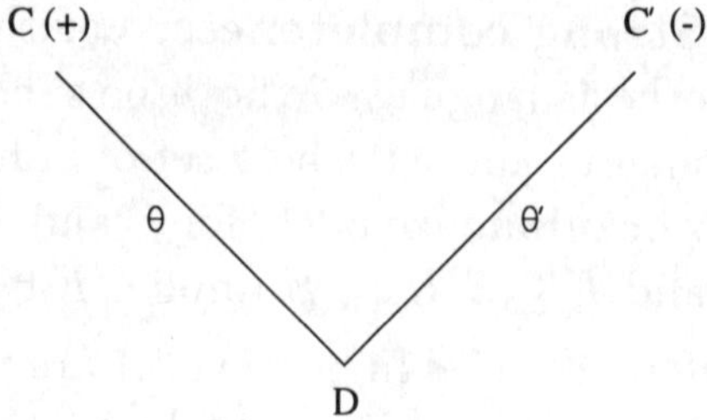

Figure 6.1. Single resolution.

$H \wedge E \not\models \square$. Let $H_{\max}$ have maximum compression within $\mathcal{H}$ relative to E and let H_0 have compression 0 relative to E. $H_{\max}$ has maximum posterior probability and H_0 has posterior probability equal to E.

Proof. According to Equation (6.6) in Appendix 15.2

$$\frac{p(H|E)}{p(E|E)} = \frac{p(H)}{p(E)} = 2^{|E|-|H|}.$$

$p(H|E)$ is maximal when $|E|-|H|$ is maximal. When $|E|-|H| = 0$ then $p(H|E) = p(E|E)$. $\square$

The hypothesis with maximum posterior probability ($H_{\max}$) has maximum expected predictive accuracy.

4 INVERSE RESOLUTION IN FIRST-ORDER LOGIC

Inverse resolution was lifted to first-order predicate calculus in Muggleton and Buntine (1988). This involved algebraic inversion of the equations of resolution below:

$$D = (C \cup C')\theta\theta'$$
$$l\theta = \overline{l'\theta'}$$

Figure 6.1 shows a resolution step. D is derived at the base of the 'V' given the clauses on the arms. In contrast, a 'V' inductive inference step derives one of the clauses on the arm of the 'V' given the clause on the other arm and the clause at the base. In Figure 6.1 the literal resolved on is positive ($+$) in C and negative ($-$) in C'. Duce's absorption rule constructs C' from C and D, while the identification rule derives C from C' and D.

Since algebraic inversion of resolution has a complex non-deterministic solution only a restricted form of absorption was implemented in Cigol.[3] However, it was shown independently in Muggleton (1991a) and Rouveirol (1992) that there is a unique most-specific solution for 'V' inductive inference rules. That is

$$C' \downarrow \; = (D \cup l\theta)$$

where θ is such that $C\theta \subseteq D$. Rather than inverting the equations of resolution we might consider resolution from the model-theoretic point of view. That is

$$C \wedge C' \models D. \tag{6.3}$$

Applying the deduction theorem gives a deductive solution for absorption.

$$C \wedge \overline{D} \models \overline{C'}$$

This is a special case of *inverting implication* (Section 7). Since D and C' are clauses, $\overline{D}$ and $\overline{C'}$ are conjunctions of ground skolemized literals. The most specific solution for C' corresponds to the most general solution for $\overline{C'}$, i.e. when $\overline{C'}$ contains the maximum set of literals derivable from $C \wedge \overline{D}$. However, this solution is neither restricted to single-depth resolutions, nor is the clause cardinality finitely bounded.

Example 6.6 Recursive list membership. Let $C = member(X,[X|Y])$ and $D = member(2,[1,2,3])$

$$
\begin{aligned}
C \wedge \overline{D} \;&\models\; \overline{member(2,[1,2,3])} \\
&\models\; member(1,[1,2,3]) \\
&\models\; member(2,[2,3]) \\
&\models\; member(3,[3]) \\
&\models\; \ldots
\end{aligned}
$$

Though clause

$$C' = member(2,[1,2,3]) \leftarrow member(1,[1,2,3]),\ldots$$

---

[3]logiC backwards.

maintains Relationship (6.3), there are at least 3 derivation steps to D. C' is θ-subsumed by all single-step resolution solutions. $\overline{C'}$ also contains the infinite sequence of atoms $member(3, [3, 3])$, $member(3, [3, 3, 3]), \ldots$.

Owing to the weak completeness results for the Duce inductive inference rules (Section 3.2) only absorption and intraconstruction were implemented in Cigol.

4.1 Compression

Like Duce, Cigol used Occam compression (Definition 6.4) to guide the choice of inverse resolution steps. The encoding measure was the total number of predicate and function symbol occurrences in a logic program. Like Duce, each such inverse resolution step was only allowed if it produced a positive compression value. This led to two difficulties.

1. **Local generalization.** Consider the recursive multiplication clause

$$mult(A, B, C) \leftarrow dec(A, D), mult(D, B, E), plus(E, B, C).$$

   When given a large set of ground instances of valid multiplications, compression is only achievable after a series of inverse resolution steps, in which all steps except the last do not produce compression.

2. **Learning from positive examples.** In Muggleton (1988) it was noted that the compression measure used in Cigol did not allow learning from only positive data since the simplest possible hypothesis, say $\forall X.p(X)$, will always be consistent. Alternative compression measures were suggested in Muggleton (1988); Muggleton *et al.* (1992b); Conklin and Witten (1992); Gillies (1992). These measures are closely allied to Rissanen's Minimal Description Length (MDL) Principle (Rissanen 1978; Li and Vitanyi 1993).

The first problem was addressed by considering the inversion of multiple resolution steps by *saturating* clauses (Rouveirol and Puget 1989; Rouveirol 1992; Muggleton 1991a; Idestam-

Almquist 1992). Clause saturation is closely related to the techniques of inverse entailment described in Section 7. However, since saturation is based on inverting resolution proof steps, it cannot deal with built-in predicates. Nevertheless, the interpretations of such predicates can be computed by calling C functions. The Progol system (Sections 8 to 11) uses mode declarations to access such interpretations.

4.2 Learning from positive data

The second problem is of a different nature. When learning from only positive data, predictive accuracy will be maximized by choosing the most general consistent hypothesis since this will always agree with new data. However, in applications such as grammar learning (Ling 1994; Quinlan 1993), only positive data are available, though the grammar which produces all strings is not an acceptable hypothesis. Let us then suppose a modification to the U-learning setting given in Appendix 15. The teacher still draws instances randomly from distribution G but only gives them to the learner if they are positive examples of the target T. In this setting we would need to find a tradeoff between the generality and complexity of an hypothesis. First let us define a measure of the generality of an hypothesis.

Definition 6.7 Generality measure. Let H be a wff and G be a probability distribution over a (possibly infinite) set of wffs X. The generality g of H is defined as

$$g(H) = \sum_{x \in X, H \models x} G(x).$$

Since G is a probability distribution it follows for every $H \in \mathcal{H}$ that $0 \leq g(H) \leq 1$. $g(H)$ is the probability that an instance drawn randomly from G will be entailed by H. Note therefore that $g(\Box) = 1$, $g(\blacksquare) = 0$ and $T_1 \models T_2$ implies $g(T_1) \geq g(T_2)$. Clearly for infinite instance spaces $g(H)$ cannot be calculated exactly. However, according to the Central Limit Theorem, given a sufficiently large random sample S from G, the proportion of S entailed by H is an arbitrarily good estimateof $g(H)$. Now consider the following probability distribution:

$$f_m(H) = c.2^{-|H|}(1 - g(H))^m.$$

m is the number of examples so far and c is a normalizing constant to ensure that for $H \in \mathcal{H}$ the function f_m sums to 1. f_m trades off the complexity of an hypothesis against its generality. Note that since f_m varies with m, it cannot be viewed as a prior distribution over hypotheses. As with MDL f_m increases the discrimination against over-generality with increasing numbers of examples. When used to choose between hypotheses given positive-only data f_m has the following convergence property.

Theorem 6.8 Finite elimination of false conjectures with positive-only data. Let T be an element of the set of wffs $\mathcal{H}$ and let G be a probability distribution over the set of wffs X such that $x \in X$ has non-zero probability in G if and only if $T \models x$. Let T' be the minimal complexity expression of T in $\mathcal{H}$. Let $\langle x_1, x_2, \ldots \rangle$ be an infinite series of wffs drawn randomly according to G. Let $f_i(H)$ have value $2^{-|H|}(1 - g(H))^i$ for all those H in $\mathcal{H}$ which entail each x_j, $1 \le j \le i$, and have value 0 otherwise. Let H be any element of $\mathcal{H}$ such that H does not entail the same subset of X as T. Then there exists a finite natural number k such that $f_k(H) < f_k(T')$.
Proof. Suppose there is an H for which there is no such k. It cannot be the case for H that $g(H) > g(T')$ and $|H| > |T'|$ since otherwise for all i, $i \ge 0$, $f_i(H) < f_i(T')$. Therefore suppose $g(H) > g(T')$ and $|H| \le |T'|$. But then since $(1 - g(H))^i$ decreases monotonically with i there must exist k such that for all $j \ge k$ it is the case that $f_j(H) < f_j(T')$. Therefore it must be that $|H| > |T'|$ and $g(H) < g(T')$. But then there exists k and x_k such that $T' \models x_k$ and $H \not\models x_k$ and therefore $f_k(H) = 0 < f_k(T')$. This contradicts the assumption and completes the proof. $\square$[4]

f_m provides the basis for a simplified version of the compression models defined in (Muggleton 1988; Muggleton *et al.* 1992b).

---

[4]At first sight, this theorem appears to clash with the fundamental result of Gold (Gold 1967) that not even the regular languages can be identified in the limit from positive data alone. However, it cannot be guaranteed after any finite number of examples that all H which are not over-general have lower values of f_m than T'.

Definition 6.9 Positive-only compression. Let H be a wff and G be a distribution over instance space X. Let $E \subseteq X$ be a set of m examples of H. Let $|H|$ and $|E|$ be the number of bits required to encode H and E. The positive-only compression of E to H is

$$
\begin{aligned}
pcomp(H, E) \;&=\; \log_2 \frac{f_m(H)}{f_m(E)} \\
&=\; |E| - |H| - m(\log_2(1 - g(E)) - \log_2(1 - g(H))) \\
&\approx\; |E| - |H| + m\,\log_2(1 - g(H)).
\end{aligned}
$$

The approximation in the last line applies for small m, in which case $g(E)$ is close to 0.

5 RELATIVE LEAST GENERAL GENERALIZATIONS

One commonly advocated approach to learning from positive data is that of taking relative least general generalizations (rlggs) of clauses (see Appendix 16). Suppose, as in the last section, that the teacher chooses target T and presents to the learner examples $E = \{x_1, x_2, ..., x_m\}$. Given background knowledge B, $H = rlgg_B(E)$ will be the hypothesis within the relative subsumption lattice with the fewest possible errors of commission (instances $x \in X$ for which $H \models x$ and $T \not\models x$). This approach to learning from positive data has the following problems.

1. **Arbitrary background knowledge.** Plotkin (Plotkin 1971) showed that with unrestricted definite clause background knowledge B there may not be any finite $rlgg_B(E)$.

2. **Extensional background knowledge.** Suppose B and E consist of n and m ground unit clauses respectively. In the worst case the number of literals in $rlgg_B(E)$ will be $(n+1)^m$, making the construction intractable for large m.

3. **Multiple clause hypothesis.** Target concepts with multiple clauses cannot be learned since $rlgg_B(E)$ is a single clause.

In contrast, none of these problems occur if H is chosen from the set of all definite clause theories $\mathcal{H}$ using maximum positive-only compression (Definition 6.9). Suppose $E \in \mathcal{H}$ and H is the hypothesis with maximum positive-only compression. As with

$rlgg_B(E)$, H will be maximally specific among clauses of the same complexity. Also H will always have complexity of at most that of E. Lastly H can be a multiple clause hypothesis.

5.1 Golem

Golem was designed to overcome the search problems of Cigol (Section 4.1). The unique construction of rlggs contrasts with the highly non-deterministic choices involved in inverting a resolution step.

Golem used extensional background knowledge to avoid the problem of non-finite rlggs. Extensional background knowledge B can be generated from intensional background knowledge B' by generating all ground unit clauses derivable from B' in at most h resolution steps. The parameter h is provided by the user. The rlggs constructed by Golem were forced to have only a tractable number of literals by requiring that $\mathcal{H}$ contain definite clause theories that were ij-determinate. The idea behind ij-determinacy is as follows. Let C be a definite clause of the form

$$\forall \vec{X}.h \leftarrow b_1, b_2, \ldots, b_n$$

where $\vec{X}$ is the vector of all variables within C. Suppose that $\vec{Y}$ are the variables in the head of C and $\vec{Z}$ are the variables found only in the body of C. C can equivalently be written

$$\forall \vec{Y}.h \leftarrow (\exists \vec{Z} b_1, b_2, \ldots, b_n).$$

Determinacy is a constraint which restricts the quantification on variables $\vec{Z}$ in the body of definite clauses to Hilbert ϵ^* (exists exactly one) quantification. This is equivalent to requiring that predicates in the background knowledge must represent functions. Thus for every example e and hypothesized clause C there must exist at most one valid substitution for the variables $\vec{Z}$ in the body of C. j-determinate clauses are constrained to having at most j variables in any literal. ij-determinate clauses are further restricted that each variable has depth at most depth i. For variable v the depth $d(v)$ is defined recursively as follows.

Definition 6.10 Depth of variables.

$$d(v) = \begin{cases} 0 & \text{if } v \text{ is in the head of } C \\ (\max_{u \in U_v} d(u)) + 1 & \text{otherwise} \end{cases}$$

where U_v are the variables in atoms in the body of C containing v.

Multiple clause theories could be learned by Golem due to the use of negative examples. Each clause was built from the rlgg of a set of positive examples. Negative examples were used to stop rlggs becoming over-general.

5.2 Application experience

Golem was the first ILP system to be applied to a wide variety of real-world applications. These included the construction of a satellite fault diagnosis model (Feng, 1992) the design of a qualitative physics model (Bratko *et al.* 1991), finite-element mesh design (Dolsak and Muggleton 1992), protein secondary structure prediction (Muggleton *et al.* 1992a) and structure-activity prediction for drugs (King *et al.* 1992). In the qualitative physics domain Golem was hampered in requiring a large tabulation of the QSIM simulator. The determinacy restriction was inappropriate in the finite element mesh design application. The restrictions of Golem and other ILP algorithms are discussed in (Muggleton 1994b).

Golem was also applied to various list and number-theoretic learning tasks involving the construction of recursive theories. Learning recursive theories was awkward using Golem partly because intensional hypothesized base cases could not be used to augment the entirely extensional background knowledge. Also Golem's search was through the subsumption lattice, rather than the lattice of implication between clauses.

6 IMPLICATION BETWEEN CLAUSES

Plotkin (1971) noted that if clause C θ-subsumes clause D (or $C \preceq D$) then $C \rightarrow D$. However, he also notes that $C \rightarrow D$ does not imply $C \preceq D$, as shown by the following example.

Example 6.11 Implication and subsumption. Consider the following clauses:

$$C = \quad \text{nat}(s(X)) \leftarrow \text{nat}(X)$$
$$D = \quad \text{nat}(s(s(Y))) \leftarrow \text{nat}(Y)$$

$C \rightarrow D$ but not $C \preceq D$.

Although efficient methods are known (see for example, van der Laag and Nienhuys-Cheng 1993) for enumerating every clause C which θ-subsumes an arbitrary clause D, this is not the case for clauses C which imply D. This is known as the problem of inverting implication between clauses. The inability to invert implication between clauses limits the completeness of inverse resolution and rlggs since θ-subsumption is used in place of clause implication in both.

Gottlob (1987) proves a number of properties concerning implication between clauses. The following lemma is notable.

Lemma 6.12 Gottlob's lemma. Let C, D be two clauses that are not tautological. Let C^+, C^- be the sets of positive and negative literals of clauses C and D^+, D^- be the same for D. $C \rightarrow D$ implies that $C^+ \preceq D^+$ and $C^- \preceq D^-$.

In an attempt to solve the inverting implication problem Lapointe and Matwin (Lapointe and Matwin 1992) introduced sub-unification, a process of matching sub-terms in D to produce C. They demonstrate that sub-unification is able to construct recursive clauses from fewer examples than would be required by ILP systems such as Golem (Muggleton and Feng 1990) and FOIL (Quinlan, 1990). Although the operations described by Lapointe and Matwin are shown to work on a number of examples it is not clear how general the mechanism is. Various general properties of implication between clauses are investigated in Muggleton (1992). In particular it is shown that Lee's subsumption lemma (Lee 1967) has the following corollary.

Corollary 6.13 Implication and recursion. Let C, D be clauses. $C \rightarrow D$ if and only if either D is a tautology or $C \preceq D$ or there is a clause E such that $E \preceq D$ where E is constructed by repeatedly self-resolving C.

Thus the difference between θ-subsumption and implication between C and D is only pertinent when, as in Example 6.11, C can self-resolve. Attempts were made to a) extend inverse resolution (Muggleton, 1992) and b) use a mixture of inverse resolution and lgg (Idestam-Almquist 1993) to solve the problem. The extended inverse resolution method in Muggleton (1992) suffers from the same problems of non-determinacy as Cigol. Idestam-Almquist's (1993) use of lgg suffers from the standard problem of intractably large clauses (see Section 5). Both approaches are incomplete for inverting implication, though Idestam-Almquist's technique is complete for a restricted form of entailment called T-implication.

In Muggleton and Page (1994a) it is shown that for certain recursive clauses D all the clauses C which imply D also θ-subsume a logically equivalent clause D'. Up to renaming of variables every clause D has at most one most specific form of D' in the θ-subsumption lattice. D' is called the self-saturation of D. The self-saturation of D in Example 6.11 is simply $C \cup D$. However, it is shown in Muggleton and Page (1994a) that there exist definite clauses which have no finite self-saturation.

6.1 Inverting entailment between clauses

This section gives a complete and efficient method for inverting implication between function-free definite clauses. The techniques used are based on inverting entailment using the deduction theorem. First we define definite sub-saturants.

Definition 6.14 Definite sub-saturants. Let $D = h \leftarrow b_1, \ldots, b_n$ be a definite clause. Let $\mathcal{B}(\overline{D})$ be the Herbrand base of $\overline{D}$ restricted to the predicate symbol of h and let $\mathcal{M}(\overline{D})$ be the minimal Herbrand model of $\overline{D}$. Let $desk(a)$ be the atom a with skolem constants in $\overline{D}$ replaced by their corresponding variables in D. Let $\mathcal{A}(D)$ be $\mathcal{B}(\overline{D}) - \mathcal{M}(\overline{D})$. The sub-saturants of D, $\mathcal{S}(D)$ are the set of all definite clauses $desk(a) \leftarrow b_1, \ldots, b_n$ for which $a \in \mathcal{A}(D)$.

Although arbitrary definite clauses can have an infinite sub-saturant set, this is not so for function-free definite clauses. It is now shown for function-free clauses that if k is a bound on the arity of predicates then the cardinality of the sub-saturant set is polynomially bounded in the number of variables in D.

Remark 6.15 Cardinality of sub-saturant set. Let D be a function-free definite clause, k be the arity of the predicate symbol in the head of D, n be the number of variables in D and $\mathcal{S}(D)$ be the sub-saturants of D. The cardinality of $\mathcal{S}(D)$ is at most n^k.

Proof. The arguments of the heads of clauses in $\mathcal{S}(D)$ are k-length permutations of variables in D. There are n^k such permutations. $\square$

We now present the main theorem concerning sub-saturants.

Theorem 6.16 Let C and D be definite non-tautological clauses and $\mathcal{S}(D)$ be the sub-saturants of D. $C \models D$ only if there exists C' in $\mathcal{S}(D)$ such that $C \preceq C'$.

Proof. Suppose $C \models D$ and there does not exist C' in $\mathcal{S}(D)$ such that $C \preceq C'$. According to Lemma 6.12 the heads of C and D have the same predicate symbol. Since $C \models D$ it follows that $C \wedge \overline{D}$ is not satisfiable. According to Herbrand's theorem this is the case if and only if $C \wedge \overline{D}$ has no Herbrand model. According to Lemma 6.12 the body of C θ-subsumes the body of D and therefore there exists a ground (skolemized) substitution θ for which all elements in the body of C are true in the least model of $\overline{D}$. Therefore with substitution θ the head of C must be false in the least Herbrand model of $\overline{D}$ since otherwise $C \wedge \overline{D}$ has a Herbrand model. But according to the construction in Definition 6.14 for every such C with the same predicate symbol as D there is a C' in $\mathcal{S}(D)$ such that $C \preceq C'$. This contradicts the assumption and completes the proof. $\square$

This theorem can be used to efficiently enumerate all function-free definite clauses C such that $C \models D$. First the finite set of sub-saturants $\mathcal{S}(D)$ is constructed. Then the clauses which θ-subsume any clause in $\mathcal{S}(D)$ are enumerated using an efficient interleaved enumeration of the subsumption lattice. Since function-free first-order predicate calculus is decidable the clauses C for which $C \models D$ can be enumerated by testing $C \wedge D \vdash \square$.

Example 6.17 Factorial. $x! = (x-2)!(x-1)x$ is an overly specific recurrence formula for the factorial function. This formula can be represented by the clause

$$D = f(I, J) \leftarrow d(I, K), d(K, L), f(L, M), m(K, M, N), m(I, N, J)$$

where the predicate symbols are f =factorial, d =decrement, m =multiply. Since there are 14 variables in D it follows from

Remark 6.15 that the cardinality of $\mathcal{S}(D)$ is at most $14^2 = 196$. $\mathcal{S}(D)$ contains the clause

$$C' = \mathrm{f}(K, N) \leftarrow d(I, K), d(K, L), f(L, M), m(K, M, N), m(I, N, J).$$

The following clause C which implies D (but does not θ-subsume D) corresponds to the most general recurrence for factorial, $x! = (x-1)!x$:

$$C = \mathrm{f}(K, N) \leftarrow d(K, L), f(L, M), m(K, M, N).$$

The following example demonstrates how clauses with function symbols, such as those in Example 6.11, can be dealt with as though they were function-free by using *flattening* (Rouveirol 1992).

Example 6.18 Flattening and inverse implication. The clause $D = \mathrm{nat}(s(s(X))) \leftarrow \mathrm{nat}(X)$ can be flattened to the function-free clause $D' = \mathrm{nat}(V) \leftarrow s(V, W), s(W, X), \mathrm{nat}(X)$ where s is defined as $s(X, s(X))$. There are two sub-saturants of D': D' itself and $C'' = \mathrm{nat}(W) \leftarrow s(V, W), s(W, X), \mathrm{nat}(X)$, which is θ-subsumed by $C' = \mathrm{nat}(W) \leftarrow s(W, X), \mathrm{nat}(X)$. C' can be unflattened to the following clause which implies but does not θ-subsume D:

$$C = \mathrm{nat}(s(X)) \leftarrow \mathrm{nat}(X).$$

7 INVERTING ENTAILMENT

Inverse resolution and other subsumption-oriented approaches to induction have been re-assessed in previous sections of this paper. It has been demonstrated that a great deal of clarity and simplicity can be achieved by approaching the problem from the direction of model-theory rather than resolution proof-theory. In Duce an inductive inference rule $\frac{X}{Y}$ is sound in the deductive sense if viewed as stating the relationship $X \models Y$. In Cigol all solutions for absorption are found by simply rewriting the inductive specification $C \wedge C' \models D$ by the equivalent deduction-oriented relationship $C \wedge \overline{D} \models \overline{C'}$. Lastly, it has been shown in this paper that a solution to Plotkin's 25-year-old problem of generalizing θ-subsumption can be achieved with relative ease by simply viewing solutions for C in $C \models D$ (given D) as clauses which eliminate Herbrand models of $C \wedge \overline{D}$.

Let us now consider the general problem specification of ILP (Section 2) in this light. That is, given background knowledge B and examples E find the simplest consistent hypothesis H (where simplicity is measured relative to a prior distribution) such that

$$B \wedge H \models E. \tag{6.4}$$

It was demonstrated in Example 6.1 that in general B, H and E could be arbitrary logic programs. Each clause in the simplest H should explain at least one example, since otherwise there is a simpler H' which will do. Consider then the case of H and E each being single Horn clauses. This can now be seen as a generalized form of absorption (Relation (6.3) in Section 4) and rearranged similarly to give

$$B \wedge \overline{E} \models \overline{H}$$

Since H and E are each single clauses, $\overline{H}$ and $\overline{E}$ will be logic programs consisting only of ground skolemized unit clauses. Let $\overline{\bot}$ be the (potentially infinite) conjunction of ground literals which are true in all models of $B \wedge \overline{E}$. Since $\overline{H}$ must be true in every model of $B \wedge \overline{E}$ it must contain a subset of the ground literals in $\overline{\bot}$. Therefore

$$B \wedge \overline{E} \models \overline{\bot} \models \overline{H}$$

and so for all H

$$H \models \bot.$$

A subset of the solutions for H can be found by considering the clauses which θ-subsume $\bot$. The complete set of candidates for H can be found by considering all clauses which θ-subsume sub-saturants of $\bot$ (Section 6.1).

Example 6.19 Various examples of $\bot$. Figure 6.2 shows various B, E and $\bot$. In the first case, the clauses which θ-subsume $\bot$ include all those which could be reached using first-order absorption (Section 4). In the second case the definite

B	E	⊥
anim(X)← pet(X). pet(X)← dog(X).	nice(X)← dog(X).	nice(X) ← dog(X), pet(X), anim(X).

hasbeak(X)← bird(X).
bird(X)← vulture(X).
	hasbeak(tweety).	hasbeak(tweety);
		bird(tweety);
		vulture(tweety).

white(swan1).	← black(swan1).	← black(swan1), white(swan1).
sentence([],[]).	sentence([a,a,a],[]).	sentence([a,a,a],[]) ← sentence([],[]).

Figure 6.2. The most-specific clause ($\perp$) for various versions of background knowledge (B) and example (E).

clauses which θ-subsume $\perp$ are those which could be reached by a first-order version of Duce's identification operator (Section 3.1). This form of identification is a general form of Kakas *et al.*'s abduction (Kakas *et al.* 1992) and is of central interest in 'theory revision' (alterations in theory revision range over all definitions within a hierarchical set of predicates which reference each other). The third case demonstrates that constraints (headless Horn clauses) can be learned from negative examples since the clause

$$\leftarrow black(X), white(X)$$

θ-subsumes $\perp$. In the fourth case one of the clauses which θ-subsumes a sub-saturant of the flattened $\perp$ (see Example 6.18) is the DCG grammar rule

$$sentence([a|X], Y) \leftarrow sentence(X, Y).$$

8 THE DEFINITE MODE LANGUAGE

In general $\perp$ can have infinite cardinality. Progol uses mode declarations to constrain the search for clauses which θ-subsume $\perp$ (see last Section).

Definition 6.20 Mode declaration. A mode declaration has either the form modeh(n,atom) or modeb(n,atom) where n, the recall, is either an integer, $n > 1$, or '*' and atom is a ground atom. Terms in the atom are either normal or place-marker. A normal term is either a constant or a function symbol followed by a bracketed tuple of terms. A place-marker is either +type, −type or #type, where type is a constant. If m is a mode declaration then $a(m)$ denotes the atom of m with place-markers replaced by distinct variables. The sign of m is positive if m is a modeh and negative if m is a modeb.

For instance the following are mode declarations.

$$\text{modeh}(1,\text{plus}(+\text{int},+\text{int},-\text{int}))$$
$$\text{modeb}(*,\text{append}(-\text{list},+\text{list},+\text{list}))$$
$$\text{modeb}(1,\text{append}(+\text{list},[+\text{any}],-\text{list}))$$
$$\text{modeb}(4,(+\text{int} > \#\text{int}))$$

The recall is used to bound the number of alternative solutions for instantiating the atom. For simplicity, we assume in the following that all the modes have the recall '*', meaning all solutions. The following defines when a clause is within Progol's definite mode language $\mathcal{L}$.

Definition 6.21 Definite mode language. Let C be a definite clause with a defined total ordering over the literals and M be a set of mode declarations. $C = h \leftarrow b_1, .., b_n$ is in the definite mode language $\mathcal{L}(M)$ if and only if 1) h is the atom of a modeh declaration in M with every place-marker +type and −type replaced by variables and every place-marker #type replaced by a ground term and 2) every atom b_i in the body of C is the atom of a modeb declaration in M with every place-marker +type and −type replaced by variables and every place-marker #type replaced by a ground term and 3) every variable of +type in any atom b_i is either of +type in h or of −type in some atom b_j, $1 \leq j < i$.

Like Golem, Progol constructs clauses of bounded depth (see Definition 6.10 in Section 5.1).

Definition 6.22 Depth-bounded mode language. Let C be a definite clause with a defined total ordering over the literals and M be a set of mode declarations. C is in $\mathcal{L}_i(M)$ if and only if C is in $\mathcal{L}(M)$ and all variables in C have depth at most i according to Definition 6.10.

Example 6.23 Factorial revisited. Reconsider Example 6.17 with M being

$$\text{modeh}(*,\text{f}(+\text{int},-\text{int})) \quad \text{modeb}(*,\text{d}(+\text{int},-\text{int})$$
$$\text{modeb}(*,\text{f}(+\text{int},-\text{int})) \quad \text{modeb}(*,\text{m}(+\text{int},-\text{int}))$$

The clause

$$f(A,B) \leftarrow d(A,C), f(C,D), m(A,D,B)$$

is only in $\mathcal{L}_i(M)$ for $i \geq 2$.

8.1 Most-specific clauses in $\mathcal{L}_i(M)$

Progol searches a bounded sub-lattice for each example e relative to background knowledge B and mode declarations M. The sub-lattice has a most general element ($\top$) which is the empty clause, $\Box$, and a least general element $\perp_i$ which is the most specific element in $\mathcal{L}_i(M)$ such that

$$B \wedge \perp_i \wedge \overline{e} \vdash_h \Box$$

where $\vdash_h \Box$ denotes derivation of the empty clause in at most h resolutions.

Definition 6.24 Most-specific clause $\perp_i$. Let h, i be natural numbers B be a set of Horn clauses, $e = a \leftarrow b_1, .., b_n$ be a definite clause, M be a set of mode declarations containing exactly one modeh m such that $a(m) \preceq a$ and $\perp$ be the most-specific (potentially infinite) definite clause such that $B \wedge \perp \wedge \overline{e} \vdash_h \Box$. $\perp_i$ is the most-specific clause in $\mathcal{L}_i(M)$ such that $\perp_i \preceq \perp$.

Progol constructs $\perp_i$ using Algorithm 6.40 in Appendix 17.1.

Theorem 6.25 Correctness of Algorithm 6.40. Let h, i, B, M be defined as in Definition 6.24. Given h, i, B, e and M Algorithm 6.40 returns an alphabetic variant of $\perp_i$.

Proof. By induction on i. Let i be 0. In step 3 the head of $\perp_0$ is within the definite mode language of M (Definition 6.21) since every +type and $-$type place-marker is replaced by variables, every #type place-marker is replaced by ground terms and every variable has depth 0 (Definition 6.10). By construction the head a_h of the returned $\perp_0$ θ-subsumes a since inverting the one-one function hash gives a substitution from the variables in a_h to the terms in a. This substitution is most specific since every variable

155

is replaced by a unique term. This proves the base case. Suppose that for all i up to and including k Algorithm 6.40 correctly constructs a most-specific clause $\bot_k$ such that $\bot_k$ is the most-specific clause in $\mathcal{L}_k(M)$ which θ-subsumes $\bot$. It is now shown that this implies the same will hold for $k+1$. Consider step 5 for $k+1$. The $+$type place-markers in the atom of m are replaced by variables of depth at most k which represent terms in InTerms. These terms must either have been placed in InTerms as $+$type in the head (step 3) or $-$type from step 5 at an earlier value of k. $-$type place-markers are replaced by variables of depth at most $k+1$ and #type by ground terms. Therefore $\bot_{k+1}$ is in $\mathcal{L}_{k+1}(M)$. Also by construction a_b subsumes an atom in the body of $\bot$ with substitution θ_b, and the substitution is most specific since all variables map to unique terms in $\bot$. $T(m)$ corresponds to all combinations of $+$type substitutions, which makes $\bot_{k+1}$ an alphabetic variant of the maximally specific clause in $\mathcal{L}_{k+1}(M)$ which θ-subsumes $\bot$. This proves the step and completes the proof. $\square$

The time-complexity of Algorithm 6.40 is proportional to the cardinality of $\bot_i$.

Theorem 6.26 Cardinality of $\bot_i$. Let h, i, B, M be defined as in Definition 6.24 and let $|M|$ denote the cardinality of M. Let the number of $+$type and $-$type occurrences in each modeh in M be bounded by constants j^- and j^+ respectively. Let the number of $+$type and $-$type occurrences in each modeb in M be bounded by j^+ and j^- respectively. Let the recall of each m in M be bounded by the constant r. The cardinality of $\bot_i$ is bounded by $(r|M|j^+j^-)^{ij^+}$.

Proof. By induction. The clause $\bot_0$ contains only a head so its cardinality is 1. This proves the base case. Assume true for all i up to and including k and show for $i = k + 1$. The number of terms associated with $+$type in the head or $-$type in the body of $\bot_k$ is $j^-(r|M|j^+j^-)^{kj^+}$. These can be used to replace j^+ $+$type place-markers in $|M|$ modeb declarations and the atom can be recalled r times, giving a cardinality of $\bot_{k+1}$ of at most $(r|M|j^+j^-)^{(k+1)j^+}$. This proves the step and completes the proof. $\square$

By default $i = 3$ in Progol and typically $j^+ \leq 2$. However, since in most cases relatively few atoms are true in the least Herbrand model of $B \wedge \bar{e}$ when $|M| < 10$ it is usually the case that $\perp_3$ has cardinality of less than 100 atoms.

9 REFINEMENT

9.1 Refinement operators

When generalising an example e relative to background knowledge B, Progol constructs $\perp_i$ and searches from general to specific through the sub-lattice of single clause hypotheses H such that $\square \preceq H \preceq \perp_i$. This sub-lattice is bounded both above and below. The search is therefore better constrained than other general to specific searches, such as those in MIS (Shapiro 1983) and FOIL (Quinlan 1990), in which the sub-lattice being searched is not bounded below.

For the purposes of searching a lattice of clauses ordered by θ-subsumption Shapiro (1983) introduced the concept of refinement operators. Suppose $\mathcal{L}$ is a (potentially infinite) set of clauses and C is an element of $\mathcal{L}$. Then the refinement operator ρ is defined such that $\rho(C) \subseteq \mathcal{L}$. ρ is said to be *sound* if and only if for each D in $\rho(C)$ it is the case that $C \preceq D$. Also $\rho^0(C) = \{C\}$ and $D \in \rho^i(C)$ if and only if there exists $D' \in \rho^{i-1}(C)$ and $D = D'$ or $D \in \rho(D')$. The closure $\rho^*(C)$ is $\rho^0(C) \cup \rho^1(C) \cup \ldots$

According to van der Laag and Nienhuys-Cheng (1994) ρ is *complete* if and only if for each D in $\mathcal{L}$ there is an alphabetic variant of D in $\rho^*(\square)$. ρ is *finite* if and only if for all $C \in \mathcal{L}$ the cardinality of $\rho(C)$ is finite. ρ is *proper* if and only if for each clause C and $D \in \rho(C)$ it is the case that $C \prec D$. It is shown in van der Laag and Nienhuys-Cheng (1994) that Shapiro's ρ is not complete. It is also shown that there does not exist ρ which is finite, proper and complete.

Redundancy of refinement operators is investigated in Grobelnik (1992) and Dormer (1993). The refinement operator ρ is redundant if and only if there exist clauses C, C', D in $\mathcal{L}$ such that $D \in \rho(C)$ and $D \in \rho(C')$ and C is not an alphabetic variant of C'. Since both MIS and FOIL employ redundant refinement operators, the same clause D can be reached repeatedly when applying ρ to various C and C'.

9.2 The refinement operator in Progol

The refinement operator in Progol is designed to avoid redundancy and to maintain the relationship $\Box \preceq H \preceq \bot_i$ for each clause H.

Since $H \preceq \bot_i$, it is the case that there exists a substitution θ such that $H\theta \subseteq \bot_i$. Thus for each literal l in H there exists a literal l' in $\bot_i$ such that $l\theta = l'$. Clearly there is a uniquely defined subset $\bot_i(H)$ consisting of all l' in $\bot_i$ for which there exists l in H and $l\theta = l'$. A non-deterministic approach to choosing an arbitrary subset S' of a set S involves maintaining an index k. For each value of k between 1 and n, the cardinality of S, we decide whether to include the kth element of S in S'. Clearly, the set of all series of n choices corresponds to the set of all subsets of S. Also for each subset of S there is exactly one series of n choices. To avoid redundancy and maintain θ-subsumption of $\bot_i$ Progol's refinement operator maintains both k and θ.

Definition 6.27 Progol refinement operator. Let h, i, B, e, M and $\bot_i$ be defined as in Definition 6.24 and let n be the cardinality of $\bot_i$. Let k be a natural number, $1 \leq k \leq n$. Let C be a clause in $\mathcal{L}_i(M)$ and θ be a substitution such that $C\theta \subseteq \bot_i$. Below a literal l corresponding to a mode m_l in M is denoted simply as $p(v_1, ..., v_m)$ despite the sign of m_l and function symbols in $a(m_l)$. A variable is *splittable* if it corresponds to a $+$type or $-$type in a modeh or if it corresponds to a $-$type in a modeb. $\langle C', \theta', k' \rangle$ is in $\rho(\langle C, \theta, k \rangle)$ if and only if either

1. $C' = C \cup \{l\}$, $k' = k$, $\langle l, \theta' \rangle$ is in $\delta(\theta, k)$ and $C' \in \mathcal{L}_i(M)$ or
2. $C' = C$, $k' = k + 1$, $\theta' = \theta$ and $k < n$.

$\langle p(v_1, .., v_m), \theta' \rangle$ is in $\delta(\theta, k)$ if and only if θ' is initialized to θ, $l_k = p(u_1, .., u_m)$ is the kth literal of $\bot_i$ and for each j, $1 \leq j \leq m$,

1. if u_j is splittable then $v_j / u_j \in \theta'$ else $v_j / u_j \in \theta$ or
2. if u_j is splittable then v_j is a new variable not in $\text{dom}(\theta)$ and $\theta' = \theta \cup \{v_j / u_j\}$.

In Definition 6.27 the variables in $\perp_i$ form a set of equivalences classes over the variables in any clause C which θ-subsumes $\perp_i$. Thus we could write the equivalence class of u in θ as $[v]_u$, the set of all variables in C such that v/u is in θ. The second choice in the definition of δ adds a new variable to an equivalence class $[v_j]_{u_j}$. This will be referred to as *splitting* the variable u_j. Note that in Definition 6.27 a variable is not splittable if it corresponds to a +type in a modeb since the resulting clause would violate the mode declaration language $\mathcal{L}(M)$ (see Definition 6.21). The following is an example of variable splitting.

Example 6.28 Applying ρ in list reversal. Suppose M consists of the following mode declarations.

modeh(*,reverse(+list,-list))   modeb(*,+list=[-int|-list]

modeb(*,+any= #any)   modeb(*,reverse(+list,-list))

modeb(*,append(+list,[+int],-list))

The types and other background knowledge are defined as follows.

$$B = \left\{ \begin{array}{l} \text{any}(\text{Term}) \leftarrow \\ \text{list}([]) \leftarrow \\ \text{list}([H|T]) \leftarrow \text{list}(T) \\ Term = Term \leftarrow \\ \text{reverse}([],[]) \leftarrow \\ \text{append}([], X, X) \leftarrow \\ \text{append}([H|T], L1, [H|L2]) \leftarrow \text{append}(T, L1, L2) \end{array} \right.$$

Let $h = 30$ and $i = 3$ and let the example be as below.

$$e = \text{reverse}([1],[1]) \leftarrow$$

In this case $\perp_i$ is as follows.

$$\perp_i = \text{reverse}(A, A) \leftarrow A = [1], A = [B|C], B = 1, C = [],$$
$$\text{reverse}(C, C), \text{append}(C, [B], A)$$

Let $\langle C', \theta', k' \rangle$ be in $\rho(\langle \square, \emptyset, 1 \rangle)$. Then all $\langle C', \theta', k' \rangle$ are shown in the first table in Figure 6.3. Suppose that $C = (\text{reverse}(D, E) \leftarrow D = [F|G])$, $\theta = \{D/A, E/A, F/B, G/C\}$, $k = 6$ and $\langle C', \theta', k' \rangle$ is in $\rho(\langle C, \theta, k \rangle)$. Then all $\langle C', \theta', k' \rangle$ are shown in the second table in Figure 6.3.

C'	θ'	k'
reverse$(D, E) \leftarrow$	$\{D/A, E/A\}$	1
reverse$(D, D) \leftarrow$	$\{D/A\}$	1
$\square$	$\emptyset$	2

C'	θ'	k'
reverse$(D, E) \leftarrow D = [F\|G], \text{reverse}(G, G)$	θ	6
reverse$(D, E) \leftarrow D = [F\|G], \text{reverse}(G, H)$	$\theta \cup \{H/C\}$	6
reverse$(D, E) \leftarrow D = [F\|G]$	θ	7

Figure 6.3. Two applications of ρ.

By analogy to Shapiro's ρ we can talk of the soundness of Progol's ρ.

Lemma 6.29 Soundness of Progol's ρ. Let h, i, B, e, M and $\perp_i$ be defined as in Definition 6.24 and let n be the cardinality of $\perp_i$. Let k be a natural number, $1 \leq k \leq n$. Let C be a clause in $\mathcal{L}_i(M)$ and θ be a substitution such that $C\theta \subseteq \perp_i$. $\langle C', \theta', k' \rangle \in \rho(\langle C, \theta, k \rangle)$ only if $C'\theta' \subseteq \perp_i$ and $C' \in \mathcal{L}_i(M)$.
Proof. Suppose the lemma is false. In that case there exists $\langle C', \theta', k' \rangle \in \rho(\langle C, \theta, k \rangle)$ and either $C'\theta' \not\subseteq \perp_i$ or $C' \notin \mathcal{L}_i(M)$. But according to Definition 6.27, $C' \in \mathcal{L}_i(M)$ or $C' = C$, in which case also $C' \in \mathcal{L}_i(M)$. Thus it must be that $C'\theta' \not\subseteq \perp_i$ in which case $C' = C \cup \{l\}$ and $k' = k$ where $\langle l, \theta' \rangle$ is in $\delta(\theta, k)$. But then according to the definition of δ, $C'\theta' \subseteq \perp_i$ which contradicts the assumption and completes the proof. $\square$

As with Shapiro's refinement operator we can define the closure set for Progol's ρ. Let X, Y, Z stand for triples of the form $\langle C, \theta, k \rangle$. Then $\rho^0(X) = \{X\}$ and $Y \in \rho^i(X)$ if and only if there exists $Z \in \rho^{i-1}(X)$ and $Y = Z$ or $Y \in \rho(Z)$. The closure $\rho^*(X)$ is $\rho^0(X) \cup \rho^1(X) \cup \ldots$ The following example shows that Progol's ρ is not complete due to the choice of ordering of $\perp_i$.

Example 6.30 Incompleteness of search. Let B contain definitions for decrementation (dec), addition (plus) and the clause $mult(0, X, 0) \leftarrow$ with appropriate mode declarations M and let the example e be the clause $mult(1, 1, 1) \leftarrow$. Then $\perp_i$ is the clause

$$\text{mult}(A, A, A) \leftarrow \text{dec}(A, B), \text{plus}(A, B, A), \text{plus}(B, B, B),$$
$$\text{mult}(A, B, B), \text{mult}(B, B, B).$$

Given this ordering over $\perp_i$ there will be no element of Progol's ρ^* containing the clause

$$\text{mult}(U, V, W) \leftarrow \text{dec}(U, X), \text{mult}(X, V, Y), \text{plus}(Y, V, W).$$

9.3 Complexity of ρ

In order to analyse the complexity of ρ we introduce an incremental variant of the Bell number (Krishnamurthy, 1986) from combinatorics. The mth Bell number is the number of ways that a set S of cardinality m can be partitioned into non-empty equivalence classes.

Lemma 6.31 Number of splits of a variable. Suppose that δ in Definition 6.27 has arguments θ, k and that the kth literal of $\perp_i$ has m splittable occurrences of only one variable u. Suppose also that the cardinality of $[v]_u$ in θ is n. The number of variants of θ' is given by the function s as follows.

$$s(n, m) = \begin{cases} 1 & \text{if } m = 0 \\ s(n, m-1)n + s(n+1, m-1) & \text{if } m > 0 \end{cases}$$

Proof. If $m = 0$ there is only one substitution, $\theta' = \theta$. If $m > 0$ consider the first occurrence of u in l_k. In δ the choice can be to not split u (case 1) or to split u (case 2). In case 1, the set of θ' variants is $\{\theta\}$ crossed with the set of n choices for v_1/u crossed with the set of $s(n, m-1)$ variants for the remaining $m-1$ occurrences of u in l_k. In case 2, if the new variable is v then the set of θ' variants is $\{\theta\}$ crossed with $\{v/u\}$ crossed with the set of $s(n+1, m-1)$ variants for the remaining $m-1$ occurrences of u in l_k. This gives a total of $s(n, m-1)n + s(n+1, m-1)$ variants of θ'. $\square$

A partial tabulation of the function s is shown in Figure 6.4.[5]

---

[5] The Bell function can be expressed simply as $B(m) = s(0, m)$.

n	0	1	2	3	4	5	6	7
m								
0	1	1	1	1	1	1	1	1
1	1	2	3	4	5	6	7	
2	2	5	10	17	26			
3	5	15	37					
4	15							

Figure 6.4. A partial tabulation of the function s.

Remark 6.32 Bounds on s. Let n, m be natural numbers. $n^m \leq s(n, m) \leq (n+m)^m$.

Proof. For $m=0$, $n^0 = s(n, 0) = (n+0)^0 = 1$. Consider s in terms of the recurrence $n^m = n^{m-1}n$. For all $n \geq 0$ and $m > 0$ it is the case that $s(n, m-1)n < s(n, m) < s(n+m, m-1)n + s(n+m, m-1)$. $\square$

Example 6.33 Suppose in Definition 6.27 that $C = p(V) \leftarrow$ and $\theta = \{V/U\}$ and $l_k = q(U, U, U)$ where the last two occurrences of U in l_k are $-$type. Then in Lemma 6.31 this gives $m = 2, n = 1$, and $s(n, m) = 5$. The 5 variants of $l_k\theta'$ are $q(V, V, V)$, $q(V, V, W)$, $q(V, W, V)$, $q(V, W, W)$ and $q(V, W, Z)$.

We are now in a position to give a function for the cardinality of ρ.

Theorem 6.34 The cardinality of ρ. Let C, θ, k and l_k be as in Definition 6.27. Suppose that l_k contains p splittable variables and q non-splittable variables. Let m_x, $1 \leq x \leq p$, and m_y, $1 \leq y \leq q$, denote respectively the number of occurrences of v_x and v_y in the splittable and non-splittable variables of l_k. Let n_x, $1 \leq x \leq p$, and n_y, $1 \leq y \leq q$, denote respectively the number of u_x and u_y such that u_x/v_x and u_y/v_y are in θ. Then the cardinality of $\rho(\langle C, \theta, k \rangle)$ is

$$|\rho(\langle C, \theta, k \rangle)| = (\Pi_{x=1}^{p} n_x^{m_x})(\Pi_{y=1}^{q} s(n_y, m_y)) + 1.$$

Proof. In Definition 6.27, ρ chooses between 2 cases. Since the second choice produces a unique solution, the cardinality of ρ is one greater than the cardinality of the associated function δ. Only the first case of δ is applicable to non-splittable variables.

Thus for each of the m_x occurrences of v_x in l_k there are n_x choices of u_x/v_x, giving $n_x^{m_x}$ variants. The set of all substitutions θ' for l_k is $\{\theta\}$ crossed with the set of variants for each v_x, $1 \leq x \leq p$ crossed with the set of variants for each v_y, $1 \leq y \leq q$. This gives a total of $(\Pi_{x=1}^{p} n_x^{m_x})(\Pi_{y=1}^{q} s(n_y, m_y))$ different substitutions θ' for the function δ and the same value plus 1 for the cardinality of ρ. $\square$

From Remark 6.32 it can be seen that $|\rho(\langle C, \theta, k \rangle)|$ is exponential in p, q, m_x and m_y. This reiterates the requirement indicated by Theorem 6.26 that for the sake of polynomial tractability p, m_x and q, m_y should be bounded respectively by constants j^+ and j^-.

In the implementation of ρ Progol simply decodes each of the natural numbers between 1 and $|\rho(\langle C, \theta, k \rangle)|$ into clauses and updates θ and k appropriately. The details of this decoding process are omitted.

10 SEARCHING THE SUBSUMPTION LATTICE

To search the subsumption lattice Progol applies an A^*-like algorithm (Nilsson, 1980) to find a clause C, $\square \preceq C \preceq \perp_i$, with maximal Occam compression (Definition 6.4). The encoding measure is the total number of atom occurrences in a *reduced* logic program. Logic programs are reduced by eliminating *redundant* clauses.

Definition 6.35 Redundant clauses. Let C be a clause and T be a set of clauses. C is redundant in $T \cup C$ if and only if $T \models C$.

Definition 6.36 Reduced set of clauses. Let T be a set of clauses. T is reduced iff T contains no redundant clauses.

Progol's algorithm for finding C with maximal Occam compression is Algorithm 6.42 in Appendix 17.2. The algorithm searches through the state space defined by elements of $\rho^*(\langle \square, \emptyset, 1 \rangle)$. A lookahead function h_s is used to increase efficiency when searching for 'variable-chaining' clauses. A clause is variable-chaining if and only if it contains a chain of variables $v_1, \ldots, v_n$ such that v_1, v_n are +type and −type respectively in the head of C and each v_i, v_{i+1} are $+$type and $-$type respectively in an atom in the body of C. The recursive clause for reversing lists

$$\text{reverse}(A, B) \leftarrow A = [C|D], \text{reverse}(C, E), \text{append}(E, [A], B) \tag{6.5}$$

(see Example 6.28) is variable-chaining. A clause C is called I/O complete if and only if each $-$type variable in the head of C is found in the body of C. Clause (6.5) is I/O complete given the mode declarations in Example 6.28.

Lemma 6.37 The function h_s defines I/O complete lookahead. Let $\perp_i$ and $s = \langle C, \theta, k \rangle$ be as in Definition 6.41 in Section 17.2. For every I/O complete C' such that $s' = \langle C', \theta', k' \rangle \in \rho^*(\langle C, \theta, k \rangle)$ it is the case that $|C'| - |C| \geq h_s$.

Proof. By mathematical induction on h_s. Suppose v is in the body of C, then $h_s = 0$ and the lemma holds in the base case. Suppose, by mathematical induction, that for all I/O complete C' and for all $s_d = \langle C_d, \theta_d, k_d \rangle$ for which $h_{s_d} = d$ it is the case that $|C'| - |C_d| \geq h_{s_d}$ and suppose that there exists such $s_d \in \rho(s)$. According to Definition 6.27 either $C_d = C$ and $\theta_d = \theta$ in which case for all I/O complete C' it is the case that $|C'| - |C| \geq h_s = d$ or else $C_d = C \cup \{l\}$ and $|C'| - |C| \geq (h_{s_d} + 1) \geq h_s$. This proves the step and completes the proof. $\square$

10.1 Correctness and time complexity

Note that in order to ensure polynomial tractability of Algorithm 6.42, the user is required to provide a bound c on the cardinality of the clause body.

Theorem 6.38 Correctness of Algorithm 6.42. Let E, h, i, B, e, M, $\perp_i$, c be as in Definition 6.41. Let $S = \rho^*(\langle \square, \emptyset, 1 \rangle)$ and S_c be the set of all elements s of S such that $c_s \leq c$. If $s = \langle C, \theta, k \rangle$ then $C(s) = C$. We say that clause C explains example e if and only if $B \wedge C \wedge \bar{e} \vdash_h \square$ and $B \wedge C \wedge E \vdash_h \square$. If S_c does not contain any s such that $C(s)$ explains e and $f_s > 0$ then Algorithm 6.42 returns 'no compression'. Otherwise Algorithm 6.42 returns $s \in S_c$ such that $C(s)$ explains e and there does not exist $s' \in S_c$ for which $C(s')$ explains e and $f_{s'} > f_s$.

Proof. By contradiction. Assume the theorem is false. Then either (a) the algorithm does not terminate or (b) there exists $s \in S_c$ such that $C(s)$ explains e, $f_s > 0$ and 'no compression' is returned or (c) s is returned and either $C(s)$ does not explain e or $f_s \leq 0$ or (d) s is returned and $C(s)$ explains e and $f_s > 0$ but there exists $s' \in S_c$ for which $C(s')$ explains e and $f_{s'} > f_s$.

First consider (a). Since ρ (Definition 6.27) either adds another literal or moves forward by one through $\perp_i$, there can only be a finite number of elements of $s \in S_c$. In each cycle at least one of these, say s, is transferred from Open to Closed in steps 3 and 4 and never reappears in Open again due to the construction in step 6. Open will never contain elements other than those in S_c due to the third condition in the predicate prune. Thus there are only a finite number of cycles and each operation terminates in finite time. This refutes (a).

Therefore instead suppose (b) there exists $s \in S_c$ such that $C(s)$ explains e, $f_s > 0$ and 'no compression' is returned in step 8. But step 8 can only be entered after step 7, in which case if Open $= \emptyset$ then terminated must have been false and therefore Closed contained no s for which $C(s)$ explained e and $f_s > 0$. But if there exists $s \in S_c$ for which $C(s)$ explains e and $f_s > 0$ then there must be $s' \in S_c$ for which prune(s') was true, since otherwise s would eventually have been transferred to Closed. But the first condition of prune could not have been true of s' since otherwise at worst s' would have succeeded as best in terminated. The second condition of prune could not have been true of s' since if $g_{s'} \leq 0$ then also $g_s \leq 0$ and thus $f_s \leq 0$. The third condition of prune could not be true either since if $c_{s'} \geq c$ then either $C(s') = C(s)$ or $C(s) \notin S_c$. This refutes (b).

Instead suppose (c) s is returned and either $C(s)$ does not explain e or $f_s \leq 0$. But if s is returned in step 7 then terminated must be true in which case $n_s = 0$ and $f_s > 0$. For all $s \in S$, by the construction of $\perp_i$ (Definition 6.24) and the soundness of ρ (Lemma 6.29) $B \wedge C(s) \wedge \overline{e} \vdash_h \square$. Also since $n_s = 0$ it follows that $B \wedge C(s) \wedge E \nvdash_h \square$. Therefore $C(s)$ explains e and $f(s) > 0$. This refutes (c).

Lastly suppose (d) s is returned and $C(s)$ explains e and $f_s > 0$ but there exists $s' \in S_c$ for which $C(s')$ explains e and $f_{s'} > f_s$. But s' cannot be in Closed since $s =$best(Closed) and therefore $f_s \geq f'_s$. Therefore on return from step 7 there must exist s'' in Open for which $s' \in \rho^*(s'')$. But in that case according to the terminated predicate $f_s \geq g_{s''} \geq g_{s'} \geq f_{s'}$. This refutes (d) and completes the proof. $\Box$

In the worst case Algorithm 6.42 will consider all elements of S_c in Theorem 6.38.

Theorem 6.39 Cardinality of S_c. Let $i, \bot_i, S_c, c$ be as in Definition 6.41. Let j^+, j^- be as in Theorem 6.26 and let $j = j^+ + j^-$. Let $|S|$ denote the cardinality of any set S. $|S_c| \leq |\bot_i|^{c+1} j(c+1)^j$.

Proof. The elements $s = \langle C, \theta, k \rangle$ of S_c are all those $s \in \rho^*(\langle \Box, \emptyset, 1 \rangle)$ for which $|C| \leq (c+1)$. Since $C\theta \subseteq \bot_i$ we can view the construction of s as the choice (with possible repeats) of $c+1$ elements from $\bot_i$ followed by the choice of θ. It is simplest to treat $C\theta$ (with repeat literals) as though it were a single atom and use the bounds in Remark 6.32 to calculate the worst case for the number of variants of θ. In this case there are at most $|\bot_i|^{c+1}$ ways of choosing the elements of $C\theta$ and $j(c+1)^j$ ways of choosing θ. Thus $|S_c| \leq |\bot_i|^{c+1} j(c+1)^j$. $\Box$

From Theorems 6.26 and 6.39 we find that $|S_c|$ is $O(r|M|^{2ij(c+1)})$. Clearly, for tractability i, j, c must be small constants.

10.2 Cover set algorithm

Progol uses a simple cover set algorithm much like that employed in Michalski's AQ family of algorithms (Michalski and Larson, 1980). It repeatedly generalizes examples in the order found in the Progol source file and adds the generalization to the background knowledge. Examples which are redundant relative to the background knowledge are then removed (redundancy is based on Definition 6.35). The cover set algorithm, Algorithm 6.44, is given in Appendix 17.3. Clearly this algorithm terminates in at most $|E|$ iterations.

Note that each clause is unflattened before being added to the background knowledge. If, as in Prolog, equality is assumed to be completely defined using only the axiom of identity ($\forall x.(x = x)$) then unflattening has no effect on the Herbrand models of a logic program. However, it does improve its readability. For instance, clause (6.5) in Section 10 can be unflattened to the following simpler clause:

$$\text{reverse}([A|B], C) \leftarrow \text{reverse}(B, D), \text{append}(D, [A], C).$$

Note that the use of modeb declarations for '=' in Example 6.28 followed by the use of unflattening in Algorithm 6.44 allows Progol to search through the term structure of hypothesized clauses. This is despite the fact that Progol's refinement operator (Definition 6.27) considers only variable/variable substitutions which map hypothesized clauses to subsets of $\perp_i$.

11   THE PROGOL SYSTEM

Progol was written in C by the author of this paper. Progol version 4.1 source code, example files and manual pages are freely available (for academic research) by anonymous ftp from ftp.comlab.ox.ac.uk in directory

$$\text{pub/Packages/ILP/progol4.1.}$$

The design methodology for Progol was to present the user with a standard Prolog interpreter augmented with inductive capabilities. The syntax for examples, background knowledge and hypotheses is Dec-10 Prolog, with the usual augmentable set of prefix, postfix and infix operators. Headless Horn clauses, representing constraints, are used to represent negative examples and constraints. These are stored internally as clauses with head 'false'. Thus the following statement can be placed in the Progol source file.

$$: -black(X), white(X).$$

This is stored internally as the following definite clause.

$$false : -black(X), white(X).$$

In this way both the testing of negative examples and of general constraints reduces to seeing whether 'false' is provable. Headless clause constraints can be learned from ground headless unit clauses by use of a modeh for the predicate 'false'. An example of this can be found in the Progol4.1 distribution dataset 'animals.pl'.

The standard library of primitive predicates described in Clocksin and Mellish (1981) is built into Progol and available as background knowledge. Thus the following command-line can be given to Progol when using the infix predicate '=<' for learning ranges of integers:

|−modeh(1,p(+int)), modeb(3,#int =< +int),
  modeb(3,+int =< #int)?

The Progol prompt is |− and int is a built-in single arity predicate which is true for all integers. Note that Progol queries are terminated by '?' rather than the usual '.' in Prolog. This allows queries to be distinguished from assertions. Assertions terminated by '.' can also be made at the Progol prompt level. The user can request examples to be generalized from the prompt by terminating the example clause by a '!'. Unless the predicate 'search' is executed first, a '!' statement will simply show the user the clause $\perp_i$ for the example. Thus the mode declarations above will allow the following interaction:

|− p(5)!
[Most specific clause is]
p(A) :- 3=<A, 4=<A, 5=<A, A=<5, A=<6, A=<7.

In this $\perp_3$ clause the modeb declarations (given above) for '=<' are used. In step 5 of Algorithm 6.40 the goals $X =< 5$ and $5 =< Y$ are both recalled 3 times and succeed with substitutions 3,4,5 for X and 5,6,7 for Y. The #int place-markers are replaced by 3,4,5 and 5,6,7 respectively and the +int place-marker is replaced by the unique variable A using the hash function described in Algorithm 6.40.

Although Progol can be used interactively, it is often more convenient to run it in batch mode. In this case, when called from the operating system shell, Progol is given the name of the example file as an argument. Progol then simply generalizes every predicate for which a modeh is declared and shows the results as output.

Progol can learn ranges and functions with numeric data. These can be either integer or floating point by simply making use of the built-in predicates 'is', '<', '=<', etc. This is best exemplified in the Progol4.1 dataset order4, in which qualitative regression is applied in conjecturing Newton's inverse square law from artificial floating point data.

The choice of engineering a complete Prolog interpreter was taken in order to make induction a first-class and efficient operation on the same footing as deductive theorem-proving. This allows implementation of low-level operations such as depth-bounding of the theorem prover and rapid virtual assertion and retraction of clauses into the clause set.

12 RESULTS

Results of a series of experiments involving Progol in learning to predict mutagenic molecules can be found in Srinivasan *et al.* 1994; Srinivasan *et al.* 1995a; Srinivasan *et al.* 1995b). A description of Progol doing qualitative regression can be found in (Muggleton and Page 1994b). Qualitative regression is carried out by using mode declarations to define a family of three different functions (linear, polynomial in one term and exponential) and using these in competition to fit the data. The equation solver is supplied as user-defined background knowledge.

Appendix 18 gives a table of runtimes on a SPARCstation 10 for learning the various examples in the distribution version of Progol4.1. The numbers of clauses in E^+, E^-, B and H are also given for each dataset. Note that the datasets 'animals', 'exp', 'family' and 'set' involve learning a series of related predicates. These runtimes are comparable with those of FOIL (Quinlan 1990), despite the fact that FOIL does incomplete heuristic search to find clauses. FOIL also uses extensional background knowledge rather than the intensional background knowledge of Progol.

13 CONCLUSION

This paper traces the line of development followed by the author in investigating induction as the inverse of deduction. It has been shown that the idea of inverting resolution proofs used in Duce and Cigol can be greatly simplified by considering this as a special case of inversion of entailment. However, the notion of inverting entailment is of a more fundamental nature than that of inverting proof, since it is based on the model-theory which underlies proof. This approach has led to the development of a new state-of-the-art ILP system called Progol, which is available for academic research purposes by anonymous ftp (see Section 11). For each example Progol develops a most-specific clause $\perp_i$ within the user-defined mode language, and uses this to guide an A^*-like search through clauses which subsume $\perp_i$. Each invocation of the search returns a clause which is guaranteed to maximally compress the data. Despite the admissibility of this search, the learning times in Appendix 18 are comparable with FOIL, an algorithm which carries out a truncated heuristic search and allows only extensional background knowledge.

Figure 6.2 in Section 7 shows various ways in which Progol could be made more powerful. At present Progol can only deal effectively with the first and third form of $\perp$. If Progol could prove not only positive ground facts but also negative ones then it would be possible to construct $\perp$ in the form of the second entry in Figure 6.2. This would have applications in theory revision. However, for the purposes of theory revision, Progol would need to have a strategy for specializing over-general clauses. The construction of sub-saturants (Section 6.1) would allow Progol to find all generalizations of recursive clauses, such as the one in the fourth entry of Figure 6.2. Both the second and fourth form of generalization in Figure 6.2 will lead to multiple definite $\perp$ clauses. Dealing with the multiplicity of $\perp$ clauses will require improvements in Progol's search techniques. The incompleteness of the present search (see Example 6.30) also needs to be addressed.

Definition 6.9 suggests a way in which Progol could be made to learn effectively when provided with only positive example data. This would have real world applications in areas such as natural language learning, in which it is common to find positive-only data sources.

No learnability results have yet been shown for Progol. U-learnability (Appendix 15) offers a promising direction for such results.

The author believes that inverse entailment offers many new

avenues in the rapidly maturing research area of Inductive Logic Programming.

Acknowledgements

The author would like to thank the *New Generation Computing (NGC)* Journal for permitting the reprinting of this paper, which appeared originally in the May 1995 edition of *NGC*. Many thanks are due to my wife, Thirza Castello-Cortes, who has not only shown super-human tolerance during the long incubation and writing of this paper but has also helped by proof-reading various versions. The author would also like to thank Donald Gillies for pointing out the foundational (but almost wholly disregarded) work of Stanley Jevons. Thanks are also due to David Page and Donald Michie for their helpful discussions and advice and to Ashwin Srinivasan, who produced the initial Prolog version of Progol. Valuable suggestions concerning the U-learnability model were given by Tony Hoare, Bill McColl, Michael Kearns and Paul Vitanyi. This work was supported partly by the Esprit Basic Research Action ILP (project 6020), EPSRC grant GR/J46623 on Experimental Application and Development of ILP and an EPSRC Advanced Research Fellowship held by the author. The author is supported by a non-stipendiary Research Fellowship at Wolfson College Oxford.

REFERENCES

Bain, M. and Muggleton, S. (1991). Non-monotonic learning. In D. Michie, editor, *Machine Intelligence 12*. Oxford University Press, Oxford.

Bratko, I. Muggleton, S. and Varsek, A. (1991). Learning qualitative models of dynamic systems. In *Proceedings of the Eighth International Machine Learning Workshop*, Morgan-Kaufmann, San Mateo, CA.

Clocksin, W.F. and Mellish, C.S. (1981). *Programming in Prolog*. Springer-Verlag, Berlin.

Cohen, W. (1993). Learnability of restricted logic programs. In S. Muggleton, editor, *Proceedings of the 3rd International Workshop on Inductive Logic Programming* (Technical report IJS-DP-

6707 of the Josef Stefan Institute, Ljubljana, Slovenia), pp. 41–72.

Conklin, D. and Witten, I. (1992). Complexity-based Induction. Technical report, Dept. of Computing and Information Science, Queen's University, Kingston, Ontario, Canada.

Dolsak, B. and Muggleton, S. (1992). The application of Inductive Logic Programming to finite element mesh design. In S. Muggleton, editor, *Inductive Logic Programming*. Academic Press, London.

Dormer, R. (1993). *An Inductive Logic Programming Implementation*. PhD thesis, Oxford University Computing Laboratory, Oxford.

Feng, C. (1992). Inducing temporal fault dignostic rules from a qualitative model. In S. Muggleton, editor, *Inductive Logic Programming*. Academic Press, London.

Gillies, D.A. (1992). Confirmation theory and machine learning. In *Proceedings of the Second Inductive Logic Programming Workshop*, Tokyo. ICOT TM-1182.

Gold, E.M. (1967). Language identification in the limit. *Information and Control*, **10**, 447–474.

Gottlob, G. (1987). Subsumption and implication. *Information Processing Letters*, **24** (2),109–111.

Grobelnik, M. (1992). Markus—an optimized model inference system. In *Proceedings of the ECAI workshop on Logical Approaches to Machine Learning*.

Idestam-Almquist, P. (1992). Learning missing clauses by inverse resolution. In *Proceedings of the International Conference on Fifth Generation Computer Systems*, 610–617, Tokyo. ICOT.

Idestam-Almquist, P. (1993). *Generalisation of Clauses*. PhD thesis, Stockholm University.

Jevons, W.S. (1870). On the mechanisation of deductive inference. *Philosophical Transactions of the Royal Society of London*, **160**, 497–518.

Jevons, W.S. (1874). *The Principles of Science: a Treatise on Logic and Scientific Method*. Macmillan, London.

Kakas, A.C., Kowalski, R.A. and Toni, F. (1992). Abductive logic programming. *Journal of Logic and Computation*, 2.

King, R., Muggleton, S., Lewis, R. and Sternberg, M. (1992). Drug design by machine learning: The use of inductive logic programming to model the structure-activity relationships of trimethoprim analogues binding to dihydrofolate reductase. *Proceedings of the National Academy of Sciences*, 89(23), 11322–11326.

Krishnamurthy, V. (1986). *Combinatorics: Theory and Applications*. Ellis Horwood, Chichester.

Lapointe, S. and Matwin, S. (1992). Sub-unification: a tool for efficient induction of recursive programs. In *Proceedings of the Ninth International Machine Learning Conference*, Los Altos. Morgan Kaufmann, Los Altos, CA.

Lee, C. (1967). *A Completeness Theorem and a Computer Program for Finding Theorems Derivable from Given Axioms*. PhD thesis, University of California, Berkeley.

Li, M. and Vitanyi, P. (1993). *An Introduction to Kolmogorov Complexity and its Applications*. Springer-Verlag, Berlin.

Ling, C.X. (1994). Learning the past tense of english verbs: the symbolic pattern associators vs. connectionist models. *Journal of Artificial Intelligence Research*, 1, 209–229.

Lloyd, J.W. (1984). *Foundations of Logic Programming*. Springer-Verlag, Berlin.

Meltzer, B. (1969). Power amplification for automatic theorem proving. In B. Meltzer and D. Michie, editors, *Machine Intelligence 5*, pages 165–179. Edinburgh University Press, Edinburgh.

Michalski, R. and Larson, J. (1980). Incremental generation of vl1 hypotheses: the underlying methodology and the description of program AQ11. ISG 83-5, Computer Science Department, Univ. of Illinois at Urbana-Champaign.

Muggleton, S. (1987). Duce, an oracle based approach to constructive induction. In *IJCAI-87*, pp. 287–292. Morgan Kaufmann, Los Altos, CA.

Muggleton, S. (1988). A strategy for constructing new predicates in first order logic. In *Proceedings of the Third European Working Session on Learning*, pp. 123–130. Pitman, London.

Muggleton, S. (1991a). Inductive logic programming. *New Generation Computing*, 8(4),295–318.

Muggleton, (1991b). Inverting the resolution principle. In *Machine Intelligence 12*. Oxford University Press, Oxford.

Muggleton, S. (1992). Inverting implication. In *Proceedings of the*

Second Inductive Logic Programming Workshop, Tokyo. ICOT (Technical report TM-1182).

Muggleton, S. (1994a). Bayesian inductive logic programming. In W. Cohen and H. Hirsh, editors, *Proceedings of the Eleventh International Machine Learning Conference*, pages 371–379, San Mateo, CA. Morgan-Kaufmann, Los Altos, CA.

Muggleton, S. (1994b). Inductive logic programming: derivations, successes and shortcomings. *SIGART Bulletin*, **5**(1),5–11.

Muggleton, S. (1994c). Predicate invention and utilization. *Journal of Experimental and Theoretical Artificial Intelligence*, **6**(1),127–130.

Muggleton, S. and Buntine, W. (1988). Machine invention of first-order predicates by inverting resolution. In *Proceedings of the Fifth International Conference on Machine Learning*, pp. 339–352. Morgan Kaufmann, Los Altos, CA.

Muggleton, S. and De Raedt, L. (1994). Inductive logic programming: Theory and methods. *Journal of Logic Programming*, **19,20**,629–679.

Muggleton, S. and Feng, C. (1990). Efficient induction of logic programs. In *Proceedings of the First Conference on Algorithmic Learning Theory*, Ohmsha, Tokyo.

Muggleton, S. and Page, C.D. (1994a). Self-saturation of definite clauses. In S. Wrobel, editor, *Proceedings of the Fourth International Inductive Logic Programming Workshop*, pp. 161–174. Gesellschaft für Mathematik und Datenverarbeitung MBH. GMD-Studien Nr 237.

Muggleton, S. and Page, C.D. (1994b). Beyond first-order learning: inductive learning with higher-order logic. Technical Report PRG-TR-13-94, Oxford University Computing Laboratory, Oxford.

Muggleton, S. and Page, C.D. (1994c). A learnability model for universal representations. Technical Report PRG-TR-3-94, Oxford University Computing Laboratory, Oxford.

Muggleton, S., King, R. and Sternberg, M. (1992a). Protein secondary structure prediction using logic-based machine learning. *Protein Engineering*, **5**(7),647–657.

Muggleton, S., Srinivasan, A. and Bain, M. (1992b). Compression, significance and accuracy. In D. Sleeman and P. Edwards, editors, *Proceedings of the Ninth International Machine Learning Conference*, pp. 338–347, San Mateo, CA, 1992. Morgan Kaufmann, Los Altos, CA.

Nilsson, N.J. (1980). *Principles of Artificial Intelligence.* Tioga, Palo Alto, CA.

Plotkin, G.D. (1969). A note on inductive generalisation. In B. Meltzer and D. Michie, editors, *Machine Intelligence 5*, pp. 153–163. Edinburgh University Press, Edinburgh.

Plotkin, G.D. (1971). *Automatic Methods of Inductive Inference.* PhD thesis, Edinburgh University, August 1971.

Popplestone, R.J. (1969). An experiment in automatic induction. In B. Meltzer and D. Michie, editors, *Machine Intelligence 5*, pp. 203–215. Edinburgh University Press, Edinburgh.

Quinlan, J.R. (1990). Learning logical definitions from relations. *Machine Learning*, **5**,239–266.

Quinlan, J.R. (1993). Past tenses of verbs and first-order learning. In Zhang C., J. Debenham, and Lukose D., editors, *Proceedings of the 7th Australian Joint Conference on Artificial Intelligence*, pp. 13–20, Singapore. World Scientific.

Reynolds, J.C. (1969). Transformational systems and the algebraic structure of atomic formulas. In B. Meltzer and D. Michie, editors, *Machine Intelligence 5*, pp. 135–151. Edinburgh University Press, Edinburgh.

Rissanen, J. (1978). Modeling by Shortest Data Description. *Automatica*, **14**,465–471.

Robinson, J.A. (1965). A machine-oriented logic based on the resolution principle. *JACM*, **12**(1),23–41.

Rouveirol, C. (1992). Extensions of inversion of resolution applied to theory completion. In S. Muggleton, editor, *Inductive Logic Programming*. Academic Press, London.

Rouveirol, C. and Puget, J-F. (1989). A simple and general solution for inverting resolution. In *EWSL-89*, pp. 201–210, Pitman, London.

Shannon, C.E. and Weaver, W. (1963). *The Mathematical Theory of Communication.* University of Illinois Press, Urbana, IL.

Shapiro, E.Y. (1983). *Algorithmic program debugging.* MIT Press, Cambridge, MA.

Srinivasan, A., Muggleton, S., King, R. and Sternberg, M. (1994).

Mutagenesis: ILP experiments in a non-determinate biological domain. In S. Wrobel, editor, *Proceedings of the Fourth International Inductive Logic Programming Workshop*. Gesellschaft für Mathematik und Datenverarbeitung MBH. GMD-Studien Nr 237.

Srinivasan, A., Muggleton, S., King, R. and Sternberg, M. (1995a). The effect of background knowledge in inductive logic programming: a case study. Technical Report PRG-TR-9-95, Oxford University Computing Laboratory, Oxford.

Srinivasan, A., Muggleton, S., King, R. and Sternberg, M. (1995b). Theories for mutagenicity: a study of first-order and feature based induction. Technical Report PRG-TR-8-95, Oxford University Computing Laboratory, Oxford.

van der Laag, P.R. and Nienhuys-Cheng, S.H. (1993). Subsumption and refinement in model inference. In P. Brazdil, editor, *Proceedings of the 6th European Conference on Machine Learning*, volume 667 of *Lecture Notes in Artificial Intelligence*, pages 95–114. Springer-Verlag, Berlin.

van der Laag, P.R. and Nienhuys-Cheng, S.H. (1994). Existence and nonexistence of complete refinement operators. In Bergadano F. and De Raedt L., editors, *Proceedings of the 7th European Conference on Machine Learning*, volume 784 of *Lecture Notes in Artificial Intelligence*, pages 307–322. Springer-Verlag, Berlin.

Wirth, R. (1989). Completing logic programs by inverse resolution. In *EWSL-89*, pages 239–250. Pitman, London.

Appendices

14 DEFINITIONS FROM LOGIC

14.1 Formulae in first-order predicate calculus

A variable is represented by an upper case letter followed by a string of lower-case letters and digits. A function symbol is a lower-case letter followed by a string of lower-case letters and digits. A predicate symbol is a lower-case letter followed by a string of lower-case letters and digits. A variable is a term, and a function symbol immediately followed by a bracketed n-tuple of terms is a term. Thus $f(g(X), h)$ is a term when f, g and h are function symbols and X is a variable. As in Prolog, integers, '[]' and '.' are function symbols and if $t_1, t_2, \ldots$ are terms then '.'(t_1, t_2) can equivalently be denoted $[t_1|t_2]$ and '.'$(t_1,$'.'$(t_2, \ldots$'.'$(t_n, [])\ldots))$ can equivalently be denoted $[t_1, t_2, \ldots, t_n]$. A predicate symbol immediately followed by a bracketed n-tuple of terms is called an atomic formula, or atom. Every atom is a well-formed formula (wff). If W and W' are wffs then $\overline{W}$ (not W), $W \wedge W'$ (W and W'), $W \vee W'$ (W or W') and $W \leftarrow W'$ (W implied by W') are wffs. $W \wedge W'$ is a conjunction and $W \vee W'$ is a disjunction. If v is a variable and W is a wff then $\forall v.W$ (for all v W) and $\exists v.W$ (there exists a v such that W) are wffs. v is said to be universally quantified in $\forall v.W$ and existentially quantified in $\exists v.W$. The wff W is said to be function-free if and only if W contains no function symbols. Both A and $\overline{A}$ are literals whenever A is an atom. In this case A is called a positive literal and $\overline{A}$ is called a negative literal. A set of literals is called a clause. The empty clause is represented by $\square$. A clause represents the disjunction of its literals. Thus the clause $\{a_1, a_2, \ldots \overline{a_i}, \overline{a_{i+1}}, \ldots, \overline{a_n}\}$ can be equivalently represented as $(a_1 \vee a_2 \vee \ldots \overline{a_i} \vee \overline{a_{i+1}} \vee \ldots \vee \overline{a_n})$ or $a_1; a_2; \ldots \leftarrow a_i, a_{i+1}, \ldots, a_n$. All the variables in a clause are implicitly universally quantified. A Horn clause is a clause which contains at most one positive literal. A definite clause is a clause which contains exactly one positive literal. A positive literal in either a Horn clause or definite clause is called the head of the clause while the negative literals are collectively called the body of the clause. A set of clauses in which no pair of clauses shares a common variable is called a clausal theory. The empty clausal theory is represented by $\blacksquare$. A clausal theory represents the conjunction of its clauses. Thus the clausal theory $\{C_1, C_2, \ldots, C_n\}$ can be equivalently represented as $(C_1 \wedge C_2 \wedge \ldots \wedge C_n)$. Every clausal theory is said to be in clause-normal form. Every wff can be transformed to an equivalent wff in clause-normal form. If $C = \forall l_1 \vee \ldots l_n$ is a clause then $\overline{C} = \exists \overline{l_1} \wedge \ldots \wedge \overline{l_n}$. In this case $\overline{C}$ is not in clause-normal form since the variables are existentially quantified. $\overline{C}$ can be put in clause-normal form by substituting each occurrence of every variable in $\overline{C}$ by a unique constant not found in C. The process of replacing (existential) variables by constants is called skolemization. The unique constants are called skolem constants. A set of Horn clauses is called a logic program. Apart from representing the empty clause and the empty theory, the symbols $\Box$ and $\blacksquare$ represent the logical constants *False* and *True* respectively. Let E be a wff or term. vars(E) denotes the set of variables in E. E is said to be ground if and only if vars$(E) = \emptyset$.

14.2 Substitutions and models

Let $\theta = \{v_1/t_1, \ldots, v_n/t_n\}$. θ is said to be a substitution when each v_i is a variable and each t_i is a term, and for no distinct i and j is v_i the same as v_j. The set $\{v_1, \ldots, v_n\}$ is called the domain of θ, or dom(θ), and $\{t_1, \ldots, t_n\}$ the range of θ, or rng(θ). Lower-case Greek letters are used to denote substitutions. Let E be a wff or a term and $\theta = \{v_1/t_1, \ldots, v_n/t_n\}$ be a substitution. The instantiation of E by θ, written $E\theta$, is formed by replacing every occurrence of v_i in E by t_i. Atom a θ-subsumes atom b, or $a \preceq b$ if and only if there exists a substitution θ such that $a\theta = b$. Clause C θ-subsumes clause D, or $C \preceq D$ if and only if there exists a substitution θ such that $C\theta \subseteq D$. The Herbrand universe of the wff W is the set of all ground terms composed of function symbols found in W. The Herbrand base of the wff W is the set of all ground atoms composed of predicate and function symbols found in W. An interpretation is a total function from ground atoms to $\{\Box, \blacksquare\}$. A Herbrand interpretation I of wff W is an interpretation whose domain is the Herbrand base of W. I can equivalently be represented as a subset of the atoms a in the Herbrand base of W for which $I(a) = \blacksquare$. Below all interpretations I are assumed to be Herbrand. The atom a is true in I if $I(a) = \blacksquare$ and false otherwise. The wff $\overline{W}$ is true in I if W is false in I and is false otherwise. The wff $W \wedge W'$ is true in I if both W and W' are true in I and false otherwise. The wff $W \vee W'$ is true in I if either W or W' is true in I and false otherwise. The wff $W \leftarrow W'$ is true in I if $W \vee \overline{W'}$ is true in I and false otherwise. If v is a variable and W is a wff then $\forall v.W$ is true in I if for every term t in the Herbrand universe of W the wff $W\{v/t\}$ is true in I. Otherwise $\forall v.W$ is false in I. If v is a variable and W is a wff then $\exists v.W$ is true in I if $\overline{\forall v.\overline{W}}$ is true in I and false otherwise. Interpretation M is a model of wff W if and only if W is true in M. A wff W is satisfiable if there exists a model of W and unsatisfiable otherwise. Consequently W is unsatisfiable if and only if $W \models \square$. Herbrand's theorem states that a wff W is satisfiable if and only if W has a Herbrand model. Every logic program P has a unique least Herbrand model M such that M is a model of P and every atom a is true in M only if it is true in all Herbrand models of P. Let W and W' be two wffs. We say that W semantically entails W', or $W \models W'$ if and only if every model of W is a model of W'. Let X, Y and Z be wffs. Then according to the Deduction theorem $X \wedge Y \models Z$ if and only if $X \models \overline{Y} \vee Z$. Let $\frac{X}{Y}$ be an inference rule. Then $\frac{X}{Y}$ is said to be sound if and only if $X \models Y$. Suppose I is a set of inference rules containing $\frac{X}{Y}$ and W, W' are wffs. Then $W \vdash_I W'$ if W' is formed by replacing an occurrence of X in W by Y. Otherwise $W \vdash_I W'$ if $W \vdash_I W''$ and $W'' \vdash_I W'$. We say that W syntactically entails W' using inference rules I, if and only if $W \vdash_I W'$. The set of inference rules I is said to be deductively sound and complete if and only if each rule in I is sound and $W \vdash_I W'$ whenever $W \models W'$. Let W and W' be two wffs. We say that W is more general than W' (conversely W' is more specific than W) if and only if $W \models W'$.

14.3 Resolution

The substitution θ is said to be a variable renaming if and only if each $u \in \mathrm{dom}(\theta)$ and $v \in \mathrm{rng}(\theta)$ are variables. Let W and W' be two wffs. If there exists a variable renaming θ such that $W\theta = W'$ then W, W' are said to be alphabetic variants of each other. Wffs W, W' are said to be standardized apart if and only if there exists a variable renaming $\theta = \{u_1/v_1, \ldots u_n/v_n\}$, $\mathrm{vars}(W) \subseteq \mathrm{vars}(\theta)$ and $W\theta = W'$. The substitution θ is said to be the unifier of the atoms a and a' whenever $a\theta = a'\theta$. μ is the most general unifier (mgu) of a and a' if and only if for all unifiers γ of a and a' there exists a substitution δ such that $(a\mu)\delta = a\gamma$. Let C and D be clauses and a be an atom. The sound inference rule

$$\frac{C \vee a \qquad\qquad D \vee \overline{a}}{C \vee D}$$

is called resolution. $(C \cup D)\theta$ is said to be the resolvent of the clauses $C \cup \{a\}$ and $D \cup \{a'\}$ whenever C and D are standardized apart and θ is the mgu of the atoms a and $\overline{a'}$. Let T be a clausal theory. Robinson (1965) defined the function $\mathcal{R}^n(T)$ recursively as follows. $\mathcal{R}^0(T) = T$. $\mathcal{R}^n(T)$ is the set of all resolvents constructed from pairs of clauses in $\mathcal{R}^{n-1}(T)$. Robinson showed that T is unsatisfiable if and only if there is some n for which $\mathcal{R}^n(T)$ contains the empty clause ($\square$).

15 HYPOTHESES, PROBABILITIES AND U-LEARNABILITY

15.1 U-learnability

The following is a variant of the U-learnability framework presented in Muggleton (1994a) and Muggleton and Page (1994c). The teacher starts by choosing distributions F and G from the family of distributions $\mathcal{F}$ and $\mathcal{G}$ over concept descriptions $\mathcal{H}$ (wffs with associated bounds for time taken to test entailment) and instances X (ground wffs) respectively. The teacher uses F and G to carry out an infinite series of teaching sessions. In each session a target theory T is chosen from F. Each T is used to provide labels from $\{\blacksquare, \square\}$ (True, False) for a set of instances randomly chosen according to distribution G. The teacher labels each instance x_i in the series $\langle x_1, \ldots, x_m \rangle$ with $\blacksquare$ if $T \models x_i$ and $\square$ otherwise. An hypothesis $H \in \mathcal{H}$ is said to explain a set of examples E whenever it both entails and is consistent with E. On the basis of the series of labelled instances $\langle e_1, e_2, \ldots, e_m \rangle$, a Turing machine learner L produces a sequence of hypotheses $\langle H_1, H_2, \ldots H_m \rangle$ such that $H_i \in \mathcal{H}$ explains $\{e_1, \ldots, e_i\}$. H_i must be suggested by L in expected time bounded by a fixed polynomial function of i. The teacher stops a session once the learner suggests hypothesis H_m with expected error less than ϵ for the label of any x_{m+1} chosen randomly from G. $\langle F, G \rangle$ is said to be U-learnable if and only if there exists a Turing machine learner L such that for any choice of δ and ϵ ($0 < \delta, \epsilon \leq 1$) with probability at least $(1 - \delta)$ in any of the sessions m is less than a fixed polynomial function of $\frac{1}{\delta}$ and $\frac{1}{\epsilon}$.

180

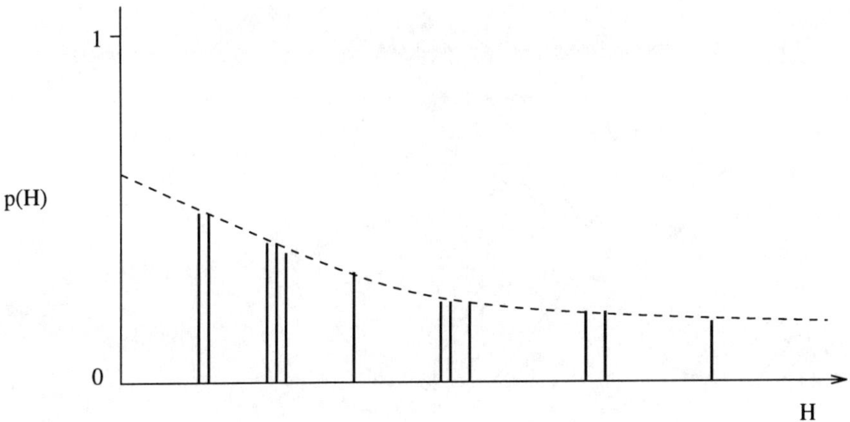

Figure 6.5. Prior and posterior probabilities of hypotheses.

15.2 Bayesian interpretation of setting

Figure 6.5 shows the effect $E = \{e_1, \ldots e_i\}$ has on the probabilities associated with hypotheses in $\mathcal{H}$. The learner's hypothesis language $\mathcal{H}$ is laid out along the X-axis with prior probability $p(H) = F(H)$ for H in $\mathcal{H}$ measured along the Y-axis, where

$$\sum_{H \in \mathcal{H}} p(H) = 1.$$

The descending dotted line in Figure 6.5 represents a bound on the prior probabilities of hypotheses before consideration of examples E. The hypotheses $\mathcal{H}_E$ ($\mathcal{H}_E \subseteq \mathcal{H}$) which explain E are marked as vertical bars. The prior probability of E, $p(E)$, is simply the sum of probabilities of hypotheses in $\mathcal{H}_E$. The conditional probability $p(E|H)$ is 1 in the case that H explains E and 0 otherwise. The posterior probability of H is now given by Bayes theorem as

$$p(H|E) = \frac{p(H)p(E|H)}{p(E)}$$

With reference to Figure 6.5, for an hypothesis H which explains all the data, $p(H|E)$ will increase monotonically with increasing E. Also for two different hypotheses H_1, H_2 which explain E the following holds:

$$\frac{p(H_1|E)}{p(H_2|E)} = \frac{p(H_1)}{p(H_2)} \tag{6.6}$$

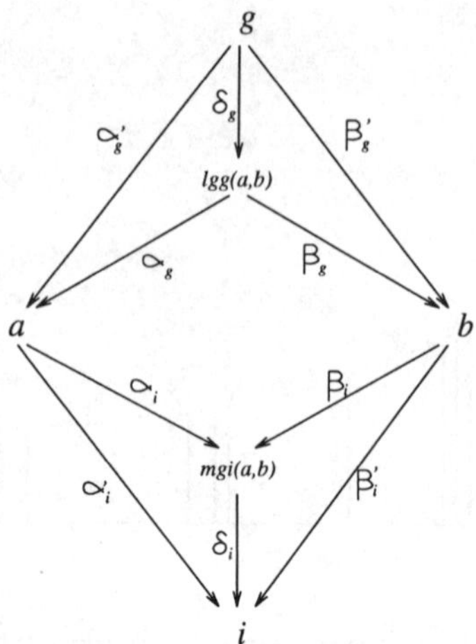

Figure 6.6. Relationship of *lgg* and *mgi*.

16   SUBSUMPTION AND LEAST GENERAL GENERALISATION

In the late 1960's the success of Robinson's (1965) resolution procedure produced considerable interest in the problem of inducing first-order formulae. Both Meltzer (1969) and Popplestone (1969) carried out initial investigations into generalization of ground formulae by replacement of constants with variables. In implementing his approach Meltzer decided to bound the number of resolutions involved in checking any hypothesis against examples. This was an important innovation which is now being used within Progol (Section 11).

In an alternative approach Reynolds (1969) and Plotkin (1969) investigated the problem of finding least general generalizations (lggs) of atoms. According to Plotkin (1971),

> The work started with a suggestion by R.J. Popplestone (private communication) that, just as the unification algorithm was fundamental to deduction, so might a converse be of use in induction.

The relationship of lgg to unification is depicted in Figure 6.6. Atom g is a common generalization of atoms a and b if an only if there exist substitutions α_g' and β_g' such that $a = g\alpha_g'$ and $b = g\beta_g'$. The atom $lgg(a, b)$ is the least general generalization of a and b if and only if $lgg(a, b)$ is a common generalization of a and b and for each common generalization g of a and b there exists a substitution δ_g such that $lgg(a, b) = g\delta_g$. The common instance i and most general instance are similarly defined for a and b (see Figure 6.6). In the case of the most general instance i of a and b Robinson (1965) calls $\alpha_i\beta_i$ the most general unifier of a and b. Robinson describes an algorithm for constructing the most-general unifier of two atoms. Robinson's unification algorithm is the basis of resolution theorem-proving. Plotkin and Reynolds describe an efficient algorithm for computing the least general generalization of two atoms.

$[a]$ is the equivalence class of all atoms which are variable renamings of a. Reynolds showed that the set of all equivalence classes of atoms augmented by the symbols $\top$ and $\bot$ form a non-modular lattice. Thus, $[a] \sqcap [b] = [lgg(a, b)]$ and $[a] \sqcup [b] = [mgi(a, b)]$, where $\sqcap$ and $\sqcup$ are both commutative and associative, though neither distributes over the other.

Plotkin (1969) extended the investigation to clauses ordered by θ-subsumption. Clause C θ-subsumes clause D, or $C \preceq D$ if and only if there exists a substitution θ such that $C\theta \subseteq D$. Just as with atoms, clause G and I are respectively a common generalization and a common instance of C and D if and only if $G \preceq C, D$ and $C, D \preceq I$. For clauses C and D there is a least general generalization $lgg(C, D)$ and most general instance $mgi(C, D)$, both unique up to renaming, such that for every common generalisation G and common instance I of C and D it is the case that $G \preceq lgg(C, D)$ and $mgi(C, D) \preceq I$. The cardinality of the least general generalization of two clauses is bounded by the product of the cardinalities of the two clauses.

Plotkin (1969) went on to define the lgg of two clauses relative to clausal background knowledge B. The relative least general generalization of clauses ($rlgg_B$) is potentially infinite for arbitrary B. When B consists of ground unit clauses only the $rlgg_B$ of two clauses is finite. However the cardinality of the $rlgg_B$ of m clauses relative to n ground unit clauses has worst-case cardinality of order $O(n^m)$, making the construction of such $rlgg_B$'s intractable.

17 PROGOL ALGORITHM

17.1 Construction of most-specific clause

Algorithm 6.40 Algorithm for constructing $\perp_i$.

1. Given natural numbers h, i, Horn clauses B, definite clause e and set of mode declarations M.

2. Let $k = 0$, $hash : Terms \to N$ be a hash function which uniquely maps terms to natural numbers, $\bar{e}$ be the clause-normal form logic program $\bar{a} \wedge b_1 \wedge \ldots \wedge b_n$, $\perp_i = \langle \rangle$ and InTerms$= \emptyset$.

3. If there is no modeh in M such that $a(m) \preceq a$ then return $\square$. Otherwise let m be the first modeh declaration in M such that $a(m) \preceq a$ with substitution θ_h. Let a_h be a copy of $a(m)$ and for each v/t in θ_h if v corresponds to a #type in m then replace v in a_h by t otherwise replace v in a_h by v_k where $k = hash(t)$ and add v to InTerms if v corresponds to +type. Add a_h to $\perp_i$.

4. If $k = i$ return $\perp_i$ else $k = k + 1$.

5. For each modeb m in M let $\{v_1, \ldots, v_n\}$ be the variables of +type in $a(m)$ and $T(m) = T_1 \times \ldots \times T_n$ be a set of n-tuples of terms such that each T_i corresponds to the set of all terms of the type associated with v_i in m (term t is tested to be of a particular type by calling Prolog with type(t) as goal). For each $\langle t_1, \ldots, t_n \rangle$ in $T(m)$ let a_b be a copy of $a(m)$ and $\theta = \{v_1/t_1, \ldots, v_n/t_n\}$. If Prolog with depth-bound h succeeds on goal $a_b\theta$ with the set of answer substitutions Θ_b then for each θ_b in Θ_b and for each v/t in θ_b if v corresponds to a #type in m then replace v in a_b by t otherwise replace v in a_b by v_k where $k = hash(t)$ and add v to InTerms if v corresponds to $-$type. Add $\overline{a_b}$ to $\perp_i$.

6. Goto step 4.

17.2 A^*-like algorithm for finding clause with maximal compression

Firstly we define some auxiliary functions used in Algorithm 6.42.

Definition 6.41 Auxiliary functions. Let the examples E be a set of Horn clauses. Let $h, i, B, e, M, \perp_i$ be as in Definition 6.24 in Section 8.1 and let C, k, θ be as in Definition 6.27 in

Section 9.2.

$$d'(v) = \begin{cases} 0 & \text{if no -type variable in head of } \perp_i \\ 0 & \text{if } v \text{ is -type in head of } \perp_i \\ \infty & \text{if } v \text{ is not in } \perp_i \\ (min_{u \in U_v} d'(u)) + 1 & \text{otherwise} \end{cases}$$

where U_v are the $-$type variables in atoms in the body of C which contain $+$type occurrences of v. Below state s has the form $\langle C, \theta, k \rangle$. c is a user-defined parameter for the maximal clause body length. $|S|$ denotes the cardinality of any set S.

$$\begin{aligned} p_s &= |\{e : e \in E \text{ and } B \wedge C \wedge \overline{e} \vdash_h \Box\}| \\ n_s &= |\{e : e \in E \text{ and } B \wedge C \wedge e \vdash_h \Box\}| \\ c_s &= |C| - 1 \\ V_s &= \{v : u/v \in \theta \text{ and } u \text{ in body of } C\} \\ h_s &= min_{v \in V_s} d'(v) \\ g_s &= p_s - (c_s + h_s) \\ f_s &= g_s - n_s \end{aligned}$$

$best(S)$ is a state $s \in S$ which has $c_s \leq c$ and for which there does not exist $s' \in S$ for which $f_{s'} > f_s$.

$$\text{prune}(s) = \begin{cases} true & \text{if } n_s = 0 \text{ and } f_s > 0 \\ true & \text{if } g_s \leq 0 \\ true & \text{if } c_s \geq c \\ false & \text{otherwise} \end{cases}$$

$$\text{terminated}(S, S') = \begin{cases} true & \text{if } s = best(S), n_s = 0, f_s > 0 \text{ and} \\ & \text{for each } s' \text{ in } S' \ f_s \geq g_{s'} \\ false & \text{otherwise} \end{cases}$$

Algorithm 6.42 Algorithm for searching $\Box \preceq C \preceq \perp_i$.

1.   Given $h, B, e, \perp_i$ as in Definition 6.24.

2.   Let Open $= \{\langle \Box, \emptyset, 1 \rangle\}$ and Closed $= \emptyset$.

3.   Let $s = best(\text{Open})$ and Open $= \text{Open} - \{s\}$.

4.   Let Closed $= \text{Closed} \cup \{s\}$.

5.   If prune(s) goto 7.

6.   Let Open $= ($Open$\cup\rho(s))-$Closed.

7.   If terminated(Closed,Open) then return best(Closed).

8.   If Open $= \emptyset$ then print 'no compression' and return $\langle e, \emptyset, 1 \rangle$.

9.   Goto 3.

17.3   Progol's cover set algorithm

Definition 6.43 Unflattening. Let $C = h \leftarrow X, Y$ be a definite clause in which $X = (s_1 = t_1, ..., s_n = t_n)$ is a conjunction of atoms with predicate symbol '=' and Y is a conjunction of atoms with predicate symbols other than '='. The clause $C' = h' \leftarrow Y'$ is called the unflattening of C if and only if C' is derived from C by successively resolving away each $s_i = t_i$ in X with the clause $(U = U \leftarrow)$.

Algorithm 6.44 Cover set algorithm

1. h, i, B, M are given as in Theorem 6.26 and E is the subset of B corresponding to atoms in modeh declarations in M.

2.   If $E = \emptyset$ then return B.

3.   Let e be the first example in E.

4.   Construct $\perp_i$ for e using Algorithm 6.40.

5.   Construct state s from $\perp_i$ using Algorithm 6.42.

6.   Let C' be the unflattening of $C(s)$ (Definition 6.43).

7.   Let $B = B \cup C'$.

8.   Let $E' = \{e : e \in E$ and $B \wedge \bar{e} \vdash_h \square\}$.

9.   Let $E = E - E'$.

10.   Goto 2.

18 PROGOL'S RUNTIMES

Data set	Predicate	$|E^+|$	$|E^-|$	$|B|$	$|H|$	Time (sec)
animals	false	42	16	105	6	0.930
	class	16	6	105	5	0.183
append	append	19	8	0	2	0.199
arch	arch	4	4	47	1	0.149
chess	move	27	12	34	11	5.080
cyclic	cyclic	3	2	69	1	0.100
delete	delete	7	6	2	2	0.365
even	even	16	15	4	3	0.216
exp	plus	6	5	13	3	0.133
	mult	6	23	10	3	0.730
	exp	5	5	8	2	0.183
family	parent_of	11	4	61	2	0.066
	grandfather_of	10	7	53	1	0.149
	grandparent_of	13	6	41	1	0.066
grammar	s	8	7	18	1	0.116
krki	illegal	341	655	51	4	17.281
last	last	7	5	2	2	0.066
min	min	14	6	4	2	1.760
nim	won	16	7	12	1	0.100
order0	f	15	3	13	1	0.382
order1	f	15	3	13	1	0.730
order2	f	8	4	13	1	0.747
order3	f	9	4	13	1	0.681
order4	f	12	4	13	1	1.079
parity4	parity	16	16	11	1	1.195
qsort	qsort	11	12	8	2	0.863
range	inrange	7	3	0	2	0.266
reverse	reverse	13	7	4	2	0.149
set	member	16	3	33	2	0.100
	pair	3	2	16	2	0.050
	subset	12	8	7	2	0.730
setuni	setuni	14	13	2	4	2.357
sumx	sumx	7	3	3	2	0.432
train	eastbound	5	5	257	1	0.100
utube	utube	5	13	173	1	1.643

7

Learning Logic Programs and Regularities from Examples by Inductive Inference

---

S. Akiba and T. Sato

Electrotechnical Laboratory, JAPAN

1 INTRODUCTION

Recently ILP (Inductive Logic Programming) has been gaining attention as a way to synthesize logic programs from examples (Muggleton 1992). What ILP does is, when the background knowledge $\mathcal{K}$, positive examples $\mathcal{E}^+$ and negative examples $\mathcal{E}^-$ are given, to find a hypothesis $\mathcal{H}$ such that $\mathcal{K} \cup \mathcal{H} \vdash \mathcal{E}^+$ and $\mathcal{K} \cup \mathcal{H} \nvdash \mathcal{E}^-$.

Given examples of the *concat* predicate, existing ILP systems can find logic programs such as

$$\left\{ \begin{array}{l} concat(X, [Y|Z], [Y|W]) \leftarrow concat(X, Z, W) \\ concat(X, [], [X]) \end{array} \right\}.$$

If also given examples of the *reverse* predicate with the above program as the background knowledge, they also can find

$$\left\{ \begin{array}{l} reverse([X|Y], Z) \leftarrow reverse(Y, W), concat(X, W, Z) \\ reverse([], []) \end{array} \right\}.$$

Creation of new predicates (*predicate invention*) is carried out automatically. For instance, a system described in Kijsirikul *et al.* (1992b) creates the following *aux* predicate (a namesake of the *concat* predicate) without any background knowledge:

$$\left\{ \begin{array}{l} reverse([X|Y], Z) \leftarrow reverse(Y, W), aux(X, W, Z) \\ reverse([], []) \\ aux(X, [Y|Z], [Y|W]) \leftarrow aux(X, Z, W) \\ aux(X, [], [X]) \end{array} \right\}.$$

In this paper, we describe an inductive inference system KISS which not only can synthesize logic programs from examples but is capable of discovering regularities among predicates such as

$$reverse(X, Y) \leftarrow reverse(Y, X)$$
$$append(X, V, W) \leftarrow append(X, Y, U), append(U, Z, W),$$
$$append(Y, Z, V).$$

Although these regularities expressed in terms of clauses cannot be part of logic programs, they are expected to play an important role in program understanding and optimization. Researchers, however, do not seem to have shown enough interest in their discovery. Actually, most ILP systems do not seek clauses beyond logic programs (Kijsirikul *et al.* 1992a, 1992b; Muggleton and Feng 1990; Shapiro 1982).

KISS first calculates *least general generalizations* (lggs) (Plotkin 1970) of subsets of the atoms in the background knowledge. It then combines them to form a logic program and clauses representing basic regularities of predicates, while removing inappropriate clauses using negative examples. Due to this *computing-lggs-first* strategy, it becomes possible to find complex regularities such as the associativity of the *append* predicate.

In the following, we describe the theoretical background of KISS in Section 2, introduce an algorithm to calculate lggs in Section 3 and give the outline of experimental implementation of KISS in Section 4. Comparison with existing ILP systems is made in Section 5 and Section 6 includes concluding remarks.

2 THEORETICAL BACKGROUND

2.1 System $\mathcal{R}$

The theoretical background of our system is an inductive inference system $\mathcal{R}$ (Sato 1992). $\mathcal{R}$ consists of the following three rules which are applied to a clause and infer one or two clauses:

- case rule: $D \xmapsto{case} A \vee D, \neg A \vee D$
- inverse-or rule: $L \vee D \xmapsto{or^{-1}} D$
- anti-substitution rule: $D\theta \xmapsto{\theta^{-1}} D$.

Here D is a clause, A an atom, L a literal and θ a substitution, respectively. $\mathcal{R}$ is *inductively complete*, i.e. it can derive from $\mathcal{E}$ every possible hypothesis $\mathcal{H}$ such that $\mathcal{H} \vdash \mathcal{E}$. Here $\vdash$ stands for provability relationship and $\mathcal{E}$ and $\mathcal{H}$ are sets of clauses, respectively.

$\mathcal{R}$ provides a theoretical framework for KISS. Although practical considerations and implementation issues obscured this relationship, we are able to understand what KISS does as systematic application of $\mathcal{R}$ as follows.

Suppose we are required to derive (using $\mathcal{R}$) a definite clause $A \leftarrow B_1, \ldots, B_n$ satisfying the following conditions:

$$\text{There exist } e^+ \in \mathcal{E}^+ \text{ and } \theta \text{ such that} \qquad (7.1)$$
$$e^+ = A\theta, \ \mathcal{K} \vdash B_1\theta, \ldots, B_n\theta,$$

$$\text{There does not exist } e^- \in \mathcal{E}^-, \theta \text{ or } \sigma \text{ such that} \qquad (7.2)$$
$$e^-\sigma = A\theta, \ \mathcal{K} \vdash B_1\theta, \ldots, B_n\theta.$$

Here $\mathcal{K}$, the background knowledge, is a set of clauses. θ and σ are substitutions. $\mathcal{E}^+$, positive examples, and $\mathcal{E}^-$, negative examples respectively, are sets of atoms such that $\mathcal{K} \cup \mathcal{E}^+$ is consistent and $\mathcal{K} \cup \mathcal{E}^+ \nvdash e^-\theta \ (\forall e^- \in \mathcal{E}^-, \forall\theta)$.

Let $A^1, \ldots, A^m$ be positive examples in $\mathcal{E}^+$, A an lgg of $\{A^1, \ldots, A^m\}$ and θ^j a substitution such that $A\theta^j = A^j$. Suppose $A \leftarrow B_1, \ldots, B_{k-1}$ which satisfies the condition (7.1) has been constructed (initially $k = 1$) by $\mathcal{R}$. Calculate an lgg, say B_k, of provable atoms and examine whether each θ^j can be extended to θ'^j such that $\mathcal{K} \vdash B_k\theta'^j$.

If such B_k and θ'^j are found, add $B_k\theta'^j$ to the body of $A\theta^j \leftarrow B_1\theta^j, \ldots, B_{k-1}\theta^j$ by the case rule, and apply the anti-substitution rule to derive $A \leftarrow B_1, \ldots, B_k$. The result is a clause satisfying the condition (7.1). Repeat this process until the generated clause satisfies the condition (7.2) as well.

Obviously, this process is an ideal one because computing the conditions (7.1) and (7.2) is an infinite process in general. So, we use modified conditions as an approximation to them for our current system:

$$\text{There exist } e^+ \in \mathcal{E}^+ \text{ and } \theta \text{ such that} \qquad (7.1')$$
$$e^+ = A\theta, \ \mathcal{K} \Vdash B_1\theta, \ldots, B_n\theta,$$

$$\text{There does not exist } e^- \in \mathcal{E}^-, \theta \text{ or } \sigma \text{ such that} \atop e^- \sigma = A\theta, \; \mathcal{K} \vdash B_1\theta, \ldots, B_n\theta. \tag{7.2'}$$

Here $\mathcal{K}$ is a finite set of clauses. $\mathcal{K} \vdash S$ means that there exist an atom $K \in \mathcal{K}$ and a substitution δ such that $K\delta = S$.

While this inevitably brings incompleteness into our system, we still expect that by using a large number of atoms as the background knowledge, we can increase a chance of narrowing the gap between two sets of conditions, one ideal, the other implementable.

We should note the problem of over-generalization. The reason that we first calculate an lgg of provable atoms B_k, and then make a clause $A \leftarrow B_1, \ldots, B_k$, is that we expect the clause to be an lgg of $\{A\theta^j \leftarrow B_1\theta^j, \ldots, B_n\theta^j\}$. Unfortunately it could be more general than the real lgg, even if it satisfies the conditions (7.1') and (7.2'). Since our objective, however, is to find clauses which satisfy the conditions (7.1') and (7.2'), it is not so important theoretically whether clauses generated by the process are the real lgg or not. As the implementation issue, since such over-generalization may cause redundant computation, we impose a weak condition on KISS in order to avoid the redundant computation (we explain a little more about this later).

2.2 Predicate invention

We should mention that predicate invention, i.e., the introduction of a new predicate not appearing in the background knowledge is straightforward in our framework. We have only to find a definite clause $A \leftarrow B_1, \ldots, B_n, F$ and a set $\mathcal{H}'$ of instances of F satisfying the following two conditions:

$$\text{There exist } e^+ \in \mathcal{E}^+ \text{ and } \theta \text{ such that} \atop e^+ = A\theta, \; \mathcal{K} \vdash B_1\theta, \ldots, B_n\theta, \; \mathcal{H}' \vdash F\theta, \tag{7.1''}$$

$$\text{There does not exist } e^- \in \mathcal{E}^-, \theta \text{ or } \sigma \text{ such that} \atop e^- \sigma = A\theta, \; \mathcal{K} \vdash B_1\theta, \ldots, B_n\theta, \; \mathcal{H}' \vdash F\theta. \tag{7.2''}$$

Here F is an atom whose predicate symbol does not occur in the background knowledge, positive examples or negative examples.

To take a closer look, let $A \leftarrow B_1, \ldots, B_n$ be a clause satisfying (7.1$'$) and $X_1, \ldots, X_p$ variables occurring in the clause. Suppose aux is a new predicate symbol. Put $F = aux(X_1, \ldots, X_p)$ and $\mathcal{H}' = \{ F\theta \mid A\theta \in \mathcal{E}^+ \text{ and } \mathcal{K} \vdash B_1\theta, \ldots, B_n\theta \}$. Then (7.1$''$) is satisfied automatically. (7.2$''$) is also satisfied because of $\mathcal{K} \cup \mathcal{E}^+ \nvdash e^-\theta$ ($\forall e^- \in \mathcal{E}^-$, $\forall \theta$).[1] Hence $A \leftarrow B_1, \ldots, B_n, F$ is a clause we seek.

In general, however, $X_1, \ldots, X_p$, the arguments of F, could include unnecessary variables. We must take F with the minimum set of variables satisfying (7.1$''$) and (7.2$''$). To choose the minimum set of variables, DBC algorithm (Kijsirikul 1992b) is available.

The main part of KISS consists of the calculation of lggs of atoms in the background knowledge and their combinations to generate clauses that satisfy (7.1$'$) and (7.2$'$), or (7.1$''$) and (7.2$''$) when predicate invention is required. In the next section, we describe the calculation of lggs.

3 CALCULATING LGGS

KISS first calculates lggs (modulo variants) of atoms in the background knowledge when it is given a finite set of available function symbols and constants together with the maximum depth of nesting of function symbols in a term. It then generates variants to add to the body of a clause. Note that the atoms used by calculating lggs need not be ground atoms.

3.1 An algorithm to calculate lggs

In this subsection we describe an algorithm to calculate all lggs (modulo variants) of subsets of a given set of atoms. One simple method is to generate all subsets of the given set and then to calculate the lgg of each subset. This method is inefficient because it calculates an exponential number of subsets and their lggs, while usually there are many subsets whose lggs are the same. We describe below a much more efficient algorithm.

---

[1] If (7.2$''$) is not satisfied, there exist $e^- \in \mathcal{E}^-$, θ and σ such that $e^-\sigma = A\theta$ and $\mathcal{H}' \vdash F\theta$. From the construction of $\mathcal{H}'$, we get $A\theta \in \mathcal{E}^+$. This means $e^-\sigma \in \mathcal{E}^+$. This is inconsistent with $\mathcal{K} \cup \mathcal{E}^+ \nvdash e^-\theta$ for any $e^- \in \mathcal{E}^-$ and θ.

First classify given atoms according to their predicate symbols P_i and put $E(P_i) = \{\ e \mid e$ is an atom whose predicate symbol is $P_i\ \}$. Then calculate $lggs(E(P_i))$ by the following algorithm. $\bigcup_{P_i} lggs(E(P_i))$ is the set of all lggs.

An algorithm to calculate $lggs(E)$ from a given set E of atoms with the same predicate symbol:

1. If E contains more than one element, perform from 2. to 6., otherwise output $lggs(E) = \phi$ and exit.

2. Calculate $t = lgg(E)$. Let $V = \{v_i\}$ be the set of all variables occurring in t.

3. For each e_j included in E, calculate a substitution $\theta_j = \{t_i^j/v_i\}$ such that $t\theta_j = e_j$.

4. For each v_i occurring in t, classify e_j included in E according to the function symbol f_k of t_i^j or the constant c_k of t_i^j to make $E_{v_i,f_k} = \{\ e_j \in E \mid t_i^j = f_k(\ldots)\}$ and $E_{v_i,c_k} = \{\ e_j \in E \mid t_i^j = c_k\}$.

5. For each $V' = \{v_{i_1}, v_{i_2}\}$ which is a subset of V and contains two elements, collect elements from E in which $t_{i_1}^j, t_{i_2}^j$ are identical, and make sets $E_{V'} = \{\ e_j \in E \mid t_{i_1}^j = t_{i_2}^j,\ v_{i_1}, v_{i_2} \in V'\}$.

6. Output $lggs(E) = \{\ t\ \} \cup \bigcup_{v_i,f_k} lggs(E_{v_i,f_k}) \cup \bigcup_{v_i,c_k} lggs(E_{v_i,c_k}) \cup \bigcup_{V'} lggs(E_{V'})$.

Example 7.1 Calculating lggs of $E = \{\ reverse([a],[a]), reverse([b],[b]), reverse([a,b],[b,a]), reverse([a,c],[c,a])\ \}$.

$$lgg(E) = reverse([X|Y],[Z|W])$$

$$E_{X,a} = \left\{ \begin{array}{l} reverse([a],[a]) \\ reverse([a,b],[b,a]),\ reverse([a,c],[c,a]) \end{array} \right\}$$

$$E_{X,b} = \{\ reverse([b],[b])\ \}$$

$$E_{Y,[]} = E_{W,[]} = \{\ reverse([a],[a]),\ reverse([b],[b])\ \}$$

$$E_{Y,cons} = E_{W,cons} = \left\{ \begin{array}{l} reverse([a,b],[b,a]) \\ reverse([a,c],[c,a]) \end{array} \right\}$$

$$E_{Z,a} = \{\ reverse([a],[a])\ \}$$

$$E_{Z,b} = \{\ reverse([b],[b]),\ reverse([a,b],[b,a])\ \}$$

$$E_{Z,c} = \{\ reverse([a,c],[c,a])\ \}$$

$$E_{\{X,Y\}} = E_{\{X,W\}} = E_{\{Y,Z\}} = E_{\{Z,W\}} = \phi$$
$$E_{\{X,Z\}} = E_{\{Y,W\}} = \{\ reverse([a],[a]),\ reverse([b],[b])\ \}$$

$$lggs(E_{X,a}) = \left\{ \begin{array}{c} reverse([a|X],[Y|Z]) \\ reverse([a,X],[X,a]) \end{array} \right\}$$

$$lggs(E_{Y,[]}) = \{\ reverse([X],[X])\ \}$$
$$lggs(E_{Y,cons}) = \{\ reverse([a,X],[X,a])\ \}$$
$$lggs(E_{Z,b}) = \{\ reverse([X|Y],[b|Z])\ \}$$

$$lggs(E_{\{X,Z\}}) = \{\ reverse([X],[X])\ \}$$

$$lggs(E) = \left\{ \begin{array}{l} reverse([X|Y],[Z|W]) \\ reverse([a|X],[Y|Z]) \\ reverse([a,X],[X,a]),\ reverse([X],[X]) \\ reverse([X|Y],[b|Z]) \end{array} \right\}$$

It is usual that we do not calculate all lggs but some of them specified in terms of available symbols and the nesting depth of function symbols in a term. For example if the available constant is only [] (the empty list), we do not calculate $E_{X,a}$, etc, and we have $lggs(E) = \{\ reverse([X|Y],[Z|W])$, $reverse([X],[X])\ \}$.

The reader might notice that $reverse([X],[X])$ is calculated twice in this example. In our implementation, we modified the above algorithm so that each lgg is calculated only once. Since the computational cost of calculating lggs depends on the number of the given atoms and the number of the calculated lggs, it is complicated to evaluate efficiency of the modified algorithm.

Table 7.1 is the result of calculating lggs of the *reverse* predicate by using the modified algorithm. It shows two good features: Time taken by calculating the same lggs is almost proportional to the number of the given atoms. If the maximum depth of nesting of function symbols in a term increases, average time taken by calculating an lgg tends to decrease.

3.2 Generating variants

In this subsection we describe how to generate variants of an atom that are to be added to a given clause. We call them *admissible variants* of the atom w.r.t. the clause. Our system

Table 7.1. Calculating lggs from non-ground instances of *reverse*

Max. length	Atoms	Max. depth	Lggs	Time (msecs)	Time per atom
2	4	0	2	3.2	0.8
3	9	0	2	5.3	0.59
4	24	0	2	11.7	0.49
5	76	0	2	44.9	0.62

Max. length	Atoms	Max. depth	Lggs	Time (msecs)	Time per lgg
5	76	0	2	45	22.5
5	76	1	5	99	19.8
5	76	2	23	236	10.3
5	76	3	200	994	5.0
5	76	4	721	3670	5.1
5	76	5	772	3783	4.9

uses them to form clauses to satisfy the conditions $(7.1')$ and $(7.2')$, or $(7.1'')$ and $(7.2'')$.

First note that we do not need to generate those variants that share no variables with the given clause (Arimura and Shinohara 1991; Kijsirikul *et al.* 1992a; Muggleton and Feng 1990) (we explain this later). We also do not need, once an atom in a clause is renamed, to further rename those variables that are existentially quantified in the clause.

Taking these two factors into account, we define admissible variants of A w.r.t. C as variants generated in the following way.

Suppose an atom A in which m variables occur and a clause C in which n variables $X_1, \ldots, X_n$ occur are given. First rename the variables of A to $Y_1, \ldots, Y_m$ that don't occur in C. Then select k variables from $X_1, \ldots, X_n$ and also from $Y_1, \ldots, Y_m$ respectively and construct a substitution $\theta = \{X_{i_1}/Y_{j_1}, \ldots, X_{i_k}/Y_{j_k}\}$ to generate a variant $A\theta$ of A.

The number of the admissible variants of A w.r.t. C is

$$\sum_{k=1}^{\min\{n,m\}} {}_nP_k \cdot {}_mP_k/k!$$

Example 7.2 The admissible variants of $reverse(U, V)$ w.r.t. $reverse([X|Y], [Z|W])$ are the following 20 atoms:

$$reverse(X, Y), \ reverse(X, Z), \ reverse(X, W)$$
$$reverse(Y, X), \ reverse(Y, Z), \ reverse(Y, W)$$
$$reverse(Z, X), \ reverse(Z, Y), \ reverse(Z, W)$$
$$reverse(W, X), \ reverse(W, Y), \ reverse(W, Z)$$
$$reverse(X, V), \ reverse(U, X), \ reverse(Y, V)$$
$$reverse(U, Y), \ reverse(Z, V), \ reverse(U, Z)$$
$$reverse(W, V), \ reverse(U, W).$$

We remark that we should avoid forming clauses which are variants of already formed clauses. For example, $P(X, Z)$ is an admissible variant of $P(W, Z)$ w.r.t. $a(X) \leftarrow q(X, Y)$. However, if $a(X) \leftarrow p(X, Y), q(X, Z)$ is already formed, we should not form $a(X) \leftarrow q(X, Y), p(X, Z)$.

To avoid redundant formation of clauses like the above, we introduced two total orders, one on the set of admissible variants, and the other on the set of formed clauses. Our system can avoid the redundancy by using these total orders without retaining formed clauses.

4 SYSTEM KISS

We have been developing an inductive inference system KISS which takes the background knowledge $\mathcal{K}$, a set of positive examples $\mathcal{E}^+$ and a set of negative examples $\mathcal{E}^-$ as input and outputs a clause C and a set of atoms $\mathcal{H}'$ satisfying the following conditions:

(1) $C = A \leftarrow B_1, \ldots, B_n$ or $C = A \leftarrow B_1, \ldots, B_n, F$. Here A is an lgg of atoms in $\mathcal{K} \cup \mathcal{E}^+$. $B_1, \ldots, B_n$ are lggs of atoms in $\mathcal{K}$. F is an atom whose predicate symbol does not occur in $\mathcal{K}$, $\mathcal{E}^+$ or $\mathcal{E}^-$.

(2) $\mathcal{H}'$ is a set of instances of F.

(3) There exist $e^+ \in \mathcal{E}^+$ and θ such that $e^+ = A\theta$, $\mathcal{K} \vdash B_1\theta, \ldots, B_n\theta$ (and $\mathcal{H}' \vdash F\theta$ if C contains F).

(4) There does not exist $e^- \in \mathcal{E}^-$, θ or σ such that $e^-\sigma = A\theta$, $\mathcal{K} \vdash B_1\theta, \ldots, B_n\theta$ (and $\mathcal{H}' \vdash F\theta$ if C contains F).

(5) For each two distinct variables X, Y occurring in C, there exist $e^+ \in \mathcal{E}^+$ and θ such that $e^+ = A\theta$, $\mathcal{K} \vdash B_1\theta, \ldots,$ $B_n\theta$, $X\theta \neq Y\theta$ (and $\mathcal{H}' \vdash F\theta$ if C contains F).

(6) If $C' \subseteq C$ and C' satisfies the condition (4) then $C' = C$.

We adopted (5) to avoid over-generalization as mentioned in Section 2. We intend to unify variables in C if possible by checking this condition.

(6) is intended as a subsumption check. Instead of checking from (1) to (5) in (6), we only check the condition (4) in (6) (Muggleton and Feng 1990). [2]

Also (6) explains why admissible variants must share variables with the clause they are added to as stated in Section 3. To see it, suppose a clause C satisfies from (1) to (6). Let C_1 and C_2 be clauses which are made from C by dividing C, or $C_1, C_2 \neq C$ and $C_1 \cup C_2 = C$, then there are variables occurring in both C_1 and C_2. If not, C_α ($= A \leftarrow B_{i_1}, \ldots, B_{i_k}$), one of C_1 and C_2, which contains A satisfies the condition (4). This contradicts that C satisfies (6). Therefore, if C satisfies from (1) to (6), C can be arranged to satisfy $var(A \leftarrow B_1, \ldots, B_{i-1}) \cap var(B_i) \neq \phi$ ($i = 1, \ldots, n$). Here, $var(S)$ denotes the set of variables occurring in S.

At the moment, we have completed experimental implementation by using Common Lisp to confirm that the computing-lggs-first strategy can derive programs from examples and definite clauses which express basic regularities of predicates without special heuristics except restrictions on available function symbols, available constants, the maximum depth of nesting of function symbols in a term, and the maximum length of inferred clauses.

Therefore the implemented system takes as input:

- the set of positive examples $\mathcal{E}^+$
- the set of negative examples $\mathcal{E}^-$

---

[2]Let (6') be the condition 'if $C' \subseteq C$ and C' satisfies the conditions from (1) to (5) then $C' = C$'. We must prove that 'C satisfies from (1) to (5) and (6') $\Leftrightarrow C$ satisfies from (1) to (6)'. If C satisfies (1) (2) (3) (5) and $C' \subseteq C$ then C' also satisfies (1) (2) (3) (5), therefore the $\Rightarrow$ part holds. The $\Leftarrow$ part is obvious.

- the background knowledge $\mathcal{K}$
- a set of available function symbols *FSym*
- a set of available constants *Const*
- the maximum length of inferred clauses *CLmax*
- the maximum depth of nesting of function symbols in heads of inferred clauses and in bodies of inferred clauses *HDmax* and *BDmax*, respectively.

It outputs all clauses (modulo variants) satisfying the conditions from (1) to (6). The whole process is automatic.

For easy implementation, it has the following two restrictions.

- Positive and negative examples are given as ground atoms. They must have the same predicate symbol.
- The output of $\mathcal{H}'$, the set of instances of a new predicate, is suppressed (though calculated in the system).

The system adopts the following algorithm.

1. Let *LGG* be the set of lggs of subsets of $\mathcal{K}$ calculated by the algorithm described in Section 3.1.
   Output atoms each of which is an lgg of a subset of $\mathcal{K} \cup \mathcal{E}^+$ and satisfies the condition (4).
   Let S be the set of atoms each of which is an lgg of a subset of $\mathcal{K} \cup \mathcal{E}^+$ and does not satisfy the condition (4).
   For each clause D in S, Let $AV(D)$ be the set of admissible variants of atoms in *LGG* w.r.t. D.

2. While S is not empty, repeat 2.1.
   Exit.

2.1. Select a clause D from S.
   If $AV(D)$ is not empty, do 2.1a. Else do 2.1b.

2.1a. Select B from $AV(D)$.
   Put $C = D \vee \neg B$.
   If C satisfies the conditions (3), (4), (5) and (6), output C.
   If the length of C is less than *CLmax* and C satisfies (3), (5) but not (4), add C to S and let $AV(C)$ be the set of admissible variants of atoms in *LGG* w.r.t. C.
   Remove B from $AV(D)$.

2.1b. Make a new predicate F.
Put $C = D \vee \neg F$.
Calculate $\mathcal{H}'$, a set $\mathcal{H}'$ of instances of F such that C satisfies the conditions (3), (4), (5) and (6).
Output C.
Remove D from S.

We need to calculate a set $\mathcal{H}'$ of instances of an atom F containing a new predicate symbol in the above algorithm. Since DBC algorithm (Kijsirikul *et al.* 1992b) is not appropriate for this purpose, we have developed a new algorithm that calculates *all* minimum sets of variables to construct new predicates. Note that DBC calculates one minimum set of variables for a new predicate.

Example 7.3 If

$$
\mathcal{E}^+ = \left\{
\begin{array}{l}
reverse([a,b,c],[c,b,a]),\ reverse([a,b],[b,a]) \\
reverse([a],[a]),\ reverse([b],[b]),\ reverse([],[])
\end{array}
\right\}
$$

$$
\mathcal{E}^- = \left\{
\begin{array}{l}
reverse([o,b,c],[c,b,a]),\ reverse([a,b],[b,a,c]) \\
reverse([a,o,c],[c,b,a]),\ reverse([a,c,b],[b,a]) \\
reverse([a,b,o],[c,b,a]),\ reverse([o,b],[b,a]) \\
reverse([a,b,c],[o,b,a]),\ reverse([a,o],[b,a]) \\
reverse([a,b,c],[c,o,a]),\ reverse([a,b],[o,a]) \\
reverse([a,b,c],[c,b,o]),\ reverse([a,b],[b,o]) \\
reverse([a,b,c],[a,b,c]),\ reverse([a,b],[a,b]) \\
reverse([a],[a,b]),\ reverse([b],[b,a]) \\
reverse([a,b],[a]),\ reverse([b,a],[b]) \\
reverse([a],[b]),\ reverse([b],[a]) \\
reverse([a],[]),\ reverse([],[b])
\end{array}
\right\}
$$

$$
\mathcal{K} = \left\{
\begin{array}{l}
reverse([],[]),\ reverse([X,Y,Z],[Z,Y,X]) \\
reverse([X],[X]),\ reverse([X,Y],[Y,X])
\end{array}
\right\}
$$

$FSym = \{\ cons\ \}$

$Const = \{\ []\ \}$

$CLmax = 3$

$HDmax = \infty$

$BDmax = 0$

is given as input, current KISS outputs

$$reverse(X, Y) \leftarrow reverse(Y, X)$$
$$reverse([X|Y], [Z|W]) \leftarrow reverse(Y, U), aux1(X, Z, W, U)$$
$$reverse([X|Y], [Z|W]) \leftarrow reverse(W, U), aux2(X, Y, Z, U)$$
$$reverse([X|Y], [Z|W]) \leftarrow reverse(U, Y), aux3(X, Z, W, U)$$
$$reverse([X|Y], [Z|W]) \leftarrow reverse(U, W), aux4(X, Y, Z, U)$$
$$reverse(X, X) \leftarrow aux5(X)$$
$$reverse(X, Y) \leftarrow aux6(X, Y)$$
$$reverse([X|Y], [Z|W]) \leftarrow aux7(X, Y, Z, W)$$
$$reverse([X, Y|Z], [W, U|V]) \leftarrow aux8(X, Y, Z, W, U, V).$$

The first clause cannot be used as part of logic programs but represents a basic regularity of *reverse*. $aux1(X, Z, W, U)$, $aux2(X, Y, Z, U)$, etc occurring in the last eight clauses are new predicates automatically generated by the system. Their positive and negative examples are also automatically calculated from those of *reverse*. Accordingly if KISS is given these ground atoms as input it generates part of programs for the new predicates (predicate invention).

The following is an example of program synthesis for $aux1$. The positive and negative examples of $aux1$ calculated by KISS are:

$$\mathcal{E}^{+\prime} = \left\{ \begin{array}{l} aux1(a, c, [b, a], [c, b]), \ aux1(a, b, [a], [b]) \\ aux1(a, a, [], []), \ aux1(b, b, [], []) \end{array} \right\}$$

$$\mathcal{E}^{-\prime} = \left\{ \begin{array}{l} aux1(o, c, [b, a], [c, b]), \ aux1(a, b, [a, c], [b]) \\ aux1(a, c, [b, a], [c, o]), \ aux1(a, b, [a], [b, c]) \\ aux1(a, c, [b, a], [o, b]), \ aux1(o, b, [a], [b]) \\ aux1(a, o, [b, a], [c, b]), \ aux1(a, b, [a], [o]) \\ aux1(a, c, [o, a], [c, b]), \ aux1(a, b, [o], [b]) \\ aux1(a, c, [b, o], [c, b]), \ aux1(a, o, [a], [b]) \\ aux1(a, a, [b, c], [c, b]), \ aux1(a, a, [b], [b]) \\ aux1(a, a, [b], []), \ aux1(b, b, [a], []) \\ aux1(b, b, [], [a]), \ aux1(a, a, [], [b]) \\ aux1(b, a, [], []), \ aux1(a, b, [], []) \end{array} \right\}.$$

With restrictions $FSym = \{cons\}$, $Const = \{[]\}$, $CLmax = 2$, $HDmax = \infty$ and $BDmax = 0$, and by putting $\mathcal{K} = \mathcal{E}^+$, KISS outputs the following clauses:

$$aux1(X, X, [], [])$$
$$aux1(X, Y, [Z|W], [Y|U]) \leftarrow aux1(X, Z, W, U)$$
$$aux1(X, Y, Z, W) \leftarrow aux9(X, Y, Z, W)$$
$$aux1(X, Y, [Z|W], [Y|U]) \leftarrow aux10(X, Z, W, U).$$

By putting together all clauses for $reverse$ and $aux1$, we obtain a program that calculates $reverse$ relation:

$$\left\{ \begin{array}{l} reverse([X|Y], [Z|W]) \leftarrow reverse(Y, U) \\ \qquad\qquad\qquad\qquad\qquad aux1(X, Z, W, U) \\ reverse([], []) \\ aux1(X, Y, [Z|W], [Y|U]) \leftarrow aux1(X, Z, W, U) \\ aux1(X, X, [], []) \end{array} \right\}.$$

Example 7.4 If

$$\mathcal{E}^+ = \left\{ \begin{array}{l} reverse([a, b, c], [c, b, a]), \ reverse([a, b], [b, a]) \\ reverse([a], [a]), \ reverse([b], [b]), \ reverse([], []) \end{array} \right\}$$

$$\mathcal{E}^- = \left\{ \begin{array}{l} reverse([o, b, c], [c, b, a]), \ reverse([a, b], [b, a, c]) \\ reverse([a, o, c], [c, b, a]), \ reverse([a, c, b], [b, a]) \\ reverse([a, b, o], [c, b, a]), \ reverse([o, b], [b, a]) \\ reverse([a, b, c], [o, b, a]), \ reverse([a, o], [b, a]) \\ reverse([a, b, c], [c, o, a]), \ reverse([a, b], [o, a]) \\ reverse([a, b, c], [c, b, o]), \ reverse([a, b], [b, o]) \\ reverse([a, b, c], [a, b, c]), \ reverse([a, b], [a, b]) \\ reverse([a], [a, b]), \ reverse([b], [b, a]) \\ reverse([a, b], [a]), \ reverse([b, a], [b]) \\ reverse([a], [b]), \ reverse([b], [a]) \\ reverse([a], []), \ reverse([], [b]) \end{array} \right\}$$

$$\mathcal{K} = \left\{ \begin{array}{l} reverse([], []), \ reverse(X, Y, Z], [Z, Y, X]) \\ reverse([X], [X]), \ reverse([X, Y], [Y, X]) \\ concat(X, [], [X]), \ concat(X, [Y], [Y, X]) \\ concat(X, [Y, Z], [Y, Z, X]) \end{array} \right\}$$

$$FSym = \{ cons \}$$

$$Const = \{\, [] \,\}$$
$$CLmax = 3$$
$$HDmax = \infty$$
$$BDmax = 1,$$

KISS outputs about 1300 clauses. Among them we can find four similar clauses:

$$reverse([X|Y],[Z|W]) \leftarrow reverse(Y,U), concat(X,U,[Z|W])$$
$$reverse([X|Y],[Z|W]) \leftarrow reverse(U,W), concat(Z,U,[X|Y])$$
$$reverse([X|Y],[Z|W]) \leftarrow reverse(W,U), concat(Z,U,[X|Y])$$
$$reverse([X|Y],[Z|W]) \leftarrow reverse(U,Y), concat(X,U,[Z|W]).$$

The first two clauses are available to construct a program of *reverse* predicate; on the other hand, the last two clauses are seldom used.

Example 7.5 The next example is a little more complex.

$$\mathcal{E}^+ = \left\{ \begin{array}{l} append([],[a,b],[a,b]), \ append([a],[b],[a,b]) \\ append([a,b],[],[a,b]) \end{array} \right\}$$

$$\mathcal{E}^- = \left\{ \begin{array}{l} append([a],[b],[]), \ append([a],[],[a,b]) \\ append([],[b],[a,b]), \ append([],[a,b],[b,a]) \\ append([a,b],[],[b,a]), \ append([a],[b],[b,a]) \end{array} \right\}$$

$$\mathcal{K} = \left\{ \begin{array}{l} append([],[],[]), \ append([],[X,Y],[X,Y]) \\ append([],[X],[X]), \ append([X],[Y],[X,Y]) \\ append([X],[],[X]), \ append([X,Y],[],[X,Y]) \end{array} \right\}$$

$$FSym = \{\, cons \,\}$$
$$Const = \{\, [] \,\}$$
$$CLmax = 4$$
$$HDmax = 1$$
$$BDmax = 0$$

KISS outputs more than 5000 clauses. Among them we can find interesting clauses such as:

$$append([X],Y,[X|Y])$$
$$append(X,Y,Z) \leftarrow append(X,W,U), append(U,V,Z),$$
$$append(W,V,Y)$$
$$append([X|Y],Z,[X|W]) \leftarrow append(Y,Z,W).$$

The second clause represents the associativity of the *append* predicate, and the third clause is part of a logic program that calculates the *append* predicate.

5 COMPARISON WITH EXISTING SYSTEMS

We aim to develop an inductive inference system which derives as many clauses as possible. In the previous section, we have seen that experimental implementation of KISS can produce programs from examples and find definite clauses that express basic regularities of the *reverse* and *append* predicates. We have done it by using the strategy that calculates lggs first and then combines them, without special heuristics except restrictions on available function symbols, available constants, the maximum depth of nesting of function symbols in a term and the maximum length of inferred clauses.

This contrasts sharply with existing ILP systems, as they are designed to synthesize one program. They are capable of producing programs of many predicates including *reverse* and *append* by using complicated heuristics and restrictions for various reasons. However, they cannot find clauses that express basic regularities. Moreover, even if they are given enough examples to produce several programs, they can find only one of them.

In the rest of this section we compare our system with two eminent ILP systems, MIS (Shapiro 1982) and GOLEM (Muggleton and Feng 1990).

5.1 Comparison with MIS

MIS generates clauses by using three refinement operators:

- instantiation of a variable
- unification of two variables
- addition of an atom to the body of a clause.

When MIS is required to generate clauses with $reverse(X, Y)$ and $concat(X, Y, Z)$ as available predicates, it will generate clauses systematically by those three refinement operators as shown in Figure 7.1.

There are a couple of problems in this method however:

- Since MIS generates clauses mechanically in a top-down manner, taking no notice of examples, it tends to generate clauses not instantiated enough. In Figure 7.1, clauses containing $reverse([X|Y], Z)$ or $reverse(X, [Y|Z])$ are generated, though both arguments should explicitly be lists.

- MIS sometimes generates clauses containing atoms whose instances are not in the given examples or derivable from the background knowledge. For example, it generates $reverse([X|Y], Y)$ and $reverse(X, [Y|X])$ though the arguments of $reverse(X, Y)$ must be lists with equal length.

- MIS generates the same clause repeatedly. For instance $reverse([X|Y], [Z|W])$ is generated twice in the figure. It appears however that MIS and other systems (Kijsirikul et al. 1992a, 1992b) lack a mechanism to eliminate these redundant clauses.

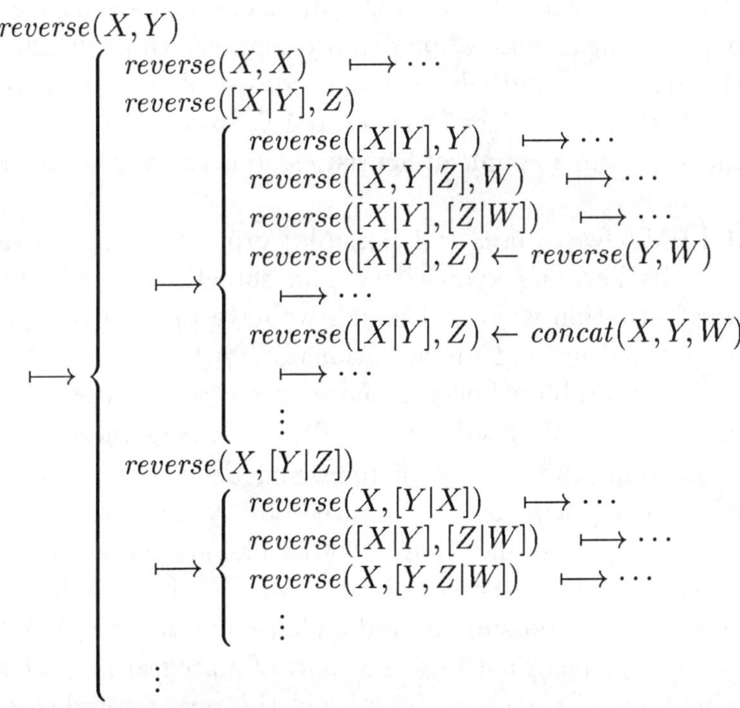

Figure 7.1. Search space of MIS

Since KISS first calculates lggs of atoms in the background knowledge and then combines them to form clauses, these problems do not arise in the following sense:

- All atoms in the generated clauses are not more abstract than is necessary because they are lggs. For example, $reverse([X|Y], Z)$ or $reverse(X, [Y|Z])$ will never be generated.

- Every atom in the generated clauses is the lgg of atoms in the background knowledge. This is why KISS does not generate clauses containing $reverse([X|Y], Y)$ or $reverse(X, [Y|X])$.

- KISS generates each clause only once by using lggs and admissible variants.

5.2 Comparison with GOLEM

GOLEM starts by calculating ground atoms provable from the background knowledge within the limit of calculation given in advance. It next makes up definite clauses whose heads are positive examples and whose bodies consist of these calculated atoms. It then takes lggs of generated definite clauses. Finally it removes, using a couple of heuristics, unnecessary atoms from these lggs.

GOLEM always uses (all possible) ground atoms provable from the background knowledge. This sometimes results in an awkward situation where, although we have $eq(X, X)$, we have to compute all ground instantiations of $eq(X, X)$. This 'over-computation' problem becomes more serious when we synthesize a program that only needs some instantiations of $eq(X, X)$.

In addition, the process of removing unnecessary atoms is computationally expensive as pointed out by the authors themselves in Muggleton and Feng (1990). The system accordingly uses a couple of heuristics to cut down on the search space, which makes it impossible to find a clause like $reverse(X, Y) \leftarrow reverse(Y, X)$ that is not usable as part of a program but clearly represents one of the characteristics of the $reverse$ predicate.

Because KISS generates clauses by simply combining lggs generated from (possibly non-ground) atoms in the background knowledge, with only information about available function symbols, available constants, the maximum depth of nesting of function symbols in a term and the maximum length of inferred clauses, it suffers neither redundancies nor the incapability mentioned above. Also thanks to this simple strategy, it is not hard to predicate what clause it can synthesize or what clause it cannot.

6 CONCLUDING REMARKS

In this paper we have described current implementation of our inductive inference system KISS. It achieves simplicity and efficiency by adopting such a strategy that it calculates lggs of atoms in the background knowledge to form clauses, instead of calculating lggs of provable atoms. Although this strategy seems irrelevant to *rlgg* (Plotkin 1971), we conjecture that it can calculate rlgg as well under some conditions.

Concerning the computation of lggs itself, we have to say that the *k-mmg* (Arimura and Shinohara 1991) algorithm calculates the set of lggs of several, not all, subsets of a given atom set E, whereas our algorithm calculates the set of lggs of all subsets of E.

Our system is based on a complete inductive inference system $\mathcal{R}$, and we have been developing KISS with the least sacrifice of completeness. We did not employ heuristics, whereas most existing ILP systems did. This has a favourable side effect that KISS can find non-program clauses which represent regularities of predicates.

We here should refer to the paper by Dehaspe *et al.* (1994) that introduced the system CLAUDIEN. It searches the space of instances of the given *clausemodels* by using refinement operators. It can find non-program non-definite clauses.

As a future topic, we need to remove various restrictions of experimental implementation described in Section 4. We plan to enable our system to use Horn clauses as the background knowledge so that we can compare its ability with that of existing ILP systems.

Due to the computing-lggs-first strategy, our system generates a smaller number of clauses than other systems using refinement operators as we discussed in Section 5.1. But the number of generated clauses is still large since the current system simply combines lggs by the depth-first method. It obviously needs a more efficient method to avoid uninteresting combinations.

Another important topic is the need for a selection mechanism of generated clauses. While our system can find a variety of clauses, there is no mechanism incorporated to filter out redundant clauses, nor mechanism for generalizing generated clauses to an appropriate degree. For example, KISS can find $reverse([X|Y],[Z|W]) \leftarrow reverse(Y,U), \; concat(X,U,[Z|W])$ from appropriate input. In this clause however, variables Z and W occur only in $[Z|W]$, so the system should generalize $[Z|W]$ and output $reverse([X|Y],V) \leftarrow reverse(Y,U), concat(X,U,V)$.

Last but not least, the current system introduces new predicates automatically whenever possible and generates clauses for them (Kijsirikul et al. 1992b). This strategy works well with Example 7.3, but when applied to the other examples, it generates too many uninteresting clauses. We therefore must look for criteria to decide whether new predicates should be introduced or not.

Acknowledgements

We are grateful to Koichi Furukawa for suggesting and giving the paper on CLAUDIEN. We are also grateful to Masayuki Numao for giving the paper. We thank anonymous referees for their helpful comments.

REFERENCES

Arimura, H. and Shinohara, T. (1991). Polynomial time inference of unions of tree pattern languages. *Proc. of the 2nd International Workshop on Algorithmic Learning Theory*, 105–114.

Dehaspe, L., Van Laer, W. and De Raedt, L. (1994). Applications of a logical discovery engine. *Proc. of the 4th International Workshop on Inductive Logic Programming*, 291–304.

Kijsirikul, B., Numao, M. and Shimura, M. (1992a). Efficient learning of logic programs with non-determinate, non-discriminating literals. In S. Muggleton (ed.), *Inductive Logic Programming*, pp. 361–372. Academic Press, London.

Kijsirikul, B., Numao, M. and Shimura, M. (1992b). Discrimination-Based Constructive Inductive Learning (in Japanese). *Journal of Japanese Society for Artificial Intelligence*, **7** (6), 1027–1036.

Muggleton, S. (ed.) (1992). *Inductive Logic Programming*, Academic Press, London.

Muggleton, S. and Feng, C. (1990). Efficient induction of logic programs. *Proc. of the 1st International Workshop on Algorithmic Learning Theory*, 368–381.

Plotkin, G. D. (1970). A note on inductive generalization. In B. Meltzer and D. Michie (eds.), *Machine Intelligence* **5**, 153–163. Edinburgh University Press, Edinburgh.

Plotkin, G. D. (1971). A further note on inductive generalization. In B. Meltzer and D. Michie (eds.), *Machine Intelligence* **6**,pp. 101–124. Edinburgh University Press, Edinburgh.

Sato, T. (1992). A complete set of rules for inductive inference. *ETL Technical Report* TR-92-44.

Shapiro, E. Y. (1982). *Algorithmic Program Debugging*, MIT Press, Cambridge, MA.

8

Variations and Local Exceptions in Inductive Logic Programming

Arul Siromoney

School of Computer Science and Engineering,
Anna University, Madras 600 025, India.

Rani Siromoney

Madras Christian College, Tambaram, Madras 600 059, India.

1 INTRODUCTION

Variations are valid departures from the normal. One pictures the classical music composer writing variations for a given theme, the jazz player improvising on a melody, or the Indian percussionist improvising on a rhythm. Each variation is valid in itself, and is a departure or variation from some normal base or theme. We note that variations are different from noise. Each variation is a valid departure from the normal, whereas noise is incorrect or illegal deviation from the normal.

The study of variations is motivated by possible application in widely differing areas such as music, molecular biology, speech recognition and distributed knowledge. In music, the classical areas of variations on a melodic theme and improvisation of drum rhythms, as well as the formalization of the presence of non-harmonic notes in harmonic music are some of the immediate applications. In molecular biology, mutations are a good application of variations. In the application area of speech recognition, it becomes possible to describe the base knowledge, and then the special characteristics of an individual's voice. In distributed applications, one can have a centralized knowledge-base, and have variations at different geographical sites based on site-specific knowledge. In these days of internationalization issues, one can think of language or cultural customization of generalized base knowledge. Variations on a string or image can be described by the edit operations of insert, substitute or delete. This has application in the areas of picture processing, linguistics and bio-informatics.

When we consider variations in knowledge, we can look at each of the variations as valid departure or deviation from the normal or base knowledge. Since each of these deviations is itself knowledge in some form or another, we consider variations as the combination of base knowledge as well as one of the many different variations in knowledge. The notion of variations in the classification problem is thus that of a concept which is described by a base set of rules (base description) as well as one of a number of variation sets of rules (variation descriptions).

One of the recent classification techniques is inductive logic programming (ILP), and we introduce the concept of variations in inductive logic programming. Inductive logic programming (Muggleton 1991) is the field of inducing logic programs from examples in the presence of background knowledge. The induced logic program consists of rules in the form of Horn clauses. In this paper, we first present our implementation of an extended version of Muggleton and Feng's (1990) ILP algorithm. The main advantage of our implementation is that it is no longer necessary to give all the data as background knowledge in the form of ground predicates. The background knowledge now consists of predicates that operate on the data sequences, and return a *true/false* value. This now makes it possible to easily handle predicates such as 'contains' (Sakakibara and Siromoney 1992) that operate on the entire example or test sequence. Our implementation of GOLEM is therefore able to easily handle examples that consist of strings or sequences. This opens up a much wider area of application of ILP techniques.

We then present an illustrative experimental example of variations from the field of molecular biology in learning the classification of an amino-acid sequence as a signal peptide (Shimozono *et al.* 1993). The classification of signal peptide sequences for 'other mammalian' data is first learnt as the base knowledge. The classification of signal peptide sequences for primates is used as the variation. This illustrates one of the many uses of variations. Here, the extensive effort spent in learning the base knowledge can be used, and modifications done to cater to the particular variation. We also see that classification is better than when directly learning that new concept. Although we have used the ILP algorithm GOLEM in our own experimental study, the concept of variations is general enough to be studied using any machine learning algorithm.

We note that variations are different from layered learning (Muggleton 1993) since in layered learning, knowledge learnt in one stage is refined at later stages to improve learning of the original concept, whereas in variations, the learning of new knowledge is in order to describe a concept that is different from the original one. Knowledge is learnt initially to describe the base concept, and additional knowledge is learnt in order to describe correctly a different concept - the variation. However, a special case of the concept of variations can also be considered, where the new knowledge to be learnt results in a more accurate form of the original knowledge.

We then see how Compton and Jansen's (1988) ripple-down rule sets can be applied to ILP to have local exceptions in ILP. We modify GOLEM to be able to learn local exceptions. Considering the variation to be a more accurate version of the base knowledge, we see how the concept of variations completely contains the concept of local exceptions. Ripple-down rule sets and local exceptions have been shown to be powerful learning approaches, and we see here that they are a special case of the general concept of variations. We also look at PAC-learnability of variations and local exceptions.

2 DIFFERENT TYPES OF VARIATIONS

The basic concept of variations may be considered as being described by a base description as well as one of a number of variation descriptions. But, the combination of the base description and the variation description can be done in different ways. Many different features need to be analysed in any application of variations, and different types of variations are based on certain combinations of these features.

The first feature is that the variation description can either restrict or extend the base description. A *specializing variation* is one in which the concept described by the variation is a subset of that described by the base. A *non-specializing variation* is one in which the concept described by the variation is not a subset of that described by the base. However, it is not necessary that the non-specializing variation be a generalizing variation. The concept described by the variation need not necessarily be a superset of that described by the base.

The second feature that needs to be considered is whether the variation is local or global. A *local variation* is one in which the variation description acts locally on each rule of the base description and a *global variation* is one in which the variation description acts globally on the base description as a whole. When the base description is a black box and the internal representation of the base knowledge cannot be seen or used, it has to be a global variation. In the case of a local variation, the base description has to necessarily be a glass box so that the rules in the base knowledge can be seen and used.

The third feature is whether the variation is a *single variation* or a *multiple variation*. In a single variation, only one particular variation is known to be applicable in a particular context. It would also be possible to have a specific example set corresponding to that particular variation. A multiple variation is one in which any one of several variations may be applicable. This feature is similar to that of learning a single concept and learning multiple concepts.

One of the other features that will play a role in certain applications is whether the base description is the default (*default-base variation*). In such a variation, if a test sample is described by the base description, and is not specifically disallowed by the variation description, then it is a valid example of the variation. Another feature that may need to be considered is whether the individual variations are required to be mutually exclusive (*mutually exclusive variation*), or whether there can be traits that are common between some of the variations.

The different combinations of these features give rise to different types of variations. Any particular application will need to consider each of the features outlined above, and will be one or more of the different types of variations.

The centralized knowledge-base and site-specific variations example is a non-specializing default-base single variation. It is a global variation if the centralized knowledge is a black box, and can be a local variation if it is a glass box. Mutations (in molecular biology) are an example of non-specializing non-default-base variations. Local exceptions are an example of specializing local default-base single variations.

All these different types of variations can be learnt by using the ILP techniques. In this paper, we look at the logic programs that capture some of these types of variations, and see how the ILP technique can be used in learning them.

3 VARIATIONS ON A WELL-KNOWN THEME

One of the ways in which variations are useful is when the base knowledge has already been learnt well (is already 'well-known') and is similar to the knowledge that needs to be learnt. The effort and expertise used to learn the base knowledge can then be used in learning the particular variation knowledge. This is useful when most examples are classified correctly by the base knowledge already learned, and only a few are left to be learnt now. So variation rules need to be learnt to add cover for the additional positive examples not covered by the base knowledge, and to delete cover for the negative examples covered wrongly by the base knowledge. Since the concept described by the variation is not a subset of the concept described by the base, these are non-specializing variations. Since the base knowledge is the default (unless modified explicitly by the variation knowledge) these are default-base variations. We consider learning only one new concept, and so this is an example of a single variation.

We can assume that the base knowledge is a black box and nothing is known about the rules and the way they are formed. In this case, the variation knowledge can only assume that given a particular test example, the central knowledge would decide whether it is a valid example or not. This is the situation that is most likely to occur. The central knowledge has been created and is available for use, but nothing is known of the internal representation. This is therefore an example of global variations. (There can also be applications where the base knowledge is a glass box, and the rules are known. In this situation, we can assume that each of the rules in the base knowledge has a stub predicate attached to it, so that variations on that specific rule can be introduced through this stub. These will then be local variations.)

Therefore this is an illustration of non-specializing global default-base single variations.

4   LEARNING A VARIATION ON A WELL-KNOWN THEME

The logic program that defines a non-specializing global default-base single variation is of the following form:

$$\text{class}(X,\dots) :- \text{baseclass}(X,\dots), \text{not } (\text{lessvar}(X,\dots)).$$

$$\text{lessvar}(X,\dots) :- \dots.$$
$$\text{lessvar}(X,\dots) :- \dots.$$
$$\dots$$

$$\text{class}(X,\dots) :- \text{morevar}(X,\dots).$$

$$\text{morevar}(X,\dots) :- \dots.$$
$$\text{morevar}(X,\dots) :- \dots.$$
$$\dots$$

where the base knowledge has *baseclass* as the target predicate and is of the form

$$\text{baseclass}(X,\dots) :- \dots.$$
$$\text{baseclass}(X,\dots) :- \dots.$$
$$\dots$$

Here the predicate *lessvar* is at the head of the rules that delete the negative variation examples wrongly covered by the base knowledge. The predicate *morevar* is at the head of the rules that add the positive variation examples that are not covered by the base description.

Let us now consider the problem of learning this logic program. The learning method is as follows:

Input:

        Background knowledge.
        Base +ve and −ve examples.
        Variation +ve and −ve examples.

Method:

Learn base:

        Form +ve examples from base +ve examples.
        Form −ve examples from base −ve examples.
        Learn *baseclass*.

Learn variation:

        Form +ve examples from variation +ve examples,
        and delete those covered by base.
        Form −ve examples from variation −ve examples
        and base −ve examples,
        deleting any variation +ve examples found.
        Learn *morevar*.

        Form +ve examples from variation −ve examples,
        and delete those *not* covered by base.
        Form −ve examples from variation +ve examples
        and base +ve examples,
        deleting any variation −ve examples found.
        Learn *lessvar*.

5 INDUCTIVE LOGIC PROGRAMMING

Inductive logic programming (Muggleton 1991) is the field of inducing logic programs from examples in the presence of background knowledge. The induced logic program consists of rules in the form of Horn clauses. Muggleton and Feng (1990) present GOLEM, an ILP implementation that uses the following 'greedy' control strategy to find each of the clauses in H, the set of hypothesized clauses which together cover all examples in E^+ and do not cover any elements of E^-.

Let E^+ be a set of positive examples.
Let E^- be negative examples.
Let M_h(B) be an h-easy model of background
    knowledge B .
Let s be a given sample limit.
Let Pairs(s) be a random sample of pairs from E^+ .
Let Lggs = {C:e,e$'$ $\in$ Pairs(s)
          and C=rlgg(e,e$'$) wrt M_h (B)
          and C consistent wrt E^- }.
Let S be the pair {e,e$'$}
whose rlgg has the greatest cover in Lggs.
DO
    Let E^+ (s) be a random sample of size s from E^+
    Let Lggs = { C: e$'$ $\in$ E^+ (s) and C = rlgg(S $\cup$ {e$'$})
          consistent wrt E^- }.
    Find e$'$ which produces the greatest cover in Lggs.
    Let S = S $\cup$ {e$'$}.
WHILE increasing-cover.
Let E^+ = E^+ - cover(rlgg(S)).

Here, the Herbrand h-easy model of B, $M_h(B)$, is the set of all Herbrand instantiations of h-easy atoms of B. An atom a is h-easy with respect to B if and only if there exists a derivation of a from B involving at most h binary resolutions, where h is a natural number.

If the sample limit is set to be twice the expected number of clauses, where the cover of each clause is disjoint, it can be shown that a randomly chosen pair of examples will be covered by one of the clauses with high probability.

Our implementation of the GOLEM algorithm in C contains the following extensions. The main advantage of this implementation over the original implementation of GOLEM is that it allows the use of C callable functions to return simple predicate values, thus allowing the use of operators such as 'contains' studied by Sakakibara and Siromoney (1992). The 'contains' operator is *true* when the search string is contained in the target string and *false* otherwise. This also means that all the data need not be given as background ground rules. Data is independent of the background predicates, and the background predicates (such as 'contains') act on the data and return *true / false*. It currently uses a compiled C function table as background knowledge rather than Prolog program clauses. It also currently internally evaluates the induced Horn clauses in their internal format rather than externally using a Prolog compiler on the Prolog program output generated. Appropriate input/output translation modules can be added to use Prolog-like input and generate actual Prolog program output.

6 PRIMATE AS A VARIATION ON WELL-KNOWN MAMMALS

We now consider an experimental illustration from the field of molecular biology. Shimozono *et al.* (1993) study the classification problem on signal peptides. They study machine learning for the classification of sequences as signal peptides for viral, bacterial, invertebrate, primate, rodent, other mammalian, other vertebrate and plant data by using three-level hydropathy-index-based regular patterns in the nodes of a decision tree. The simple pattern language actually used in their practical implementation is the equivalent of the 'contains' operator.

We use our extended implementation of the GOLEM algorithm with the predicates used in the background knowledge as the contains and abstains operators on indexed sequences using the hydropathic index and acidity/basicity/neutrality of the amino acids. The operator 'abstains' is the opposite of contains, and is *true* when the search string is not contained in the target string.

The illustrative study is made using the 'other mammalian' data as the base, and the 'primate' data as the variation. The actual sequence data kindly sent to us by Professor Miyano was sorted, with duplicates removed, and then placed in random order. Eighty sequences each were taken as the training and test examples. We present below the results of the experiment.

Learning from the primate training set of 80 positive and 80 negative examples, and using this learnt knowledge on the primate test set of 80 positive and 80 negative examples yielded the following results:

	Positive	Negative	Total
Correct	75.00%	77.50%	76.25%
	(60/80)	(62/80)	

Learning the base knowledge from the other mammalian training set of 80 positive and 80 negative examples, and then learning the variation knowledge from the primate training set of 80 positive and 80 negative examples, using the method outlined in the earlier section, and then using this knowledge on the primate test set of 80 positive and 80 negative examples yielded the following results:

	Positive	Negative	Total
Correct	81.25%	87.5%	84.38%
	(65/80)	(70/80)	

All learning was done using a 90% negative consistency check in the GOLEM algorithm and by choosing a 1 out of 4 sample for forming the seed example pairs.

The highlight of the results of this illustrative experiment is that this method of learning variations shows improvement over the normal learning method and will be of extensive use in contexts where what is to be learnt is a variation of what is already learnt, and is very similar to it. However, much more detailed experimentation is required with larger and more completely covered training and test sets.

7 PAC-LEARNABILITY OF VARIATIONS

Dzeroski *et al.* (1993) have proved that the ILP problem of learning a set of constrained non-recursive function-free program clauses is PAC-learnable. Each query to the background knowledge should take time polynomial to the maximum arity of the background predicates.

The problem of learning variations on a well-known theme is decomposable into the problems of learning the base knowledge, learning the knowledge that describes positive examples of the variation that are not covered by the base knowledge, and learning the knowledge that describes negative examples of the variation that are covered by the base knowledge.

Learning variations on a well-known theme is PAC-learnable, if and only if each one of these three learning problems is PAC-learnable. Each one of these is PAC-learnable for the set of constrained non-recursive function free program clauses, where each query to the background knowledge takes time polynomial to the maximum arity of the background predicates, and therefore, learning variations on a well-known theme is PAC-learnable.

When we consider learning using strings or sequences as examples, and some background knowledge predicate like 'contains' that operates on the entire string, we note that the above PAC-learnability result is valid only when each query to the background knowledge takes time polynomial to the maximum arity of the background predicates. Therefore, any string parameters used in the predicates should have a constant maximum length, if we are to study the PAC-learnability of learning from string or sequence examples.

8 VARIATIONS AND NOISE

When noisy real-world data is considered, it is difficult to distinguish between valid variations and noise. We do not study this problem in detail in this paper. However, there are a number of broad approaches to tackling this problem.

One approach is the threshold approach. Occurrences below a particular threshold are taken as noise, and only those above the threshold are taken as valid variations. This approach can be used both for attribute noise as well as for classification noise. Attribute noise is when the example is correctly classified, but there are errors in the values of some of the attributes. Differences in the attributes form a variation only if they involve a sufficiently large number of attributes. A difference in only a single attribute could well have been due to noise, rather than a genuine variation. So, in handling attribute noise, the number of attributes that are different have to be larger than a threshold.

Classification noise is when some examples are wrongly classified. In handling classification noise, the threshold is in the number of examples that are involved. A change is a variation only if it has a sufficiently large number of examples.

It is possible that in the threshold approach, genuine variations can easily be classified as noise, if they do not pass the threshold. However, this approach has the advantage of being relatively simple to understand and implement.

Srinivasan *et al.* (1992) have done much work in the area of distinguishing exceptions from noise. It may be possible to extend this work to distinguish valid variations from noise.

9 VARIATIONS AND INCREMENTAL LEARNING

Layered learning (Muggleton 1993) first takes a small sample from a stream of data and uses this to construct an approximately correct theory. A second approximately correct theory is then constructed based on the errors of the first theory in a new sample which is a superset of the first, and further layers of correcting theories are added using successively larger samples until a specified level of overall theory accuracy is achieved. This builds successive approximately correct theories, gradually bringing them to the required level of accuracy.

Non-monotonic learning (Bain and Muggleton, 1991) is a learning area where the coverage of a learnt model changes non-monotonically. As new examples are received, the original knowledge changes so as to either include describing the new example (generalization) or exclude description of the new counter-example (specialization).

Non-monotonic learning and layered learning are both forms of incremental learning, where some knowledge is known initially, and more knowledge is then learnt incrementally. Variations also involve the incremental learning of knowledge, but the learning of new knowledge is in order to describe a concept that is different from the original one. Knowledge was learnt initially to describe the base concept, and now knowledge is learnt in order to describe correctly another concept - the variation.

Incremental learning can however be considered as a special

case of the concept of variations, where the new knowledge to be learnt results in a more accurate form of the original knowledge. The concept of variations contains within it as a special case, many forms of incremental learning. We now look at local exceptions in inductive logic programming and see how these are also a particular type of variations.

10 LOCAL EXCEPTIONS IN ILP

Ripple-down rule sets were introduced by Compton and Jansen (1988). From a knowledge representation point of view, one of the main features of rules is that they tend to have exceptions. Realistic rules are of the form ' *if* P *then* u *unless* Q'. To represent such a rule, an exception rule ' *if* Q *then* v ' may be placed before the rule ' *if* P *then* u'. However, this raises serious problems because of the global ordering of the rules. The exception rule thus introduced may interfere with other rules that do not have the same exceptions as the rule ' *if* P *then* u'. Hence, there is a need for representing exceptions in a more localized manner.

Ripple-down rule sets provide a formalism for representing exceptions in a localized manner. For instance, assigning x to class + if and only if it satisfies exactly one of the conditions P_1 and P_2 is easily achieved by the following two ripple-down rules.

<table>
<tr><td>if P_1 then</td><td>if P_2 then</td></tr>
<tr><td>   if P_2 then -</td><td>   if P_1 then -</td></tr>
<tr><td>   else + fi</td><td>   else + fi</td></tr>
<tr><td>else - fi</td><td>else - fi</td></tr>
</table>

Note that by giving all the exceptions locally, the need for a global ordering of the rules has been eliminated. The ripple-down rule set given above is of depth 2, since 2 is the depth of the nesting of the *if* statements. If the exception rules are allowed to have exception rules etc, then depth t ripple-down rule sets are obtained for $t > 2$.

Let us now consider the following general example of a logic program that can be learnt using inductive logic programming:

$$q(X,\ldots) :- p1(X,\ldots), \ldots .$$
$$q(X,\ldots) :- p2(X,\ldots), \ldots .$$

$$.$$
$$.$$
$$.$$
$$q(X,\ldots) :\text{-} pk(X,\ldots), \ldots.$$

Using the concept of local exceptions of depth 2 in ILP we get the following logic program that can be learnt:

$$q(X,\ldots) :\text{-} p1(X,\ldots), \ldots, not\ (r1(X,\ldots)).$$
$$r1(X,\ldots):\text{-} p11(X,\ldots), \ldots.$$
$$r1(X,\ldots):\text{-} p12(X,\ldots), \ldots.$$
$$.$$
$$.$$
$$r1(X,\ldots):\text{-} p1k(X,\ldots), \ldots.$$

$$q(X,\ldots) :\text{-} p2(X,\ldots), \ldots, not\ (r2(X,\ldots)).$$
$$r2(X,\ldots):\text{-} p21(X,\ldots), \ldots.$$
$$.$$
$$.$$
$$r2(X,\ldots):\text{-} p2k(X,\ldots), \ldots.$$

$$.$$
$$.$$
$$.$$

$$q(X,\ldots) :\text{-} pk(X,\ldots), \ldots, not\ (rk(X,\ldots)).$$
$$rk(X,\ldots):\text{-} pk1(X,\ldots), \ldots.$$
$$.$$
$$.$$

This can be extended to cover depths > 2.

11   LEARNING LOCAL EXCEPTIONS IN ILP

We modify the ILP algorithm GOLEM to take care of local exceptions as well.

E^+ is the set of given positive examples and E^- is the set of given negative examples. The GOLEM learning algorithm is first applied using E^+ as the set of positive examples, and E^- as the set of negative examples (as usually done). However, now rules are learnt even if they also cover some of the negative examples, as long as they cover more positive examples than negative. Once the best rule is learnt, then the same learning algorithm is recursively applied, but now, the set of positive examples used is that of the examples covered by that learnt rule in E^-; and similarly, the set of negative examples now used, is that of the examples covered by that learnt rule in E^+. The rule now being learnt will cover the exceptions to the rule learnt at the first level of learning. Similarly, at the next level of recursion, the set of positive examples used is the set of examples covered by the previous level rule in its set of negative examples, and so on.

This recursive process continues for a fixed maximum level of recursion (as much as is felt feasible computationally, as well as in being able to understand the rules learnt), or until the required number of examples are already covered.

When any particular rule is under consideration, it is checked to see that the number of examples it covers in the set of negative examples is less than the number of examples it covers in the set of positive examples. However, when the lowest level of recursion is reached, then there will be no further recursion, and so the negative examples covered by this rule cannot be learnt as an exception rule in the next round of learning. Therefore, the rule being learnt now is ensured to not cover more than a threshold number of examples in the current set of negative examples. This threshold is set at such a level that stray misclassification of examples (some amount of classification noise) will be eliminated.

Using the threshold value helps to filter out noise in the example sets. This also means, however, that very specific exceptions will not be learnt as exceptions, but would rather be treated as noise. The exception examples would be used to learn an exception rule only when there are a sufficient number of them, and this number of exception examples is greater than the threshold value. Srinivasan *et al.* (1992) present a method that would distinguish exceptions from noise without losing genuine exceptions.

> Let E^+ be a set of positive examples.
> Let E^- be negative examples.
> Let $M_h(B)$ be an h-easy model of background
>   knowledge B .
> Let s be a given sample limit.
> Let $D^+ = E^+$ and $D^- = E^-$.

Let minthreshold be the threshold value used to elimi-
nate stray (noise) coverage in the negative example set.
Let maxdepth be the maximum depth of local exceptions
allowed.
Let depth $= 1$.
Call do_proc(D^+ ,D^- ,depth,maxdepth).

do_proc (D^+ ,D^- ,depth,maxdepth):

DO

> Let Pairs(s) be a random sample of pairs from D^+ .
> Let Lggs = { C: e,e' $\in$ Pairs(s)
>   and C = rlgg({e,e'}) wrt $M_h(B)$
>   and cover of C in D^- less than M }
> where M, the threshold value to be used, is
>   the cover in D^+ , if depth < maxdepth;
>   minthreshold, otherwise.
> Let S be the pair {e,e'}
>   whose rlgg has the greatest cover in Lggs.
> DO
> > Let $T^+ = D^+$.
> > Let $T^+(s)$ be a random sample of size s from T^+
> > Let Lggs = {C:e' $\in T^+(s)$ and C = rlgg(S $\cup$ {e'})
> >   and cover of C in D^- less than M }
> > where M, the threshold value to be used, is
> >   the cover in D^+ , if depth < maxdepth;
> >   minthreshold, otherwise.
> > Find e' which produces the greatest cover in Lggs

Let S = S $\cup$ {e'}.
WHILE increasing-cover.
Let T$^+$ = T$^+$ - cover(rlgg(S),T$^+$).

Add rlgg(S) to the current set of rules.

Let T$^+$ = cover(rlgg(S),D$^-$).
Let T$^-$ = cover(rlgg(S),D$^+$).
If maximum depth not reached (depth < maxdepth),
    call do-proc (T$^+$,T$^-$,depth+1,maxdepth)

Let D$^+$ = D$^+$ - cover(rlgg(S) along with
    exceptions, D$^+$)
WHILE required number of examples in D$^+$ not covered.

12 PAC-LEARNABILITY OF LOCAL EXCEPTIONS IN ILP

In order to show PAC-learnability of local exceptions in ILP, we follow the method used by Dzeroski *et al.* (1993) in proving that the ILP problem of learning a set of constrained non-recursive function-free program clauses is PAC-learnable. The ILP problem is first shown to be convertible to propositional form in polynomial time, and then existing propositional PAC-learning results applied to prove PAC-learnability in inductive logic programming.

The ILP problem of learning a set of constrained nonrecursive function-free program clauses defined by a set of m examples E of the target predicate $q(X_1, X_2, \ldots, X_n)$, and background predicates $p_1, \ldots, p_b$ of maximum arity j, can be converted to a propositional form in $O(\text{poly}(j)mbn^j)$ time, if each query to the background knowledge takes $O(\text{poly}(j))$ to answer. This conversion results in the list of features used for propositional learning and transforms the examples to propositional form. The list of features used for propositional learning is the list of all literals that use predicates from the background knowledge and variables from the set of variables in the target predicate. The examples are converted to propositional form by determining for each example the truth value of each of the above propositional features by calls to the background knowledge. This conversion to the list of features and examples in propositional form is shown to be in polynomial time.

The list of features and examples in propositional form are then used to learn a ripple-down rule set (rules with local exceptions). Kivinen *et al.* (1993) have shown that for a constant depth t, learning the ripple-down rule set is PAC-learnable.

The resulting ripple-down rule set can finally be transformed to program clause form. Each rule in the ripple-down rule set at a given depth is transformed by replacing each feature with the corresponding literal and finally *and*ing with these the *not* of a corresponding exception target. The rules for each exception target are transformed by using the rules for that exception in the ripple-down rule set. This transformation is in polynomial time, for a constant depth t.

Thus we see that local exceptions in inductive logic programming for a set of constrained nonrecursive function-free program clauses are PAC-learnable.

13 VARIATIONS AND LOCAL EXCEPTIONS

A variation is in general a deviation from the base knowledge, but one kind of variation is that where the variation is considered to be a more accurate version of the base knowledge. This particular kind of variation corresponds to the concept of local exceptions. Local exceptions are a form of specializing local default-base single variations. They are specializing variations because the knowledge learnt with local exceptions will describe a subset of the original concept learnt, a subset, since exceptions to the original concept are now deleted. The exceptions are local, since they act locally on the individual rules of the original knowledge. Exceptions are default-base variations, since they modify the original rules only when necessary. As we have seen earlier, in default-base variations, if a test sample is described by the base description, and is not specifically disallowed by the variation description, then it is a valid example of the variation. Local exceptions disallow only the exceptions from the general rule. Local exceptions are single variations, since there is only one variation being considered (that is the more accurate version of the original knowledge). (They are not multiple variations, where any one of several variations may be applicable.)

The logic program for specializing local default-base single variations is of the following form.

```
class(X,...) :- baseclass(X,...).

varforruleone(X,...):-neededone(X,...),
                         not (exceptone(X,...)).
neededone(X,...) :- ....
neededone(X,...) :- ....
...
exceptone(X,...) :- ....
exceptone(X,...) :- ....

...

varforruletwo(X,...):-neededtwo(X,...),
                        not (excepttwo(X,...)).

...


...

baseclass(X,...) :- ..., varforruleone(X,...).
baseclass(X,...) :- ..., varforruletwo(X,...).
...
```

The concept is described by the predicate *class*, and the base description is given by the rules that have *baseclass* as the head. The predicates *varforruleone*, *varforruletwo*, and so on are stub predicates provided in each of the baseclass rules. They are then used as the head of the rules that correspond to the variations acting on rule one, rule two, etc of the base description.

It is apparent from the above logic program that local exceptions are a subcase of this category, and corresponds to the above logic program when neededone, neededtwo, ... are all set to *true*. This is shown in the following logic program.

```
class(X,...) :- baseclass(X,...).

varforruleone(X,...) :- not (exceptone(X,...)).
exceptone(X,...) :- ....
exceptone(X,...) :- ....
...

varforruletwo(X,...) :- not (excepttwo(X,...)).
...


...

baseclass(X,...) :- ..., varforruleone(X,...).
baseclass(X,...) :- ..., varforruletwo(X,...).
...
```

This is the same as the usual local exceptions logic program.

```
exceptone(X,...) :- ....
exceptone(X,...) :- ....
...

excepttwo(X,...) :- ....
...


...

class(X,...) :- ..., not (exceptone(X,...)).
class(X,...) :- ..., not (excepttwo(X,...)).
...
```

14 CONCLUSION

In this paper we have presented the concept of variations on a base theme as applied to the machine learning context. Different features that characterize different types of variations are discussed, and then the concept of variations on a well-known theme discussed in detail.

We present our extended implementation of the ILP algorithm GOLEM. The GOLEM method has been extended so that it is no longer necessary to give all the data as background knowledge in the form of ground predicates. The background knowledge now consists of predicates that operate on the data sequences, and so it is now possible to easily handle predicates such as 'contains' that operate on the entire example or test sequence.

An illustrative experimental example is presented from the field of molecular biology in learning the classification of an amino-acid sequence as a signal peptide. The classification of signal peptide sequences for mammalian data is first learnt as the base knowledge, and then sequences for primates learnt as a variation.

The formalism of ripple-down rule sets is used as local exceptions in ILP, and the GOLEM algorithm is modified to learn local exceptions. It is seen that local exceptions are a special form of variations. PAC-learnability of variations and local exceptions is studied.

The concept of variations is also applicable to other knowledge representation and learning techniques and further work is to be done in using other machine learning techniques to learn variations in different application areas. More work is also required in using and further extending the ILP learning algorithm to other string-based applications.

REFERENCES

Bain, M. and Muggleton, S.H. (1991). Non-monotonic learning. *Machine Intelligence 12* , ed. J. E. Hayes-Michie and E. Tyugu. Oxford University Press, Oxford.

Compton, P. and Jansen, R. (1988). Knowledge in context: a strategy for expert system maintenance. *Proceedings of AI'88: 2nd Australian Joint Artificial Intelligence Conference*, 292–306. Springer-Verlag, Berlin.

Dzeroski, T., Muggleton, S.H. and Russell, S. (1993). Learnability of constrained logic programs. *Machine Learning: ECML-93 European Conference on Machine Learning, Vienna, Austria*, ed. Pavel B. Brazdir, 342–347. Springer-Verlag, Berlin.

Kivinen, J., Mannila, H. and Ukkonen, E. (1993). Learning rules with local exceptions. *Proceedings Euro-COLT*, December.

Muggleton, S.H. (1991). Inductive logic programming. *New Generation Computing*, **8** , 295-318.

Muggleton, S.H. (1993). Optimal layered learning: a PAC approach to incremental sampling. *Proceedings of the Fourth International Workshop on Algorithmic Learning Theory*, 37–44. Springer-Verlag, Berlin.

Muggleton, S.H. and Feng, C. (1990). Efficient induction of logic programs. *Proceedings of the First International Workshop on Algorithmic Learning Theory*, 368–381.

Sakakibara, Y. and Siromoney, R. (1992). A noise model on learning sets of strings. *Proceedings of the Fifth Annual ACM Workshop on Computational Learning Theory*, 295–302. ACM Press.

Shimozono, S., Shinohara, A., Shinohara, T., Miyano, S., Kuhara, S. and Arikawa, S. (1993). Finding alphabet indexing for decision trees over regular patterns: An approach to bioinformatical knowledge acquisition. *Proceedings of the 26th Hawaii International Conference on System Sciences*, 763–72.

Srinivasan, A., Muggleton, S. and Bain, M. (1992). Distinguishing exceptions from noise in non-monotonic learning. *Proceedings of the Second Inductive Logic Programming Workshop*.

9

Inductive Logic Programming With Large-Scale Unstructured Data

Michael Bain

Artificial Intelligence Laboratory, School of Computer Science and Engineering, University of New South Wales, PO Box 1, Kensington, NSW, Australia 2033.

Ashwin Srinivasan

Oxford University Computing Laboratory

Abstract

We report some recent developments from an ongoing project in which a chess endgame domain is providing benchmark experimental tests for the study of concept learning. The King and Rook against King (KRK) endgame is simple enough in chess terms but provides concept learning tasks which can be demanding, as evidenced in previous studies by a number of authors. For learning systems these tasks have highlighted problems of representation, such as the ability to express the structural relationships to be found in learning examples, and other issues like correctness, compression and comprehensibility. Our current focus is on inductive logic programming methods which are based on previously developed systems for the generalization and specialization of normal logic programs. In the current work we are principally concerned with improving these methods to be able to handle more examples during learning. The main contribution of this work consists of a new method of incremental learning, together with new results on a set of concept learning problems taken from the KRK endgame domain.

1 INTRODUCTION

In recent years a theme has been present in a number of commentaries on the state-of-the-art of artificial intelligence in general and machine learning in particular. This is usually expressed as a requirement that research should focus on the 'scaling-up' of laboratory techniques to make ready for their application to real-world problems. A frequent criticism is that workers do not customarily test the methods they have developed beyond applying them to a small set of 'toy' problems. It might be assumed that the effort required to proceed further than these routine experiments lies outwith scientific research and is more properly the concern of technological development. However, it has been the experience of a number of workers in the area of machine learning applied to chess that the problems encountered in such a large domain have forced significant attention to be devoted to basic issues like knowledge representation for learning systems, efficient generalization and confirmation. It might be thought that chess is not representative of the class of real-world problems. In fact relatively simple chess problems have in the past defeated machine learning systems which have otherwise proved rather successful on a range of real-world tasks, e.g. Dolsak and Muggleton (1992); Feng (1992); King *et al.* (1992); Muggleton *et al.* (1992a).

In this work the general approach is to let the induction system operate at any given time with a subset of the total problem domain. Incremental learning is then implemented by iteratively generalizing and specializing the current approximate concept expression. Such a system should eventually converge to the target concept expression, or theory. Our system combines minimal generalization methods with minimal specialization of the current concept expression with respect to a single counterexample. This is then extended to enable the batch generalization and specialization of the current concept expression. These concepts are defined in the paper and the algorithm is presented.

Testing of concept learning systems on the King and Rook against King (KRK) chess endgame domain is reviewed from the illegality tasks of previous work to the optimal depth of win classifiers being currently studied. Issues raised include the need for a relational representation, the ability to use background knowledge in theory construction and rule refinement. It is also clear that efficient generalization allows larger sample sizes. As in the current work, this is further extended by the use of large virtual sets of examples in learning via theory-guided sampling. The technique implies incremental learning, in this case using batches of examples.

We explore different incremental algorithms employing the above methods in order to extend the approach. We discuss two strategies of incremental specialization, which differ in the degree of commitment shown to the elements of partially constructed theories.

An exhaustive database for the KRK domain is a source of example positions, each of which has associated with it optimal depth of win information. The depth of win scale is measured by the number of moves to checkmate. In the current empirical framework the learning task is set as a number of separate sub-problems. A separate set of classification rules is learned for each sub-concept 'black-to-move KRK position won optimally for white in N moves'. Each may be seen as a classification step exactly predicting the optimal distance in moves from a set of positions to the final goal position (i.e. checkmate).

First it is shown that the main problem to be overcome is not generalization, since existing methods are largely adequate. Results are given for the accuracy of classifiers induced by Golem (a generalization-only learning system). These show the need for specialization methods.

Second we report that exact classifiers for 'won in 0 moves' up to 'won in 5 moves' have been learned using two versions of an incremental algorithm. The two approaches are compared and aspects of the induced classification rules are discussed.

Finally we note that the methods described in the paper may be insufficiently powerful to tackle the remaining sub-problems in the domain. This is primarily due to the large numbers of examples involved and the increasing difficulty of the concepts to be learned. Some directions for further work are suggested which may avoid these difficulties.

2 DEFINITIONS

The current work is within the framework of inductive logic programming (ILP) due to Muggleton (1993) which is defined as follows.

Definition 9.1 Inductive logic programming (ILP).

$$
\begin{aligned}
B   &= C_1 \wedge C_2 \wedge \ldots && \text{background} \\
E   &= E^+ \wedge E^- && \text{examples} \\
E^+ &= e_1 \wedge e_2 \wedge \ldots && \text{atoms} \\
E^- &= \overline{f_1} \wedge \overline{f_2} \wedge \ldots && \text{negative literals} \\
H   &= D_1 \wedge D_2 \wedge \ldots && \text{clauses}
\end{aligned}
$$

A is an ILP algorithm iff

$$H = A(B, E) \text{ where for each } D_i$$

$$B \wedge D_i \models e_1 \vee e_2 \vee \ldots$$

and

$$B \wedge H \wedge E^- \not\models \square.$$

We follow Lloyd (1987) in defining normal logic programs.

Definition 9.2 Normal program clause. A normal program clause is a clause of the form $A \leftarrow L_1, \ldots, L_n$ where A is an atom and $L_1, \ldots, L_n$ are literals.

Definition 9.3 Normal logic program. A normal logic program is a finite set of normal program clauses.

In the remainder of this section we will assume that all normal logic programs under discussion are *stratified* as defined in Lloyd (1987).

We now give definitions for the semantics of normal logic programs under SLDNF resolution. For simplicity we will assume that the model of a normal logic program P is equivalent to the success set of P under SLDNF resolution. The set of all ground atoms which can be constructed from predicates and function symbols in P is the Herbrand base of P, $H(P)$. The success set of P is the set of ground atoms $A \in H(P)$ such that there is a (finite) SLDNF-refutation for $P \cup \{\leftarrow A\}$. We use the notation $Ms(P)$ to denote the set of models of a program P. $Ms(P)$ is a subset of the power set of the Herbrand base of P, $Hs(P)$. We now prove a basic theorem in the semantics of normal logic programs.

Theorem 9.4 Unique model for normal logic program.
For a normal logic program P, $M(P)$ is unique.
Proof. Assume the opposite, that there is a normal logic program P with more than one model, call them M1 and M2. Let M1 contain a ground atom a entailed by P which is not in M2. But a is entailed by P, and so M2 cannot be a model for P, which contradicts the assumption. This proves that there is at most one model for a normal logic program. A program P' containing the empty clause has no models, but the empty clause is not a normal program clause by Definition 9.2, so P' is not a normal logic program by Definition 9.3. $\square$

In Bain (1994) we defined the generality relation between sets of clauses in terms of entailment. Then $P \models P'$ iff $Ms(P) \subseteq Ms(P')$. If, as above, $Ms(P)$ and $Ms(P')$ are singletons (unit sets), then this condition only applies if $P = \square$, which is not a normal logic program, or $P' \models P$, i.e. $P \equiv P'$. Consequently we cannot use entailment to define the generality lattice for normal logic programs. In the remainder of this section, we will restrict our attention to the semantics of normal logic programs, and write $M(P)$ to denote the unique model for such a program P. This model is a subset of $H(P)$.

Following Lloyd (1987) we refer to the *definition* of a particular predicate symbol p in a normal logic program P. The definition is taken to be the set of all program clauses in P which have p in their head. We consider the semantics for the definition of a predicate in normal logic programs. This is because our algorithm may introduce a new predicate into the first-order language for specialized programs, thus complicating the semantical relation between the program and its specialization. We use $M(p|P)$ to denote the model for a particular predicate p in a program P. This model is a subset of the Herbrand base for p in P which we write as $H(p|P)$.

Definition 9.5 Predicate model. $M(p|P) = \{a : a \in M(P),\ \mathrm{pred}(a) = p\}$, where $\mathrm{pred}(a)$ denotes the predicate symbol of atom a.

Since we cannot use entailment, we use the result of Theorem 9.4 on the unique model for a normal logic program to define a specialization relation between programs.

Definition 9.6 Generality by model inclusion. Let P_1 and P_2 be normal logic programs. Then P_1 is more general than P_2 iff $M(P_1) \supseteq M(P_2)$. Alternatively we say that P_2 is a specialization of P_1. Similarly, the definition of predicate symbol p in P_1 is more general than the definition of p in P_2 iff $M(p|P_1) \supseteq M(p|P_2)$.

We require the concept of 'intended interpretation', which can be thought of as the abstract model for some target program. In the context of inductive logic programming, a learning example is an element of this intended interpretation. More formally, we have the following definition.

Definition 9.7 Learning examples. Let $\oplus$ be a set of positive examples and $\ominus$ a set of negative examples, such that each $e \in \oplus \cup \ominus$ is a ground atom and $\oplus \cap \ominus = \emptyset$. Then for the intended interpretation $M(P)$ of a target normal logic program P, $e^+ \in \oplus$ only if $e^+ \in M(\mathrm{pred}(e^+)|P)$ and $e^- \in \ominus$ only if $e^- \notin M(\mathrm{pred}(e^-)|P)$.

In Bain (1994) we defined the most general correct specialization (MGCS) of a predicate in a normal logic program with respect to a single negative example. We presented an algorithm, Closed-World Specialisation, and proved that it constructed an element of the MGCS. In this paper we have extended the algorithm to generalize a normal logic program with respect to a single positive example. This algorithm, called UPDATE, is presented in Fig. 9.1. We expect that it will be possible to show using the methods in (Bain 1994) that $P' = \mathrm{UPDATE}(P, e)$ is a minimally corrected transformation of P with respect to e.

Algorithm UPDATE

Input: Normal logic program P and ground atom e such that either
      (1) $P \not\vdash e$ and $e \in \oplus$, or
      (2) $P \vdash e$ and $e \in \ominus$.

Case (1):   /* update w.r.t. a single positive example */

If there is a normal clause $C \in P$ such that
  the body of C does not contain a literal *not(B)* and
  C resolves with e in a finitely failed SLDNF-tree for $P \cup \{\leftarrow e\}$
Then $P' = P \cup \{e \leftarrow\}$.

If there is a normal clause $C \in P$ such that
  the body of C contains a literal *not(B)*, and C resolves with
  e in a finitely failed SLDNF-tree for $P \cup \{\leftarrow e\}$, and there is
  an SLDNF-refutation of $P \cup \{\leftarrow not(B)\}$ with substitution θ
Then either $P' = P \cup \{e \leftarrow\}$ or
$P' = \textbf{UPDATE}(P, B\theta)$, whichever maximizes compression.

Case (2):   /* update w.r.t. a single negative example */

If there is a normal clause $C \in P$ such that
  the body of C does not contain a literal *not(B)* and
  C resolves with e in an SLDNF-refutation of $P \cup \{\leftarrow e\}$
Then
  Let C be the clause $A \leftarrow (B_1, \ldots, B_m)$
  Let $\{V_1, .., V_n\}$ be the variables in A
  Let q be a predicate symbol not found in P
  Let B be $q(V_1, .., V_n)$
$P' = P - \{C\} \cup \{A \leftarrow (not(B), B_1, \ldots, B_m)\} \cup \{B\theta\}$.

If there is a normal clause $C \in P$ such that
  the body of C contains a literal *not(B)*, and there is
  an SLDNF-refutation of $P \cup \{\leftarrow not(B)\}$ with substitution θ
Then $P' = \textbf{UPDATE}(P, B\theta)$.

Output: P'

Figure 9.1. UPDATE algorithm schema.
Recursive algorithm schema for the generalization or specialization of a single clause of a target predicate in a normal logic program with respect to a single positive or negative learning example.

2.1 Incremental learning

The UPDATE algorithm transforms a single clause of a target predicate in a normal logic program given a single example. However, in practice it is often required that a program be updated with respect to a set of examples. Furthermore this situation may occur many times within an incremental learning process which includes alternate training and testing phases. We now discuss a framework within which the UPDATE algorithm may form a component of an incremental learning system. This is based on that of E. Shapiro's formulation of incremental learning (Shapiro 1983). In this framework the incremental learning of a target program is a process in which a sequence of programs is generated. It is assumed that an oracle for the target model, i.e. the intended interpretation of the target program, is available. Let the current program in the incremental sequence be P_i with model M_i, and the target program be P_n with model M_n. At any time, if $M_i \setminus M_n \neq \emptyset$ then P_i is *incorrect*, otherwise P_i is *correct*. Similarly, if $M_n \setminus M_i \neq \emptyset$ then P_i is *incomplete*, otherwise P_i is *complete*.

In the sequence of programs $P_0, P_1, P_2, \ldots$ generated by an incremental learning system, for $i < j < k$, if P_i contains a clause C found to be incorrect, and P_j does not contain C, then no P_k will contain C. This definition leads to the following general schema for an incremental learning system.

For a logic program P with respect to a target model :

> **repeat**
> > **if** P is incorrect **then** *specialize P*
> > **if** P is incomplete **then** *generalize P*
>
> **until**
> > P is complete and correct.

For a learning task we envisage a sequence of programs P_0, P_1, P_2, ... generated by an incremental learning system. The intended interpretation M_n for the target program P_n is a set of ground atoms from which learning examples in the sense of Definition 9.7 are sampled. Learning begins with a training set $T_0 \subseteq M_n$ provided as input to the learning system which outputs program P_0. This is the initializing step of the incremental process. All subsequent steps consist of the following pattern. First, program P_{i-1} is tested with respect to a set of learning examples $\oplus \cup \ominus$ to produce a set of exceptions. The exceptions consist of the elements of $\ominus$ (negative examples) which are entailed by P_{i-1} and the elements of $\oplus$ (positive examples) which are not entailed by P_{i-1}. Second, the exceptions are used in the batch specialization and generalization of P_{i-1}. The processes of batch specialization and generalization, described below, transform clauses in P_{i-1} and produce a set of ground unit clauses. In the final step, these ground unit clauses are themselves generalized and added to P_{i-1}, thus giving the new program P_i.

Note that the test set of learning examples at any step in the incremental process is expected to be disjoint from the training set. If the exceptions set is empty then the incremental process is terminated. At each step a new training set is formed from the union of the previous training set and the exceptions set.

We proceed to describe batch specialization and generalization relative to a set of exceptions. The batch specialization (resp. generalization) P' of a normal logic program P with respect to a set of exceptions $E^- \subseteq \ominus$ (resp. $E^+ \subseteq \oplus$) is constructed by calling the UPDATE algorithm on each element of E^- (resp. E^+) in turn. Using these batch transformations within a single step of an incremental process in which a possibly incorrect and incomplete program undergoes least specialization and least generalization will return a program which will be complete and correct with respect to the examples in the current test set. This is an important property of our incremental method. In contrast, ID3 with windowing (Quinlan 1983) has no equivalent stage where the hypothesis is minimally specialized and generalized with respect to exceptions in the current test set.

Following the steps of batch specialization and generalization the current theory contains ground atoms. These atoms may be generalized with respect to the theory and negative examples in the training and test sets. Generalizing the set of positive examples added by batch generalization may produce an over-general, i.e. incorrect program with respect to the target model. However, such over-generalizations can obviously be corrected on the subsequent cycles of the incremental process. Generalizing the set of instances of an exception predicate will specialize its parent clause. When such generalizations are made, it is important to ensure that consistency between the exception predicate and its parent is maintained. In our method this is accomplished by storing the set of all training examples used to induce the initial theory and all exception examples used to update subsequent versions of the theory. This prevents any generalization which covers negative examples, and any specialization which does not cover positive examples.

We note that in this incremental method no clause will contain more than one negated literal, i.e. the exception literal. Additionally, we do not consider the incremental learning of programs where the target predicate is invoked by some other predicate. In such cases, changing the model of the target predicate by generalization or specialization affects the model of the invoking predicate. It may be possible to formalize this constraint on the invocation of the target predicate by defining the stratification restrictions required.

3 THE KRK DOMAIN

In a number of commercial applications machine learning has delivered significant cost benefits (Michie 1987; Michie 1989). Many of these successes in real world applications depended on methods originally developed and extensively tested in the laboratory on problems of inducing classifiers for chess endgame positions. This work was typically concerned, as is ours, with domain-independent general purpose inductive inference, despite the fact that chess endgames were the common experimental domain, e.g. Michalski and Negri (1977); Quinlan (1983); Altman *et al.* (1979); O'Rorke (1982); Shapiro (1987); Paterson (1983); Muggleton (1987).

As indicated in Section 1 chess endgame tasks have highlighted issues such as knowledge representation for learning systems. A well-studied case in the recent ILP literature comes from the domain of the chess endgame King and Rook against King (KRK). The target concept is the predicate 'White-to-move position is illegal'. In a comparative study (Muggleton *et al.* 1989) it was concluded that the ability to produce high performance in this domain was almost entirely dependent on the ability to express first-order predicate relationships.

This domain has since become something of a benchmark test for relational learning algorithms by a number of authors, e.g. Quinlan (1990); Lavrac *et al.* (1991). The same KRK illegality domain has served to illustrate issues including correctness (specialization) and compression (noise tolerance) for ILP algorithms, e.g. Bain (1991); Pazzani *et al.* (1991); Brunk and Pazzani (1991); Muggleton *et al.* (1992b). Employing an incremental ILP algorithm based on generalization in first-order logic (Muggleton and Feng 1990) and specialization by predicate invention (Bain and Muggleton 1991) enabled the induction of a complete and correct solution for the KRK illegality problem (Bain 1992).

A much harder problem in the KRK domain is the following. Could a machine learn to play a simple chess endgame *optimally* given only example positions and some simple facts about the geometry of the board? In the remainder of this paper we consider results from induction experiments which could legitimately form part of a feasibility demonstration for such a project. First we describe the representation and form of learning examples used in this task.

Chess endgames are complex domains which are enumerable. Endgame databases are tables of stored game-theoretic values for the enumerated elements (legal positions) of the domain. The game-theoretic values stored denote whether or not positions are won for either side, or include also the depth of win (number of moves) assuming minimax-optimal play. From the point of view of experiments on computer induction such databases provide not only a source of examples but also an oracle (Roycroft 1986) for testing induced rules. However a chess endgame database differs from, say, a relational database containing details of parts and suppliers in the following important respect. The combinatorics of computing the required game-theoretic values for individual position entries independently would be prohibitive. Therefore all the database entries are generated in a single iterative process using the 'standard backup' (retrograde analysis) algorithm (Thompson 1986).

A database is an ordered list of game-theoretic values for all positions in the endgame. In our case, the truth value for the predicate 'won-for-white with black-to-move' for every position is stored. The depth of win is also recorded for each position. This allows the database to be used to play the endgame 'optimally', using only a legal-move generator and a database look-up program. The size of databases is governed by the total number of piece combinations (positions) for the pieces on the board. Without removal of redundancies, an endgame contains on the order of 64^N positions, where N is the number of pieces in the ending. The combinatorial explosion makes an exhaustive enumeration impossible for endgames of more than a few pieces.

Reductions of roughly an order of magnitude in the size of an endgame domain are possible through various symmetries. The potential reduction is less if there are pawns in the endgame. Symmetry in the space of positions of an endgame is exploited in an attempt to minimize the storage size and generation complexity of a database for that endgame. Symmetries reduce the number of positions in the database by storing only one value for a set of positions equivalent by combinations of reflections or rotations.

The retrograde analysis method for generating chess endgame databases employs reduction of the space of positions by removing from consideration those positions equivalent to a canonical set by symmetry. Consequently, any legal position which could be encountered for example in over-the-board play must be translated to its canonical equivalent before its database value may be retrieved. The exact symmetries which may be exploited vary according to the pieces in the endgame. In the KRK database used to provide examples for the current work three types of symmetrical translation were applied. These are diagrammed in Fig. 9.2.

Only information on black-to-move (BTM) positions was extracted from the database. However, this is sufficient to allow optimal play using only a legal move generator which is operated with 2-ply (1 move) lookahead. Since every won position is tagged in the database with its minimax-optimal depth of win value, and the learned definitions contain the same values, this method holds also to allow the output of the learning-from-

Table 9.1. Depth of win, optimal play.

Depth is depth of win for white in moves with black-to-move; Number is number of positions. There are a total of 25 260 wins. Together with 2796 draws this gives a total of 28 056 positions used for positive and negative example sets.

Depth	Number	Depth	Number
0	27	9	1712
1	78	10	1985
2	246	11	2854
3	81	12	3597
4	198	13	4194
5	471	14	4553
6	592	15	2166
7	683	16	390
8	1433	Total	25260

examples method to play optimally.

By the removal of redundancy due to symmetries the total space of legal canonical positions in the KRK endgame is reduced from a potential 262 144 to 28 056. In the BTM database used in our experiments the number of legal positions won-for-white was 25 260. Each of these positions is tagged with its depth of win value. The number of positions in each depth of win class is given in Table 9.1.

Using a Prolog syntax, the examples and target program have the top-level predicate krk/7. The first argument gives the depth of win in moves for a minimax-optimal strategy. The other six arguments specify positions by the file and rank (x and y) chessboard coordinates of, respectively, the White King, White Rook and Black King.

4 INDUCING COMPLETE CLASSIFIERS (NOT GUARANTEED CORRECT)

As can be seen from Table 9.1, in the KRK endgame the maximum depth of win for BTM positions is 16 moves. If draws are thought of as infinite-depth wins then the BTM database can be partitioned by depth of win into 18 disjoint subsets.

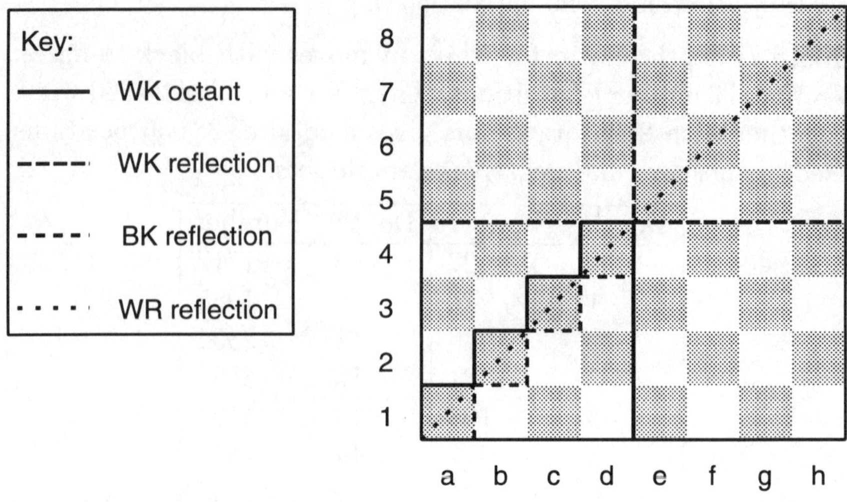

Figure 9.2. Canonical KRK positions.

WK octant—the ten squares {a1, b1, c1, d1, b2, c2, d2, c3, d3, d4}
are the canonical locations for the White King (WK).

WK reflection—reflection about the axes indicated places the WK in
a canonical location:

> if the WK is above the central horizontal (rank 5 or greater),
> reflect the WK below (into the lower half of the board);

> if the WK is right of the central vertical (file e or greater),
> reflect the WK to the left of (into the left half of the board);

> if the WK is above the diagonal a1 to h8,
> reflect the WK below this diagonal (into the WK octant).

BK reflection—with the WK on squares a1, b2, c3 or d4 and
the Black King (BK) above the diagonal a1 to h8, reflect the BK
about this axis to place it below the diagonal.

WR reflection—with both WK and BK on the diagonal a1 to h8
and the White Rook (WR) above the diagonal, reflect the WR
about this axis to place it below the diagonal.

Each subset can be viewed as a separate classifier, answering
database queries relating to its depth of win. We begin the task
of learning optimal strategies for the endgame by treating each
classifier separately. For each depth of win, the relevant subset

provides the positive training examples, and the remaining sub-sets provide the negative training examples. The first stage is to generalize these examples. We expect generalization to compress the positive examples, in the sense that the description complexity of the generalized examples, or hypothesis, is less than that of the original examples. It is to be expected that the gain in compression will be at the expense of introducing some incorrectness into the hypothesis. Whereas the original examples were complete and correct (in the sense discussed in Section 2) for a fixed depth of win, the hypothesis is likely to cover positions at other depths of win.

The method described in Section 4.1 produced separate classifiers for each depth of win. These were tested against the database as described in Section 4.2.

4.1 Induction method

The learning method treated the problem of learning an optimal KRK strategy as 18 independent sub-problems. Each depth of win was a separate sub-problem. The learning method was to generalize the example positions for each depth of win using GOLEM. This guarantees completeness but not necessarily correctness. For instance, to induce a classifier for depth of win D three example sets would be constructed. All positions won at depth D formed the set of positive examples. All other positions formed the universe of negative examples. From this universe a subset of the same size as the set of positive examples was chosen randomly (sampling with replacement) to form the set of negative examples. The background examples consisted of ground instances of the predicates 'symmetric difference' (defined below in Section 5.1) and 'strictly less than' ($<$) for all unordered pairs of the file values $\{a, \ldots, h\}$ and all unordered pairs of the rank values $\{1, \ldots, 8\}$.

For large example sets or problems involving few regularities GOLEM may fail to find a generalization. In such cases the algorithm simply outputs the set of positive training examples as its hypothesis. This occurred once in the current work, when no generalization was found for the depth 14 sub-problem. Although draws are treated as one of the depths of

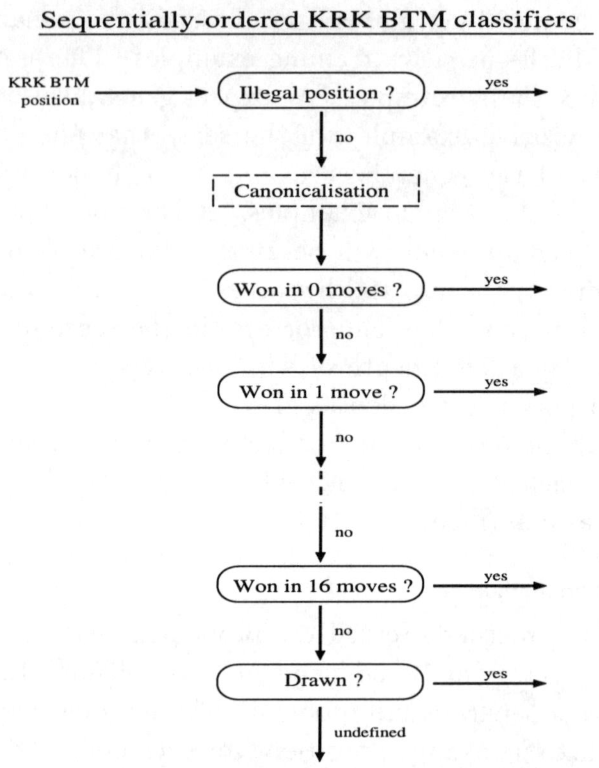

Sequentially-ordered KRK BTM classifiers

Figure 9.3. Top-level structuring of KRK BTM position classifiers.

win in our framework, no separate classifier was induced for this sub-problem. By default, therefore, in the testing phase the set of positive training examples consisting of all drawn positions was used as the corresponding hypothesis. Consequently, the classifiers for depth 14 and draw were complete and correct. However, a considerable penalty is paid for these properties in terms of description complexity.

4.2 Testing sequentially ordered classifiers

The method of testing the induced classifiers treated all eighteen as ordered sub-problems (see Fig. 9.3). To test the classifier at depth D three example sets were constructed. All positions won at depth D formed the test set of positive examples. All positions won at depth greater than D formed the test set of negative examples. The background examples were as for the training stage as described in Section 4.1.

248

A classifier for depth D has two outputs, yes and no. The total number of 'machine guesses' made in each of these categories for the test sets of positive and negative examples was recorded. In Table 9.2 some of these results are shown.

Table 9.2 also highlights in column four the penalty paid in terms of description complexity by the depth 14 and draw classifiers. Although both complete and correct, they are more than two orders of magnitude greater in complexity (4553 and 2796 clauses, respectively) than most of the other classifiers.

Issues of completeness and correctness are manifested in greater detail in Table 9.3. The completeness of all classifiers is clearly illustrated, in that no classifier for depth D fails to account for all positions it sees which are in fact won in D moves. Also clearly apparent from this confusion matrix is the fact that the depth 14 classifier is complete and correct. The level of incorrectness for depth < 16 classifiers is such that all 390 positions won optimally in 16 moves are misclassified, primarily by the depth 15 and depth 13 classifiers.

A similar effect is seen for draws, but with a striking difference. Whereas for other depths most misclassifications of positions won in D occur in classifiers for $D - 1$, $D - 2$, in other words close to D, with draws the misclassification profile is much more evenly spread. The number of misclassified draws peaks at 455 with the depth 6 classifier. A possible reason for this is that most draws in the domain are due to the white rook being *en prise*. These are likely to contain positional patterns quite similar to those in won positions, where the rook is safe.

4.3 Summary

From Table 9.3 we can see that since all classifiers are complete, there are no positions predicted as won in D moves which are actually won in $< D$ moves. This is because any position which is in fact won at depth D will be correctly identified as such by the classifier for depth D. For each depth D classifier (except for depths 14, 16 and draw) there are many positions actually won at depth $> D$ which are predicted as won optimally in D moves. This illustrates the incorrectness of these classifiers. In view of the obvious incorrectness of the induced theory in this work, it

Table 9.2. Incorrectness of sequentially ordered BTM classifiers by depth of win.

Depth is the depth in moves of a win for white with black-to-move; Correctly predicted is the number of positions correctly classified as won at Depth; Total predicted (not shown in table) is the total number of positions classified as won at Depth; Incorrectly predicted is Total predicted less Correctly predicted. Description complexity is the number of Prolog clauses in each classifier. Classifiers for depth 14 and draw are the respective sets of ungeneralized positive training examples (see text for details).

Depth	Correctly predicted	Incorrectly predicted	Description complexity
0	27	99	2
1	78	433	3
2	178	178	5
3	48	418	4
4	63	1098	8
5	181	2022	9
6	67	2793	9
7	90	3427	11
8	76	1118	23
9	183	4441	23
10	221	2276	25
11	143	634	53
12	359	2517	77
13	473	1696	109
14	1163	0	4553
15	1146	410	22
16	0	0	12
draw	0	0	2796
Total	4496	23560	7744

Table 9.3. Confusion matrix for sequentially ordered BTM classifiers.

The ordering of the complete classifiers results in zeroes for cells above the leading diagonal. All positions won at depth 16 or drawn are incorrectly classified as won at depths less than 16, and hence left nothing for the depth 16 classifier to work on. Note that the pattern of misclassification of draws differs from other depths of win. See text for further details.

Actual depth of win from BTM database against depth of win predicted by BTM classifiers

Predicted → / Actual ↓	0	1	2	3	4	5	6	7	8	9	10	11	12	13	14	15	16	draw	Total
0	27	0	0	0	0	0	0	0	0	0	0	0	0	0	0	0	0	0	27
1	0	78	0	0	0	0	0	0	0	0	0	0	0	0	0	0	0	0	78
2	0	68	178	0	0	0	0	0	0	0	0	0	0	0	0	0	0	0	246
3	0	1	32	48	0	0	0	0	0	0	0	0	0	0	0	0	0	0	81
4	0	3	26	106	63	0	0	0	0	0	0	0	0	0	0	0	0	0	198
5	0	6	26	178	80	181	0	0	0	0	0	0	0	0	0	0	0	0	471
6	0	16	13	27	160	309	67	0	0	0	0	0	0	0	0	0	0	0	592
7	0	33	16	24	69	245	206	90	0	0	0	0	0	0	0	0	0	0	683
8	0	23	6	41	147	432	451	257	76	0	0	0	0	0	0	0	0	0	1433
9	4	59	1	11	83	373	330	569	99	183	0	0	0	0	0	0	0	0	1712
10	11	68	6	6	75	164	379	623	122	310	221	0	0	0	0	0	0	0	1985
11	16	63	10	0	118	198	344	678	174	805	305	143	0	0	0	0	0	0	2854
12	20	60	17	0	92	112	265	571	209	943	761	188	359	0	0	0	0	0	3597
13	10	9	9	0	71	35	212	289	120	1057	432	229	1248	473	0	0	0	0	4194
14	6	0	0	0	58	5	147	218	78	874	332	57	846	769	1163	0	0	0	4553
15	0	0	0	0	14	0	4	27	30	148	175	17	128	477	0	1146	0	0	2166
16	0	0	0	0	0	0	0	0	1	3	37	0	1	121	0	227	0	0	390
draw	32	24	16	25	131	149	455	195	285	301	234	143	294	329	0	183	0	0	2796
Total	126	511	356	466	1161	2203	2860	3517	1194	4624	2497	777	2876	2169	1163	1556	0	0	28056

<u>Algorithm GCWS</u>

<u>Input</u> : P_i, training, test, background

  <u>if</u> training $= \emptyset$ <u>then</u>

    $P_f = P_i$

  <u>else</u>

    $P = \mathrm{Gen}(\text{training}, \text{background})$

    $P' = P_i \cup P$

    $\langle P'', \text{exceptions}\rangle = \mathrm{Spec}(P', \text{test}, \text{background})$

    $P_f = \mathrm{GCWS}(P'', \text{exceptions}, \text{test}, \text{background})$

<u>Output</u> : P_f

Figure 9.4. GCWS algorithm schema.

is worth recalling that the problem we are attacking is a difficult one. That this is so is apparent from a past failed attempt made by unaided human experts to construct by analysis an optimal classifier theory. Clarke (1977) established (by constructing a database) that, contrary to previously published statements in standard texts, KRK was won for white in a maximum of sixteen moves.

5 INDUCTION OF COMPLETE AND CORRECT CLASSIFIERS

From the results of the previous section it is notable that although complete and in most cases compressed (more concise than the training examples) the classifiers at all depths of win where generalization took place are incorrect. This seems a suitable test, therefore, of the specialization methods discussed in Section 2. In this section we describe the induction of complete and correct classifiers for depths of win from 0 to 5 moves.

5.1 Method

We adopted an inductive logic programming approach, using a new version of an algorithm called GCWS ('Generalising Closed-World Specialisation') which was originally developed in Bain

(1994). The implementation of the new version was done by Ashwin Srinivasan. GCWS is closely related to the UPDATE algorithm presented in Section 2. In particular, the generalization and specialization steps of GCWS incorporate methods corresponding to the processes of batch generalization and batch specialization. GCWS is an incremental learning algorithm which can select its examples through theory-guided sampling. This means that at any stage in the incremental sequence it will ignore examples which are redundant with respect to its current hypothesis. A large number of examples are tested against the current hypothesis. Only those found to be exceptions are used in subsequent learning. This has the benefit that concepts can be learned from 'virtual' example sets possibly very much larger than could be be handled by a 'one-shot' learning system. The principle was notably demonstrated by Quinlan (1983) in the ID3 system where it was termed 'windowing'.

The top-level algorithm of GCWS is in Fig. 9.4. The generalization step of GCWS appears as a function call 'Gen(training, background)'. In the current version this is implemented using an algorithm based on Muggleton and Feng's GOLEM system (1990) developed by Ashwin Srinivasan. This system is called *CWSGolem* due to its ability to perform closed-world specialization. It is additionally equipped with a confirmation method using HP-compression (Muggleton *et al.* 1992b).

Testing of the current hypothesis to select exceptions appears in Fig. 9.4 as a function call 'Spec(P', test, background)'. In Bain (1994), where Golem was used as the generalization step of GCWS, the specialization step used closed-world specialization to transform the current hypothesis with respect to the exceptions. Under this method any clause in the current hypothesis found to be incorrect or incomplete was transformed as in the UPDATE algorithm. Any ground atoms generated during this step were then added as input to the generalization step. This is referred to in the current work as Strategy 1 specialization. However we have also implemented an alternative specialization method which we refer to as Strategy 2 specialisation.

The idea behind Strategy 2 is to make less commitment to clauses in the current hypothesis than is the case during closed-world specialization. The method requires maintaining for each clause the set of positive and negative examples used to construct that clause. If a clause is found to be incorrect by covering some exceptions, under Strategy 2 the clause is deleted and a new set of examples is constructed by adding the exceptions to the set of examples associated with that clause. This new set of examples is then used as input for the subsequent generalization step. The main consequence is that whereas in Strategy 1 a corrected clause would remain substantially the same as it was before exceptions were discovered, in Strategy 2 it may be replaced by a completely new clause or set of clauses.

To avoid bias of the method by supplying the learning algorithm with a large number of predefined domain-specific background predicates, the background knowledge was restricted to contain only one specifically chess-oriented geometrical relation, namely the symmetric difference between files and between ranks. This is defined as follows: for two file (resp. rank) values V_1 and V_2 the symmetric difference is $\mathrm{abs}(V_1 - V_2)$, where $V_1, V_2 \in \{1, \ldots, 8\}$ and $\mathrm{abs}(X)$ is X if $X \geq 0$ or $0 - X$ otherwise. Other background predicates available were num/1, specifying the ranks 1–8 and files a–h, and edge/1, specifying the edges of the board along rank and file.

These background predicates were selected as basic building blocks for the expression of piece relations in terms of the geometry of the chess board. In particular, they facilitate expression of the types of attack and counter-attack relationships which would seem to be essential for the expression of higher-level chess concepts such as capture, safety, check, etc. Thus they supply some of the raw materials for relevant predicate invention in chess domains.

Each depth of win was treated as a separate learning problem, in line with the structure shown in Fig. 9.3. At each depth of win, the positive examples are exactly those positions in the database which are won for white at that depth, and the negative examples are those positions won at higher depths. Negative examples are selected randomly, in samples of at most 1000 at a time. Note that this learning framework therefore assumes a control strategy in which learned rules will always be tested in increasing order of depth of win, as in Fig. 9.3. This affects the declarative meaning of the independently induced classifiers. Only legal, canonical positions will be correctly classified. Any classifier for depth D is only complete and correct for positions at depths $\geq D$.

5.2 Results

krk(0, c, 2, a, A, a, 2) :- not(ab3(0, c, 2, a, A, a, 2)).
krk(0, c, A, a, B, a, 1) :- not(ab2(0, c, A, a, B, a, 1)).
krk(0, A, 3, B, 1, A, 1) :- not(ab1(0, A, 3, B, 1, A, 1)).

ab1(0, A, 3, B, 1, A, 1) :- diff(A, B, d1).

ab2(0, c, A, a, 2, a, 1).

ab3(0, c, 2, a, A, a, 2) :- diff(2, A, d1).

Figure 9.5. BTM WFW depth 0 classifier in Prolog.

5.2.1 *Complete and correct classifiers for depths 0 to 5*

The GCWS incremental algorithm was run to induce six separate complete and correct classifiers for depths of win of 0 to 5 moves. This was done using both specialization strategies discussed in the previous section. For comparison, batch learning of these sub-problems was also attempted using *CWSGolem*, although this was only successful for depths of win 0 to 2 moves. In this section we show in Figs. 9.5 and 9.6 classifiers in Prolog for depths 0 and 1 respectively, learned under the Strategy 2 condition. We also represent graphically in Fig. 9.7 the classifier for depth of win 2, learned under the Strategy 2 condition.

In Fig. 9.7 the Prolog classifier is represented as an and–or tree. The top-level predicate is krk/7, the first argument of which is always 2 and is therefore omitted in this diagram. The other six arguments are ordered as for krk/7, described in Section 3. Boxes indicate terminal nodes. These are unit clauses either of the top-level predicate, a machine-invented (i.e. abnormality) predicate or a background predicate. Ovals indicate

```
krk(1, A, 3, B, C, D, 1) :- diff(A, B, d2), diff(A, D, d1), diff(B, D, d1),
                    not(ab5(1, A, 3, B, C, D, 1)).
krk(1, c, A, B, C, a, D) :- diff(A, C, d2), diff(A, D, d1),
                    not(ab4(1, c, A, B, C, a, D)).
krk(1, c, 2, A, B, a, 1) :- not(ab3(1, c, 2, A, B, a, 1)).
krk(1, c, 2, A, 3, a, 2) :- not(ab1(1, c, 2, A, 3, a, 2)).

ab1(1, c, 2, a, 3, a, 2).

ab3(1, c, 2, A, 2, a, 1).
ab3(1, c, 2, A, B, a, 1) :- diff(2, B, d1).

ab4(1, c, A, a, B, a, C).
ab4(1, c, A, b, B, a, C).

ab5(1, A, 3, B, 2, C, 1).
ab5(1, A, 3, B, 1, C, 1).
```

Figure 9.6. BTM WFW depth 1 classifier in Prolog.

non-terminal nodes. Non-terminal nodes are clauses either of
the top-level or a machine-invented predicate. Prolog conventions are used for variables (upper-case) and constants (lower-
case).

For brevity we have not included the classifiers for depths 3
to 5 in this paper.

5.2.2 *Comparison of specialization strategies*

The two specialization strategies discussed above were compared both on the number of clauses and invented predicates
appearing in the final theory (see Table 9.4) and on the relative
compression of the examples by the final theory (see Table 9.5).

In Table 9.4 the complexity of induced classifiers is measured
simply by counting the number of Prolog clauses and the number
of machine-invented abnormality predicates. This was done for
all classifiers from depth 0 to 5 corrected by both specialization
strategies, i.e. incrementally learned, and for classifiers from
depth 0 to 2 where all examples were initially available, i.e.
batch learned. To a reader familiar with Prolog these figures
give an indication of the ease of understanding of each classifier.

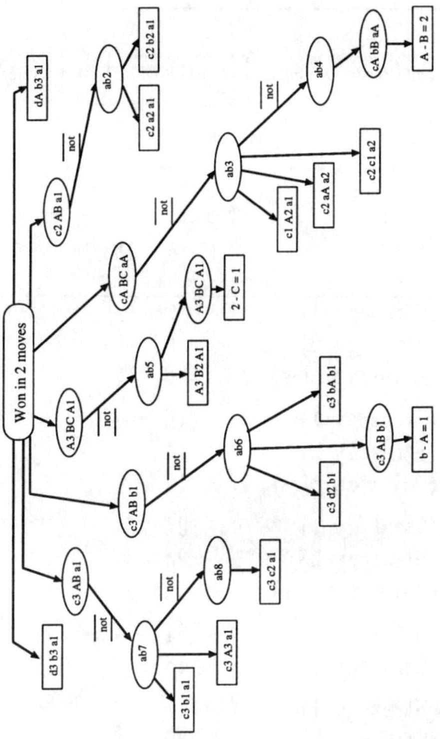

Figure 9.7. Tree-structured representation of depth 2 classifier.
The Prolog classifier is represented as an and–or tree. Nodes labelled 'abN'
indicate machine-invented predicates. Prolog conventions are used for variables and constants. Arguments as for krk/7, without depth.

Table 9.5 contains results of the complexity of the induced
classifiers measured in terms of their encoding size in bits. Within the Hypothesis-Proof (HP) compression framework proposed
in Muggleton *et al.* (1992b) a Universal Turing Machine model is
used to represent the induction process. The learning examples
appear on the output tape of this machine, while the hypothesis (a logic program) plus a specification of the derivation of the
examples from the hypothesis appear on the input tape. If the
encoding size in bits of the input tape is less than that of the
output tape then the hypothesis is judged to be more compact
than the examples. This is expressed as positive compression of
the examples by the hypothesis. For the induced classifiers, under both specialization strategies and the batch learning method

Table 9.4. Comparison of specialization strategies—representation change.

Theory	No. of clauses	No. of ab predicat es invented
Depth 0 (Strategy 1)	9	5
Depth 0 (Strategy 2)	6	3
Depth 0 (All examples)	6	3
Depth 1 (Strategy 1)	16	7
Depth 1 (Strategy 2)	11	4
Depth 1 (All examples)	12	4
Depth 2 (Strategy 1)	31	7
Depth 2 (Strategy 2)	23	7
Depth 2 (All examples)	12	6
Depth 3 (Strategy 1)	61	17
Depth 3 (Strategy 2)	44	12
Depth 4 (Strategy 1)	116	38
Depth 4 (Strategy 2)	89	22
Depth 5 (Strategy 1)	338	88
Depth 5 (Strategy 2)	185	40

where applicable, the hypothesis and proof encoding sizes appear in Table 9.5 as a sum (hypothesis plus proof equals input tape). The encoding size for the examples (output tape) is given on the line below the entries for each classifier.

5.2.3 *Learning common sub-concepts for depths 0 to 1*

Learning classifiers independently has the disadvantage that common sub-concepts across different depths of win are not detected. In Fig. 9.8 we give results from an attempt to learn sub-concepts common to classifiers at different depths of win. Within the current learning framework this was only attempted for depths 0 and 1. The combined set of exceptions to the classifiers shown in Figs. 9.5 and 9.6 provided as learning examples

Table 9.5. Comparison of specialization strategies—HP compression.

Theory	encoding size in bits
Depth 0 (Strategy 1)	3491(+88935 = 92426)
Depth 0 (Strategy 2)	3174(+77524 = 80698)
Depth 0 (All examples)	3177(+77524 = 80701)
Examples	278893
Depth 1 (Strategy 1)	4310(+112116 = 116426)
Depth 1 (Strategy 2)	3633(+96964 = 100597)
Depth 1 (All examples)	3588(+100482 = 104070)
Examples	278608
Depth 2 (Strategy 1)	4931(+138474 = 143405)
Depth 2 (Strategy 2)	4381(+126438 = 130819)
Depth 2 (All examples)	4329(+120802 = 125131)
Examples	277833
Depth 3 (Strategy 1)	7322(+164311 = 171633)
Depth 3 (Strategy 2)	5784(+151253 = 157037)
Examples	275388
Depth 4 (Strategy 1)	12608(+189444 = 202052)
Depth 4 (Strategy 2)	9035(+178885 = 187920)
Examples	274583
Depth 5 (Strategy 1)	30974(+230402 = 261376)
Depth 5 (Strategy 2)	15445(+206555 = 222000)
Examples	272614

to induce a common abnormality theory. The resulting classifier for depths 0 and 1 appears in Figure 9.8.

5.3 Discussion

The three top-level clauses in the depth 0 classifier (Fig. 9.5) have a similar structure. Typically the clause head arguments constrain the White King (WK) and the Black King (BK) to be in opposition, with the White Rook (WR) attacking the BK. However, clause 2 also covers six positions where the kings are not in opposition, with WK on c2 and BK on a1. In this classifier the exception predicates ab1, ab2 and ab3 all exclude positions in which the WR is *en prise*. This is a typical exception since capture of the WR by the BK is an automatic draw.

It should be borne in mind that the execution order for clas-

---

```
krk(0, c, 2, a, A, a, 2) :- not(ab(0, c, 2, a, A, a, 2)).
krk(0, c, A, a, B, a, 1) :- not(ab(0, c, A, a, B, a, 1)).
krk(0, A, 3, B, 1, A, 1) :- not(ab(0, A, 3, B, 1, A, 1)).
krk(1, A, 3, B, C, D, 1 ) :- diff(A, B, d2), diff(A, D, d1), diff(B, D, d1),
                             not(ab(1, A, 3, B, C, D, 1)).
krk(1, c, A, B, C, a, D) :- diff(A, C, d2), diff(A, D, d1),
                            not(ab(1, c, A, B, C, a, D)).
krk(1, c, 2, A, B, a, 1) :- not(ab(1, c, 2, A, B, a, 1)).
krk(1, c, 2, A, 3, a, 2) :- not(ab(1, c, 2, A, 3, a, 2)).


ab(A,B,C,D,2,E,1).
ab(A,c,B,a,C,a,D) :- diff(C,D,d1).
ab(A,B,C,D,E,F,G) :- diff(B,D,d1), diff(C,E,d2), diff(D,F,d1),
                     not(ab1(A,B,C,D,E,F,G)).
ab(1,A,3,B,1,C,1).
ab(1,c,2,A,B,a,1) :- diff(2,B,d1).


ab1(1,c,2,b,4,a,1).
```

Figure 9.8. BTM WFW combined depths 0 and 1 classifier in Prolog.

---

sifiers shown in Fig. 9.3 affects the example set from which each
classifier is induced. Therefore, for example, no illegal positions
need to be excepted from the coverage of a clause since none appear in the example set for any classifier. Additionally, a different ordering of classifiers might save more exceptions. Checking
for draws first instead of last should be investigated, since many
exceptions concern coverage of drawn positions.[1] The reader
should also bear in mind when inspecting classifiers that only
canonical positions appear in the database from which learning
examples are taken, which excludes many positions equivalent
by symmetry to the canonical set (see Fig. 9.2).

Inspection of the depth 1 classifier in Fig. 9.6 illustrates how
the independent classifiers could be linked via a legal move generator for canonical positions to play the endgame optimally.
Clause 1 of the depth 1 classifier covers the position WK:c3,
WR:a5; BK:b1. From this position there is a 1-move forced se-

---

[1]This was suggested to us by Ross Quinlan.

quence, with the BK moving from b1 to c1 and the WR coming from a5 to a1 to force checkmate. The final position WK:c3, WR:a1; BK:c1 is covered by clause 3 of the depth 0 classifier in Fig. 9.5.

The classifiers for depths 0 and 1 are similar to those for the same tasks learned as part of an earlier study (Bain 1994). As part of that work depth 0 and 1 classifiers were validated as meaningful by a chess expert. Expert validation of the induced classifiers has not been attempted for this work, but if it could be done it would mark a significant result, particularly for depths of win ≥ 2.

By referring to the database, certain features of the depth 2 classifier shown in tree form in Fig. 9.7 can be elucidated. The branch headed 'c3 AB a1' represents a clause covering examples where the BK is in a corner of the board and the WK is in diagonal opposition. Again, the clause represented by the branch headed 'A3 BC A1' has the Kings in opposition with the BK on the edge. This clause alone covers about $\frac{1}{3}$ of the 246 positions won at depth 2. In fact, together with the clause 'cA BC aA' about $\frac{2}{3}$ of the total positions are covered, due to the large board area for Rook placement. There is an interesting range of exceptions to these clauses, from depths 3, 4 and 7, as well as drawn positions. The clause 'dA b3 a1' groups together three positions such that the WK is one move away from the defending WR. Several clauses in the depth 2 tree contain exceptions to exceptions, a feature which is not seen at depths 0 or 1. Further work is necessary to test whether these machine learned concepts could be readily taught to humans and used by them in classification.

Since the KRK database used to supply the learning examples in this work is exhaustive, and the rules comprising our classifiers for depths 0 to 5 are complete and correct with respect to this database as discussed above, the question arises as to what evaluation method is appropriate for these classifiers. We discussed above some aspects of classifiers for depths 0 to 2 in terms of concept descriptions, even whether as concept descriptions the classifiers might be assimilable by humans.

We now turn to consider whether the induced classifiers are

more compact than their respective example sets. The results in Table 9.5 show that for both specialization strategies the classifiers for depths 0 to 5 are more compact than their respective example sets, i.e. they show positive compression. Within the framework of HP-compression (Muggleton *et al.* 1992b) this result indicates that the classifiers may be regarded as significant hypotheses [2]. However, the size of this positive compression for classifiers decreases as depth of win increases. A similar trend in increasing classifier complexity is apparent from Table 9.4, measured by number of clauses and invented predicates in each classifier. The relatively low compression gained for the depth 5 classifier, together with the time required to complete the incremental learning of this classifier, led us to conclude that application of the current approach to depth 6 was unlikely to be successful.

The alternative specialization strategies used with GCWS for correcting the faulty definition of a culprit predicate in an incorrect theory may be summarized as follows. We refer to the top-level predicate krk/7 and the background predicates as *fixed*. The definition of all other predicates can be revised during the learning process. Strategy 1 recursively corrects the definition of one or more predicates used in the definition of the culprit predicate. Strategy 2 discards the definitions of all non-fixed predicates used in the definition of the culprit predicate and re-learns the definition of this predicate.

Strategy 2 is clearly reminiscent of decision-tree induction using windowing. However, unlike windowing only some part of the theory (i.e. that which is involved in the incorrect definition) is reconstructed. In general, there is a distinct difference in theories obtained by the two strategies. Strategy 1 is biased toward correcting theories by introducing new predicate symbols. This is apparent in Table 9.4, where Strategy 2 classifiers consistently have fewer clauses and abnormality predicates. From Table 9.5 it is clear also that Strategy 2 classifiers are more compressive

---

[2]The significance of a hypothesis is estimated from the data compression it produces. The meaning of a k-bit compression is that the probability of obtaining positive k-bit compression by chance is at most 2^{-k}.

than those for Strategy 1. These results show the tendency of Strategy 1 to produce more complex theories. Since it would appear advisable to minimize this complexity, Strategy 2 seems to provide an efficient alternative.

Within the current learning framework classifiers are induced independently. However, use of common concepts (for example, Rook safety) can result in further savings in the number of clauses constructed and the number of new predicates that are invented. As can be seen from Fig. 9.8 the combined theory for depths 0 and 1 contains a total of 13 clauses, 7 for the top-level krk predicate and 6 for the 2 invented abnormality predicates. This compares with a total of 17 clauses and 7 invented abnormality predicates from the independently learned classifiers for depths 0 and 1.

6 CONCLUDING REMARKS

Although progress may seem modest, we believe some aspects of the current work are significant. The datasets used in these KRK experiments qualify as large-scale and unstructured in the following usage of those terms. Informally, large-scale data may be thought of as at the limit or beyond the capabilities of the existing ML methods we customarily use. Again, unstructured data does not contain explicit problem decomposition relations. On both of these (admittedly loose) definitions the problem seems to be a challenging one. Because of this, progress is likely to be slow.

The current work has produced results which exceed our best previous solution, which only included classifiers for depth of win 0 (checkmate) and depth of win 1 positions. More importantly, we would suggest, they demonstrate the potential applicability of this method of incremental learning in a non-monotonic logic representation. To date the principal successes with ILP applications have been restricted to a definite clause logic representation. In addition such successes have required all examples to be present at the start of learning. For many real-world problems this will not be the case. For instance, the problem of learning integrity constraints from logic databases typically requires dealing with database updates over time, necessitating a continuously changing theory.

However it appears unlikely that the current methods will be successfully applicable to learning optimal depth of win classifiers for more than 5 moves to checkmate in our KRK domain. The depth 5 classifier comprises 187 clauses, with 471 positions in the database won optimally in 5 moves. Recall that the number of positions won optimally in 14 moves is 4553. It seems that further progress will depend on approaching the learning task in a different way, or changing the learning methods being used.

One way to change the learning task would be to change the context in which the separate classifiers are used. For example, instead of a sequential organization in which classifiers are interrogated in ascending order from depth 0, a tree-structured regime containing a hierarchy of sub-concepts might be used. In such a scheme the top-level theory would classify a position as 'won in greater than 8 moves'; the next level in the binary tree would adjudicate positions 'won in greater than 4 moves' or 'won in greater than 12 moves'; etc. Another alternative could be to have a similar, flatter tree containing a top-level with classifiers such as 'won in at most 2 moves', 'won in at most 5 moves', 'won in at most 8 moves', etc, and lower levels containing closer-to-optimal classifiers. Finally, the constraint on optimality could also be relaxed.

The decline in compression for classifiers as depth of win increases does however suggest that more powerful predicate invention methods may be be required if the framework of learning separate classifiers for each optimal depth of win is to be retained.

Acknowledgements

Support was provided to Ashwin Srinivasan by SERC under contract GR/J05699, the Rule-Based Systems Project. This work would not have been possible without the facilities made available to the authors by the Department of Statistics and Modelling Science at Strathclyde University and the Turing Institute. We thank Donald Michie for his invaluable comments and suggestions regarding this work, and Stephen Muggleton who originally proposed the problem and assisted us by running Golem to produce the even-numbered KRK BTM classifiers described in Section 4.

REFERENCES

Altman, M., Cheng, A. and Galeota, S. (1979). 'AQ11: Experiments and Evaluation', C.S. 397. University of Illinois at Urbana Champaign.

Bain, M. (1991). Experiments in non-monotonic learning, *in* L. Birnbaum and G. Collins, eds, ML-91: *Proceedings of the Eighth International Workshop on Machine Learning*, Morgan Kaufmann, San Mateo, CA, pp. 380–384.

Bain, M. (1992). Learning optimal chess strategies, *in* S. Muggleton, ed., *ILP 92: Proc. Intl. Workshop on Inductive Logic Programming*, Vol. ICOT TM-1182, Institute for New Generation Computer Technology, Tokyo, Japan.

Bain, M. (1994). *Learning Logical Exceptions in Chess*, PhD thesis, University of Strathclyde.

Bain, M. and Muggleton, S. H. (1991). Non-monotonic learning, *in* J. E. Hayes, D. Michie and E. Tyugu, eds, *Machine Intelligence 12*, Oxford University Press, Oxford, pp. 105–119.

Brunk, C. and Pazzani, M. (1991). An investigation of noise-tolerant relational concept learning examples, *in* L. Birnbaum and G. Collins, eds, 'ML-91: *Proceedings of the Eighth International Workshop on Machine Learning*, Morgan Kaufmann, San Mateo, CA, pp. 389–393.

Clarke, M. R. B. (1977). A quantitative study of king and pawn against king, *in* M. R. B. Clarke, ed., *Advances in Computer Chess*, Vol. 1, Edinburgh University Press, Edinburgh, pp. 108–118.

Dolsak, B. and Muggleton, S. (1992). The application of Inductive Logic Programming to finite element mesh design, *in* S. Muggleton, ed., *Inductive Logic Programming*, Academic Press, London, pp. 453–472.

Feng, C. (1992). Inducing temporal fault diagnostic rules from a qualitative model, *in* S. H. Muggleton, ed., *Inductive Logic Programming*, Academic Press, London, pp. 473–493.

King, R., Muggleton, S. and Sternberg, M. (1992). Drug design by machine learning: The use of inductive logic programming to model the structure-activity relationships of trimethoprim analogues binding to dihydrofolate reductase, *Journal of the National Academy of Sciences*.

Lavrac, N., Dzeroski, S. and Grobelnik, M. (1991). Learning non-recursive definitions of relations with LINUS, *in* Y. Kodratoff, ed., 'EWSL-91: *Proceedings of the European Working Session on Learning*, Springer-Verlag, Berlin, pp. 265–281.

Lloyd, J. W. (1987). *Logic Programming*, 2nd Edition, Springer-Verlag, Berlin.

Michalski, R. S. and Negri, P. (1977). An experiment in inductive learning in chess end-games, *in* E. W. Elcock and D. Michie, eds, *Machine Intelligence*, Vol. 8, Edinburgh University Press, Edinburgh, pp. 168–201.

Michie, D. (1987). Current developments in expert systems, *in* J. R. Quinlan, ed., *Applications of Expert Systems*, Turing Institute Press in association with Addison-Wesley, Wokingham, pp. 137–156.

Michie, D. (1989). Problems of computer-aided concept formation, *in* J. R. Quinlan, ed., *Applications of Expert Systems* (Vol. 2)', Turing Institute Press in association with Addison-Wesley, Wokingham, pp. 310–333.

Muggleton, S. H. (1987). Duce, an oracle-based approach to constructive induction, *in IJCAI-87*, Kaufmann, Los Altos, CA, pp. 287–292.

Muggleton, S. H. (1993). 'Mode-directed Inverse Resolution'.

Muggleton, S. H. and Feng, C. (1990). Efficient induction of logic programs, *in Proceedings of the Workshop on Algorithmic Learning Theory*, Ohmsha, Tokyo, pp. 368–381.

Muggleton, S. H., Bain, M. E., Hayes-Michie, J. and Michie, D. (1989). An experimental comparison of human and machine learning formalisms, *in* A. Segre, ed., *Proceedings of the Sixth International Workshop on Machine Learning*, Kaufmann, Los

Altos, CA, pp. 113–118.

Muggleton, S., King, R. and Sternberg, M. (1992a). Predicting protein secondary structure using inductive logic programming, *Protein Engineering* **5**, 647–657.

Muggleton, S., Srinivasan, A. and Bain, M. (1992b). Compression, significance and accuracy, *in* D. Sleeman and P. Edwards, eds, *ML-92: Proceedings of the Ninth International Workshop on Machine Learning*, Morgan Kaufmann, San Mateo, CA, pp. 338–347.

O'Rorke, P. (1982). A comparative study of inductive learning systems AQ11P and ID3 using a chess end-game test problem, ISG 82-2, Computer Science Department, Univ. of Illinois at Urbana–Champaign.

Paterson, A. (1983). An attempt to use cluster to synthesise humanly Intelligible Subproblems for the KPK Chess Endgame, Technical Report UIUCDCS-R-83-1156, University of Illinois, Urbana, IL.

Pazzani, M., Brunk, C. and Silverstein, G. (1991). A knowledge-intensive approach to learning relational concepts, *in ML-91: Proceedings of the Eighth International Workshop on Machine Learning*, Morgan Kaufmann, San Mateo, CA, pp. 432–436.

Quinlan, J. R. (1983). Learning efficient classification procedures and their application to chess end games, *in* R. Michalski, J. Carbonnel & T. Mitchell, eds, *Machine Learning: An Artificial Intelligence Approach*, Tioga, Palo Alto, CA, pp. 464–482.

Quinlan, J. R. (1990). Learning logical definitions from relations, *Machine Learning* **5**(3), 239–266.

Roycroft, A. J. (1986). Database 'oracles': Necessary and desirable features, *ICCA Journal* **8**(2), 100–104.

Shapiro, A. D. (1987). *Structured Induction in Expert Systems*, Turing Institute Press with Addison-Wesley, Wokingham, UK.

Shapiro, E. Y. (1983). *Algorithmic Program Debugging*, MIT Press, Cambridge, MA.

Thompson, K. (1986). Retrograde analysis of certain endgames, *ICCA Journal* **8**(3), 131–139.

APPLIED MACHINE LEARNING

10

Discovery of Protein Structural Constraints in a Deductive Database using Inductive Logic Programming

Ross D. King, Dominic A. Clark, Jack Shirazi, and Michael J.E. Sternberg

Imperial Cancer Research Fund, 44 Lincoln's Inn Fields, London, WC2A 3PX, UK, rd_king@icrf.ac.uk

Abstract

This paper describes a framework for the use of machine learning as a tool to aid scientists in the discovery of patterns in data. The framework is tested by the application of the inductive logic programming (ILP) program GOLEM to the discovery of constraints in the packing of beta-sheets in alpha/beta proteins. These constraints (rules) play a part in the protein folding problem, an important unsolved problem in molecular biology. Constraints were learnt for four features of beta-sheet packing: the winding direction of two sequential sheets, whether two sequential sheets pack parallel or anti-parallel, whether two sheets pack adjacently, and whether a beta-sheet is at an edge. Investigation of the constraints found revealed interesting patterns, some of which were previously known, others that were novel. Novel features include the discovery that the relationship between pairs of sequential strands is in general one of decreasing size, and that more sequential pairs of strands wind in the direction out than the direction in. We conclude that machine learning has a role for scientists as a pattern discovery tool.

1 INTRODUCTION

1.1 Machine learning as a tool for scientists

In this paper, machine learning is viewed as a tool to aid scientists in the discovery of patterns in data. It is considered to be an alternative method to examining data 'by eye' (perhaps using sophisticated visualization software), or the use of statistical methods. We see the process of applying machine learning to a scientific problem as an interactive cycle between the scientist and a machine learning program (Fig. 10.1).

- The scientist first identifies the biological problem of interest.

- A formal data representation is created that is intended to capture the important features of the problem.

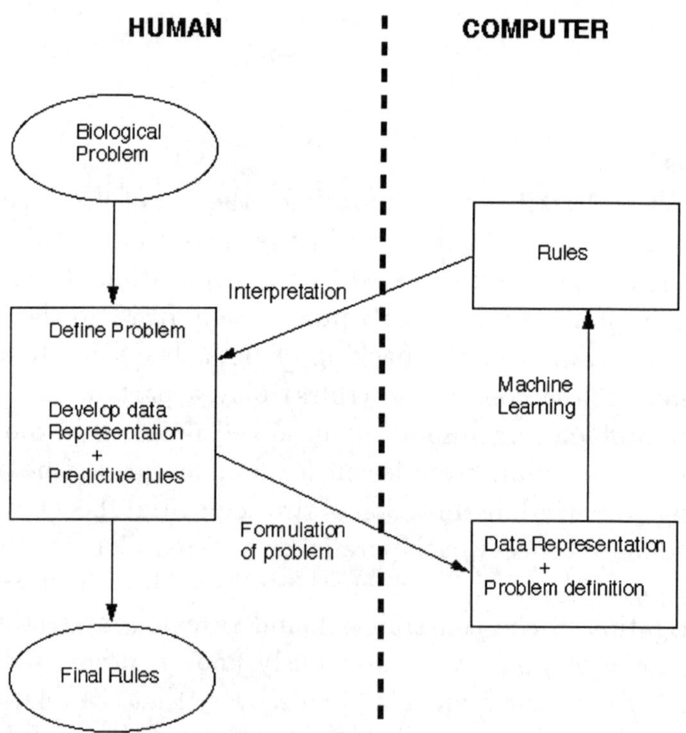

Figure 10.1. Diagram illustrating the cycle of interaction between scientist and machine learning program.

- The actual data is then translated into this formalism to produce a model of the problem.

- This data is input into the machine learning system and rules generated.

- The scientist then examines the rules to gleam any regularities and patterns in the data that are of scientific interest.

- If this cycle is successful the newly discovered regularities can be used to form a better data representation and the cycle repeated.

To test this view of machine learning we have applied the inductive logic programming (ILP) program GOLEM to the discovery of constraints in the packing of beta-sheets in alpha/beta proteins.

The application of machine learning to the discovery of patterns in scientific data is known as 'scientific discovery'. Even by the standards of AI it has had a controversial history. For example, it has been claimed that Boyle's, Kepler's, and Ohm's Laws were 'rediscovered' by the program Bacon (Langley *et al.* 1987), and that the program AM 'rediscovered' the concept of the natural numbers (Lenat and Brown 1984) . Whether such laws and concepts were really rediscovered has been a matter of debate (e.g. Shaffer 1989; Gray *et al.* 1988) . But what is clear is that the application of machine learning to current scientific problems is essential for the development of the field: e.g. Gray *et al.* (1988) state that 'a project that attempts to demonstrate the effectiveness of some chosen scheme for learning or discovery really does require a predictive component and should attempt to work with real-world data'.

1.2 The problem

A problem from structural molecular biology was chosen to test the application of machine learning to the discovery of patterns in scientific data. Molecular biology is currently undergoing an outburst in the amount of data and is therefore in great need of automatic tools to aid scientists. The particular problem studied was the discovery of constraints in the folding patterns of alpha/beta proteins. To understand the relevance of this problem it is necessary to understand a little about the structure of proteins.

Proteins consist of linear chains of amino-acids (Schulz and Schirmer 1978) . These chains spontaneously fold up to form complicated three-dimensional shapes, which particular shape depending on the sequence of amino-acids. The shape formed by the protein defines its properties, e.g. whether it is an enzyme, antibody, etc. The problem of predicting what shape will form from a sequence is known as the *protein folding problem.* It remains one of the most important and intractable problems in molecular biology. Its solution is increasingly urgent, as it is much easier to determine the amino-acid sequence of proteins ($>$ 50 000 sequences known) than their shape ($<$ 1000 structures known). Although both number are increasing rapidly, the mismatch between the number of sequences is set to grow with the continued progress of the human genome project. There is now so much available data that the traditional methods of examining it are becoming infeasible. For example, at one time a crystallographer would intimately know the structure of every crystallized protein—this is no longer possible. Automatic methods of pattern discovery are therefore needed to cope with the large amount of data.

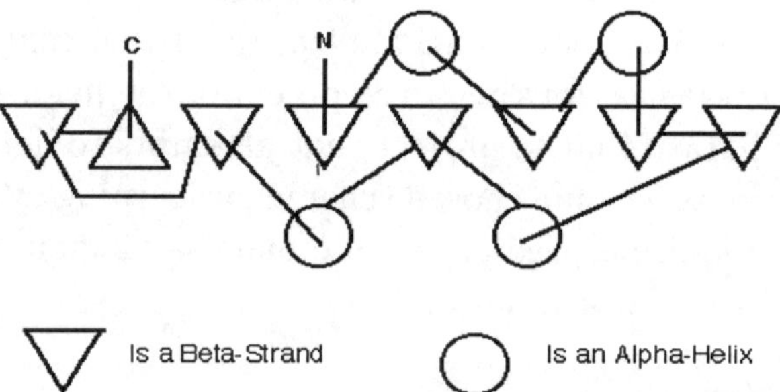

Figure 10.2. Schematic diagram showing how the secondary structure elements in the protein dihydrofolate reductase pack together.

A common approach to the protein folding problem is to exploit the existence of several levels of structure in the shape of proteins—a divide and conquer strategy. At the lowest level of

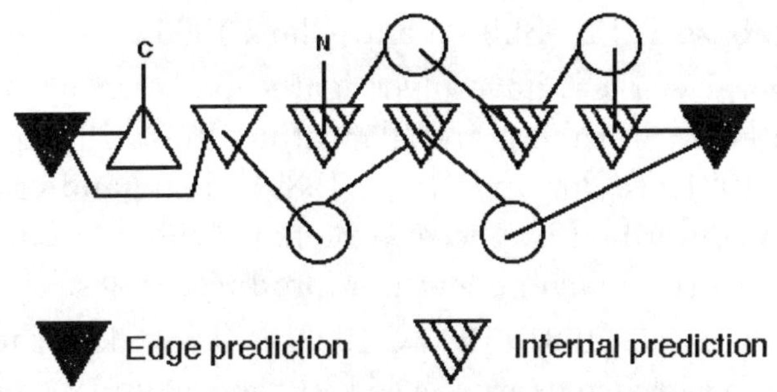

Figure 10.3. Schematic diagram showing edge and not_edge predictions for the protein dihydrofolate reductase.

structure is secondary structure; two main types of secondary structure have been recognized, alpha-helices, and beta-strands. Many methods have been proposed for predicting protein secondary structure from amino-acid sequences (Garnier *et al.* 1978; Muggleton *et al.* 1992a; Rost and Sander 1993). However, the success of these predictions has been limited to a ceiling of about 70%. It is generally believed that the reason for this is that there are constraints on secondary structure imposed by higher levels of protein structure. Such higher levels of structure include the packing together of beta-strands to form beta-sheets, the clustering together of beta-sheets and alpha-helices to form protein domains, etc. In this paper constraints are learnt relating how beta-strands can pack together to form sheets (Fig. 10.2).

A further way of simplifying the general protein folding problem is to consider only one sub-type of protein at a time. One of the most important sub-types of proteins consists of those formed by only alpha/beta domains, that is they consist of repeated alpha-helices and beta-strands. These domains were chosen as a test bed for our application of machine learning. Several factors make these proteins particularly suitable for testing the application of machine learning.

- The relevant data for the problem exists in a form suitable for machine learning. The data consists of Prolog clauses using the symbolic representation scheme developed for the TOPOL database of protein topology (Rawlings *et al.* 1985) . This data is embedded in the deductive database PIPS (Shirazi and Clark 1993).

- Several workers have investigated patterns in alpha/beta proteins (Sternberg and Thornton 1977a, 1977b; Richardson 1981; Taylor and Green 1989). The hand-crafted patterns described by these workers provide a useful comparison to the machine learning produced rules.

- Clark *et al.* (1991, 1993a, 1993b) have taken the existing hand-crafted patterns, checked their validity, and formalized them, in the process additionally formalizing some rules of their own. They have used these rules in an algorithm for predicting the domain packing structure of a protein from its secondary structure. The rules are formalized as constraints in the constraint logic programming language ElipSys (Vernon *et al.* 1993). The rules generated by machine learning can be directly tested against the hand-crafted rules on the task of predicting protein domain structure.

1.3 Machine learning

The ILP program GOLEM Muggleton and Feng (1990) was chosen as the inductive method for pattern discovery. The reasons for this were that the data already exists in a data format suited to ILP, we consider ILP to be better suited than attribute methods to machine discovery problems in general, and we have successfully applied GOLEM to other related problems in biological structures. GOLEM has previously been applied to the prediction of protein secondary structure (Muggleton *et al.* 1992a), and the design of drugs to fit into proteins (King *et al.* 1992). The protein data exists in a logic programming format; this data consists of complicated relations that reflect the complicated structures of proteins. These relations would be difficult to represent using attributes. We consider ILP programs more suitable for machine discovery than attribute-based ones because: they can better express background knowledge (there is commonly a great deal of relevant background knowledge in scientific discovery problems), and they can learn a more general set of concepts (it is difficult to represent many scientific concepts using attributes).

2 METHODS

2.1 Database of proteins

The proteins chosen were of class alpha/beta. The original data comes from the PIPS deductive database of protein topologies (Shirazi and Clark, 1993) , which is in turn derived from the IDITIS relational database (marketed by Oxford Molecular and developed by Gardner and Thornton, extending the work of Islam and Sternberg (1989)). The PIPS database is a deductive database implemented in the constraint logic-programming language ElipSys. The selection of proteins was carried out using the non-homologous set of protein folds described by (Orengo *et al.* 1993). All protein domains were chosen that are in the IDITIS database and the Orengo sub-classes (80 Str) Alpha/Beta; Doubly Wound, Alpha/Beta; One Doubly Wound, and Alpha/ Beta; Two Doubly Wound. Domains in the Orengo sub-class Alpha/Beta Tim Barrel were excluded because of problems in the designation of barrels in IDITIS database. The data was further filtered by removal of homologous beta-sheets, so that for each protein only non-homologous sheets were included. This gave the following set of proteins: 1CSE: Substilin Carlsberg (*B. Subtilis*), 2FCR: Flavodoxin (*C. Crispus*), 2TRX: Thioredoxin (*E. Coli*), 3ADK: Adenylate Kinase (Porcine), 3CHY: Chey Protein (*E. Coli* B), 3PGM: Phosphoglycerate Mutase (*S. cerevisiae*), 4DFR: dihydrofolate Reductase (*E. Coli* B), 4FXN: Flavodoxin (*Clostridium MD*), 5CPA: Carboxypeptidase A (Bovine), 5P21: Ras P21 Protein (Human), 1GD1: Glyceraldehyde Phosphate Dehydrogenease (*B. Stearothermophilus*), 1PHH: P Hydroxybenzoate Hydroxylase (*P. Fluorenscens*), 2TS1: Tyrosyl–Transfer RNA Synthetase (*B. Stearothermophilus*), 3GRS: Glutathione Reductase (Human), 6LDH: Lactate Dehydrogenase (Dogfish), 8ADH: Alcohol Dehydrogenase (Horse), 8CAT: Catalase (Bovine), 1RHD: Rhodenase (Bovine), 2LIV: Leucine/Isoleucine/Valine Binding Protein (*E. Coli*), 2YHX: Yeast Hexokinase B (*S. cerevisiae*), 3GBP: Glucose Binding Protein (*S. Typhimurium*) Orengo uses *E. Coli*, 3PGK: Phosphoglyerate Kinase (*S. cerevisiae*), 4PFK: Phosphofructokinase (*B. Stearother-mophilus*). From this set the following proteins were randomly chosen as a test set (7 from 23): 3ADK, 3CHY, 4FXN, 1GD1, 8ADH, 1RHD, 3GBP. The remaining proteins were used as a training set.

2.2 Representation in Prolog

The ILP program GOLEM was used in this study. GOLEM takes as input: positive examples, negative examples, and background knowledge described as Prolog ground clauses. The Prolog representation used in GOLEM is a modified version of that used in TOPOL (Rawlings *et al.* 1985) . It draws on the experience of the representations used to represent protein sequences in (Muggleton *et al.* 1992a) and drugs in (King *et al.* 1992, 1993).

1°   ...A C F C I L W Y A A P L M T R V G F W M L M P V G ...

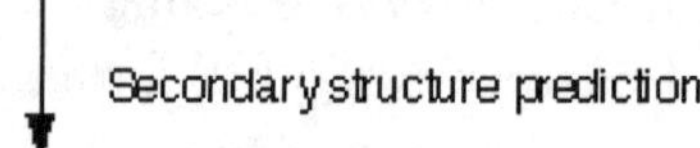

2°   ...H H H H H H H T T T T T T T B B B B B B B B B B B B B ...

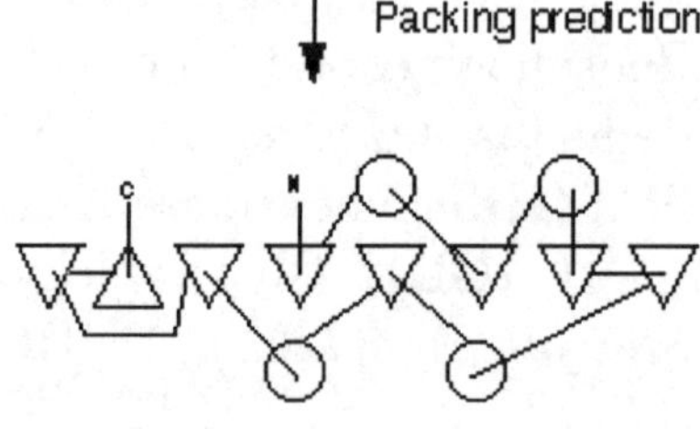

Figure 10.4. Hierarchical prediction of protein structure. Secondary structure is first predicted from primary structure, then secondary structure packing is predicted. This paper is concerned with rules to aid in packing prediction.

In the learning experiments a basic set of background facts was used. Using these facts, a number of different predicates describing alpha/beta proteins were learned. The basic idea is that the background knowledge consists of facts that could be assumed to be known after a successful secondary structure prediction (Fig. 10.4). From this information it is possible to predict the next level of protein structure, how the secondary structure elements pack together. The learnt descriptive predicates describing alpha/beta proteins will aid in this prediction of protein structure. For each descriptive predicate, rules were learned for it and its negation: e.g. predicate foo(A), and not foo(A). It was aimed to produce rules that had high accuracy and statistical significance. It was not intended that rules would necessarily cover all the examples, i.e. discriminate between examples with and without the foo predicate. The reasons for this are: the rules are intended to be input into a constraint–satisfaction algorithm, and the rules are intended to be understandable to protein chemists. The constraint–satisfaction algorithm deals with uncertain rules by minimizing a linear cost function based on individual costs of the form $-K\log(\text{Odds})$.

2.2.1 *Descriptive predicates*

The four types of packing rules were learnt, they are represented by PROLOG facts as follows:

$edge(P, S)$.

In protein P strand S is positioned at the edge of a sheet.

$parallel(P, S1, S2)$.

In protein P consecutive strands S1 and S2 are parallel.

$adj(P, S1, S2)$.

In protein P strands S1 and S2 are adjacent in a sheet.

$in(P, S1, S2)$.

In protein P consecutive strands S1 is closer to the edge than strand S2.

2.2.2 *Background structural knowledge*

Background knowledge about proteins secondary structure is needed to learn packing constraints. This relates to the lengths of beta-strands, and the lengths and composition of the connections between the strands. This type of information is very difficult to represent by traditional statistical or neural-network type approaches. The structural background knowledge was represented as PROLOG facts as follows:

$seql(P, S, L)$.

In protein P strand S has length L.

$con\_helix(P, S1, S2, H)$.

In protein P strands S1 and S2 are joined by H helices.

$con\_length(P, S1, S2, R)$.

In protein P strands S1 and S2 are joined by R residues.

$con\_to\_helix1(P, S1, S2, N)$.

In protein P between S1 and S2 the first helix has id. N.

$con\_to\_helix2(P, S1, S2, N)$.

In protein P between S1 and S2 the last helix has id. N.

$con\_to\_chain1(P, S1, S2, N)$.

In protein P between S1 and S2 the first coil has id. N.

$con\_to\_chain2(P, S1, S2, N)$.

In protein P between S1 and S2 the last coil has id. N.

2.2.3 *Background hydrophobic knowledge*

It has previously been recognized that the hydrophobicity and relative hydrophobicity of beta-strands plays an important place in determining their packing. Therefore, background knowledge representing this information was put into GOLEM (using the scale of Kyte and Doolittle). This is represented as PROLOG facts as follows ('In P,E' means in protein P sheet E: 'hydro. energy' is hydrophobic energy the sum of hydrophobicities of the residues in the strand):

$th(P, E, S, Ht)$.

In P,E, strand S has a hydro. energy of Ht.

$avh(P, E, S, Ha)$.

In P,E, strand S has an average hydro. energy of Ha.

$rth(P, E, S, Htr)$.

In P,E, strand S has a rank of hydro. energy of Htr.

$rhy(P, E, S, Har)$.

In P,E, strand S has a rank of average hydro. energy of Htr.

2.2.4 *Background arithmetical knowledge*

Each piece of secondary structure (strand, helix, turn, and loop) has a number that allows its position to be related in sequence to the other structures using arithmetic relational predicates. Typed arithmetical information is also given for the various predicates above. The use of types disallows the finding of spurious rules, e.g. equating the rank of total hydrophobic energy to the number of helices separating it to the next strand (it is an inductive bias).

2.2.5 *Data size*

For each of the data sets there were 9263 background facts in the training data and 8047 background facts in the test data. The training data for the predicate edge consisted of 71 foreground examples and 91 negative examples [71 : 91]. The test data consisted of [27 : 42] examples. The training data for the predicate parallel consisted of [66 : 46] examples. The test data consisted of [39 : 11] examples. The training data for the predicate adjacency consisted of [127 : 786] examples. The test data consisted of [58 : 360] examples. The training data for the strand direction predicate consisted of [36 : 60] examples. The test data consisted of [18 : 26] examples.

3 RESULTS

3.1 Rules for the edge of a sheet

3.1.1 *Rules*

Three rules were learnt for edge, and one rule for not_edge. These rules covered in the training examples all but [14 : 35] examples and all but [6 : 14] test examples. The coverage and accuracy of each rule is that for each rule taken in isolation.

Rule edge1:
Train cov. 0.465, acc. 0.891: Test cov. 0.482, acc. 0.765
$edge(A, B) : -rth(A, C, B, rth0).$
A strand is at the edge if
it has the lowest rank of total hydrophobic energy in its sheet.

Rule edge2:
Train cov. 0.310, acc. 0.880: Test cov. 0.148, acc. 0.500
$edge(A, B) : -seql(A, B, l3), pairs2(A, C, B),$

$pairs2(A, D, C)$.
A strand is at the edge if
it has length 3 and at least two strands precede it.

Rule edge3:
Train cov. 0.197 acc. 1.000: Test cov. 0.296, acc. 1.000
$edge(A, B) : -seql(A, B, l2)$.
A strand is at the edge if
it has length 2.

Rule not_edge1:
Train cov. 0.550, acc. 0.909: Test cov. 0.4681, acc. 0.815
$non\_edge(A, B) : -con\_to\_chain2(A, B, C), rhy(A, D, B, E)$,
$pred(F, E), rth(A, D, B, G), pred(H, G), pred(I, H)$.
A strand is not at the edge if
it does not have the lowest rank of average hydrophobic
energy in its sheet and its rank of total hydrophobic
energy in its sheet is at least 2 and the following strand
is in the same sheet.

3.1.2 *Rule interpretation*

The ordering of strands in sheets by their hydrophobic energy
was first stressed by Sternberg and Thornton (1977a) who noted
that 'the most hydrophobic strand is buried and the remaining
strands are arranged in decreasing hydrophobicity outwards in
both directions. Rule edge1 is implied by the Sternberg and
Thornton statement. It is interesting that this rule is still valid
with the current much expanded dataset. It would not have
been possible to learn the rule that the most hydrophobic strand
was not at an edge (because of the representation used of ranks
from 0 to n, where n varies with each strand). In fact, the
simplest implementation of this rule would not perform very
well on the IDITIS data because of the existence of a number
of sheets consisting of two strands each of two residues; these
sheets may be artefacts of the use of a poor definition for beta-
strands. Attempting to extend the rule manually by reasoning,

that as a sheet has two edges the strand with the second lowest total hydrophobic energy should also be an edge strand doesn't work very well (training cover 0.310, accuracy 0.629, test cover 0.296, accuracy 0.615). The reason for this is that the second lowest strand, following the Sternberg and Thornton rules, could also be placed between the lowest strand and the centre. The best way found by GOLEM to characterize the remaining edge strands was to examine strand length (which is closely related to total hydrophobic energy). Sternberg and Thornton further noted that total hydrophobic energy was a better measure than average hydrophobic energy to show the ordering of strands. This is still true, and is reflected in GOLEM's choice of the rule using total hydrophobic energy. If the rule using average hydrophobic energy is used it produces the following results: training cover 0.648, accuracy 0.630; test cover 0.630, accuracy 0.548.

The features of rule not_edge1 dealing with hydrophobic energy are consistent with the current understanding of protein structure. They state that for a strand to be internal, the strand should have a sufficient amount of average and total hydrophobic energy. The other condition, that the following strand should be in the same sheet, is more difficult to understand. It may just be a statistical artefact: or it may point to something more important; removal of this clause in the rule adds about equal numbers of positive and negative examples in the training and test data (training cover 0.803, accuracy 0.851: test cover 0.926, accuracy 0.781). It may be that the connecting to a strand in another sheet disrupts hydrophobic ordering because of the packing of the edge to the other sheet.

3.2 Rules for parallel packing

3.2.1 *Rules*

Two rules were learnt for parallel, and one rule for not parallel. In the training examples these rules covered all but [7 : 8] examples and [8 : 2] test examples. The coverage and accuracy of each rule is that for each rule taken in isolation.

Rule parallel1:
Train cov. 0.636, acc. 0.977; test cov. 0.564, acc. 1.000
$parallel(A, B, C) : -rhy(A, D, B, E), pred(F, E),$
$con\_helix(A, B, C, G), pred(H, G).$
Two consecutive strands B and C are parallel if
B does not have the lowest rank of average hydrophobic
energy in its sheet and B and C are connected by
at least 1 helix.

Rule parallel2:
Train cov. 0.500, acc. 0.868; test cov. 0.410, acc. 0.833
$parallel(A, B, C) : -con\_length(A, B, C, D), succ(D, E),$
$con\_helix(A, B, C, F), pred(G, F), rth(A, H, C, I), pred(J, I),$
$seql(A, C, K), seql(A, B, L), succ(L, M), lt(K, M).$
Two consecutive strands B and C are parallel if
C does not have the lowest rank of total hydrophobic energy
in its sheet and B and C are connected by at least 1 helix
and the length of B $\geq$ C.

Rule not_parallel1:
Training cov. 0.696, acc. 0.865; test cov. 0.727, acc. 0.667
$not\_parallel(A, B, C) : -con\_helix(A, B, C, hi0), pred(D, B),$
$pred(E, D).$
Two consecutive strands B and C are not parallel if
they are not connected by a helix and
there are at least two strands before B.

3.2.2 *Rule interpretation*

In rule parallel1 the condition for parallel packing that the
strands are connected by at least 1 helix is consistent with the
current understanding of protein structure. In the absence of a
helix most connections between the strands would not be long
enough to allow the protein chain to loop back to the start of
the first strand. It has been previously recognized (Sternberg
and Thornton, 1977a) that beta–alpha–beta secondary structure
elements tend to occur in parallel sheets, and beta–coil–beta el-

ements tend to occur in anti-parallel sheets. The condition that strand B should be of sufficient average hydrophobic energy is more unusual; the rule suggest that parallel strands are more hydrophobic than anti-parallel strands. This idea is supported by the work of Lifson and Sander (1979) . Removal of the condition gives: training cover 0.894, accuracy 0.819; test cover 0.897, accuracy 0.946. Rule parallel2 is very similar to Parallel1, the main difference is that it is the second strand that must have sufficient total hydrophobic energy. The change to total hydrophobic energy from average hydrophobic energy makes little difference.

The significance of the condition concerning length is unclear. There seems to be a relatively greater chance of being anti-parallel when the second strand is of greater length than the first. But it is of interest that such strands are relatively rare (46 examples) compared to pairs where the first strand is of greater length (71 examples). It is important to note how the relation $A \geq B$ is represented by the Prolog program induced by GOLEM. The relation is not given in the background knowledge, where only $A > B$ is given. The relation is therefore expressed by $A + 1 > B$.

Rule not_parallel1 is basically the negation of rules parallel1 and parallel2. Its most important condition that no helix separates the strands. The second condition, concerning the number of strands before B, does not make a significant improvement to the rule.

It should be noted that the ratio of positive to negative examples in the test data is not the same as in the training data. This is makes it easier to predict parallel strands in the test data, and more difficult to predict anti-parallel strands. This difference is ratio is due to chance in the random selection of data.

3.3 Rules for strand adjacency

3.3.1 *Rules*

Two rules were learnt for adjacent, and three rules for not adjacent. In the training examples these rules covered all but [60

: 234] examples and [18 : 89] test examples. The coverage and accuracy of each rule is that for each rule taken in isolation.

Rule adj1:
Train cov. 0.441, acc. 0.849: Test: cov. 0.345, acc. 0.833
$adj(A, B, C) : -con\_length(A, B, C, D), succ(D, E),$
$seql(A, C, F), succ(F, G), seql(A, B, H), pred(I, H),$
$lt(I, G), succ(H, J), pred(K, F), lt(K, J).$
Strands B and C are adj. when C follows B in seq. if
C directly follows B in sequence in a sheet and
they differ in length by < 2 and
they are connected by < 50 residues.

Rule adj2:
Train cov. 0.354, acc. 0.818: Test: cov. 0.349, acc. 0.870
$adj(A, B, C) : -con\_helix(A, B, C, D), pairs2(A, E, B),$
$rth(A, F, B, G), pred(H, G), seql(A, C, I), seql(A, B, J),$
$succ(J, K), lt(I, K).$
Strands B and C are adj. when C follows B in seq. if
C directly follows B in sequence in a sheet and
B does not have the lowest rank of total hydrophobic energy
in its sheet and the length of B $\geq$ C and a strand
precedes B.

Rule not_adj1:
Train cov. 0.396, acc. 0.978: Test cov. 0.386, acc. 0.979
$not\_adj(A, B, C) : -th(A, D, B, E), succ(E, F), succ(F, G),$
$rhy(A, H, C, I), rhy(A, D, B, J), succ(J, K), lt(I, K),$
$pairs1(A, B, L), pairs1(A, L, M), pred(N, C), pred(O, N),$
$lt(M, O).$
Strands B and C are not adj. when C follows B in seq. if
at least four strands separate B and C and
the rank of average hydrophobic energy of B $\geq$ C and
the total hydrophobic energy of B is < 18.

Rule not_adj2:
Train cov. 0.313, acc. 0.984: Test cov. 0.397, acc. 0.960

$not\_adj(A, B, C) : -avh(A, D, B, E), pairs2(A, F, B),$
$avh(A, D, F, G), pairs2(A, H, C), lt(B, H), pred(I, F),$
$pred(J, I), pairs1(A, B, K), rth(A, L, K, M), pred(N, M).$
Strands B and C are not adj. when C follows B in seq. if
at least 1 strand separates B and C and
the strand immediately following B has not the lowest rank
of total hydrophobic energy and the strand immediately
preceding B is in the same sheet and at least three strands
precede B.

Rule not_adj3:
Train cov. 0.350, acc. 0.984: Test cov. 0.419, acc. 0.968
$not\_adj(A, B, C) : -pairs1(A, C, D), con\_length(A, C, D, E),$
$succ(E, F), th(A, G, B, H), succ(H, I), succ(I, J),$
$con\_to\_chain1(A, C, K), pred(L, K), pred(M, L), succ(B, N),$
$pred(O, C), pred(P, O), lt(N, P).$
Strands B and C are not adj. when C follows B in seq. if
at least three strands separate B and C and
the total hydrophobic energy of B is < 18 and
strand C is followed by a strand in the same sheet in less
than 50 residues and a turn or helix follows C
(not just a loop).

3.3.2 *Rule interpretation*

The most important feature of rules for predicting adjacency
is the condition that the two strands follow in sequence (see
Richardson 1981). It was not possible to find any successful
rules for predicting the adjacency of strands that did not directly follow in sequence. This illustrates the importance of
short-range interactions in sheet formation. However, note that
in the context of packing prediction, short range means a far
greater distance than it would in predicting secondary structure. The reason that sequentially adjacent strands are likely to
pack adjacently in space is probably due to their having a far
greater chance of interacting during the folding process.

In rule adj1 the condition that the stands differ in length by
less than two residues is consistent with the current understand-

ing of protein structure. Adjacent strands should be about the same length so that they can form hydrogen bonds. It is interesting how this condition is represented in GOLEM. It is not given as part of the background knowledge, but is instead built up from the greater-than relation ($>$) and the successor relation ($+1$) in the following way: $((((A + 1) + 1) > B)$ and $(((B + 1) + 1) > A))$. The discovery of such a complicated relation between two lengths illustrates the power of the ILP methodology. A conventional attribute-based learning system would not have been able to learn this concept, unless it was explicitly given as a possibility. The last condition of rule adj1, concerning connection length, is relatively unimportant as most adjacent strands are connected by less than 50 residues.

Rule adj2 has the same essential condition as rule adj1 that the two strands follow in sequence. The second condition, that the first strand in sequence of the pair should not have too low hydrophobic energy is interesting, as it implies that the formation of hydrogen bonds between sequential beta strands can be disrupted by hydrophobic effects. The third condition, that the length of the first strand should be longer than the following strand, is reminiscent of rule Parallel2 and may have a similar cause. The fourth clause is relatively unimportant.

The rules for predicting that two strands will not be adjacent in a sheet are the most complicated found for predicting protein folding constraints. This reflects the larger number of examples of non-adjacency compared to adjacency, and the need for highly accurate rules. A better method of determining the statistical validity of the addition of new clauses needs to be found; the work of Muggleton *et al.* (1992b) may offer one way towards this end. The most important condition preventing strands becoming adjacent is that the strands are separated by a sufficient distance. This is the reverse of the most important condition for strands being adjacent—that sequential separation of the strands decreases the probability that the strands will interact in the folding process. In rule not_adj1 the strands are separated sequentially by at least four other strands. The condition concerning the relationship between the rank of average hydrophobic energy is the reverse of rule adj2; its inclusion appears to slightly favour non-adjacency. In rule not_adj2, the strands must be separated by at least one intervening strand. Condition 2 suggests, as in rule adj2, that contact with the hydrophobic effects disrupt predictions about strand packing; it is however unclear why the preceding strand should be important. In rule not_adj3, the only important condition is the first condition, that the strands be separated by three intervening strands; the other conditions appear to be statistical artefacts.

3.4 Rules for strand direction

3.4.1 *Rules*

One rule was learnt for in, and one rule for out (not in). In the training examples these rules covered all but $[10 : 11]$ examples and $[2 : 3]$ test examples. The coverage and accuracy of each rule is that for each rule taken in isolation.

Rule in1:

Train cov. 0.500, acc. 0.818: Test cov. 0.556, acc. 0.833

$in(A, B, C) : -con\_to\_chain1(A, B, D),$

$con\_length(A, B, C, E), succ(E, F), rth(A, G, B, H),$

$rth(A, G, C, I), pred(J, I), lt(H, J).$

B is closer to the edge than consecutive strand C if

the rank of total hydrophobic energy of C is 2 greater

than B and they are connected < 50 residues.

Rule out1:

Train cov. 0.750, acc. 0.849: Test cov. 0.808, acc. 0.777

$out(A, B, C) : -con\_to\_chain2(A, B, D), succ(D, E),$

$succ(E, F), rth(A, G, C, H), rth(A, G, B, I), succ(I, J),$

$lt(H, J).$

B is further from the edge than consecutive strand C if

the rank of total hydrophobic energy of B $\geq$ C and

B is not the last strand in the sheet and

there are < 128 ss elements.

3.4.2 *Rule interpretation*

Considering rule in1, the most important condition is that the rank total hydrophobic energy of C should be two ranks greater than B. This is consistent with the analysis of Sternberg and Thornton (1977a), who proposed that strands are ordered by their hydrophobicities, with the most hydrophobic strands in the centre. There is not enough data to test the importance of the second condition.

In rule out1 the most important condition is that the total hydrophobic energy of B $\geq$ C. This is almost the reverse of rule in1, although it is interesting that the condition for moving in is more strict than moving out, i.e. it is easier to wind out. There is not enough data to test the importance of the other conditions. To illustrate the application of the rules learned by GOLEM the results of applying rules in1 and out1 are shown in Fig. 10.5.

It is important to note that there are more connections in the direction towards the edge than there are away from the edge (significant at 1% level); this is illustrated in Fig. 10.6. This figure also neatly illustrates why the discrimination between rules in1 and out1 in terms of difference in total hydrophobic energy is placed where it is. Where the difference in ranks is two or greater then there are examples of in compared to out: where the difference is zero or less there are more examples of out: the case is ambiguous where the difference is 1.

4 DISCUSSION

4.1 Winding direction

A number of the rules found by GOLEM on investigation are thought to be consequences of the fact that beta-sheets in alpha-beta proteins are more likely to start winding from the centre out, than from the edge in. This tendency has been hinted at in the literature (Richardson 1981), but the logical consequences of it have not been fully appreciated. The consequences were discovered by consideration of the rules generated by GOLEM. One consequence is that because proteins are roughly globular in shape, the relationship between pairs of sequential strands is

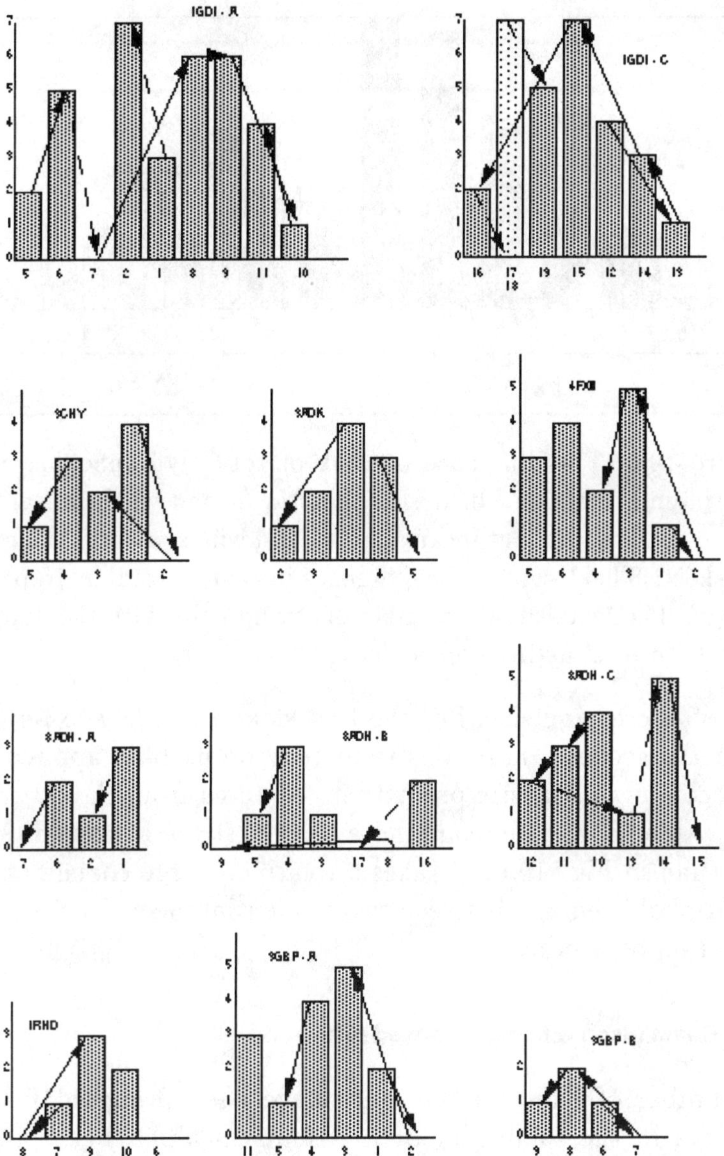

Figure 10.5. The predictions of winding direction. The 11 sheets of the seven test proteins are illustrated. The Y-axis is the rank of total hydrophobic energy. The X-axis is the sequential number of strand, i.e. strand no. n is the nth in sequence. Arrows show the prediction of winding direction; dotted arrows are incorrect predictions. In sheet 1GD1–C, strands 17 and 18 have the same position in the sheet, causing two prediction errors.

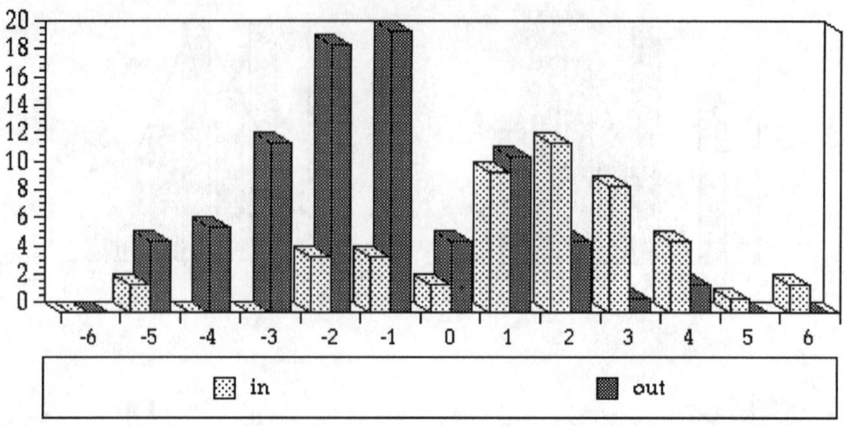

Figure 10.6. The difference in rank of total hydrophophic energy by winding direction. In means that the strand winds towards the centre of the sheet: out means that strand winds towards the edge of the sheet. The X-axis is the difference in rank of total hydrophophic energy. The Y-axis is the number of strand pairs with the difference in rank of total hydrophophic energy.

one of decreasing size, i.e. the first strand is likely to be larger than the second. This constraint may be usefully applied back to secondary structure prediction. Winding from the centre out also explains why there are more pairs of strands in the direction out than in Fig. 10.6. It takes a relatively large change in total hydrophobic energy between two sequential sheets to change the direction of winding.

4.2 Comparison with hand-derived rules

A number of hand-crafted rules have been proposed for constraints in the folding of beta strands in alpha/beta proteins (Clark *et al.* 1991; ESPRIT III project EP 6708 report). It is interesting to compare these rules with those found by GOLEM:

- Some rules were found to be identical, e.g. the rule: 'the least hydrophobic strand is on the edge of the sheet (using total hydropathies)' is identical in meaning with rule edge1. This rule originated in the work of Sternberg and Thornton (1977).

- Other rules are closely related but are somewhat more general, e.g parallel beta–alpha–beta connections should contain at least 10 residues in the coil (Taylor and Green 1989).

- However, some of the proposed rules appear to be rather poor. For example, the proposed rule that the initial strand in sequence is not an edge sheet. This can be translated into Prolog as:

  Train cov. 0.127, acc. 0.600: Test cov. 0.185, acc. 0.833
  $not\_edge(A, S) : -lt(1, S).$
  This rule has rather a low accuracy and coverage compared to the rules found by GOLEM.

- Other proposed rules could not have been found because of the limitation of the representation used. For example, Taylor and Green (Taylor and Green 1989) proposed that unconserved strands are at the edge. This rule could not have found as the concept of conservation of sequence is not represented in the background knowledge; it relates to the rate of mutation across homologous proteins. Similarly, Richardson (1981) proposed that there is only one change in winding direction in a sheet. Such a rule could not have been found because the concept of change in winding direction is second order compared to strand direction.

4.3 ElipSys rules

The existing hand-produced rules relating to the secondary structure packing of alpha/beta proteins have been gathered together by Clark *et al.* (1991, 1993a, 1993b). These rules were formalized and translated into logic programs and used as part of an overall structural packing program. This program inputs one or more protein secondary structure assignments and outputs a predicted packing for the protein. Currently the rules and program are implemented in the parallel constraint logic programming language ElipSys. The success of these hand-produced rules at predicting protein packing patterns is currently being evaluated by a systematic prediction of the database. The rules discovered by GOLEM have also been translated into ElipSys. It is intended to directly compare the success of these rules with the hand-produced ones on the systematic prediction of the database. The rule below is the ElipSys version of rule edge1.

$not\_edge([])$.

$not\_edge([Y - F|T]) : -Y + F\# > 2, not\_edge(T)$.

The rule is called with a list of length N of key value finite domain variables Y and F which may be in any state of groundedness. Y is the Strand sequence position and F is the position of the strand in the sheet.

5 CONCLUSIONS

This paper describes an interactive cycle for the use of machine learning as a tool to aid scientists in the discovery of patterns in data. This framework has been successfully tested by the application of the inductive logic programming (ILP) program GOLEM to the discovery of constraints in the packing of beta-sheets in alpha/beta proteins. Constraints (rules) were learnt for four features of beta-sheet packing: the winding direction of two sequential sheets (two rules found), whether two sequential sheets pack in a parallel or anti-parallel (three rules found), whether two sheets pack adjacently (five rules found), and whether a beta-sheet is at an edge (four rules found). Investigation of the rules revealed interesting patterns, some of which were previously known, others that are novel. Novel features include two previously unrecognized consequences of the bias of winding direction to start from the centre: that the relationship between pairs of sequential strands is in general one of decreasing size, i.e. the first strand is likely to be larger than the second; and that more sequential pairs of strands wind in the direction out than in. We conclude that machine learning, in particular ILP, has a potential role as a tool for pattern discovery for scientists.

Acknowledgements

We would like to thank Chris Rawlings and Steve Garner (Oxford Molecular) for making IDITIS raw data available. We would also like to thank Steve Muggleton for supplying GOLEM. Dominic A. Clark and Jack Shirazi were partly funded by the EU under ESPRIT Project 6708 'APPLAUSE'.

REFERENCES

Clark, D. A., Shirazi, J. and Rawlings, C.J. (1991). Protein topology prediction through constraint-based search and the evaluation of topological folding rules. *Prot. Engng.* **4**, 751–760.

Clark, D. A., Rawlings, C. J., Shirazi, J., Veron, A. and Reeve, M. (1993a). Protein topology prediction through parallel constraint logic programming. In *Proceedings of the First International Conference on Intelligent Systems for Molecular Biology*, (eds. Hunter, L., Searls, D., and Shavlik, J), AAAI/MIT Press, Menlo Park.

Clark, D. A., Rawlings, C. J., Shirazi, J., Reeve, M., Schumeran, K. and Vernon, A. (1993b). Solving large combinatorial problems in molecular biology using the ElipSys parallel constraint logic programming system. *The Computer Journal* **36**, 69–701.

Garnier, J., Osguthorpe, D. J. and Robson, B. (1978). Analysis of the accuracy and implications of simple methods for predicting the secondary structure of globular proteins. *J. Mol. Biol.* **120**, 97–120.

Gray, N. A. B., Sleeman, D. H. and Stacey, M. K. (1988). Machine Discovery and the Operationalization of Scientific Theories. *Aberdeen University Computer Science Technical Report AUCS(TR8801)*.

Islam, S. A. and Sternberg M. J. E. (1989). A relational database of protein structures designed for flexible enquires about conformation. *Prot. Engng.* **2**, 431–442.

King, R. D., Muggleton, S., Lewis, R. and Sternberg, M. J. E. (1992). Drug design by machine learning: the use of inductive logic programming to model the structure–activity relationships of trimethoprim analogues binding to dihydrofolate reductase. *Proc. Natl. Acad. Sci. USA* **89**, 11322–11326.

King, R. D., Muggleton, S., Lewis, R., Srinivasan, A., Feng, C. and Sternberg M. J. E. (1993). Drug design using inductive logic programming. In *Proceedings of the 26th Annual Hawaii In-*

ternational Conference on System Sciences 1: 646–655. IEEE Computer Society Press, Los Alamitos.

Langley, P., Simon, H.A., Bradshaw, G. L. and Zytkow, J. M. (1987). *Scientific Discovery: Computational Explorations of the Creative Process* MIT Press, Cambridge, MA.

Lenat, D. B. and Brown J. S. (1984). Why AM and Eurisko appear to work. *Artificial Intelligence* **23**, 269–294.

Lifson, S. and Sander, C. (1979). Antiparalell and parallel beta-strands differ in amino acid residue preferences. *Nature 282*, 109–110.

Muggleton, S. and Feng C. (1990). Efficient induction of logic programs. In *Proceedings of the First Conference on Algorithmic Learning Theory* Jpn. Soc. Artifical Intelligence.

Muggleton, S., King, R. D. and Sternberg, M. J. E. (1992a). Protein secondary structure prediction using logic-based machine learning. *Protein Engng* **5**, 647–657.

Muggleton, A. Srinivasan, S. and Bain M. (1992b). Compression, Significance and Accuracy. In *Proceedings of 9th International Conference on Machine Learning* Morgan-Kaufman, San Diego, CA.

Orengo, C. A., Flores, T. P., Taylor, W. R. and Thornton, J. M. (1993). Identification and classification of protein fold families. *Protein Engng* **6**, 485–500.

Rawlings, C. J. E., Taylor, W. R., Nyakairu, J. Fox, J. and Sternberg, M. J. E. (1985). TOPOL. *J. Mol. Graphics* **3**, 151–157.

Richardson, J. S. (1981). The anatomy and taxonomy of protein structure. *Advances in Protein Chemistry* **34**, 167–339.

Rost, B. and Sander C. (1993). Prediction of protein secondary structure at better than 70% accuracy. *J. Mol. Biol.* **232**, 584–599.

Schulz, G. E. and Schirmer R. H. (1978). *Principles of Protein Structure*. Springer-Verlag, Berlin.

Shaffer, C. (1989). Bacon, data analysis and artificial intelligence. In *Proceedings of the Sixth International Workshop on Machine Learning*, Cornell University, Ithaca, N.Y., Morgan Kaufmann, Los Altos, CA.

Shirazi, J. and Clark, D. A. (1993). Combining Databases and Constraints in Protein Structural Analysis. *Technical report ESPRIT*

Project 6708 'APPLAUSE'.

Sternberg, M. J. E. and Thornton J. M. (1977a). On the conformation of proteins: hydrophobic ordering of strands in beta-pleated sheets. *J. Mol. Biol.* **115**, 1–17.

Sternberg, M. J. E. and Thornton J. M. (1977b). On the conformation of proteins: towards the prediction of strand arrangements in beta–pleated sheets. *J. M. Biol.* **113**, 401–418.

Taylor, W. R. and Green N. M. (1989). The predicted secondary structure of the nucleotide-binding sites of six cation-transporting ATPases leads to a probable tertiary fold. *European Journal of Biochemistry* **179**, 241–248.

Vernon, A., Schuerman, K., Reeve, M. and Li, L.-L. (1993). *PARLE '93 (Lecture Notes in Computer Science 694)*. Springer-Verlag, Heidelberg, Berlin.

11

Controlling a Steel Mill with BOXES

Michael McGarity, Claude Sammut and David Clements

The University of New South Wales

Abstract

We describe an application of the BOXES learning algorithm of Michie and Chambers (1968) to a large-scale, real-world problem, namely, learning to control a steel mill. By applying BOXES to a model of a skinpass mill (a type of steel mill), we find that the BOXES algorithm can be made to produce a robust controller relatively quickly. Various aspects of the BOXES algorithm are adapted for the higher dimensionality and noise present in the skinpass mill. These changes are critically examined to find those which give a better controller.

1 INTRODUCTION

BOXES began as an exploration into the possibility that many small tasks may be easier for a computer to learn than one large one. That is, it was thought that by breaking up a complex problem, difficult to solve as it stood, into many smaller and more tractable problems, the original problem could be solved with greater speed or ease. Although some information is always lost by splitting the problem into sub-problems, it was hoped that the advantages gained with the improvements in complexity would offset this. The heart of the BOXES algorithm is that within each sub-problem, a simple decision-array control strategy is altered by an incremental process based on the success or failure of the controller on the last trial.

The BOXES algorithm has traditionally been applied to unstable, linearizable, low noise, single input plants [1] such as the pole and cart (Michie and Chambers 1968; Sammut 1994). We might therefore ask what changes we might have to make to adapt the algorithm to be suitable for a larger class of tasks. Some of the issues to be considered are as follows.

- A much larger action space due to multiple inputs will make it harder to learn to choose a good action within a reasonable time.

- Most viable controllers for physical systems need to minimize the number of changes in actions sent to the actuators, as this behaviour carries with it high running and maintenance costs.

- Typical industrial plants are designed to be stable and therefore the plant will not present examples of marginal failure to the controller during learning. The large amount of noise usually present may offset this effect.

To explore these problems, we apply BOXES to a model of a working steel mill. The skinpass mill is a plant designed to flatten a strip of steel. It does this by passing the strip between two rollers which are forced together. The aim of this process is to improve certain physical properties of the strip, such as uniform stretchability. This means that much of the deformation due to the rollers occurs in the surface (or skin) of the strip, giving a highly nonlinear relationship between force and elongation. The skinpass mill is therefore a nonlinear plant with multiple inputs and outputs, described in the following section, with all of the inputs and outputs linked. The skinpass mill is designed to be relatively stable.

2 THE SKINPASS MILL

The reduction of the steel strip applied by the skinpass mill is very small (usually less than 5%), and needs to be controlled

---

[1]Note that we use here the convention of control engineers where the plant is the system under control and the input to the plant is the control action.

to within fine limits. The result of this small reduction is to improve the yield point properties of the thin strip product. In terms of yield point flattening, a temper rolling mill is different from a hot rolling mill, which may perform reductions of 50% on very thick steel ingots or plate, with the aim of reducing the thickness of the strip, plate or ingot. Thus the skinpass mill is one of the final stages in the rolling of the steel strip and has different requirements from the earlier processes. In addition to this, the physical processes involved in skinpass rolling are not as well understood as either hot or cold rolling is, which makes the mathematical model needed for control purposes harder to find (Roberts 1972). Naturally, the mill stand is only a small part of the mill, but as this is the object of most of the control design, we will concentrate our attention on it. The primary aim of the control task is to keep the elongation as close as possible to the *setpoint*, or desired level of elongation, while keeping the other parameters (roll tilt and strip shape) within acceptable bounds.

The skinpass mill has three inputs and outputs. The outputs are elongation (related to the average of the main roll force), Roll Tilt (related to the difference in the roll forces) and the roll bending (related to special roll bending actuators) as shown in Fig. 11.1. The relationships between these three main systems is complex, and is difficult to describe analytically. Therefore, we modelled the mill using a static nonlinear block in series with a simple linear second-order dynamic system. The nonlinear element was found using steady-state empirical data. The three sub-systems, elongation, crown and roll tilt were treated as separately as possible.

2.1 Actuators

The *actuators* apply pressure to the cylinders which, in turn, transfer force to the strip. The effect of the actuators to alter the strip shape is effectively instantaneous.

2.2 Measurements

Thinning the strip of steel results in *elongation* of the strip. Distortion in the strip can cause *roll tilt*, which will result in buckle.

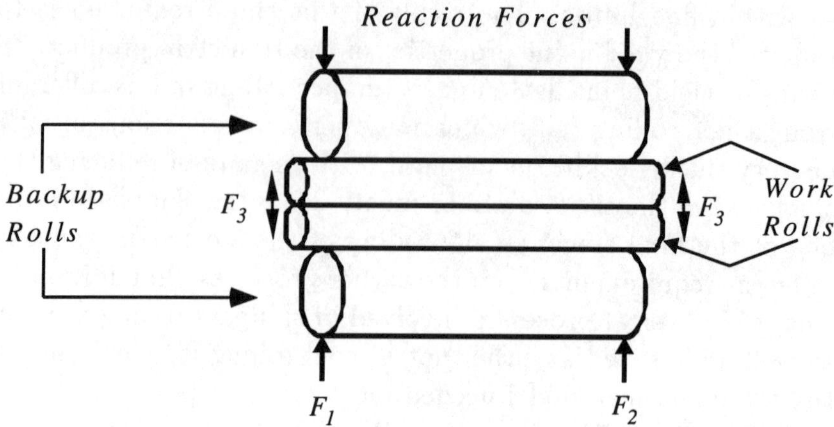

Figure 11.1. Inputs and outputs of the mill.

Heating of the strip as a result of rolling causes expansion and more thinning in the middle. This is called *negative crown*.

2.3 Noise

The noise is mainly due to roll eccentricities and strip irregularities and so the bandwidth of the noise is very closely linked to the strip speed.

Some mill dynamics are fast, with an open loop step disturbance lasting about 5 ms. These are mostly hydraulic resonances (damped by gas cylinders) and are ignored in the current implementation. This is because we cannot control them without a dedicated controller and because they die out in between step inputs from the BOXES controller. Note also that in the commercial version of this mill controller, a dedicated controller implementing a PID controller is used to control fast valve and hydraulic dynamics.

The dynamics that are of interest to us concern the shape and elongation of the steel strip and are much slower. The strip runs through the mill at speeds between 30 m/min and 400 m/min. At the fastest speed (1.2 mm strip) undulations in strip thickness are caused by elliptical flattening of the rolls. The work rolls are smaller and so contribute a higher frequency (although a lower amplitude). In the experiments described in this paper, a strip thickness of 4 mm is always used, with a corresponding strip speed of 150 m/min. The work rolls have a diameter of roughly 400 mm (circumference of 1250 mm) which corresponds to a disturbance bandwidth of approximately 2 Hz. The total disturbances introduced by the irregularities in original strip thickness are limited to about 2–3 Hz. A sample time of 100 ms is 4–5 times as fast as the fastest plant dynamics, and is therefore reasonable for most cases. The experiments are therefore conducted with a sample time of 0.1 s.

3 BOXES AND THE SKINPASS MILL

This section deals with the performance of the BOXES algorithm while learning to control the skinpass mill and the changes that have been made to cope with the increased number of dimensions and noise. Our main aim with these modifications is to improve the robustness of both the controller and the learning agent.

There are three critical elements of a BOXES style algorithm:

- It succeeds by avoiding failure.
- BOXES avoids global failure by changing local variables.
- Each local variable is changed independently from every other local variable.

The BOXES algorithm relies on a state-space representation, in which each input (including dynamic information such as derivatives and integrals) is divided into several intervals. Thus, a given input parameter might be divided into three categories, for example, large negative, near zero, and large positive. Each input may be divided into a different number of divisions. In this way, the divisions of the total space form 'boxes' within which all of components of the state-space vector stay inside their respective boundaries.

When applied to the skinpass mill, there are four inputs to BOXES (i.e. outputs from the plant), these are the elongation (and its integral of error), roll tilt, and crown. Each of these four inputs is partitioned, giving $5 \times 3 \times 3 \times 3$ boxes.

The output of the control system is similarly quantized. Each box contains an output, and this output does not change during a control run. The action only changes when the whole system

303

fails. The skinpass mill has three independent actuators: operator side pressure, drive side pressure, and bending pressure. Each of this is quantized into large negative, small negative, zero, small positive and large positive. Thus there is a total of 125 different combinations of actions. This represents a large increase in complexity over the pole and cart which only has two actions.

Time is quantized as well. The current action is treated as a constant output for the duration of each time step, so the model for the plant to be controlled needs to be step invariant. Adjustment of the sample or step time is not part of the learning procedure. During the control run, then, the BOXES algorithm is simply a lookup table.

The goal of learning is to coerce the performance of the closed loop into a heuristically defined specification or boundary of acceptable performance. The way this is done is very simple to describe, but it is difficult to guarantee convergence.

The algorithm performs a local search within a global failure definition. The underlying assumption behind this learning algorithm is that an action output by the boxes has a causal relationship with the success or failure of the global system. However, this relationship is usually not directly causal: instead, it is a probabilistic link. The strength of the link between a box and the outcome depends on the behaviour of the boxes around it and, in the case of failure, on the time between the activation of the box and the eventual failure. Since the behaviour of the surrounding boxes is difficult to predict and may be seen as somewhere between a random action and the 'correct' action, they must be treated stochastically. Thus the causal link between a given action and the ensuing success and failure would probably depend on the relative certainty with which the box holds its action, and so would change over the course of the learning process.

Sammut and Cribb (1990) claimed that a tradeoff exists between speed of learning and the generality of the learned controller. The controller produced by BOXES is not guaranteed to be robust in the sense that it can control the same plant from different starting conditions. This is also true of other reinforcement learning algorithms.

In order to test the robustness of our algorithms, we run each of the modifications, with various noise levels, on two different plants: the skinpass mill and the pole and cart as described by Anderson (1987). When running the algorithms, we continued for 10 000 trials before resetting the learning algorithm. In order to show the performance over this time, we recorded the highest number of successes *in a row* that has been achieved. By 'success' we mean that the system has been kept stable for 10 000 time steps, where one time step is defined by a single loop through the simulation. In the case of the pole and cart, failure occurs when either the pole angle exceeds some predefined limit or the cart hits the end of the track, which has a finite length.

3.1 Background

After each trial when the system fails, the algorithm collects the time indices at which each box is entered. They are collected into one number which indicates the proportion of the failure that is due to the action currently set in the box. This number, termed *Life*, is a function of the elapsed time between use and failure of the box:

$$Life = \sum_{i=0}^{n}(T_{final} - T_i).$$

The *Life-time*, which gives some indication of the proportion of blame for failure, is a discounted accumulation of the past life-times for a particular action. This is done using a sliding average. The number of times, n, that a box is entered during a trial is similarly accumulated:

$$Life\text{-}time' = DK \times Life\text{-}time + Life$$

$$Usage' = DK \times Usage + n,$$

where DK is the discount factor (a number between 0 and 1).

This second term is used as the divisor when working out the 'life expectancy' of a given action and as a measure of how much is known about this action:

$$Average\ life\text{-}time = \frac{life\text{-}time}{usage}.$$

The average life-time can be seen as an estimate of the life expectancy of the entire system if this particular box chooses this action. In order to encourage exploration, this average life-time is modified to bias the choice of action towards those actions with which BOXES has little experience. Thus, we define *merit* as

$$merit = \frac{\textit{life-time}}{usage^k} \text{ where } k > 1.$$

Several variations of this measure have been used for BOXES. The one above was described by Sammut (1994). These merits are then used to compare the various actions and the one which will most likely avoid failure for the controller, in the long run, is chosen. This choice may simply be taking the action with the highest score,

$$merit_{action} > merit_i \ \forall i \neq action$$

or may be probabilistic:

$$Probability(action = i) \propto merit_i.$$

The probabilistic strategy we use proceeds by choosing a particular action with a probability proportional to its merit.

Deterministic action choices are based on the maximum score given by the appropriate scoring technique. That is, the action chosen would have the best balance, given the information known at the time, between experience and chance of success. A probabilistic choice of action would most often pick the same choice as the deterministic one, but would have some chance of choosing a different one.

4 ANNEALING

The deterministic method for choosing actions works well for the pole and cart. This may be because the range of actions is very limited, so the algorithm can obtain experience for the entire range of actions. However, the mill has a large number of actions available, 3 independent actions with 5 choices, giving

125 possible actions. Thus, there is ample scope for a complex decision surface to include local minima. Additionally, it is too large a surface to hope that the BOXES algorithm will gain global knowledge before a local minimum is found. For these reasons, we tried to use a probabilistic notion of action choice.

There are two ideas behind annealing. First, there is a need for constant excitation. It is important, when modelling a process from dynamic data, to excite all of the modes of the process so that the model includes these modes. This is often done by using a white noise input to an unknown plant after which the usual system identification procedures take place. In our simulation, plant disturbances are modelled by pseudo-random noise. However, annealing provides a second input of noise and can also be used for this purpose.

The second reason for using annealing is to prevent the algorithm being caught in local minima. As previously mentioned, each action available to a box must have a corresponding lifetime that is indicative of the action's average time to failure. Thus, each action must have a chance to find out what its time to failure is, and with a large number of actions available this may not be possible. Instead, one or two relatively successful actions take over, not allowing other actions a chance to obtain a statistically large number of example runs. Annealing is different from other ways of combating this problem in that instead of boosting the score of inexperienced actions, annealing simply chooses a random action. Each action has a probability proportional to its score and from this sample space an action is chosen. Thus, the higher scores are chosen more often, but any score can be chosen.

One variation that can be added is to provide a cut-off level. Annealing is noise, so it should produce a deterioration in the performance of the plant. After annealing has done its job, namely, to give all of the actions a chance to find their own average time to failure, it can be reduced. This is done in the current simulation by only including those actions that have a score above a certain cut-off level. This level can be fixed or it can be raised as the learning procedure progresses, reducing the noise input by the annealing procedure.

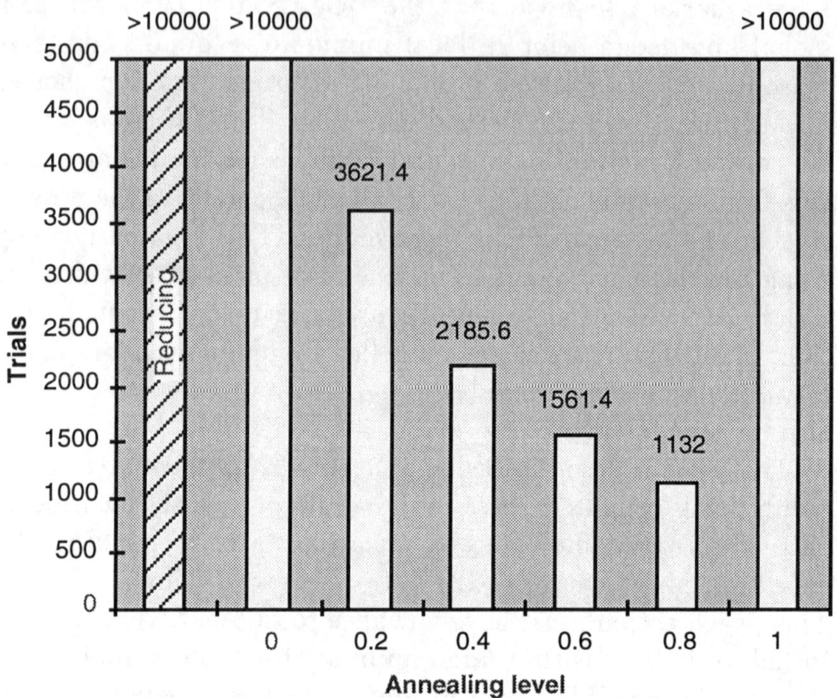

Figure 11.2. The effect of annealing on learning to control the pole and cart. Note that the criterion for success is to keep the system stable for 10 000 time steps and repeat that 10 times in a row. The number of trials plotted is the time taken to succeed for the first time.

In order to test these ideas, the pole and cart and the skinpass mill were tested with various annealing types and levels. In the three graphs shown, the columns represent fixed annealing at a certain level, the level being shown on the x-axis of Figs 11.2, 11.3 and 11.4. Two types of annealing are shown, constant annealing and reducing annealing.

Constant annealing chooses the action according to the following rule:

$$Probability(action = i) \propto AvLife\text{-}time_i, \text{ if } AvLife\text{-}time_i >$$
$$\beta \times MaxAvLife\text{-}time$$

$$Probability(action = i) = 0, \text{ otherwise.}$$

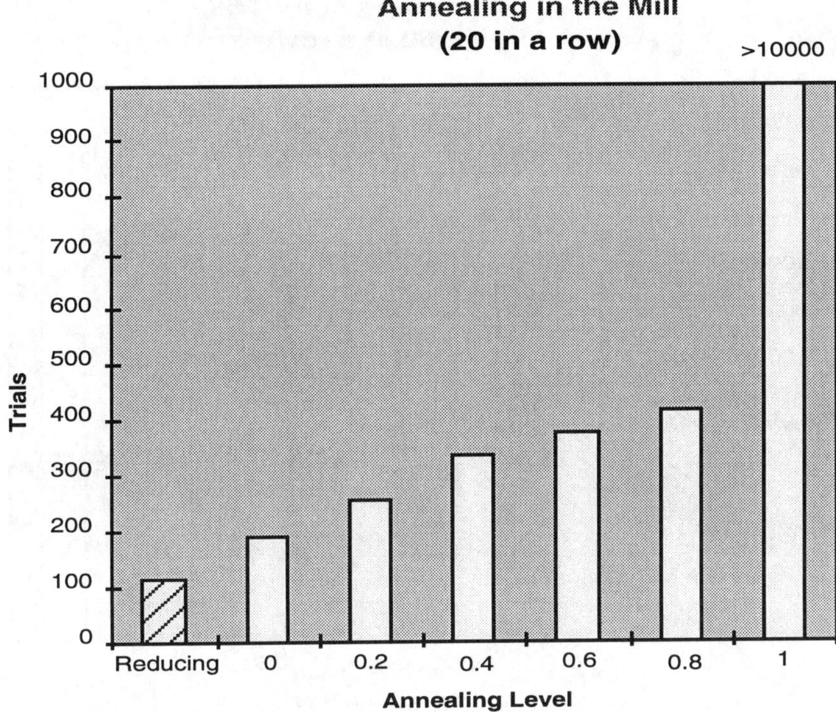

Figure 11.3. The effect of annealing on learning to control the skin-pass mill. The criterion for success is to balance the pole for 10 000 time steps and repeat that 20 times in a row. The number of trials plotted is the time taken to succeed for the first time.

That is, the probability of choosing action i is proportional to the average life-time for that action in a particular box. In addition, a cut-off level is defined such that if the average life-time is less than β times the highest average life-time of an action in the same box, then that action will never be chosen.

In the constant annealing scheme, the value of β is constant throughout a complete learning sequence. Under reducing annealing, the value of β changes according to the formula:

$$\beta = \frac{GlobalLife\text{-}time}{TargetLife\text{-}time},$$

where the global life-time is the current life-time of the system, as a whole, and the target life-time is the success criterion

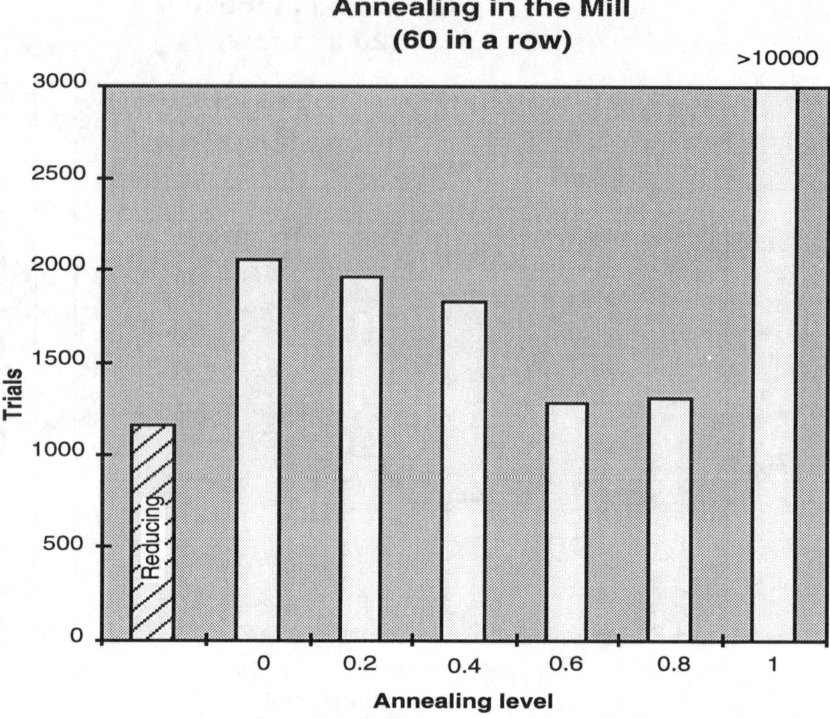

Figure 11.4. The effect of annealing on learning to control the skin-pass mill. The criterion for success is to balance the pole for 10 000 time steps and repeat that 60 times in a row. The number of trials plotted is the time taken to succeed for the first time.

of 10,000 time steps (in the present experiments). With this method the cut-off level is raised as performance increases.

Interestingly, the versions of the BOXES algorithm described by Sammut (1994) consistently failed the robustness tests used here. While that algorithm learns to control the pole and cart system quickly, it cannot achieve a consistent level of performance by retaining the box statistics from one learning sequence to the next as annealing does. We have previously proposed a method of voting (Sammut and Cribb 1990) to construct a robust controller for the pole and cart. Unfortunately, this method does not scale to problems that have a large number of control actions. The combination of annealing and not resetting the statistics kept in each box after a successful sequence appears to be more promising.

5 TRAINING FOR NOISE

Previous research in machine learning (Quinlan 1986) suggests that it is necessary to train a learning system in a noisy environment if the final system is to be used in a noisy environment. As can be seen in Figs 11.5 and 6, the performance of the algorithm when trained in this way is in accord with our expectations.

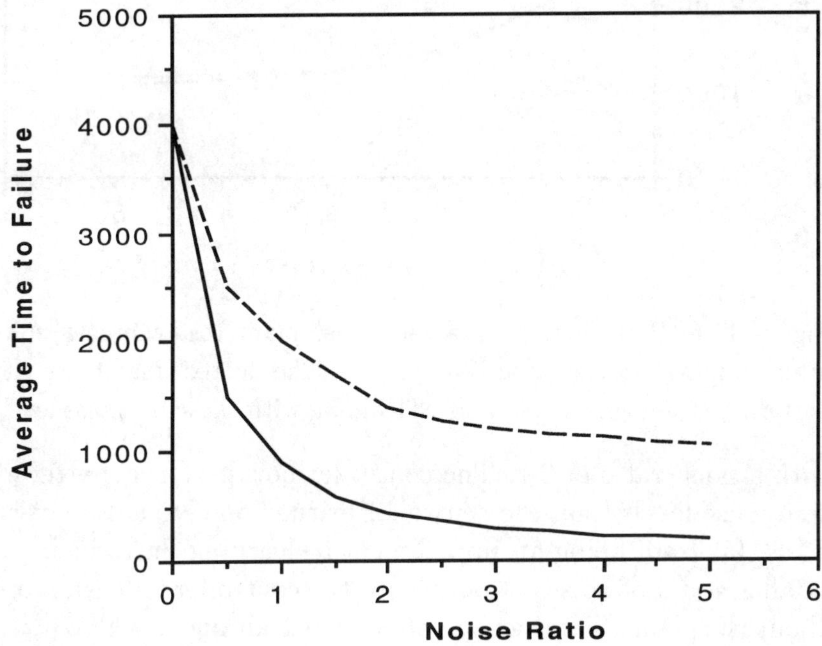

Figure 11.5. Performance on a zero noise plant after training on the zero noise plant. The dotted line shows the performance on a noisy plant.

The average time to failure of the mill with a noise ratio of 0.1 is about 1000 s when using actions learned with no noise. Actions learned with the same noise ratio of 0.1 achieve an average time to failure of about 2000 s. It seems from this result that learning on a low-noise plant does not improve performance on higher-noise plants. However, further tests were conducted, this time with the initial training being done on a low-noise plant

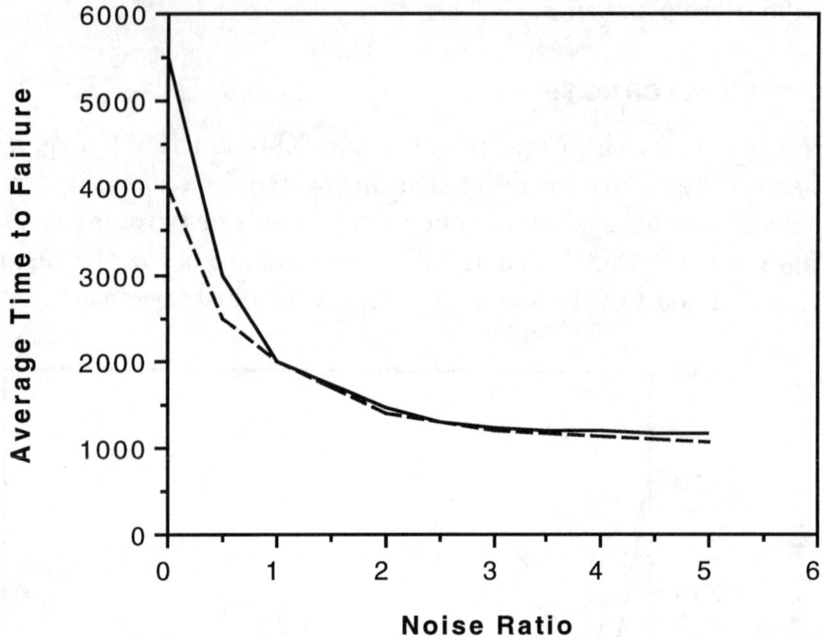

Figure 11.6. Performance on a zero noise plant (the skinpass mill) after training with a noise level of 0.1. The dotted line shows the performance on a noisy plant after training with the same noise level.

with a noise ratio of 0.1. The controller now performs better at zero noise levels than the controller learned on zero noise levels. Thus, far from being an impediment to learning, introducing a small amount of noise actually helps the controller to learn more about the plant. These graphs show that training on a zero noise plant produced a poor controller for a noisy plant, while conversely, a controller trained on a noisy plant produces a robust controller useful for all noise levels that is actually better for the zero noise plant than the zero noise controller. This supports the earlier suggestion that noise, or excitation of all modes of the plant, is important for good modelling of the plant.

6   ACTUATOR OUTPUT

The BOXES algorithm requires that the actuator output be quantized. The problem with this is that coarse quantization leads to unnecessarily large actuator changes. This would be highly detrimental to a commercial plant, coming with the attendant maintenance problems. Three methods were investigated in an attempt to alleviate this problem.

6.1 Smoothing the output

An attempt was made to filter the output to the actuator in the time domain. Such a filter is usually a running average of previous actuator outputs. This type of filtering introduces a delay and so to minimize the effects of the delay, the filter is generally first-order. That is, the new output is only a function of the immediately preceding output and the input:

$$u_t = u_{t-1} + \alpha(u'_t - u_{t-1}),$$

where u' is produced by BOXES and u_i is output to the plant.

By varying the filter coefficient, α, a smoother response can be obtained. However, substantial drop-off in performance occurs when the filtering is present, as shown in Fig. 11.7.

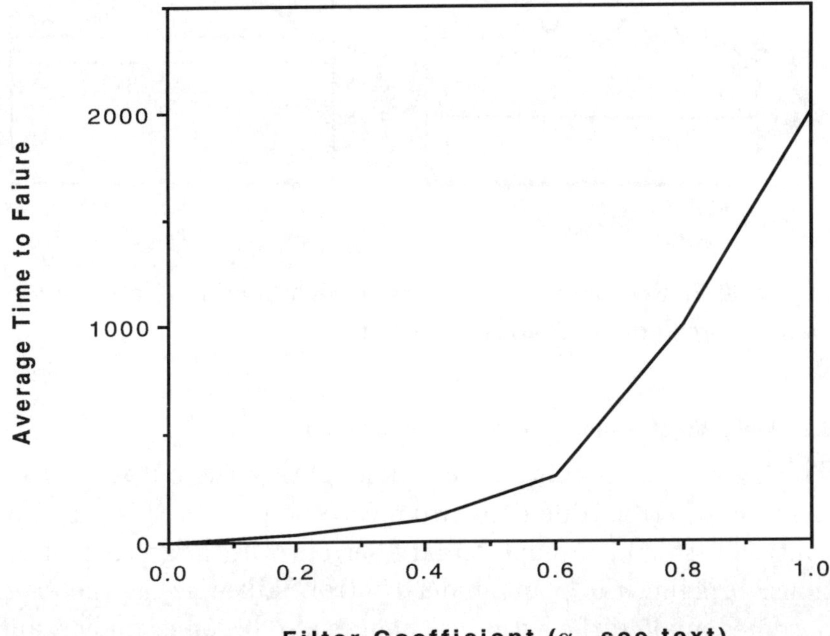

Figure 11.7. Performance of the mill as actuator output is filtered.

In order to explain why the performance is reduced, we looked at the response of BOXES in the time domain. The large damped oscillations in Fig. 11.8 provides one explanation. As can be seen, filtering the output in this way, while producing a smoother controller, also results in delays in the control loop, and large, slow oscillations in the controlled variable.

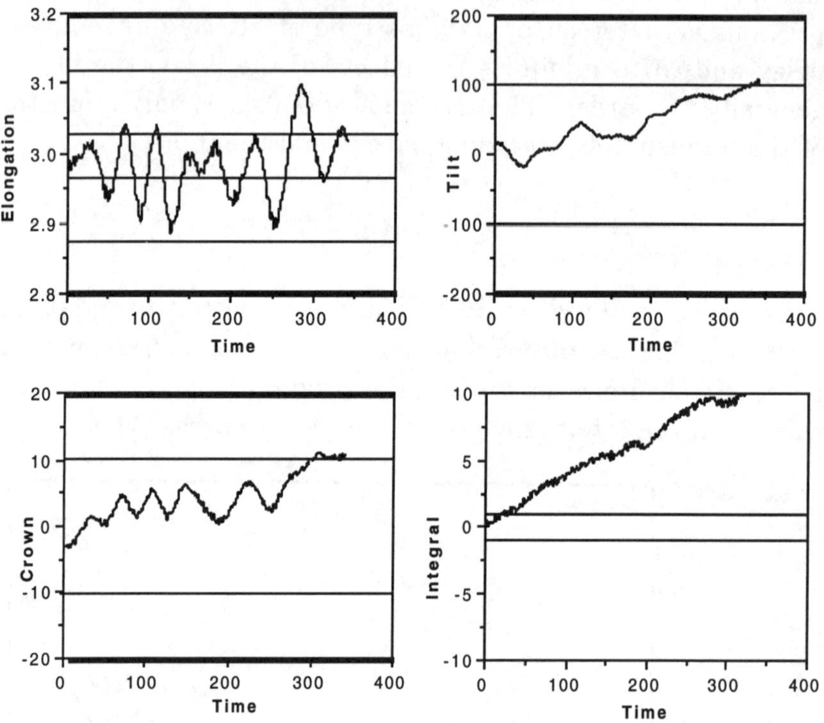

Figure 11.8. Response of one run with high filtering. Note the long damped oscillations. X-axis in seconds.

6.2 Weighting the output with error magnitude

This type of smoothing relies on weighting the output with a function of error (difference from a setpoint). In this way, the controller should respond to large errors with large control actions, bringing the plant under control. Likewise, as the error becomes smaller, the actuator changes also become smaller, and a smoother controller results. To test this theory, the following function of actuator weighting was used:

$$Action'(e) = \left| \frac{2e}{e_{max}} \right|^{\alpha} \times Action(e)$$

where e_{max} is the error at the failure boundary.

The output of the actuator is thus weighted by a function of the absolute value of the error. To test the effectiveness of weighting the output in this way, and perhaps to find a good weight curve, 20 test runs of selected algorithms with different weighting parameters were allowed to learn from 30 000 trials. The average final value of the time to failure was recorded for selected weighting parameters. Note that the results from this example, like many in these experiments, may be specific to the skinpass mill. The results are not meant to be useful for all plants, but simply to show the viability of the idea. The results from this test are given in Fig. 11.9.

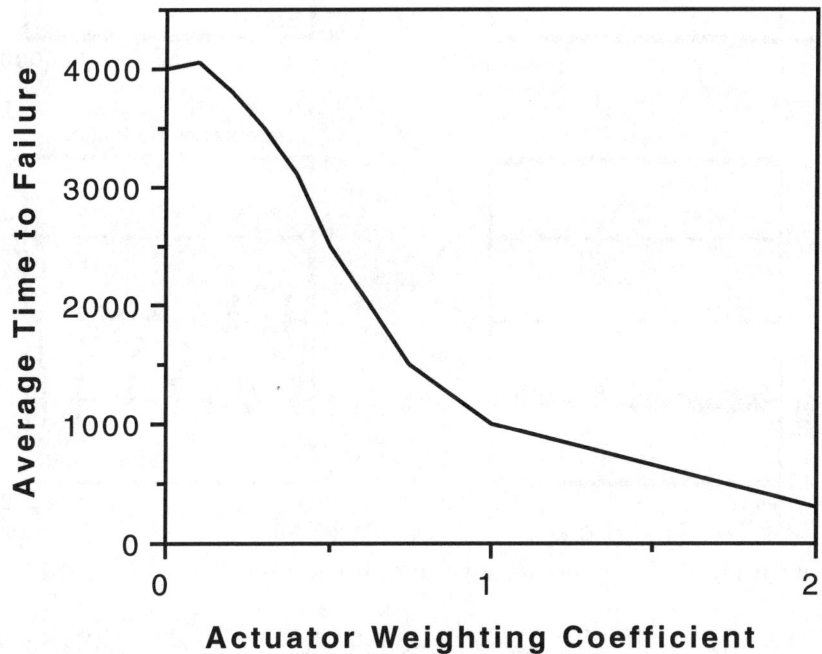

Figure 11.9. Actuator weighting vs performance. No significant best value is observed.

These are disappointing, in that no significant best weighting curve was found. However, the sharp decline in performance around the actuator weighting coefficient of 0.5 warranted further attention. Again, we turn to the time domain behaviour of BOXES controlling the mill, and take a typical example from weighting parameter of 0.3, and one at 0.5. Both examples are at a noise ratio of 0.5, which is quite high. These are shown on Figs 11.10 and 11.11 respectively.

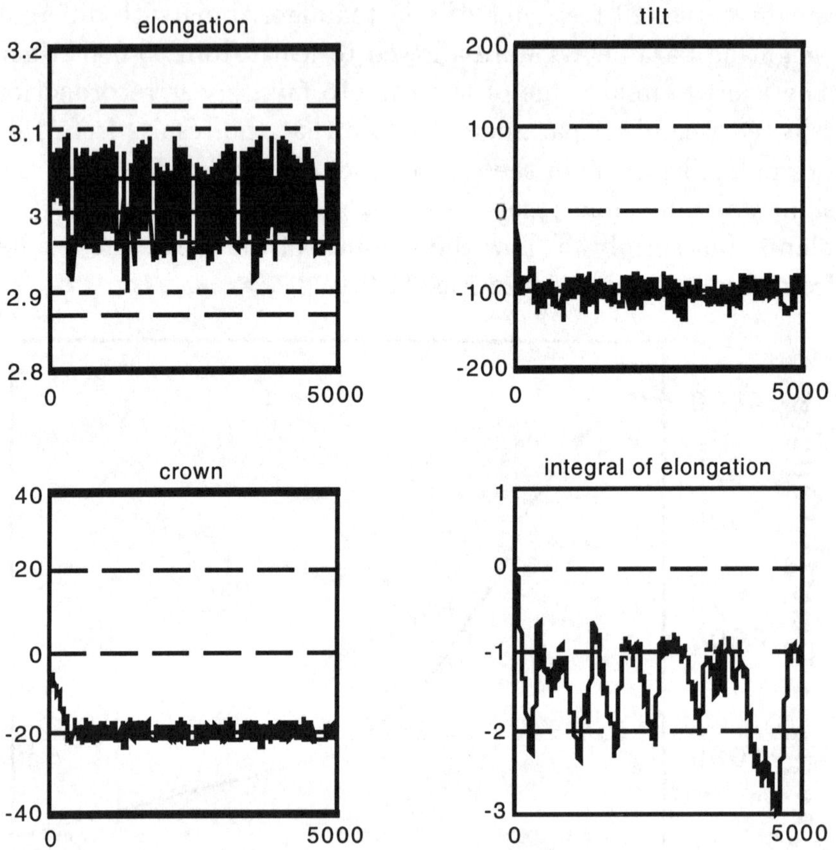

Figure 11.10. Large oscillations due to wide zero.

We speculate that the drop-off is due to larger oscillations occurring around the setpoint. These oscillations are in turn due to the lack of control and the large noise amplitude. If this is the case, then smaller weighting parameters produce narrower regions where the controller has little effect, which leads to smaller oscillations. Conversely, a large weighting parameter

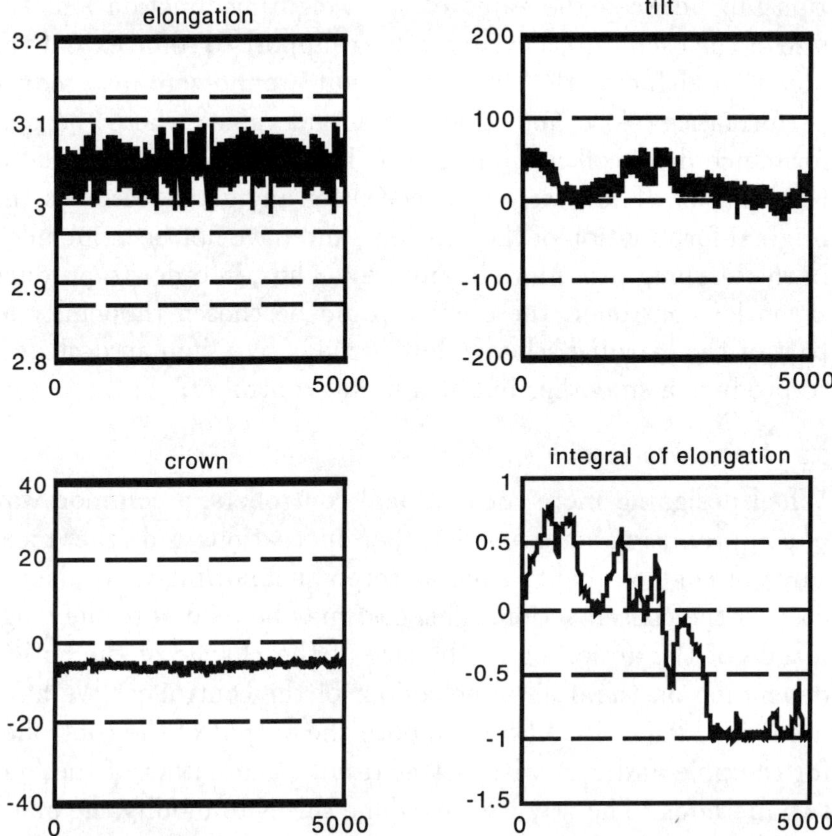

Figure 11.11. Smaller oscillations due to narrower zero. Both runs (Figs 11.10 and 11.11) had the same external noise level.

would produce larger regions where the controller has little effect. If the oscillations became larger than the size of the boxes, this would possibly produce instability and poor performance.

Figure 11.10 shows a successful controller with larger oscillations around the setpoint. The amplitude of these oscillations is about ±0.08%, or about 40% of the failure boundaries. This algorithm has a weighting parameter of 0.5, so the weighting function should have a value of about 0.65 at the limit of oscillations. In Fig. 11.11, the size of the oscillation is smaller, about 25% of the failure boundary, and the weighting parameter is 0.3. This gives a similar weighting function value, about 0.65. While this is hardly convincing proof that a direct relationship between the value of the weighting function and the size of the oscillations exists, it does support to some extent the idea that reducing the actuator output around zero may reduce performance. Also note that the actual values where the performance drops off are related to the choice of gains available to each box. These were not chosen for any good reason in the original formulation of the problem, and have not been included in the learning procedure in any way. Thus, in order to produce a gentler controller, these gains could be chosen (hopefully as part of the learning scheme, but perhaps by a human designer) to produce a smoother but still useful controller.

6.3 Control effort cost

When designing more conventional controllers, a common way of compromising between controller fluctuations and other measures of control quality such as setpoint following is to place a cost on the chosen action. This cost may be related to the magnitude of the action or to the size of the change of the action depending on the desired behaviour of the controller. We have used this idea in BOXES to smooth the output of the controller for the pole and cart with better results than either of the first two methods. The way we have done this is to modify the merit equation, as shown below:

$$merit = weight \times \frac{Life\text{-}time}{Usage^k}.$$

A 'do nothing' action was introduced into the pole and cart system. This action was given a large weighting ($w = 3$) in comparison to the push-left and push-right actions ($w = 1$). Figure 11.12 shows how the original, unweighted BOXES controller performs on this task, with the solution being characterized by jerky, unnecessary actions.

Figure 11.13 shows how BOXES performs with weighting. This second graph shows a marked difference in control strategy (which is also evidenced in the rules developed by the learning agent). In comparison with the earlier methods of actuator smoothing, there is only a minimal increase in learning time to reach the same level of average time to failure for the pole and

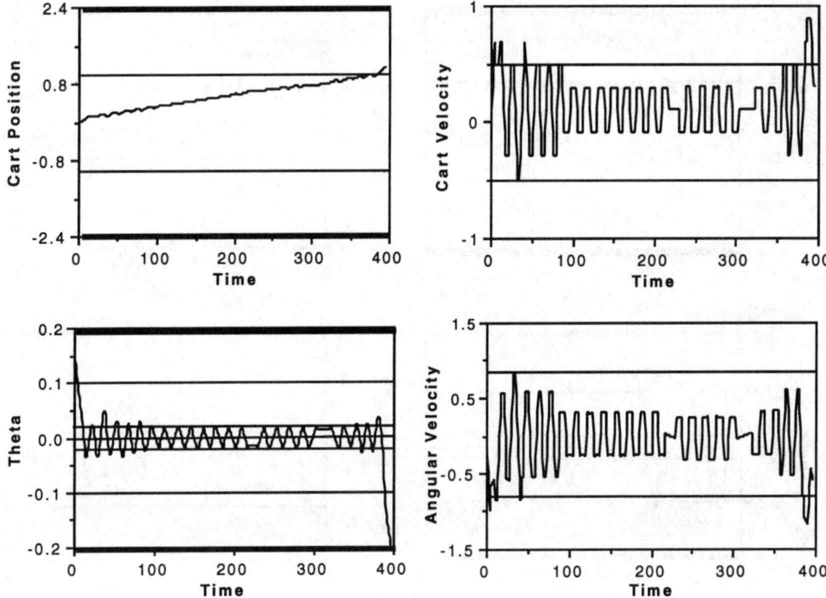

Figure 11.12. The behaviour of the pole and cart using a controller without a cost on the action.

cart. More importantly, the number of actions has been reduced significantly, resulting in a corresponding reduction in cost.

Because the mill has 125 actions, providing a weighting is somewhat more complicated and experiments are still proceeding.

7 CONCLUSIONS

Reducing annealing allows most of the actions in a box to gain experience. This means that a more complete model of expected time to failure can be built up for each action. As a result a more robust controller for the mill could be constructed.

It was noticed that adding noise to systems with no annealing or no noise improved the performance of the mill. It was suggested that this is because the noise excites the plant, enabling the BOXES model of the plant to be made more complete. This effect was not evident for the pole and cart, probably because the instability of the plant caused enough excitation by itself to make it possible to model the plant.

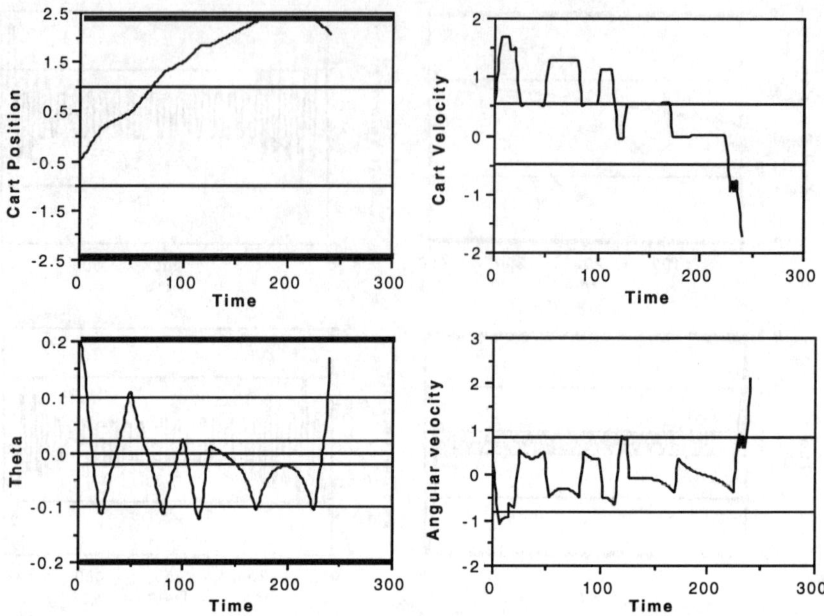

Figure 11.13. The behaviour of the pole and cart using a controller with a cost on the action

Three methods were attempted to improve the quality of the BOXES control. Filtering the output had the effect of introducing a delay into the control loop. As might be expected, this produced a marginally stable controller, exhibiting long, slow oscillations. Very poor performance was found. It was hoped that by weighting the output to be smaller near to zero error, a smoother controller might result. Instead, the small weighting near zero error produced a zone where the controller had little effect, and the oscillation usually found in a BOXES controlled plant increased in amplitude to fill this zone. Only very steep weighting showed any sign of improving performance. Placing a cost on a control action was the most useful of the three. Using a BOXES learning agent that places a cost on action magnitude, we found learning times were not significantly affected. The resulting controller, however, was far more economical with its outputs, resulting in a controller which produced an output only when really necessary. Unfortunately, no systematic way of choosing the cost for each action has yet been found, but our results do show that this technique is worth pursuing.

REFERENCES

Anderson, C. W. (1987). Strategy learning with multilayer connectionist representations. In P. Langley (Eds.), *Proceedings of the Fourth International Workshop on Machine Learning* (pp. 103–114). Los Altos: Morgan Kaufmann.

Michie, D. and Chambers, R. A. (1968). BOXES: An experiment in adaptive control. In E. Dale and D. Michie (Eds.), *Machine Intelligence 2*. Edinburgh: Oliver and Boyd.

Quinlan, J. R. (1986). The effect of noise on concept learning. In R.S. Michalski, J.G. Carbonell and T.M. Mitchell (Eds.), *Machine Learning: An Artificial Intelligence Approach, Vol. 2*. Los Altos: Morgan Kaufmann.

Roberts, W.L. (1972). An approximate theory of temper rolling, *Iron and Steel Engineer YearBook*, pp. 530–542.

Sammut, C. A. (1994). Recent progress with BOXES. In K. Furukawa, S. Muggleton and D. Michie (Eds.), *Machine Intelligence 13*. Oxford: The Clarendon Press.

Sammut, C. and Cribb, J. (1990). Is learning rate a good performance criterion of learning? In B. W. Porter and R. J. Mooney (Eds), *Proceedings of the Seventh International Machine Learning Conference*. (pp. 170–178). San Mateo, CA: Morgan Kaufmann.

12

A Reasoning System for Legal Analogy

Makoto Haraguchi

Dept. of Systems Science
Tokyo Institute of Technology

1 INTRODUCTION

This paper presents a reasoning system that performs analogical reasoning for legal rules under an order-sorted representation. Analogy is often used in the domain of law to derive an appropriate conclusion for a particular case not covered by any legal rule. For such a case, lawyers are considered to find a legal rule whose requirement is similar to the case with respect to some significant points. Then the rule is analogically applied to the case for which the same or a similar conclusion of the rule is derived.

To develop a system for reasoning by analogy in law, it is necessary to have knowledge for deciding the similarities at a conceptual level. This is because both legal rules and cases are described in terms of legal concepts. It is well known that a taxonomic hierarchy on legal concepts is useful for this purpose. Those concepts with the same super concept in the hierarchy can be understood as similar ones. From a logical point of view, such a hierarchy is represented as an ordered set of sort symbols denoting concepts. Then our legal rules will be represented as well-sorted formulas of an order-sorted logic with the sort hierarchy.

The purpose of this paper is first to show that an order-sorted logic (Beierle 1992; Walther 1988) is more appropriate in representing legal rules than a standard unsorted logic. In particular, a new symbol system is introduced to consider a predicate that takes another predicate's instances as its arguments. Such a predicate frequently appears in legal texts, as shown in Section 2 and 3. A similar symbol system based on unsorted Horn logic can be found in Yoshino (1987) in which predicates have their identifiers to be referred by other predicates. Since the notion of identifiers goes beyond the scope of semantics of first-order logic, it is hard to understand what the identifiers mean. On the other hand, it is not a difficult task to have a formal semantics based on sorted Herbrand models, although the present paper does not concern such a model theory. In addition to the model theoretic aspect, it is widely known that the sorted logic or a typed system can well control the inference processes because of its type-checking mechanism. The system presented in this paper also enjoys this property.

The second purpose of this paper is to show a computational method for analogical reasoning for legal rules under the order-sorted representation of legal knowledge. Although we can find many studies (see Russell 1986; Greiner 1988; Indurkhya 1990; Dierbach 1992 for instance) on computational analogy, few studies which emphasize the importance of sorted representations are found. In Harao (1993), an idea of using a type theory for analogical reasoning is described. However the details of how we make use of the typed knowledge in analogical reasoning and what operations are necessary to realize the idea are not fully developed. This paper, on the other hand, tries to present a set of concrete computational operators for doing that for legal rules based on our order-sorted representations.

The analogical reasoning in this paper can be viewed as a combined process of both deduction and generalization along the sort hierarchy. We classify the generalization into the following: extension of the applicability of legal rules, generalization of predicates, and abstraction of individual objects or acts. These three types of generalization are carried out by the corresponding three generalization rules: sorted generalization, predicate generalization and term generalization. All of these are applied to goal clauses of a standard deductive interpreter for order-sorted Horn logic.

At first, the sorted generalization replaces a variable appearing in a rule with another variable of more general sort to eliminate type errors occurring in applying the rule analogically. Although the applicability of rules is restricted to sorts of variables, the sorts are now extended by the generalization. Thus, our sorted generalization produces a rule with wider applicability than the original one. Moreover, it is easy to compute the generalization and therefore to apply the rule analogically, since the sorted generalization is determined by a simple algebraic operation for our sort hierarchy. Compared with the previous study (Yoshino *et al.* 1993) on analogy in law, which concerns the same legal case as this paper does, a great computational reduction is achieved due to the algebraic operation.

The term generalization, the second generalization rule, abstracts an individual instance of a sort to a variable of more general sort. The variable is then instantiated with another instance of a more specific sort. The latter instance is treated as a candidate for an analogue of the original one. This is because their sorts share the generalized sort as their common super sort. Thus, the term generalization together with the instantiation is used to find an analogue.

Finally, the predicate generalization has an effect of replacing a predicate with another one of more general extension. In contrast with the first two generalization rules, it does not depend on our sort hierarchy. A logical structure of (object-level) rules completely determines the generalization. Technically speaking, the generalization of this type is necessary to eliminate some type errors invoked by term generalization.

In the research field of machine learning, we can find many studies on generalization. Especially the notion of absorption, defined in Muggleton (1990) and Muggleton and Buntine (1988), becomes important also in this paper to realize the generalizations along the legal taxonomy. Our sorted generalization is a natural extension of the absorption. The basic idea thus comes from Muggleton. Similarly both the predicate generalization and the term generalization can be kinds of absorption, if we translate the sorted representations into unsorted ones. However, the process of controlling how we apply the absorption is strongly constrained due to the sort information given by our sort hierarchy, as we will see in Section 4. This point distinguishes this paper from the others.

We organize this paper as follows: In Section 2, a preliminary definition of order-sorted logic is described, and then a symbol system for representing legal rules is presented based on the order-sorted logic. In Section 3, a legal rule appearing in Japanese Civil Code and a real case for which the rule has been applied analogically are presented and analysed. All the necessary knowledge to realize the analogy is shown and is also represented as sorted clauses. In Section 4, the three generalization rules as well as some control rules are presented. Some examples to show why the rules are needed and how they behave are described. In the final section, some future works are discussed.

2 AN ORDER-SORTED REPRESENTATION OF LEGAL RULES

We first present preliminary definitions of order-sorted logic, and then introduce a new symbol system under which legal rules are represented.

2.1 Preliminaries

It is necessary to have a large taxonomic hierarchy to describe legal knowledge. The hierarchy consists of legal conceptual classes linked with *ISA* relations.[1] According to standard logic, each *ISA* link is represented as a definite clause. For instance, a clause meaning that s_1 is a subclass of s_2 can be written as

$$\forall x. \ s_1(x) \to s_2(x),$$

where $s_j(x)$ is true iff x is an instance of the conceptual class which s_j denotes. Some studies (Nebel 1990, Walther 1988, Beierle *et al.* 1992) have already pointed out that it is unnatural to have ISA relations in the forms of logical rules as in the above. For instance, suppose we have another clause expressing that s_2 is a subclass of s_3. In order to conclude a fact that s_1 is

---

[1]Although there exist several ways of explaining *ISA* relation (Waragai 1994), this paper interprets it as 'is_a_subclass_of'.

also a subclass of s_3, we must apply inference rules like Modus Ponens. However, the fact is a direct consequence of the transitive law of partial ordering, provided we have the taxonomic hierarchy in the form of a partially ordered set. From this simple observation, each conceptual class and the taxonomic hierarchy are now formalized as a sort symbol and a partially ordered set $(S, \leq)$ of sort symbols, respectively (Walther 1988; Beierle *et al.* 1992). In what follows, the statement that s_1 is a subclass of s_2 is denoted by $s_1 \leq s_2$.

Each non-logical symbol is supposed to have a corresponding sorted specification. A function symbol f of arity n has its sorted specification written as $f : s_1, ..., s_n \rightarrow s$, which means that the function (denoted by) f takes instances of $s_1, ..., s_n$ and returns an instance of s. Similarly, a predicate symbol p of arity n has its sorted specification $p : s_1, ..., s_n$ meaning that the predicate p is defined for n-tuples whose j-th arguments are instances of s_j. Moreover any variable x is assumed to have its sort s, and is written as $x : s$. The sort s specifies the range of possible instances for the variable x to have.

Given this sorted specification of symbols, $[t]$ of a term t, called a principal sort of t, is defined by

(1) If t is a variable $x : s$ then $[t] = s$.
(2) If $t = f(t_1, ..., t_n)$ for some $f : s_1, ..., s_n \rightarrow s$ $(n \geq 0)$, then $[t] = s$.

Moreover, a first-order term t is said to be well sorted if, for any subterm $f(t_1, ..., t_n)$ with a specification $f : s_1, ..., s_n \rightarrow s$, $[t_j] \leq s_j$ holds for each j. An expression $t : s$ denotes that t is a well sorted term such that $[t] \leq s$. Similarly a substitution $\theta = \{x_j/t_j\}$, which replaces the variable x_j with the term t_j, is called well sorted if t_j is well sorted and $[t_j] \leq [x_j]$. Thus, by the well-sorted substitution, possible instances of a variable $x : s$ are restricted to well sorted terms of sorts s' such that $s' \leq s$.

Given a sort hierarchy $(S, \leq)$, a unification that takes the sorted information into account is called an order-sorted unification. Intuitively speaking, the order-sorted unification matches two or more well sorted terms and forms them into a single well sorted term, where the matching is done by applying well sorted substitutions. For instance, suppose we have an ordering in which $s \leq s_1$ and $s \leq s_2$ hold for sorts s, s_1, and s_2. Then the terms $x_1 : s_1$ and $x_2 : s_2$ can be unifiable, since they become the same well sorted term $x : s$ by the well sorted substitution $\{x_1/x, x_2/x\}$. On the other hand, if s_1 and s_2 has no common subsort, then the order-sorted unification fails.

Formally a unifier τ for a set E of well sorted terms is a substitution such that $e_1\tau = e_2\tau$ for all $e_1, e_2 \in E$. An order-sorted unifier for a set of well sorted terms is defined as a unifier of the set that is well sorted. Furthermore, for order-sorted unifiers θ_1 and θ_2 of a set E of well sorted terms, an ordering $\theta_1 \leq \theta_2$ is defined as:

> $\theta_1 \leq \theta_2$ iff there exists an well sorted substitution τ such that $x\theta_1\tau = x\theta_2$ for any variable x in E

In this case, we say that the substitution θ_1 is more general than θ_2. It is well known that, for a set of well sorted terms that have an order-sorted unifier, there always exists a maximally general order-sorted unifier (mgosu, for short), provided our sort hierarchy is finite (Walther 1988). An order-sorted resolution is now defined as the standard resolution for well sorted clauses, where all the unifiers should be mgosu. For more details, see Beierle *et al.* (1992) for instance.

2.2 A symbol system

Legal rules generally govern individual human acts and events in our social life. Their effectiveness and validity depend on what properties they have, what legal concepts they belong to, and what relations hold between them. Since our order-sorted logic is basically a first-order logic, the properties and the relations should be formalized as first-order predicates that take individual acts as their arguments. For the same reason, once we decide to adopt order-sorted representations, the individual acts and their legal conceptual classes must be expressed as well sorted terms and their sorts, respectively. Thus, they are distinguished at symbol level. In most legal texts, however, the individual acts and their classes are sometimes confused at symbol level. For instance, consider the following sentence in the form of natural language:

a contract that is made by a person a with a person b for an object c is a contract.

The first occurrence of the term 'contract' given an indefinite article denotes an individual contract whose attributes are specified by the phrase followed by the relative pronoun. Thus, it works as a name for some individual act. On the other hand, 'is_a' is a copula that connects the individual contract and a class named 'contract'. The second occurrence of 'contract' therefore works as a general name. A symbol system defined now in this section distinguishes each individual name from a general name. For this purpose, a sort symbol and a functor are associated with a legal conceptual class on actions. Formally we need the following definition.

Definition 12.1 Sorts of event type. We first assume that we have a designated sort symbol *event* in our set S of sorts. Each sort s more specific than *event* is called a sort of event type. Otherwise, s is called a sort of object type.[2] We assume the greatest sort *object* among sorts of object type. A functor f whose codomain sort s is event type is called an event formation functor for s. If there exists the unique event formation functor f for s, f is rather denoted by s_f.

For instance, the sort *contract* ($\leq$ *event*) is supposed to have the unique event formation functor

$$contract\_f : person, person, object \rightarrow contract,$$

meaning that an instance of *contract* is determined by specifying two persons and an object for the contract. Then, given constants $a : person$, $b : person$ and $imm\_X : object$, the sentence we have examined in the preceding page corresponds to the following well sorted term:

$$contract\_f(a, b, imm\_X) : contract.$$

The arguments a, b and imm_X work as 'attributes' or 'features' of that term of *contract*. To get the attributes from a term of event type, we consider the following 'attr'-predicates. For each

---

[2] Precisely speaking, s is called a sort of object type, if $\neg(s \leq event)$ and $s \neq label$.

event formation functor $f : s_1, ..., s_n \to s$, we assume a unit clause

$$attr(f(X_1 : s_1, ..., X_n : s_n), a_j, X_j),$$

where a_j is an attribute name[3] (or a feature name) associated with the j-th domain sort s_j of f. For instance, using an attribute name $agt2$, one of the attr-predicates for $contract\_f$ can be written as

$$attr(contract\_f(X : person, \ Y : person, \ Z : object), agt2, Y),$$

meaning that the second agent of $contract\_f(X, Y, Z)$ is Y. In what follows, the sorted specification for an event formation functor $f : s_1, ..., s_n \to s$ with its attribute names $a_1, ..., a_n$ is instead written as

$$f(a_1 : s_1, \quad ..., \quad a_n : s_n) : s$$

We understand this expression as a statement that a_j of f is s_j and that f forms an instance of s. The sorted specification for $contract\_f$ can be now written as

$$contract\_f(agt1 : person, agt2 : person, obj : object) : contract.$$

In contrast with the usual first-order terms, any term of event type is a theoretical concept, and is not assumed always to have a real denotation. In order to designate that something specified by such a term really happens, we introduce a special predicate $oc : event$.[4] For instance, an atomic formula $oc(contract\_f(a, b, c))$ means that the contract made by a and b for c really occurs in a world we are going to axiomatize.

A query is a well sorted goal clause. $\leftarrow oc(X : lawful\_act)$ is an example meaning the question 'Does some lawful act X occur?'. Our order-sorted resolution directly solves this goal by finding an order-sorted unifier

$$\theta = \{X : lawful\_act/contract\_f(a, b, c)\},$$

---

[3]The attribute names are constant symbols of a designated sort *label*. *label* is assumed to be incomparable to any other sort in our sort hierarchy. Moreover it can be neither a domain sort nor a co-domain sort of a functor as well as a predicate except *attr*.

[4]The use of the *oc* predicate is introduced in Waragai (1994) for an unsorted case to analyse higher-order ISA relations.

provided our sort hierarchy includes

$$contract \leq juristic\_act \leq lawful\_act \leq human\_act \leq event.$$

3 ANALOGICAL REASONING FOR LEGAL RULES

Now we are ready to show a legal rule, Clause 2, Article 94 of Japanese Civil Code, which judges have applied analogically for many cases. Article 94 is normally considered to concern the difference between external appearances and real intentions of contracts. We describe the article in a simplified form so that we can understand how the article is applied to resolve conflicts on contracts.[5]

Clause 1: A contract with a false declaration of intention made by a party to the contract is null and void.

Clause 2: From the nullity of the contract in the preceding clause, one cannot set up against a person in good faith, who does not know the falsity that the declared intention is different from the real intention.

According to Clause 1, the contract with the false declaration of intention is null for the party to the contract. However, the nullity is not applied to the other person, provided he believes the false declaration without knowing its real intention. The right of the person will be protected by Clause 2.

The Clause 2, for instance, can be encoded in the form of order-sorted representation followed by its sorted specifications:

Rule 1 (Article94, Clause2)
$oc(Ctrct1 : contract),$
     $attr(Ctrct1, agt1, X), attr(Ctrct1, agt2, Y)$
     $attr(Ctrct1, obj, Object)$
$oc(Falsity : falsity), attr(Falsity, obj, Ctrct1),$
$oc(Ctrct2 : contract), attr(Ctrct2, agt1, Y),$
     $attr(Ctrct2, agt2, Z), attr(Ctrct2, obj, Object),$
$good\_faith(Z, Falsity)$
     $\rightarrow cannot\_set\_up(X, Z, Ctrct2)$

Sorted Specifications:
     $contract\_f(agt1 : person, agt2 : person, obj : object) : contract.$

---

[5]The original article is stated more abstractly, and requires a contract to be made in collusion with its parties.

$$contract \leq juristic\_act \leq lawful\_act \leq human\_act \leq event.$$
$$good\_faith : person, event. \qquad person \leq object.$$
$$cannot\_set\_up : person, person, contract.$$
$$falsity\_f(obj : human\_act) : falsity \leq event.$$

Rule 1 is concerned with two contracts, *Ctrct1* and *Ctrct2*. The variable *Falsity* will be bound to the falsity of the first contract $Ctrct1$, as we see in the next section. The atom *cannot_set_up(X,Z,Ctrct2)* means that X cannot claim the invalidity of $Ctrct2$ which Z made.

The meaning of falsity is clarified by the theory interpretation rule 2, which states that a contract is concluded as false if the representation and the state of affairs are different.

Rule 2 (Falsity of Contracts)
$$oc(Ctrct : contract)$$
$$repr\_of\_ctrct(Ctrct, ReprCts),$$
$$soa\_of\_ctrct(Ctrct, RealCts),$$
$$ReprCts \neq RealCts$$
$$\rightarrow oc(falsity\_f(Ctrct)).$$
Sorted Specifications:
$$(repr\_of\_ctrct : contract, top.), (soa\_of\_ctrct : contract, top.)$$
Abbreviations:
    'repr' : representation, 'soa': state of affairs.

The predicate *good_faith* is defined as follows:

$$(oc(Evt) - > not(know(Agt, Evt)))$$
$$\rightarrow good\_faith(Agt : person, Evt : event)$$

where *not* and $A - > B$ are a negation defined by negation as failure rule and a built-in predicate meaning 'if A then B', respectively. The predicate $know : person, top^6$ is defined so that an atom $know(Agt, Evt)$ succeeds iff the Evt, which will be bound to a term of event type, is proved under the set of facts Agt knows. We use an auxiliary predicate $know\_fact : person, top$. All the possible instances of $know\_fact$ as well as rules for inferring 'knowing' relations are initially present in our fact database, as Fact 1. According to such a representation of facts, the predicate *know* is easily realized as a kind of meta-interpreter of Prolog.

---

[6]*top* is the least upper bound of *event* and *object*.

Now we present a legal case for which Clause 2 of Article 94 is applied analogically. In the case, since p_b sold the house to p_c without its real ownership, p_a, who was the real owner, claimed his ownership right. However, the judge approved that p_c had the real ownership right by legal analogy.

Case of a petition against registration of passage of a house's title ((O)No.107-1951, judgment of the second petty bench, 20 August, 1951).

Case: After p_a bought a house, which p_o owned, from p_o, he approved the registration of passage of title from p_o to p_b without his real intention of the passage. Having registered the passage of title, p_b sold the house to p_c, who acted in good faith, and did not know the real intention of p_a but only that p_b registered. p_c registered the passage of ownership title. p_a claimed that p_c must do cancellation procedure of passage of title and others because the ownership of the house in the case should belong to p_a, and p_b and p_c did not have the ownership of the house.

Judgment: By analogical application of Clause2, Art. 94 of Japanese Civil Code, the nullity of the registration of p_b cannot be set up against the good faith of p_c, who did not know the real intention of p_a, so that p_a cannot claim that p_c must do cancellation procedure of passage of title and others of the registration.

We represent the legal case by a set of facts approved by the court.

Facts 1 (Facts representing the legal case)
Relations:
$oc(sale\_of\_immovables\_f(p\_o, p\_a, imm\_X))$.
$ownership(p\_a, imm\_X)$.
$oc(reg\_of\_ptitle\_f(p\_o, p\_b, imm\_X))$.
$oc(reg\_f(p\_b, imm\_X))$.
$oc(approval\_f(p\_a, reg\_of\_ptitle\_f(p\_o, p\_b, imm\_X)))$.
$oc(sale\_of\_immovables\_f(p\_b, p\_c, imm\_X))$.
$oc(reg\_of\_ptitle\_f(p\_b, p\_c, imm\_X))$.
$know\_fact(p\_c, reg\_of\_ptitle\_f(p\_o, p\_b, imm\_X))$.
$know\_fact(p\_c, reg\_f(p\_b, imm\_X))$.
$know\_fact(p\_c, sale\_of\_immovables\_f(p\_b, p\_c, imm\_X))$.
$know\_fact(p\_c, reg\_of\_ptitle\_f(p\_b, p\_c, imm\_X).$)

Sorted Specifications:

p_o, p_a, p_b, p_c : *person*. imm_X : *house*.

ownership : *person, object*.

$reg\_of\_ptitle\_f(agt1 : person, agt2 : person, obj : imm\_prop)$
$: reg\_of\_ptitle$

$house \le imm\_prop \le prop \le object$

$reg\_f(agt : person, obj : imm\_proprop) : reg$

$reg\_of\_ptitle \le reg \le quarsi\_juritstic\_act \le lawful\_act$

$sale\_of\_imm \le sale \le human\_act$

$approval\_f(agt : person, obj : human\_act) : approval \le event$

$sale\_of\_imm\_f(agt1 : person, agt2 : person, obj : imm\_prop)$
$: sale\_of\_imm$

Abbreviations:

agt: agent	*prop*: property	*reg*: registration
imm_prop: immovable property		*ptitle* : passage of titles
prop: property		
sale_of_imm: sale of immovable properties		
reg_of_ptitle: registration of passage of titles		

Rule 1 and the case represented by Fact 1 concern contracts and registrations, respectively. The judges thus seem to have applied a rule on contract to a case of registration. Moreover, the notion of falsity that Article 94 mentions is restricted to the falsity of contracts, as defined in Rule 2. Hence, for the analogy the judges used, the following conceptual operation might have been performed:

(1) The rule about contract is generalized so that it can be applied to registrations.

(2) The registration instances in Fact 1 are treated as analogues of contract instances.

(3) The notion of falsity bound to the class of contracts is generalized to a more general notion of falsity that covers registrations.

It suffices to have three generalization rules, introduced in the next section, to realize both (1) and (2). In addition to these generalization rules, we need to have a knowledge used to judge the falsity of registrations (3). Such knowledge can be supplied by the following rules:

Rule 3 (Knowledge of Registration)

$$oc(Regp : reg\_of\_ptitle),$$
$$attr(Regp, agent2, Agt), attr(Regp, object, Obj)$$
$$\rightarrow repr\_of\_reg(Regp, Agt).$$
$$oc(Regp : reg\_of\_ptitle), attr(Regp, object, Obj),$$
$$ownership(Agt, Obj)$$
$$\rightarrow soa\_of\_reg(Regp, Agt).$$
$$repr\_of\_ctrct(X : contract, Y : top) \rightarrow repr(X, Y).$$
$$soa\_of\_ctrct(X : contract, Y : top) \rightarrow soa(X, Y).$$
$$repr\_of\_reg(X : registration, Y : top) \rightarrow repr(X, Y).$$
$$soa\_of\_reg(X : registration, Y : top) \rightarrow soa(X, Y).$$

Sorted Specifications:

$$repr : human\_act, top. \qquad soa : human\_act, top.$$
$$repr\_of\_reg : human\_act, top. \qquad soa\_of\_reg : human\_act, top.$$

The falsity Rule 2 has two predicates: one is soa_of_ctrct (state of affairs) and the other is $repr\_of\_ctrct$ (representation). The Rule 2 decides the falsity of a contract if the arguments of soa_of_ctrct and $repr\_of\_ctrct$ are different. Since Rule 3 on registrations can decide both soa_of_reg and $repr\_of\_reg$ for registrations, a rule obtained by generalizing the falsity Rule 2 for contracts will succeed for our case of registrations with the aid of Rule 3. All the techniques for carrying out such a task will be presented in the next section.

4 ORDER-SORTED GENERALIZATIONS

Now we are ready to show how to utilize legal knowledge and how to carry out legal reasoning in an order-sorted symbol system for which order-sorted resolution and generalization are applied.

First suppose that we try to construct a legal argument to protect the right of good faith person p_c appearing in the case presented in Section 3. Since the plaintiff p_a claimed that p_c should do a cancellation procedure of passage of title, it suffices to show that he cannot set up p_c with respect to the passage of title. Hence we first make the following goal expressed as a well sorted goal clause:

$$\leftarrow cannot\_set\_up(p\_a, p\_c, reg\_of\_ptitle\_f(p\_b, p\_c, imm\_X)) \quad (12.1)$$

Our system is basically a backward reasoner just like a Prolog interpreter. It first applies order-sorted resolution to a given goal clause, whenever there remains an atom in the goal clause with which some rule or a fact can be resolved.

Control Rule 1 Let $\leftarrow A_1, ..., A_n$ be a given well sorted goal clause. If there exists an atom A_j with which some rule or a fact can be resolved, then do order-sorted resolution to produce the next goal.[7] If otherwise, apply Generalization Rule 1, called a sorted generalization, for an atom A_j and a rule $A \leftarrow W$ satisfying the following precondition.

Control Rule 2 *(Precondition for sorted generalization)*
Let $(A \leftarrow W)$ and A_j be a rule and an atom in a goal clause, respectively. Generalization Rule 1 is applied for $A \leftarrow W$ and A_j, if A and A_j does not have any order-sorted unifier, but are unifiable in the sense of Robinson's standard (unsorted) unification algorithm (for instance, see Lloyd 1984).

In our example case, Rule 1 and the atom (12.1) are unifiable. However they fail in order-sorted unification due to the type constraint for the third argument of *cannot_set_up*. Generalization Rule 1 is tried so that it weakens the type constraints and makes the rule applicable to the atom.

Generalization Rule 1 *(Sorted generalization)*   Let θ be a computed most general unifier (mgu) of A and B, where A and B are the head of $A \leftarrow W$ and an atom in a goal clause, respectively. The precondition means that, for some nontrivial equivalence class $M = \{x, t_1, ..., t_n\}$ containing a variable x, $[M] = \{[t] | t \in M\}$ has no lower bound in our sort hierarchy $(S, \leq)$.[8] We call such an equivalence class M a failure class. Then, for each failure class M, our sorted generalization tries to replace variables x_j appearing in the rule $A \leftarrow W$ with other

---

[7] Normally the left-most atom is selected, if there exist several atoms that can be resolved with some rules.

[8] Two terms t and s are defined to be equivalent with respect to θ iff $t\theta = s\theta$. Moreover, the reason why such an equivalence class of terms exists is explained in detail in Walther (1988).

variables x'_j of more general sorts in order to obtain a new hypothetical rule

$$A\{x_j/x'_j\} \leftarrow W\{x_j/x'_j\}.$$

This is done according to the following cases:

Case1: A failure class M consists of only variables.

Suppose $M = \{x_1, ..., x_n, y_1, ..., y_m\}$, where x_i and y_j are variables in A and B, respectively.

1. If $\{[y_1], ..., [y_m]\}$ does not have a lower bound, then our sorted generalization fails.

2. If otherwise, find a minimal n-tuple of variables $x'_1, ..., x'_n$ such that

   (a) $[x'_j] \geq [x_j]$,

   (b) $\{[x'_1], ..., [x'_n], [y_1], ..., [y_m]\}$ has a lower bound,

   where the minimal n-tuple of variables is determined by the ordering defined as:

   $$x'_1, ..., x'_n \leq x''_1, ..., x''_n \Leftrightarrow [x'_j] \leq [x''_j] \text{ holds for any } j.$$

Case2: A failure class M has a proper term:

Let $M = \{x_1, ..., x_n, y_1, ..., y_m, t_1, ..., t_k\}$, where x_j, y_j and t_j are a variable in A, a variable in B and a proper term, respectively. Note that $[t_1] = ... = [t_k] = s$ for some sort $s \in S$, since M is unifiable.

1. If there exists y_j such that $\neg([y_j] \geq s)$ then our sorted generalization fails.

2. If otherwise, there exists at least one x_j such that $\neg([x_j] \geq s)$. For each x_j satisfying this condition, find a variable x_j' such that $[x_j'] \in mub\{s, [x_j]\}$.[9]

This completes the description of Sorted Generalization.

In the present case, we have three nontrivial equivalence classes containing variables:

$$M_1 = \{X : person, p\_a\}, \qquad M_2 = \{Z : person, p\_c\},$$
$$M_3 = \{Ctrct2 : contract, reg\_of\_ptitle\_f(p\_b, p\_c, imm\_X)\}.$$

M_3 is the unique failure class classified into Case 2 of Sorted Generalization. Since $mub(\{contract, reg\_of\_ptitle\}$ is a singleton set $\{lawful\_act\}$, so the $Ctrct2$ should be replaced with a

---

[9] $mub\ D$ denotes the set of all minimal upper bounds of $D \subset S$.

variable $Lawful\_act : lawful\_act$. As a result, Rule 1 is transformed to the following rule:

Rule 4 (Article94, Clause2: generalized one)
$$oc(Ctrct1 : contract),$$
$$attr(Ctrct1, agent1, X : person), attr(Ctrct1, agent2, Y : person),$$
$$attr(Ctrct1, agent1, Obj),$$
$$oc(Falsity : falsity),$$
$$attr(Falsity, obj, Ctrct1),$$
$$oc(Lawful\_act : lawful\_act),$$
$$attr(Lawful\_act, agent1, Y), attr(Lawful\_act, agent1, Z : person),$$
$$attr(Lawful\_act, agent1, Obj),$$
$$good\_faith(Z, Falsity)$$
$$\rightarrow cannot\_set\_up(X, Z, Lawful\_act)$$

Clearly Rule 4 is applicable to our top goal (12.1). Hence we have the following as the next goal clause:

$$\leftarrow oc(Ctrct1 : contract),$$

$$attr(Ctrct1, agt1, p\_a), attr(Ctrct1, agt2, Y), \tag{12.2}$$

$$attr(Ctrct1, agt1, Obj : object), \tag{12.3}$$

$$oc(Falsity : falsity),$$

$$attr(Falsity, obj, Ctrct1), \tag{12.4}$$

$$oc(reg\_of\_ptitle\_f(p\_b, p\_c, imm\_X)), \tag{12.5}$$

$$attr(reg\_of\_ptitle\_f(p\_b, p\_c, imm\_X), agt1, Y), \tag{12.6}$$

$$attr(reg\_of\_ptitle\_f(p\_b, p\_c, imm\_X), agt2, p\_c), \tag{12.7}$$

$$attr(reg\_of\_ptitle\_f(p\_b, p\_c, imm\_X), object, Obj), \tag{12.8}$$

$$good\_faith(p\_c, Falsity)$$

According to Control Rule 1, every possible resolution is tried first. In this case, for the atoms (12.2), (12.3), (12.4), (12.6), (12.7) and (12.8) are eliminated from the goal clause from the unit clauses defining the $attr$ predicate. Furthermore the atom (12.5) is really a fact, so it is also eliminated. As a result, we have the following new goal clause after several steps of order-sorted resolutions:

$$\leftarrow oc(contract\_f(p\_a, p\_b, imm\_X),$$

$$oc(falsity\_f(contract\_f(p\_a, p\_b, imm\_X), \tag{12.9}$$

$$good\_faith(p\_c, falsity\_f(contract\_f(p\_a, p\_b, imm\_X))).$$

Now from the legal theory rule in Figure 2, the atom (12.9) is resolved, and the goal clause becomes:

$$\leftarrow oc(contract\_f(p\_a, p\_b, imm\_X),$$
$$repr\_of\_ctrct(contract\_f(p\_a, p\_b, imm\_X), ReprCts),$$
$$soa\_of\_ctrct(contract\_f(p\_a, p\_b, imm\_X), RealCts),$$
$$ReprCts \neq RealCts,$$
$$good\_faith(p\_c, falsity\_f(contract\_f(p\_a, p\_b, imm_X)))) (12.10)$$

It should be noted here that every atom in the above goal clause fails. In particular, (12.10) cannot succeed from the definition of *good_faith*, for

$$oc(contract\_f(p\_a, p\_b, imm_X))$$

fails. From Control Rule 1, we should apply Sorted Generalization Rule. However, no rule is unifiable with any atom in the goal clause, so Generalization Rule also fails to produce a new hypothetical rule.

Thus we need another type of generalization to accomplish our task. Recall that our sorted generalization tries to generalize sorts of variables appearing in a rule. It is also possible to consider a 'term generalization' that generalizes a term to a variable of more general sort. To investigate the condition for this type of generalization, let us consider a simple example. Suppose we have sorts s_3, s_4 of event type such that $s_3 \leq s_4$ and two functors $g : s_1 \rightarrow s_2$, and f with its sorted specification $f(l : s_2) : s_3$. Then the following is a logical deduction:

$$\frac{\exists z : s_1 \quad oc(f(g(z)))}{\exists x : s_4 \; \exists z : s_1 \quad oc(x) \wedge attr(x, l, g(z))}$$

The term $f(g(z))$ of sort s_3 is replaced with a variable x of more general sort s_4. Hence a goal derivation from $\leftarrow oc(f(g(z : s_1)))$ to $\leftarrow oc(x : s_4), attr(x, l, g(z : s_1))$ should be a generalization of goal. Now we present here our second generalization rule under some additional condition.

Generalization Rule 2 *(Term generalization)*   Suppose we have a goal clause

$$\leftarrow oc(f(t_1, ..., t_n)), Bs \qquad (12.11)$$

where $f(l_1 : s_1, ..., l_n : s_n) : s$. Then find a super sort[10] s' of s such that a goal clause defined by

$$\leftarrow oc(y : s') \wedge \overset{n}{\underset{i=1}{\bigwedge}} attr(y, l_j, t_j)$$

is provable by standard order-sorted resolution. If this succeeds with an answer substitution θ, then remove the first atom $oc(f(t_1, ..., t_n))$ from the original goal (12.11) and replace all its occurrences in (12.11) with $y\theta$.

In the present case we are examining, the goal

$$oc(X : lawful\_act), attr(X, agt1, p\_a),$$
$$attr(X, agt2, p\_b), attr(X, object, imm\_X) \qquad (12.12)$$

is generated $oc(contract\_f(p\_a, p\_b, imm\_X))$ and proved with the following answer:[11]

$$\theta = \{X/reg\_of\_ptitle\_(a, b, imm\_X)\}$$

Thus we have the next goal clause from the original goal (12.11), according to Generalization Rule 2:

$$\leftarrow repr\_of\_ctrct(reg\_of\_ptitlet\_f(p\_a, p\_b, imm\_X), ReprCts), \qquad (12.13)$$
$$soa\_of\_ctrct(reg\_of\_ptitlet\_f(p\_a, p\_b, imm\_X), RealCts) \qquad (12.14)$$
$$ReprCts \neq RealCts,$$
$$good\_faith(p\_c, falsity\_f(reg\_of\_ptitle\_f(p\_a, p\_b, imm_X)))$$

---

[10] When there exist several sorts s' satisfying the condition, we choose a minimal one.

[11] Strictly speaking, we assume the following additional rules to make the goal (12.12) succeed:

$$oc(reg\_of\_ptitle\_f(X : person, Y : person, W : imm\_prop)$$
$$\leftarrow oc(reg\_of\_ptitle\_f(Y, Z : person, W)),$$
$$ownership(X, W).$$

This rule is used to derive a hypothetical fact on the registrations. The registration of passage of title from Y to Z does not imply a passage from the real owner X to the nominal owner Y. However, from the standpoint of the third person Z, it can be assumable that the passage of title from X to Y was registered. Although we should distinguish two types of facts under a framework of 'abductive logic programming', we leave this issue as a future work.

Since our term generalization generalizes a term to a variable of more general sort, the replacement performed by the generalization may introduce some type errors. In the present case, the atoms (12.13) and (12.14) are not well sorted, because the domain sort of *repr_of_ctrct* is *contract*. Thus we need to have a type error elimination rule whenever the term generalization succeeds and some illegal terms appear in the new goal clause. The elimination is also carried out by a generalization.

Control Rule 3 *(Type check)* We assume a check is made of whether a goal clause obtained by Generalization Rule 2 is well sorted or not, whenever it is applied. If some ill-sorted expression is found, then execute Generalization Rule 3. Precisely speaking, suppose $oc(f(t_1, ..., t_n))$ is replaced with $y\theta$ in Generalization Rule 2 to produce the next goal clause G. Let $A_1(y\theta), ..., A_n(y\theta)$ be all the ill-sorted atoms appearing in G. Apply Generalization Rule 3, called Predicate Generalization, to a set of atoms: $A_1(y\theta), ..., A_n(y\theta)$.

The predicate generalization is originally introduced in Haraguchi (1991) as a kind of abductive goal reduction rule, and is now extended so as to cope with well sorted expressions. The major function of predicate generalization is to apply our (object-level) rules to the ill-sorted goal clause to eliminate the ill-sorted expressions. Before describing it formally, we present here a simple illustration.

Suppose symbols a and b denote

$$contract\_f(p\_a, p\_b, imm\_X) \text{ and } reg\_of\_ptitle\_f(p\_a, p\_b, imm\_X),$$

respectively. Assume furthermore that a well sorted atom

$$repr\_of\_cntrct(a, Cntrct) \tag{12.15}$$

holds as a hypothetical premise for predicate generalization. Recall that the ill-sorted expression $repr\_of\_cntrct(b, Cntrct)$ is obtained from the premise (12.15) by replacing a with b. In contrast, our predicate generalization first generalizes the premise so that the replacement for a generalized premise $B(a)$ produces a well sorted expression $B(b)$.

(PG1): $B(a)$ is provable from (12.15)

341

(PG2): $B(b)$ is well sorted.

From the conditions (PG1) and (PG2), both $B(a)$ and $B(b)$ are well sorted. Hence there exists a sort s such that

(PG3): $B(x : s)$ is well sorted, where x is a variable,

(PG4): $contract \leq s$ and $registration \leq s$.

From the syntactic assumption for our symbol system, there exist just two atoms as candidates of B that satisfy (PG3) and (PG4):

$$oc(falsity\_f(X : lawful\_act)), \qquad (12.16)$$
$$repr(X : lawful\_act, Cntrct) \qquad (12.17)$$

From the condition (PG1), we can conclude that the atom (12.16) is rejected and the atom (12.17) is accepted. As a result, our predicate generalization replaces all the occurrences of the ill-sorted atom $repr\_of\_cntrct(b, Cntrct)$, appearing by Term Generalization, with the well sorted $repr(b, Cntrct)$.

As a result, we have

$$\leftarrow \quad repr(reg\_of\_ptitlet\_f(p\_a, p\_b, imm\_X), ReprCts),$$
$$soa(reg\_of\_ptitlet\_f(p\_a, p\_b, imm\_X), RealCts),$$
$$ReprCts \neq RealCts,$$
$$good\_faith(p\_c, falsity\_f(reg\_of\_ptitle\_f(p\_a, p\_b, imm_X)))$$

Now it is clear that all the atoms in the above are refutable by standard order-sorted resolution.

Finally we present the generalization rule in its general form:

Generalization Rule 3 *(Predicate generalization)*
Let $A_1(a), ..., A_n(a)$ be a set of well sorted atoms, where a is a term of event type. Furthermore suppose $A_1(b), ..., A_n(b)$ is ill-sorted, where b is an well sorted term of event type. Then find a set of well sorted atoms $B_1(a), ..., B_k(a)$ such that $k \leq n$, $A_1(a), ..., A_n(a) \vdash B_1(a), ..., B_k(a)$, and $B_1(b), ..., B_k(b)$ is well sorted.

From the definition of predicate generalization, it is possible to consider two kinds of computational rules. One is to generate possible deductions until the ill sorted expression disappears.

The other one is to enumerate atom sets $B_1(x), ..., B_n(x)$ that meet our syntactic constraints, and then check if they are provable or not. For our present example, these two methods entail similar computational costs.

5 CONCLUDING REMARKS

We have defined an order-sorted symbol system, represented various types of legal knowledge, and shown how three generalization rules are applied. The order-sorted Horn logic with sorted generalizations has been already implemented. The implemented system is basically an order-sorted SLD-refutation procedure, where it tries to find a minimal generalization of sorts when order-sorted unification fails. The detail can be found in (Haraguchi and Kakuta 1994). The predicate generalization and the term generalization are now under development. The implemented system will be equipped with these two additional generalization rules.

Now we briefly discuss some important issues not yet mentioned in this paper. First the sorted generalization has been introduced so as to make a unification failure recover by generalizing sorts of variables. For this purpose, we required that the generalized sorts have their common lower bound which will be a sort of unified terms after sorted generalization. Here we want to call the generalized sort and the sort of unified term a generalization point and a unification point, respectively. The process for our sorted generalization thus involves finding the generalization points for which a unification point exists. Such a process might become complex when we have a large sort hierarchy in which multiple super sorts are allowed to exist. Hence we must have a more efficient method to compute the generalization points. The author is now developing such an algorithm according to the following strategy:

1. Mapping the sort hierarchy into a set of primitive elements corresponding to minimal sorts in the hierarchy. This transforms the hierarchy into a partially ordered subset of a set boolean lattice.
2. Before finding the generalization points, computing candi-

dates for the unification points by set-theoretic operations.

3. Once such a unification point is found, it is easy to find the generalization points by simple algebraic operations.

The second problem we have to discuss is how we handle hypothetical rules. The rules obtained by sorted generalization are clearly hypothetical ones. In addition, we have used another type of hypothetical rules in Section 4 to infer hypothetical facts that are substantially assumable but are not explicitly recorded as approved facts. Furthermore one may assert that even our sort hierarchy might be hypothetical. For instance, when we are talking about some issues about some legal concepts and cases, we may choose particular super sorts to emphasize some aspects of the concepts. In such a case, other super sorts should be neglected or blocked to prevent useless and harmful arguments. The studies focusing their themes on such a problem are well known collectively as default reasoning or as multiple inheritance.

Default reasoning is generally concerned with a situation that is incompletely specified by a set of evidences supporting hypothetical facts or rules. The problem is to select some hypotheses from the evidences and to conclude that they might hold in the situation. Some evidence can distinguish some useful default rules from the others, and block some irrelevant hypothetical rules. A mechanism which can behave in such a way is known as conditional entailment (Geffner and Pearl 1992). In addition to the function of conditional entailment, some experimental enviroment under which we can get additional evidences to test whether the hypothetical rules are relevant to the situation or not seems to be necessary. The author is now trying to design a system that is basically a conditional entailment system but has additional function to achieve such an experimental environment.

REFERENCES

Beierle, C. *et al.* (1992). An order-sorted logic for knowledge representation systems, *Artif. Intell.*, **55**, 149–191.

Dierbach, C. (1992). A formal basis for analogical reasoning, *Proceedings of the Second International Conference on Knowledge Representation and Reasoning*, 139–150.

Geffner, H. and Pearl, J. (1992). Conditional Entailment: bridging two approaches to default reasoning, *Artif. Intell.* **53**, 209–244.

Greiner, D. (1988). Abstraction-based analogical reasoning, in D.H. Helman ed., *Analogical Reasoning*, Kluwer Academic Publishers, 147–180.

Haraguchi, M. (1991). A form of analogy as an abductive inference, *Proc. 2nd Workshop on Algorithmic Learning Theory*, pages 266–274, Japanese Society for Artificial Intelligence.

Haraguchi, M. and Kakuta, T. (1994). A sorted generalization for legal reasoning, *Proc. Workshop on Application of Logic Programming to Legal Reasoning*, pages 61–72.

Harao, M (1993). Generalized-knowledge acquisition and reasoning based on similarity (in Japanese), in *Proc. of 7th Annual Conference of JSAI*, pages 41–44.

Indurkhya, B. (1990). On the Role of Interpretive Analogy in Learning, *Proc. ALT'90*, pages 174–189.

Lloyd, J.W. (1984). *Foundation of Logic Programming*, Springer-Verlag, Berlin.

Muggleton, S. (1990). Inductive logic programming, in *Proc. 1st Workshop of Algorithmic Learning Theory*, pages 42–66.

Muggleton, S. and Buntine, W. (1988). Machine invention of first-order predicates by inverting resolution, *Proc. Workshop on Machine Learning*, pages 339–352.

Nebel, B. (1990). Reasoning and Revision in Hybrid Representation Systems, Springer LNAI, **422**, 270 pages

Russell, S.J. (1986). Analogical and Inductive Reasoning, STAN-CS-87-1150, Dept. Computer Science, Stanford University.

Walther, C. (1988). Many sorted unification, *JACM*, **35**, 1, 1–17.

Waragai,T. (1994). A natural extension of predicate calculus in which ISA relation is expressible, Ph.D. Thesis, Tokyo Institute of Technology.

Yoshino, H. (1987). Legal expert system LES-2, *Springer Lecture Notes in Computer Science, Logic Programming '86* pages 34–45.

Yoshino, H., Haraguchi, M.,Sakurai, S.,Kagayama, S. (1993). Towards a legal analogical reasoning system: knowledge representation and reasoning methods, *Proc. 4th ICAIL*, pages 110–116, 1993.

FURTHER READING

Guarino, N. (1991). A concise presentation of ITL, *Proc. of Processing Declarative Knowledge*, 141-190, Springer-Verlag, Berlin.

Haraguchi, M. (1992). What kinds of knowledge and inferences are needed to realize legal reasoning? (in Japanese), *Proc. 6th Symposium on Knowledge Representation and Legal Reasoning System*, Legal Expert System Association in Japan.

Rouveirol, C. (1991). ITOU: Induction of First Order Theories, in *Proceedings of the first Inductive Learning Programming Workshop*, Viana de Castelo.

Tanaka, H. (1974). *Introduction to the study of positive law* (in Japanese), University of Tokyo Press.

13

A Concept Learning Algorithm with Adaptive Search

Kazumi Saito and Ryohei Nakano

NTT Communication Science Laboratories

Abstract

This chapter describes a concept learning algorithm called RF4 which adaptively improves its concept learning efficiency. RF4 performs a depth-first search on the basis of five criteria for pruning undesirable formulae and five transformation rules for combining formulae. The attribute search order is determined dynamically by estimating each attribute's probability of being a component of the concept. In a KRK chess endgame problem, after learning a few sets of training examples, RF4 quickly improved its learning efficiency as well as predictive accuracy. In a set of visual pattern recognition problems called Bongard problems, using primitive knowledge of graphical objects, RF4 solved 41 out of 100 problems efficiently; other learning algorithms, e.g. GOLEM, INDUCE, or FOIL solved much less. After solving the 41 training problems, the average time for RF4 to solve the same set of problems was reduced to about one-third. Through statistical tests, a piece of useful knowledge to improve the problem-solving efficiency was extracted from a set of probabilities used in RF4.

1 INTRODUCTION

One of the essential aspects of intelligence is to learn substantially new knowledge from a set of examples (problems). Included in this knowledge are concepts capable of discriminating new examples adequately, and procedures capable of improving the concept learning (problem-solving) efficiency.

Concept learning can be thought of as a search for a suitable formula in a space of formulae (Mitchell 1982). In this respect, most existing methods (Quinlan 1983; Michalski 1983; Quinlan 1990; Muggleton and Feng 1990) employ heuristic search: by a given heuristic evaluation function based on a few criteria (accuracy, complexity, etc), the formulae having larger heuristic values are stored and used iteratively to search for concepts. This strategy is efficient, but apt to miss some types of desirable concepts, i.e. those described by formulae whose heuristic values are not large enough. Since this may happen sometimes, any formulae having no explicit reason to be pruned should be stored to search for concepts. We believe that one of the promising approaches to concept learning is to perform pruning-based search together with multiple criteria.

Most concept learning algorithms, when presented with the same set of examples repeatedly, always execute the same processing steps, and do not improve their learning efficiency on the basis of their experiences. The methods for acquiring meta-level search-control knowledge should be investigated in a wider range of applications. One approach to improving the efficiency is to utilize explanation-based learning techniques (Mitchell *et al.* 1986; Laird *et al.* 1986), but it may suffer from the utility problem (Minton 1990). Another interesting approach adopted here is to learn the probability of each formula being a component of the target concept from a set of examples. Thus, as the estimated probabilities become more reliable, its learning efficiency will be improved.

This chapter describes a learning algorithm called RF4 which adaptively improves its learning efficiency. First, a framework for concept learning is explained. Next, the RF4 algorithm is described in detail. Then, RF4 is evaluated on the KRK chess endgame problem. Finally, how RF4 worked for a set of visual pattern recognition problems called Bongard problems is shown.

2 FRAMEWORK

A concept that discriminates examples is assumed to be describable by a formula. Each example is labelled as class1 (positive) or class2 (negative) on the basis of the unknown discriminating concept (formula). Concept learning restores the formula from a set of labelled examples.

For the sake of usefulness and readability, first-order predicate calculus having aggregate functions is adopted here to express formulae. Formally, formulae are defined recursively as in the following. A term is a variable/constant, or is formed by applying an aggregate function (count, sum, average, max, min) to a formula. An atomic formula is formed by two terms and an arithmetic comparator ($>$, $\geq$, $<$, $\leq$). A formula is an atomic formula, or is formed recursively using logical operators ($\wedge$, $\vee$) or quantifiers ($\forall$, $\exists$).

3 RF4 ALGORITHM

RF4 performs a depth-first search on the basis of five criteria for pruning undesirable formulae and five transformation rules for combining formulae. The attribute search order is determined dynamically by estimating the probability that the attribute is a component of the concept.

3.1 Skeleton feature

The algorithm performs a depth-first search together with multiple criteria pruning. The general flow of RF4 is shown in Fig. 13.1. The following procedure is iterated until a generated formula satisfies the goal condition. First, a basic formula is generated from the attributes describing the given problem. If this basic formula does not satisfy the goal and is pruned, another basic formula is generated. Otherwise, it is stored to be used to generate compound formulae together with formulae previously stored. A newly stored formula is utilized for generation prior to the other formulae. If a newly generated compound formula does not satisfy the goal and is pruned, another compound formula is generated. If no compound formula can be generated, a new basic formula is generated. The coverage of formula α for class i is defined as the ratio of the number of examples covered by α in class i to the number of examples in class i.

Four types of basic formulae can be generated from input descriptions. Examples are shown in Fig. 13.1-[1]. The simplest type is a nominal selection formula. When an attribute is nominal, the corresponding atomic formula is generated straightforwardly. When an attribute is numerical, a simple clustering method is applied: first, numerical values are sorted in ascending order; then, the biggest gap between adjacent values is used to generate two formulae: 'less than' and 'greater than'. For example, when $att(X)=\{88, 96, 99, 125, 140, 180, 192, 215, 231, 250\}$ is given, two resultant conditions are $att(X) \leq 160$ and $att(X) > 160$. This method can also be applied recursively to the subset of values to get more conditions. In our experiment, the top two gaps are used to generate conditions.

If there is more than one object, comparing the attributes of two different objects may be a good strategy. This type of formula is called a join formula. In a nominal attribute, nominal join formulae are generated using an existential quantifier. In a numerical attribute, numerical join formulae are generated using the differences between values.

Since a large number of formulae are generated, effective inductive biases to prune undesirable formulae are essential to the efficiency of the algorithm. In RF4, five biases (simplicity, usefulness, improvement, nontriviality and minimality) are employed. The formal conditions of each inductive bias are shown in Fig. 13.1-[2]. The simplicity bias requires the number of atomic formulae appearing in any of the formulae to be not more than the threshold, say five. The usefulness bias requires any formula to exceed a certain coverage threshold K, say 30%. The improvement bias requires that a compound formula improves the coverage of any component formula. The nontriviality bias discards any formula covering all objects in both classes. The minimality bias prevents the equivalent formulae from being expressed by using more complex formulae.

The formal conditions of each transformation rule are shown in Fig. 13.1-[3]. A formula should be made less general if it covers examples in class2 as well as in class1. Conversely, a formula

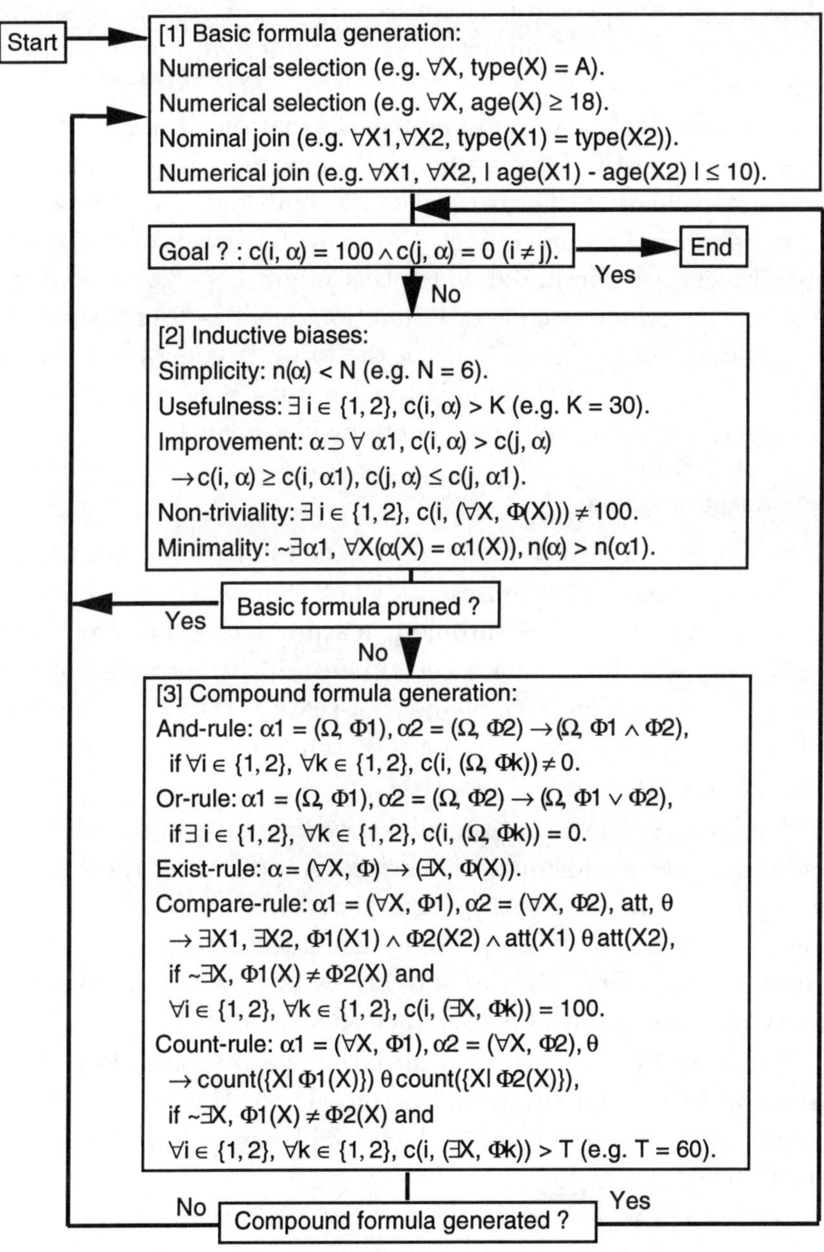

Note: any variable X is quantified as ∀F ∈ facts, X ∈ F;
F, X : variables; θ : comparator; Ω : quantifier; Φ : condition; α : formula;
n(α): number of atomics; c(i, α): coverage.

Figure 13.1. General flow of RF4.

should be less specific if it covers only a part of the examples in only one class. Conjunctive and disjunctive transformations are therefore used to make a formula less general and less specific, respectively. As another transformation, if a variable for objects is quantified by a universal quantifier, it is changed to an existential quantifier to weaken its condition. Additionally, if there is more than one object, the same attributes of two different objects are compared, since this might be a good strategy. Finally, introducing aggregate functions such as count, sum, average, max, and min, will enrich the formula generation involving numbers. Only the count function has been implemented; however, extension to other functions is straightforward.

3.2   Adaptive feature

We introduce a situation vector $\mathbf{s} = (\mathbf{f}, \mathbf{r})$: $\mathbf{f}$ represents what a problem is like and $\mathbf{r}$ represents what the current search state is like. An element of problem feature $\mathbf{f}$ is a boolean value indicating whether or not a certain descriptive formula holds in the present problem. An element of search state $\mathbf{r}$ is a boolean value indicating whether or not a certain atomic formula is used as a node in the current search.

Under a certain situation, where we know the probabilities of individual atomic formulae of $\mathbf{r}$ being components of the discriminating concept, the expected search cost to find the discriminating concept can be minimized, by using the formula having the largest probability. RF4 adaptively estimates the probabilities on the basis of growing experience as shown below.

Let $\mathbf{s} = (s_1, \ldots, s_d)$ be a situation vector, and $P(\mathbf{s})$ be a probability for the situation vector. Then, the first-order approximation to the Bahadur–Lazarsfeld expansion (Duda and Hart 1973) of $P(\mathbf{s})$ is

$$P_1(\mathbf{s}) \;=\; \prod_{i=1}^{d} p_i^{s_i} (1 - p_i)^{1-s_i}$$

where $p_i = P(s_i = 1)$. This approximation is equivalent to assuming that the elements of $\mathbf{s}$ are statistically independent.

Table 13.1. Observation and estimated probabilities.

Observation: $\{(x_1,x_2,x_3)\} = \{ (0, 1, 0), (1, 0, 1) \}$					
Estimated probabilities:					
(x_1,x_2,x_3)	$P_1(\mathbf{x})$	$P_2(\mathbf{x})$	(x_1,x_2,x_3)	$P_1(\mathbf{x})$	$P_2(\mathbf{x})$
(0, 0, 0)	0.125	0	(0, 0, 1)	0.125	0
(1, 0, 0)	0.125	0	(1, 0, 1)	0.125	0.5
(0, 1, 0)	0.125	0.5	(0, 1, 1)	0.125	0
(1, 1, 0)	0.125	0	(1, 1, 1)	0.125	0

The second-order approximation is

$$P_2(\mathbf{s}) \;=\; P_1(\mathbf{s})\Big(1 + \sum_{i=2}^{d}\sum_{j=1}^{i-1}(p_{ij} - p_i p_j)y_i y_j\Big)$$

where $p_{ij} = P(s_i = 1, s_j = 1)$ and $y_i = (s_i - p_i)/(p_i(1 - p_i))$. The kth-order approximation to $P(\mathbf{s})$ requires $O(d^k)$ terms and a very large number of probabilities must be estimated. Since we usually have only a small number of examples, we employ the second-order approximation here.

Table 13.1 shows a shortage of the first-order approximation, comparing the probabilities estimated by each approximation after two three-dimensional vectors were presented. This table shows that all the vectors have the same probability in the first-order approximation while those vectors appearing in the observation have the largest probabilities in the second-order approximation.

Based on the concept-learning experiences, the probabilities (p_i, p_{ij}) are re-estimated using the maximum likelihood estimation; each of them is estimated to be the ratio of the number of problems having a true situation vector element value to the number of problems. The final values of the situation vector elements are determined as follows: the problem feature element is true if the corresponding formula covers all the examples in one class; otherwise false. The search state element is true if the corresponding atomic formula is a component of the discriminating concept; otherwise false.

Let s_k be a search state element whose corresponding atomic formula has not yet been used to generate compound formulae. If the values of $\{s_1, \ldots, s_h\}$ $(h < k)$ are known, the conditional probability that s_k comes true is

$$P_2(s_k \mid s_1, \ldots, s_h) = p_k + \frac{\alpha}{\beta}$$

where

$$\alpha = \sum_{i=1}^{h}(p_{ki} - p_k p_i)y_i,$$

$$\beta = 1 + \sum_{i=2}^{h}\sum_{j=1}^{i-1}(p_{ij} - p_i p_j)y_i y_j.$$

RF4 explores the next node by selecting the search state element having the largest conditional probability.

In some applications, it is inefficient to calculate all the problem feature elements in advance. Here, we adopt an incremental strategy. Suppose the values of $\{s_1, \ldots, s_{h-1}\}$ are known. If the value of s_h is calculated during further search, the values of $\alpha^{(h)}$ and $\beta^{(h)}$ are calculated efficiently by the use of the following recursive definitions:

$$\alpha^{(h)} = \alpha^{(h-1)} + (p_{kh} - p_k p_h)y_h,$$
$$\beta^{(h)} = \beta^{(h-1)} + \alpha^{(h-1)}y_h.$$

where $\alpha^{(0)} = 0$, $\beta^{(0)} = 1$.

4 CHESS END-GAME

Capabilities of RF4 were evaluated on a concept learning problem called the KRK chess endgame problem (Muggleton *et al.* 1989). The KRK problem is the game White King and Rook versus Black King, the goal is to find out the concept indicating that the position is not a legal Black-to-move position. The number of possible positions (examples) is $64 \times 63 \times 62$, and about two-thirds of the examples belong to this concept. In order to express examples, three relations (equal, adjacent, less-than) were used on both row and column for each pair of pieces.

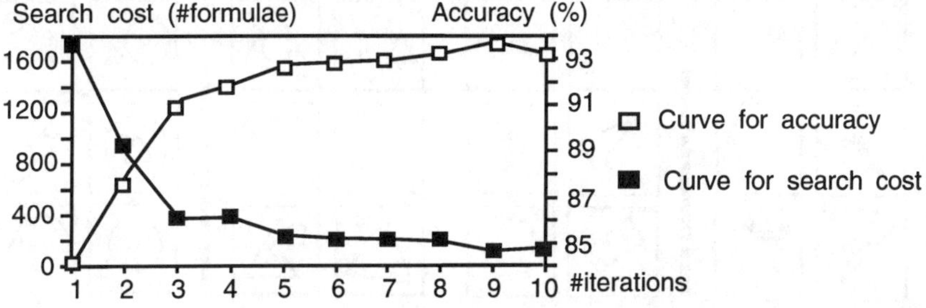

Figure 13.2. Learning curves for the KRK problem.

In this problem, we did not use problem features as situation vector elements, since the pieces appearing in examples are fixed.

In the experiments, RF4 estimated the probabilities by generating the concept from 50 training examples. This trial was successively repeated 10 times using a sequence of independent sets of training examples. The search costs (the number of formulae generated) to find out the concept and accuracy for 5,000 unseen examples are shown in Fig. 13.2, where these values were averaged on 100 trials. The figure shows that, when presented with several set of examples repeatedly, RF4 quickly improved its learning efficiency as well as predictive accuracy on the basis of its experiences.

5 BONGARD PROBLEMS

Bongard problems are puzzles in visual pattern recognition given by M. Bongard (Bongard 1970; Hofstadter 1979); they are widely used in psychology, in aptitude tests. These problems can also form an extremely interesting and useful test suited for machine learning, because they offer a wide range of difficulty (Michalski and Kodratoff 1990). Regrettably, they have hardly been explored by AI researchers. Examples of Bongard problems are shown in Fig. 13.3. Each problem consists of twelve boxes and in each box one or more graphical objects are drawn. It is assumed that the left six boxes belong to class 1, and the right six belong to class 2. The problem is to determine the concept discriminating between class 1 and class 2.

Primitive symbolic formulae utilized to solve Bongard problems can be obtained by drawing graphical objects. For exam-

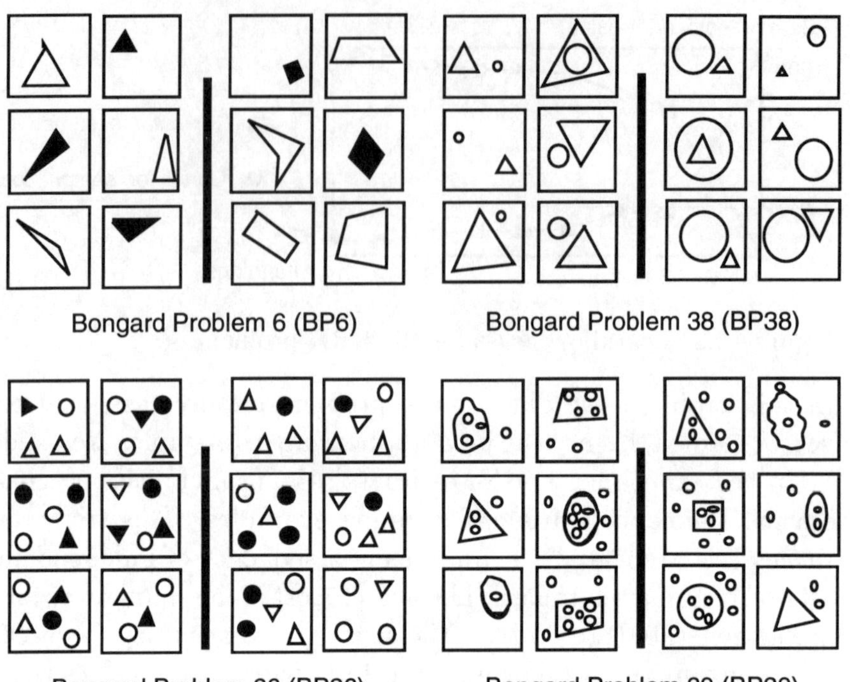

Bongard Problem 6 (BP6) Bongard Problem 38 (BP38)

Bongard Problem 26 (BP26) Bongard Problem 29 (BP29)

Figure 13.3. Examples of Bongard problems.

ple, consider drawing a black oval; at first, the item 'oval' is selected as the object type, and the top-left and bottom-right coordinates are determined by a mouse. Then, the value 'black' is selected from the 'texture' menu. Since these selected factors are nothing but compact input information, our program is designed on the basis of this idea. In our current input interface, the values of original attributes (shape, texture, shade, rotation angle, line width) are determined by a user, and the values of derived attributes (size, convexity, relation, number of angles, roundness, aspect ratio, gravity) are calculated from the original attribute values.

Let N be the number of atomic formulae used in problem-solving, and K be the largest number of atomic formulae allowed to be combined by logical connections ($\land$, $\lor$). The order of these combinations is $O(N^K)$. Moreover, each combined formula can be used as a condition for counting objects, and any pair of counted values can be compared (e.g. BP29 shown in Fig. 13.3).

Table 13.2. Major characteristics of four algorithms.

Name	Search	Major heuristics
GOLEM	random	determinate literals
INDUCE	beam	accuracy & complexity
FOIL	greedy	information gain
RF4	depth-first	five biases

Thus, the order of these combinations is $O(N^{2K})$. Here, since N is more than 50, and even if K is restricted to 5, the number of all possible formulae is at least 10^{17}. This value is beyond the scope of any exhaustive search without pruning.

5.1 Evaluation of performance

Experiments were done to explore the concept learning ability of RF4 in Bongard problem-solving. A program implemented on a personal computer in C solved 41 out of 100 Bongard problems within a few seconds for each problem. The problems solved by RF4 can be classified into four categories depending on the operations employed to get the discriminating concept: the first is characterized by a single graphical object (Single), the second by the existence of a certain graphical object (Existence), the third by comparing between graphical objects (Comparison), and the fourth by counting the number of certain graphical objects (Counting). Typical examples for each category are shown in Fig. 13.3, and the output descriptions of these examples are shown below:

BP6: $\forall B \in boxes, \forall X \in B, angles(X) = 3 \rightarrow class1.$

BP26: $\forall B \in boxes, \exists X \in B, texture(X) = black \wedge$

               $shape(X) = polygon \rightarrow class1.$

BP38: $\forall B \in boxes, \exists X_1 X_2 \in B, shape(X_1) = polygon \wedge$

               $shape(X_2) = oval \wedge size(X_1) > size(X_2) \rightarrow class1.$

BP29: $\forall B \in boxes, count(\{X \in B; relation(X) = inner\})$

               $> count(\{X \in B; relation(X) = outer\}) \rightarrow class1.$

To evaluate the concept learning ability of RF4 in comparison to that of other algorithms, we applied existing algorithms,

GOLEM (Muggleton and Feng 1990), INDUCE (Michalski 1983), FOIL (Quinlan 1990) to the Bongard problems. The involved versions were 'Golem alpha version', 'Induce 3 - version as of Feb. 10, 1984', and 'FOIL.2', respectively, and the default settings of all parameters were used. The major characteristics of the four algorithms are summarized in Table 13.2.

In order to compare the four algorithms under the same conditions, derived formulae generated by RF4 were given as input to the existing three algorithms. As an example to illustrate this point, if the sizes of two graphical objects X_1, X_2 were almost equivalent, a predicate $eqsize(X_1, X_2)$ was given to the input descriptions of the algorithms.

Figure 13.4 compares the results of these algorithms in four categories. The reasons why the existing algorithms worked poorly are as follows:

- When there are two or more graphical objects in each box, GOLEM fails to solve such problems, because it adopts heuristics called determinate literals, that is, in a new literal, bindings of variables must be determined uniquely by bindings of variables occurring earlier in the clause. In Bongard problems, the form of any solution is expressed as $class1(B) :- contain(B, X), ...$ It is therefore clear that the bindings of X cannot be determined uniquely by the bindings of B.

- FOIL fails to solve comparison type problems, and INDUCE fails to solve more than half of such problems, because they adopt heuristic search: the former adopts greedy search, while the latter adopts beam search. For example,

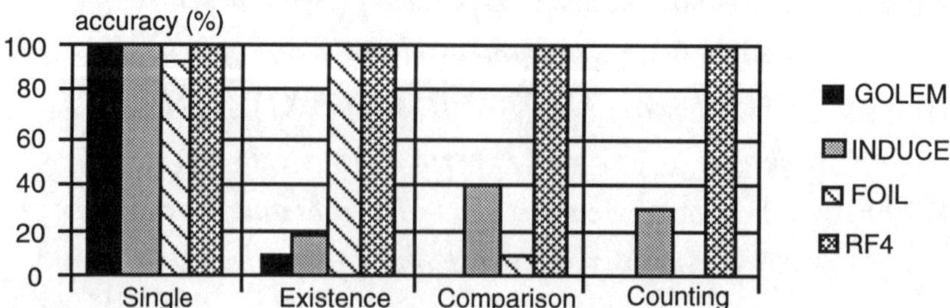

Figure 13.4. Comparisons with other algorithms.

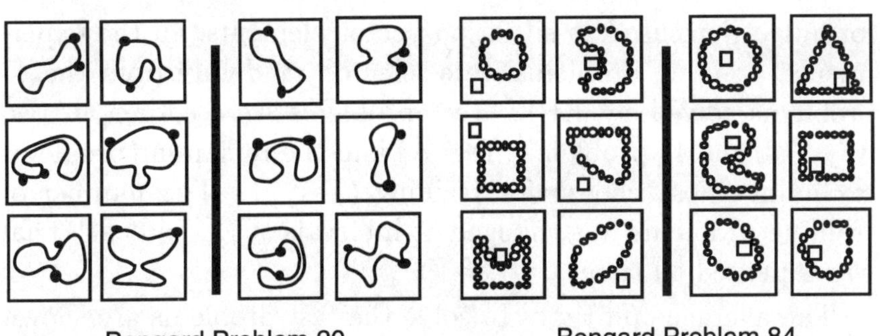

Bongard Problem 20   Bongard Problem 84

Figure 13.5. Unsolved problems.

consider BP38 shown in Fig. 13.3. The solution concept is: $class1(B) :\text{-} contain(B, X_1), contain(B, X_2), polygon(X_1), oval(X_2), gtsize(X_1, X_2)$. FOIL and INDUCE unfortunately will not select $polygon(X_1)$ since it has no positive gain; consequently, they cannot find the solution concept.

- for counting type problems, both GOLEM and FOIL cannot solve any problems, while INDUCE can only solve a few. This is because both GOLEM and FOIL have no function to count objects, while INDUCE has one, but no function to compare the values counted.

Why RF4 failed to solve about sixty problems can be reduced to two reasons: the lack of primitive knowledge and the lack of concept matching (graphical recognition) capabilities. Typical examples are shown in Fig. 13.5. In the left problem the primitive knowledge of the 'neck' is not given to RF4. In the right problem the capability to regard a group of small circles as one graphical object is not implemented in RF4. The former problem is expected to be solved by developing a sophisticated knowledge acquisition algorithm, while the latter by a powerful graphical recognition algorithm.

5.2 Evaluation of adaptability

To evaluate how far RF4's adaptive features improve its concept learning efficiency, a method based on the frequency of attributes used in discriminating concepts was employed for comparison. Here, problem features derived from nominal atomic

359

formulae were used as situation vector elements. In the experiments, training problems were selected randomly from the 41 problems solved by RF4. Test problems were chosen in two ways: all the 41 problems (Test A) and the remaining problems excluding those chosen for training (Test B). The number of training problems was changed at intervals of 10, and each trial was repeated 40 times.

The average cpu times to solve the test problems are shown in Fig. 13.6, where the training examples were given to each method in the same order. A few observations in the experiments are as follows:

- For RF4, after solving the 41 training problems, the average time to solve the same set of problems was reduced to about one-third (Test A). After solving 30 training problems, the average time to solve the remaining test problems was reduced to about two-thirds (Test B). Thus, RF4's adaptive features worked very well.

- When the number of training problems was small, the problem-solving efficiency of the frequency-based method was superior to that of RF4. This may be due to the fact that RF4 needs two extra tasks, that is, probability estimation and attribute selection. If the estimated probabilities are not so reliable, these tasks are apt to be a simple overhead to RF4.

- Although the number of training examples increased, the frequency-based method did not improve its performance monotonically. This may indicate that the frequency-based method approaches its limitation very soon.

The fact that RF4's adaptive feature improves the efficiency comes from the probability estimation. However, since the probabilities are expressed by a large number of numerical values, we cannot explicitly know what they mean. To extract a few outstanding pieces of knowledge, χ^2-tests were performed.

Let e_1 be the event a problem feature element is on, e_2 be the event a search state element is on, and e_{12} be the event the two events e_1 and e_2 happen simultaneously. Also, let m be the number of problems used, and $\hat{p_1}$, $\hat{p_2}$, and $\hat{p_{12}}$ be the estimated

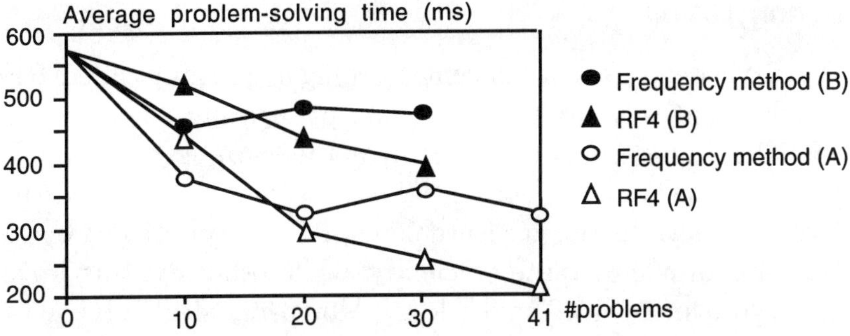

Figure 13.6. Learning curves for Bongard problems.

probabilities of events e_1, e_2, and e_{12}, respectively. If the two events e_1 and e_2 are statistically independent,

$$\chi^2 = m\frac{(\hat{p_{12}} - \hat{p_1}\hat{p_2})^2}{\hat{p_1}(1 - \hat{p_1})\hat{p_2}(1 - \hat{p_2})}$$

is an approximate χ^2-distribution with one degree of freedom. If this value exceeds a tabulated value, the hypothesis that the events e_1 and e_2 are statistically independent can be rejected with the specified confidence. In the experiment, the confidence level was set at 95% ($\chi^2 \leq 3.84$).

The extracted results can be expressed as follows: if there are ovals, examine the inside/outside relation of graphical objects ($\chi^2 = 5.45$); if there are polygons, examine the number of angles of graphical objects ($\chi^2 = 4.97$); or if there are rectangles, examine the inside/outside relation of graphical objects ($\chi^2 = 4.14$). The second rule indicates that counting the number of angles is a good strategy if almost all of the graphical objects are polygons (e.g. BP6 shown in Fig. 13.3). The first and third rules coincide with the fact that ovals or rectangles are used as small graphical objects located in another big graphical object (e.g. BP29 shown in Fig. 13.3). Thus, a piece of useful knowledge in the problem domain was extracted through the statistical tests. Incidentally, we were completely unaware of the first and third rules.

6 CONCLUSION

We have developed a concept learning algorithm called RF4 which adaptively improves its concept learning efficiency. In the KRK chess endgame problem, as the learning goes on, RF4 quickly improved its learning efficiency as well as its predictive accuracy. In Bongard problems, RF4 solved 41 out of 100 Bongard problems quite efficiently, while other existing learning algorithms solved much less. Moreover, after solving the 41 training problems, the average time to solve the same set of problems was reduced to about one-third, and a piece of useful knowledge for problem-solving was extracted from RF4.

REFERENCES

Bongard, N. (1970). *Pattern Recognition*. Spartan Books, New York.

Duda, R.O. and Hart P.E. (1973). *Pattern Classification and Scene Analysis*. John Wiley & Sons, New York.

Hofstadter, D.R. (1979). *Gödel, Escher, Bach: an Eternal Golden Braid*. Basic Books, New York.

Laird, J.E., Rosenbloom, P.S. and Newell, A. (1986). Chunking in SOAR: the anatomy of a general learning mechanism. *Machine Learning*, **1**, 11–46.

Michalski, R.S. (1983). A theory and methodology of inductive learning. In *Machine Learning: an Artificial Intelligence Approach* (eds R.S. Michalski, J.G. Carbonell and T.M. Mitchell) pp. 83–134, Tioga, Palo Alto, CA.

Michalski, R.S. and Kodratoff, Y. (1990). Research in machine learning: recent progress, classification of methods, and future directions. In *Machine learning: an artificial intelligence approach* (eds R.S. Michalski and Y. Kodratoff), **3**, pp. 3–30, Morgan Kaufmann, San Mateo, CA.

Minton, S.N. (1986). Quantitative results concerning the utility of explanation-based learning. *Artificial Intelligence*, **42**, 363–392.

Mitchell, T.M. (1982). Generalization as search. *Artificial Intelligence*, **18**, 203–226.

Mitchell, T.M., Keller, R.M. and Kedar-Cabelli, S.T. (1986). Explanation-based generalization: a unifying view. *Machine Learning*, **1**, 47–80.

Muggleton, S. and Feng C. (1990). Efficient induction of logic programs. In *Proceedings of the First International Workshop on Algorithmic Learning Theory*, pp. 368–381, Ohmsha, Tokyo.

Muggleton, S., Bain, M., Hayes-Michie, J. and Michie D. (1989). An experimental comparison of human and machine learning formalisms. *Proceedings of the sixth International Machine Learning Workshop*, pp. 113–118, Morgan Kaufmann, San Mateo,CA.

Quinlan, J.R. (1983). Learning efficient learning procedures and their applications to chess end games. In *Machine learning: an artificial intelligence approach* (eds R.S. Michalski, J.G. Carbonell and T.M. Mitchell), pp. 463–482, Tioga, Palo Alto, CA.

Quinlan, J.R. (1990). Learning logical definitions from relations. *Machine Learning*, **5**, 47–80.

DYNAMIC CONTROL

14

Deriving Qualitative Control for Dynamic Systems

Ivan Bratko

Faculty of Electrical Engineering and Computer Science
Ljubljana University, Ljubljana, Slovenia

Abstract

This paper investigates how qualitative reasoning can be applied to deriving control rules for dynamic systems. The balancing of pole and cart is used as an example problem. A qualitative control rule is derived from a qualitative model of the pole-and-cart system. This rule is shown to be a qualitative abstraction of the 'classical' control rule derived from the differential equations model of this system.

1 INTRODUCTION

It has been shown that qualitative models are better suited for several tasks than the traditional quantitative, or numerical models. These tasks include diagnosis (e.g. Bratko *et al.* 1989), generating explanation of the system's behaviour (e.g. Falkenheiner and Forbus 1990) and designing novel devices from first principles (e.g. Williams 1990). This paper is concerned with another important task: dynamic system control. We will be interested in particular in dynamic systems which are conventionally modelled by differential equations.

Control rules can be synthesized at various levels of abstraction. The conventional procedure is

physical system $\longrightarrow$ quantitative model $\longrightarrow$ control rule

Another interesting alternative is to derive a control rule through qualitative reasoning based on a quantitative model. When a quantitative model is known, an alternative is to further abstract this model into a qualitative model and reason about control in terms of this qualitative model. The following alternative, however, completely eliminates a quantitative model:

$$\text{physical system} \longrightarrow \text{qualitative model} \longrightarrow \text{control rule}$$

Here we address the second step of this route: How to reason about a qualitative model to derive a control rule.

An important decision to be made is concerned with the choice of a formalism for defining qualitative models of dynamic systems. In this study we choose qualitative differential equations (QDE) as the representation formalism. So our modelling primitives are similar to those in the QSIM qualitative simulation algorithm (Kuipers 1986). In this paper we use a QDE model to reason about the dynamic system from the control point of view. As our example study shows, it is possible to derive qualitative properties useful with respect to constructing a control strategy. It should be noted that the straightforward use of QSIM-type simulation for reasoning about control would suffer from deficiencies analysed by Makarovič and Mars (1989), and Makarovič (1991a).

We will first introduce our example problem (pole and cart). We will then consider the modelling primitives and some useful relations among these primitives. We will then use these relations to reason about control for our example system.

2 THE POLE-AND-CART PROBLEM

In the pole-and-cart problem, illustrated in Fig. 14.1, the task is to prevent the pole from falling while keeping the cart within the bounded track. Also, if the cart is not centred, the task is to bring the cart towards the centre of the track. The problem has been often used as an exercise in the control of dynamic systems. For example, Eastwood (1968) uses it as an illustration task for classical control engineering. The problem has also been used by many authors as an example task for neural nets (e.g. Anderson 1987). Michie and Chambers were the first to experiment with it within AI, and in their classical paper (1968) developed a general and robust learning scheme (called BOXES) capable of learning this task. The learning scheme of Selfridge *et al.* (1985) is similar in spirit. Recent results of BOXES-type learning applied to the more difficult two-pole problem (another pole hinged on the top of the first one) are in Michie and Bain (1989). Sammut (1988) and Urbančič (1990) review some of these 'non- classical' approaches. Urbančič and Bratko (1994) review some other approaches to learning to control, again using pole-and-cart as a frequent example problem. Varšek *et al.* (1992) explore the use of genetic and symbolic learning at various stages of inducing a solution. Makarovič (1991a,b) in his interesting study derived an elegant control rule for the two-pole problem by a kind of qualitative reasoning about the differential equations model of the system. Several ideas in this paper are similar to those discovered by Makarovič within his framework. Urbančič (1990; 1991) investigated improvements to the Michie–Chambers BOXES learning. She also derived control from a kind of probabilistic qualitative model, derived as an approximate, interval arithmetic evaluation of a proper quantitative model. A somewhat similar approach to balancing the pole-and-cart system, by means of non-deterministic automata, was studied by Lunze (1992).

The usual approach to the pole-and-cart problem in classical control engineering is to assume that the angle, θ, is small enough that the trigonometric functions in the differential equations in Fig. 14.1 can be approximated. By approximating them with the first term of the Taylor series, these equations become linear. For a control regime in which the control force can be continuously varied and unlimited force is available, this is a known control rule:

$$F = a * x + b * \dot{x} + c * \theta + d * \dot{\theta};$$

a, b, c and d are constants. This control rule minimizes a quadratic error measure (integral of the sum of squares of the errors in the four state variables and control force) for the linearized

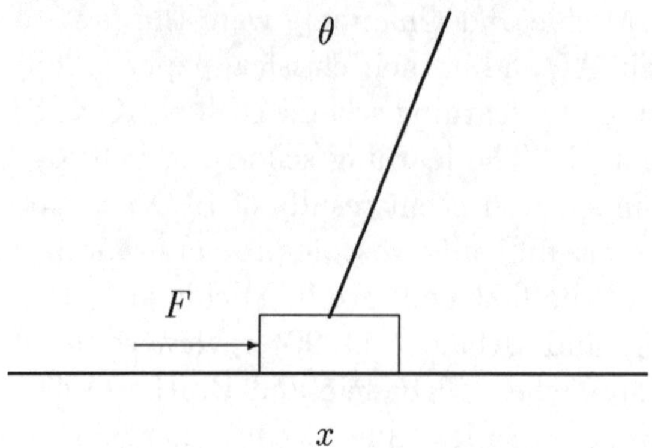

$$\ddot{x} = \frac{4F + 2lm\dot{\theta}^2 \sin\theta - 1.5mg\sin 2\theta}{4M + 4m - 3m\cos^2\theta}$$

$$\ddot{\theta} = 6\frac{(m+M)g\sin\theta - F\cos\theta - 0.5ml\dot{\theta}^2\sin\theta\cos\theta}{(4M + 4m - 3m\cos^2\theta)l}$$

Figure 14.1. The pole-and-cart system. $\theta = 0$ for pole upright, $x = 0$ for cart centred. M is the mass of the cart, m is the mass of the pole, and l is its length.

differential equations model. This can be shown by the calculus of variations.

The control regime that is usually adopted in the AI literature is that of bang–bang. In this regime the amount of force is fixed and all that the controller can do is to change its direction (left or right). Changes can only occur at the boundaries between 'sample time' intervals. Sampling time is typically chosen to be 0.02 s, which corresponds to the rate 50 Hz at which decisions are made.

3 QDE CONSTRAINTS

Our qualitative models will be stated in terms of types of constraints usually used in qualitative differential equations (QDE; as in QSIM, Kuipers 1986). For a short introduction to QDE and associated problems see (Bratko 1992). These constraints are time derivatives, arithmetic constraints, and monotonic functions. We write

$$y = M^+(x)$$

to say that y is a monotonically increasing function of x. The monotonically increasing constraint M is typical of naive physics work. In this paper we will always assume that such a function is continuous and smooth. A special case is

$$y = M_0^+(x)$$

where $y(0) = 0$. For the purpose of this work we introduce some useful additional constraints: S, A and E. We write

$$y = S(x)$$

for the special case when $y = M_0^+(x)$ and $f(-x) = -f(x)$, and f is smooth and smoothly derivable. Such a function has the property $y''(0) = 0$. For convenience we introduce two other piecewise monotonic constraints A and E. We define

$$y = A(x)$$

as: for $x < 0$, y is a monotonically increasing function of x, and for $x > 0$, y is a monotonically decreasing function of x. Also, $y(0) > 0$, $y'(0) = 0$, and $y(-x) = y(x)$. An A function is also continuous and smooth.

We write

$$y(x_1, x_2, ...) = E(x_1, x_2, ...)$$

if $y(0, x_2, x_3, ...) = 0$ for any value of x_2, x_3, ... , and for any $\epsilon > 0$ there is a $\delta = \delta(x_2, x_3, ...)$, $\delta > 0$, such that: if $|x_1| \leq \delta$ then $|y(x_1, x_2, ...)| \leq \epsilon$.

4 SOME PROPERTIES OF QDE CONSTRAINTS

In reasoning about control, some properties of the QDE constraints will be exploited. Figure 14.2 gives a set of such properties, stated as if–then rules (meaning logical implications). These properties can be easily proved. As an example consider the property

$$S(x) = S(y) \implies y = S(x).$$

Let us prove a more general property:

$$M^+(x) = M^+(y) \implies y = M^+(x).$$

This can be proved as follows. The left hand-side $M^+(x) = M^+(y)$ means: there exist two functions f and g, such that $f, g \in M^+$ and $f(x) = g(y)$. Then

$$f' = \frac{dg}{dy} y',$$

$$y' = f' / \frac{dg}{dy},$$

$$\text{sign}(y') = \text{sign}(f') * \text{sign}(\frac{df}{dy}) > 0 \implies y = M^+(x).$$

In a similar way, the property

$$y = M^+(M^+(x)) \implies y = M^+(x)$$

can be proved:

$$y = f(g(x)), \quad f, g \in M^+,$$

$$y' = \frac{df}{dg} g',$$

$$\text{sign}(y') = \text{sign}(\frac{df}{dg}) * \text{sign}(g') > 0 \implies y = M^+(x).$$

5 A QUALITATIVE MODEL OF POLE-AND-CART

A qualitative model of the pole-and-cart system can be obtained from the differential equations model. As a starting point we can use a set of basic constraints on the quantities in our system and then turn them into QDEs. Makarovič (1991b) gives such a set of basic constraints for the more complicated two-poles-and-cart system. His set of primitive constraints can be adapted for our case as follows.

The forces in the system are:

$F_m = -mg =$ gravity acting vertically on the pole at the centre of mass;

$$y = kx, \quad k \text{ const.} > 0 \Longrightarrow y = S(x)$$

$$y = x + S(x) \Longrightarrow y = S(x)$$

$$y = kS(x), \quad k \text{ const.} > 0 \Longrightarrow y = S(x)$$

$$x = S(y) \Longrightarrow y = S(x)$$

$$S(x) = S(y) \Longrightarrow y = S(x)$$

$$y = S(S(x)) \Longrightarrow y = S(x)$$

$$y = \frac{S(x)}{A(x)} \Longrightarrow y = S(x)$$

$$y = S(x) \Longrightarrow y''(x) \text{ approaches } 0 \text{ when } x \text{ approaches } 0$$

$$y = E(x_1, ...) \pm E(x_1, ...) \Longrightarrow y = E(x_1, ...)$$

$$y = x_1 A(x_2) \Longrightarrow y = const * x_1 + E(x_1, x_2)$$

Figure 14.2. Properties of QDE constraints.

F_b = reaction force from the cart acting on the pole at the bottom of the pole;
F_{bx} = horizontal component of F_b;
F_{by} = vertical component of F_b;
F = external force applied horizontally on the cart, positive if pushing from the left;
F_c = net force acting horizontally on the cart.

The coordinates of the pole and the cart are:
x = x-coordinate of the cart; $x = 0$ when the cart is in the middle of the track;
x_m = x-coordinate of the middle of the pole;
y_m = y-coordinate of the middle of the pole;
θ = the angle of the pole; $\theta = 0$ when pole is upright, and θ is measured clockwise.

The following constraints relate the forces, torques and accelerations, and reflect the mechanical connection between the cart and the pole so that this connection permits rotation of the pole:

$$F_c = F - F_{bx},$$

$$\ddot{x}_m = \frac{F_{bx}}{m},$$

$$\ddot{y}_m = \frac{-mg + F_{by}}{m},$$

$$\ddot{\theta} = \frac{6}{lm}(-F_{bx}\cos\theta + F_{by}\sin\theta),$$

$$\ddot{x} = \frac{F_c}{M},$$

$$x_m = x + \frac{l}{2}\sin\theta,$$

$$y_m = \frac{l}{2}\cos\theta.$$

The interval of interest of θ is $-\pi/2 < \theta < \pi/2$. For this interval we have $\sin\theta$ is $S(\theta)$ and $\cos\theta$ is $A(\theta)$. Thus the equations above abstract into the following qualitative constraints:

(C1) $F_c + F_{bx} = F$,
(C2) $\ddot{x}_m = a_1 F_{bx}$,
(C3) $\ddot{y}_m = a_2 F_{by} - a_3$,
(C4) $\ddot{\theta} = F_{by}S(\theta) - F_{bx}A(\theta)$,
(C5) $\ddot{x} = a_4 F_c$,
(C6) $x_m = x + S(\theta)$,
(C7) $y_m = A(\theta)$,

where a_1, a_2, a_3 and a_4 are positive constants.

Instead of abstracting the original differential equations, these constraints can be, at least to a large extent, constructed directly through common sense reasoning about the pole on the cart. For example, constraint C6 can be obtained as follows: when the angle is 0, the x-coordinates of the cart and the middle of the pole are equal. If the angle increases, the difference between both x-coordinates also increases monotonically.

We will now illustrate that it may be possible to systematically construct an adequate control rule for a dynamic system by reasoning based on a qualitative model of the system.

6 SOME CONTROL PRINCIPLES

We here look into ways of controlling a variable indirectly using a monotonic constraint, or an integrator or a chain of integrators. These should be viewed as elementary control principles that can also be found in traditional control engineering and correspond to PID-type controllers. Later we will show how a qualitative model of a system can be used to combine such controllers.

First we consider the case where y is a variable to be controlled and x is a control variable (one that can be set directly), and $y = M^+(x)$. Then it is possible to force y to approach some goal value y_g by properly varying x. An adequate control rule is: $\dot{x} = S(y_g - y)$. A special case of this is: $\dot{x} = k * (y_g - y)$. This corresponds to the I-controller.

Next, let us assume that x is the variable to be controlled and that the control variable is $\dot{x}$. Because of the relation between x and $\dot{x}$ we can indirectly control x through $\dot{x}$. Let x_g be the goal value of x. One policy to control x through $\dot{x}$ is to make $\dot{x}$ proportional to the error in x, that is $(x_g - x)$:

$$\dot{x} = k * (x_g - x),$$

where k is a constant. This corresponds to the P-controller and produces an exponential approach to the goal value:

$$x = x_g + (x_0 - x_g) * e^{-kt},$$

where x_0 is the initial value of x.

Now assume that $\dot{x}$ cannot be directly controlled, but the control variable is $\ddot{x}$. The same control principle can now be recursively applied: indirectly control $\dot{x}$ through $\ddot{x}$, and x through $\dot{x}$. This determines the goal value for $\dot{x}$ and then the control value for $\ddot{x}$:

$$\dot{x_g} = k_1(x_g - x),$$
$$\ddot{x} = k_2(\dot{x_g} - \dot{x}).$$

This control regime is equivalent to the PD-controller when the plant's transfer function is s^2. The solution of the differential equations above is

$$x = x_g + C_1 e^{p_1 * t} + C_2 e^{p_2 * t},$$

where C_1 and C_2 are constants depending on the initial conditions, and

$$p_{1,2} = -k_2 * \frac{1 \pm \sqrt{1 - 4k_1/k_2}}{2}.$$

Increasing k_1 and k_2 results in faster approach to x_g (faster reaction of the system). If $4k_1 > k_2$ then the response is oscillatory. A compromise between fast and oscillatory response, known from control engineering, is the criterion

$$1 - \frac{4k_1}{k_2} = -1.$$

This forces p_1 and p_2 to lie in the complex plane on the 45° diagonals. Accordingly, this partially determines the choice of the two constants: $k_2 > 0$ to ensure stability, and $k_1 = k_2/2$ to ensure a good compromise between the speed of response and oscillation.

The above principles of controlling x by integration or double integration through $\dot{x}$ or $\ddot{x}$ will be referred to as the P and PD control respectively. It should be noted that these principles are only one possible way of controlling a variable through its derivatives.

7 DERIVING CONTROL RELATIONS

We will now use the properties of QDE constraints to derive some relations useful for controlling the pole-and-cart system. We start with the model stated by the qualitative constraints C1-7.

Let us first consider the special case when θ is constant ($\ddot{\theta} = \dot{\theta} = 0$). From qualitative constraint C6 we have

$$x_m = x + const.,$$

$$\ddot{x}_m = \ddot{x}.$$

Using this result in constraints C2 and C5, we have

$$\ddot{x}_m = S(F_{bx}) = \ddot{x} = S(F_c),$$

so
$$F_{bx} = S(F_c).$$

Using this in constraint C1,

$$F_c + S(F_c) = F.$$

From this it follows that

$$F_c = S(F).$$

Also
$$F_{bx} = S(F_c) = S(S(F)),$$

so
$$F_{bx} = S(F).$$

From C7 we have $y_m = const.$, and then from C3,

$$F_{by} = k$$

for k constant and $k > 0$. Using this in C4,

$$0 = kS(\theta) - F_{bx}A(\theta).$$

Therefore
$$S(F)A(\theta) = S(\theta),$$

$$S(F) = \frac{S(\theta)}{A(\theta)} = S(\theta).$$

This gives finally for θ constant

$$F = S(\theta)$$

and
$$\ddot{x} = S(\theta).$$

Notice that in the derivation above, weaker constraints were used in several places instead of the stronger constraints in the model. For example, a linear function was replaced by an S-function. This, however, does not affect the final result of the derivation.

Now let us consider the relation between $\ddot{\theta}$ and external force F. From C6, after double differentiation w.r.t. time, we have

$$\ddot{x} = \ddot{x}_m - H(\theta, \dot{\theta}, \ddot{\theta}),$$

where

$$H(\theta, \dot{\theta}, \ddot{\theta}) = \frac{d^2 S(\theta)}{d\theta^2}\dot{\theta}^2 + \frac{dS(\theta)}{d\theta}\ddot{\theta}.$$

From C7, after double derivation w.r.t. time, we have

$$\ddot{y}_m = G(\theta, \dot{\theta}, \ddot{\theta}),$$

where

$$G(\theta, \dot{\theta}, \ddot{\theta}) = \frac{d^2 A(\theta)}{d\theta^2}\dot{\theta}^2 + \frac{dA(\theta)}{d\theta}\ddot{\theta}.$$

From C1 and C5,

$$F - F_{bx} = \frac{\ddot{x}}{a_4}.$$

Using relations between $\ddot{x}$ and $\ddot{x}_m$ gives

$$F - F_{bx} = \frac{\ddot{x}_m - H(\theta, \dot{\theta}, \ddot{\theta})}{a_4},$$

$$F - F_{bx} = \frac{a_1}{a_4}F_{bx} - \frac{H(\theta, \dot{\theta}, \ddot{\theta})}{a_4},$$

$$F_{bx}\left(1 + \frac{a_1}{a_4}\right) = F + \frac{H(\theta, \dot{\theta}, \ddot{\theta})}{a_4},$$

$$F_{bx} = a_5 F + a_6 H(\theta, \dot{\theta}, \ddot{\theta}),$$

where a_5 and a_6 are constants and $a_5, a_6 > 0$. From C3 and C7,

$$F_{by} = M^+(\ddot{y}_m) = M^+(G(\theta, \dot{\theta}, \ddot{\theta})).$$

Inserting expressions for F_{bx} and F_{by} into C4 we get

$$\ddot{\theta} = M^+(G(\theta, \dot{\theta}, \ddot{\theta}))S(\theta) - A(\theta)(a_5 F + a_6 H(\theta, \dot{\theta}, \ddot{\theta})).$$

By the properties of S functions

$$H(\theta, \dot{\theta}, \ddot{\theta}) = \frac{d^2 S(\theta)}{d\theta^2}\dot{\theta}^2 + \frac{dS(\theta)}{d\theta}\ddot{\theta} = \frac{dS(\theta)}{d\theta}\ddot{\theta} + E(\theta, \dot{\theta})$$

and

$$S(\theta)M^+(G(\theta,\dot{\theta},\ddot{\theta})) = E(\theta,\dot{\theta},\ddot{\theta}).$$

Thus

$$\ddot{\theta} = E(\theta,\dot{\theta},\ddot{\theta}) - A(\theta)F - E(\theta,\dot{\theta}),$$

so

$$\ddot{\theta} = -A(\theta)F + E(\theta,\dot{\theta},\ddot{\theta}) = -a_7F + E(\theta,\dot{\theta},\ddot{\theta},F)$$

for a_7 constant, $a_7 > 0$. Note that $|E(\theta,\dot{\theta},\ddot{\theta},F)|$ can be made arbitrarily small by making $|\theta|$ sufficiently small. For $|\theta|$ sufficiently small, $|E(\theta,\dot{\theta},\ddot{\theta},F)|$ is small compared with $|a_7F|$ unless $|F|$ is extremely small. It is not possible, on the basis of the qualitative model, to tell numerically how small $|\theta|$ has to be. However, it does not have to be necessarily extremely small. Also the upper bound on 'sufficiently small' θ depends on the external force F.

We are now ready to state the complete control rule that consists of the following relations:

$$\ddot{x}_g = k_2 * (k_1 * (x_g - x) - \dot{x}),$$

$$\theta_g = S(\ddot{x}_g),$$

$$\ddot{\theta}_g = k_4 * (k_3 * (\theta_g - \theta) - \dot{\theta}),$$

$$F = -k_5\ddot{\theta}_g,$$

where k_5 is a constant, $k_5 > 0$. The index g in x_g and $\ddot{\theta}_g$ indicates the *current goal* values for x and $\ddot{\theta}$. The rule applies to situations where the cart is to be moved to some goal position x_g, and stay there with the pole upright. Of course, the rule assumes that $|\theta|$ is always sufficiently small. It is not known how small is 'sufficiently small'. But it is known that there exists such an interval for θ where the qualitative rule above works. It can be verified, using the qualitative control rule, that achieving the goal $x = x_g, \dot{x} = 0$, coincides with $\theta_g = \theta = \dot{\theta} = 0$.

Of course, for an actual application of the derived control rule we need concrete values for parameters k_i and an actual S-function $\theta_g = \theta_g(\ddot{x}_g)$. A first attempt at guessing an appropriate

S-function is $\theta_g = k\ddot{x}_g$. For θ_g and $\ddot{x}_g$ small, this attempt complies with the fact that the second derivative of an S-function at 0 equals 0.

Adequate values for the parameters k_i can be found relatively easily in an *ad hoc* way with a few trials. Let pole-and-cart have the following parameters:

$$M = 1\,\text{kg}, m = 0.1\,\text{kg}, l = 1\,\text{m}, F = \pm 1\,\text{N}$$

One set of control parameters that works well, although it is not optimal, is

$$k = 0.1, k_1 = 0.25, k_2 = 1, k_3 = 5, k_4 k_5 = 5.$$

Under the bang–bang regime the computed control force is simply approximated by its sign and the available force magnitude. There is a large range of adequate settings of the parameters that perform similarly.

It is interesting to observe what happens if the controller (without being aware of that) works with a defective, asymmetrical motor that generates different amount of force in one direction than in the other. It turns out that the control rule is rather robust with respect to such a defect in the motor. For example, the rule still works adequately with a motor whose force is $1.5\,\text{N}$ in one direction and $0.5\,\text{N}$ in the other.

8 CORRESPONDENCE BETWEEN QUALITATIVE AND 'CLASSICAL' CONTROL

An interesting question is what is the correspondence between our control rule derived from a qualitative model and the 'classical' control rule derived from the proper differential equations model that minimizes the quadratic error criterion. The 'classical' rule, which assumes that the goal position $x_g = 0$, is

$$F = ax + b\dot{x} + c\theta + d\dot{\theta}.$$

Here the force may vary continuously. For the system's parameters as above, the values of the parameters of the rule are (Džeroski 1989)

$$a = 1.0873, b = 2.1747, c = -26.5349, d = -6.7831.$$

Under the bang–bang regime (when both time and force are discrete) this rule can be approximated as

$$F = \text{sign}(ax + b\dot{x} + c\theta + d\dot{\theta}).$$

Combining the constraints in our qualitative control rule, derived from the qualitative model, we have

$$\theta_g = S(k_1(x_g - x) - \dot{x}),$$

$$F = -K(k_3(\theta_g - \theta) - \dot{\theta}),$$

where $K = k_4 k_5$. What is the relation between this and the 'classical' control? This is in fact an abstraction of the classical rule when concrete real-valued parameters are replaced by symbolic parameters, and a linear function is abstracted into the S-constraint. This correspondence between the qualitative rule and the classical rule can be established as follows. Let us replace the S-constraint with a linear function, giving

$$\theta_g = k_2(k_1(x_g - x) - \dot{x}).$$

Then

$$F = -K(k_3(k(k_1(x_g - x) - \dot{x}) - \theta) - \dot{\theta}).$$

For $x_g = 0$, as assumed in the classical rule, we have

$$F = k_1 k_2 k_3 K x + k_2 k_3 K \dot{x} + k_3 K \theta + K \dot{\theta}.$$

The following parameter setting results in the same control as the classical rule:

$$k_1 = 0.5000, k_2 = -0.08196, k_3 = 3.118, K = -6.7831.$$

This correspondence was stated, in a slightly different form, by Džeroski (1989).

9 DISCUSSION

It was shown with a detailed example how a qualitative modelling approach can be used in the control of a dynamic system. A correct, although qualitative control rule for the pole-and-cart system was derived from a qualitative model of the system.

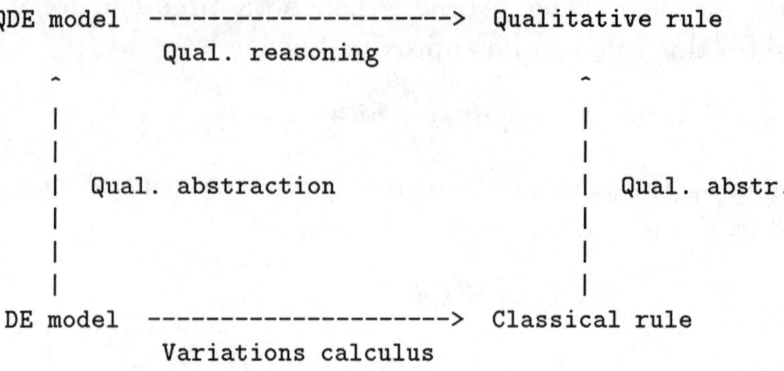

Figure 14.3. Correspondence between differential equations treatment and its qualitative abstraction.

The rule was correct in the sense that it prevents the pole from falling while bringing the cart towards a goal position on the track. It should be noted that the rule is qualitative. So its parameters have to be instantiated to concrete numerical values before the rule can be applied to the control of an actual pole-and-cart system. However, the structure of the rule was shown to be equivalent to the structure of the 'classical' control rule derived from the differential equations model using traditional means of control theory. This correspondence between the differential equations treatment and its qualitative abstraction is illustrated in Fig. 14.3. The rule was experimentally shown to be quite robust in that it can tolerate a considerable amount of asymmetry in the motor. For example, the controller still performs correctly with a defective motor that exerts a three times greater force in one direction than in the other. Details of this can be found in Bratko (1989).

An important question is: What is the utility of our qualitative control rule? One argument could be that it is trivial to satisfy the abstraction relation in Fig. 14.3 by simply stating a 'very abstract' control rule: namely, that the control force F has to be always between $-\infty$ and ∞. This is correct and completely useless. So, how useful is our qualitative control rule? How much guidance does it provide?

The original control problem is to determine F as a function of four variables (given that the goals are fixed: $x_g = 0, \theta_g = 0$):

$$F = F(x, \dot{x}, \theta, \dot{\theta}) =?$$

Given the qualitative control rule, the remaining problem is to determine the parameters k_1, k_3 and $K = k_4 k_5$, and a function of one variable:

$$\ddot{\theta}_g = \ddot{\theta}_g(\ddot{x}_g) =?$$

where we know that this function is an S-function which also helps to determine the function. This remaining problem is certainly easier than the original one of determining a function of four variables.

A question associated with this last conclusion is: How difficult is it to determine the parameters of the qualitative rule? Varšek *et al.* (1992) experimented with genetic algorithms to determine these parameters. They also developed a control rule with a genetic algorithm starting with the original problem without the guidance provided by the qualitative control rule. Their comparison shows that the guidance provided by the qualitative control rule is worth roughly two orders-of-magnitude speed-up of the genetic optimization process. However, more recent results by Tanja Urbančič and Bogdan Filipič (1993; unpublished) indicate a more cautious conclusion. The effects of qualitative rule guidance seem to be not as strong when the required performance criterion for the controller is weaker (allowing larger oscillations). The effects, however, sharply increase when this criterion is stronger. The effects also largely depend on the representation and encoding of the problem in the genetic algorithm and there is no obvious representation for both learning problems (with and without qualitative guidance) allowing direct comparison.

Another question of interest is: How sophisticated a model of the controlled system is needed to enable the derivation of useful control strategies? This question is relevant in the context of automated qualitative modelling, as studied for example in Coiera (1989); Bratko *et al.* (1991); Richards (1992). In this respect it is interesting to note that a very simple *approximate* and *incorrect* qualitative model of our system suffices for deriving very similar qualitative control as derived from our more sophisticated qualitative model. Such a simple model is

$$(C1) \quad \ddot{x} = S(F),$$

$$(C2) \quad \ddot{\theta} = S(\theta) - S(F).$$

For θ constant, C2 gives

$$F = S(\theta).$$

Using this in C1:

$$\ddot{x} = S(\theta).$$

Further, for $|\theta|$ small, C2 gives

$$\ddot{\theta} = -S(F).$$

It should be emphasized that this useful conclusion has been derived from an incorrect model, so the question of justification arises. On the other hand, the advantage of this simple approximate model is that it has a very simple and straightforward naive-physics interpretation and can be easily constructed.

Acknowledgements

I would like to thank Sašo Džeroski who wrote the pole-and-cart simulator used in this study, and observed the correspondence between the classical control rule and the qualitative rule derived in this paper. Donald Michie discovered inconsistency in an earlier version of this paper which required major changes. Other people who helped with suggestions and discussion include: Z. Bing, D. Clements, P.C. Franzone, E. Grant, L. Ironi, D. Juričič, A. Makarovič, D. S. Muggleton, T. Niblett, C. Sammut, S. Strmčnik and T. Urbančič. This work was partly done while the author was visiting the Basser Dept. of Computer Science, Sydney University, Australia.

REFERENCES

Anderson, C.W. (1987). Strategy learning with multilayer connectionist representation. *Proc. 4th Int. Conf. on Machine Learning.* Morgan Kaufmann, Los Altos, CA.

Bratko, I. (1989). Pole balancing: a study in qualitative reasoning about control. ISSEK Workshop 89, Udine, Italy, September 1989.

Bratko, I. (1992). Dynamic system simulation with qualitative differential equations. In *Advanced Topics in Artificial Intelligence* (V. Marik and O. Stepankova, eds.) Springer-Verlag, Berlin.

Bratko, I., Mozetič, I., Lavrač, N. (1989). *KARDIO: a Study in Deep and Qualitative Knowledge for Expert Systems*. MIT Press, Cambridge, MA.

Bratko, I., Muggleton, S., and Varšek, A. (1991). Learning qualitative models of dynamic systems. Inductive Logic Programming Workshop 91, Viana do Castelo, Portugal, March 1991. Also in Muggleton (1992); short version in *Proc. Machine Learning Conf. 91*, Evanston, Ill. Morgan Kaufmann, Los Altos, CA.

Coiera, E. (1989). Generating qualitative models from example behaviours. DCS Report No. 8901, School of Electr. Eng. and Computer Sc., University of New South Wales, Sydney, Australia.

Džeroski, S. (1989). Control of inverted pendulum. University of Ljubljana: Faculty of Electr. Eng. and Computer Sc., BSc Thesis (in Slovenian).

Eastwood, E. (1968). Control theory and the engineer. *Proc. IEE*, **115** (1), 203–211.

Falkenheiner, B. and Forbus, K. (1990). Self-explanatory simulations: an integration of qualitative and quantitative knowledge. *4th International Workshop on Qualitative Physics*, Lugano, July.

Kuipers, B.J. (1986). Qualitative simulation. *Artificial Intelligence*, **29**, 289–338.

Lunze, J. (1992). Qualitative modelling of continuous-variable systems by means of non-deterministic automata. *Intelligent Systems Engineering*, 1, 22–30.

Makarovič, A. (1991a). *Parsimony in Model-Based Reasoning*. Enschede: Twente University, Computer Sc. Department (Ph.D. Thesis).

Makarovič, A. (1991b). A qualitative way of solving the pole-balancing problem. *Machine Intelligence 12* (eds. J.E.Hayes, D.Michie and E.Tyugu) Oxford: Oxford University Press.

Makarovič, A. and Mars, N.J.I. (1989). Fundamental limitations of qualitative simulation. Univ. of Twente, Enschede, The Netherlands: *Memoranda Informatica*, 89–56.

Michie, D. and Bain, M. (1989). Machine acquisition of concepts from sample data. *Artificial Intelligence and Tutoring Systems*, 1989 Spring Symposium at the University of Maine.

Michie, D. and Chambers, R.A. (1968). Boxes: and experiment in adaptive control. In *Machine Intelligence 2* (eds. E.Dale and D.Michie) Edinburgh: Edinburgh University Press.

Richards, B. L. (1992). *An Operator-based Approach to First-order Theory Revision.* University of Texas at Austin, Artificial Intelligence Laboratory: AI92-181 (Ph.D. Thesis).

Sammut, C. (1988). Experimental results from an evaluation of algorithms that learn to control dynamic systems. *Proc. 5th Int. Machine Learning Conf.*, Ann Arbor, Michigan. Morgan Kaufmann, Los Altos, CA.

Selfridge, O.G., Sutton, R.S. and Barto, A.G. (1985). Training and tracking in robotics. *Proc. 9th Int. Joint Conf. on Artificial Intelligence.* Morgan Kaufmann, Los Altos, CA.

Urbančič, T. (1990). *Automatic Synthesis of Knowledge for System Control.* Ljubljana University, Faculty of Electr. Eng. and Computer Sc.: M.Sc. Thesis.

Urbančič, T. (1991). Automatic model-based synthesis of control rules for inverted pendulum. *First European Workshop on Qualitative Reasoning about Physical Systems*, Genova, January.

Urbančič, T. and Bratko, I. (1994). Learning to control dynamic systems. In: *Machine Learning, Neural and Statistical Classification* (eds. D. Michie, D. Spiegelhalter, C. Taylor) Ellis–Horwood, Chichester.

Varšek, A., Urbančič, T. and Filipič, B. (1992). Genetic algorithms in controller design and tuning. *Proc. ISSEK Workshop 92*, Bled, Slovenia, September 1992. An extended version to appear in *IEEE Transactions on Systems, Man and Cybernetics*.

Williams, B. (1990). Interaction-based invention: designing devices from first principles. *4th International Workshop on Qualitative Physics*, Lugano, July.

15

Behavioural Clones and Cognitive Skill Models

Donald Michie

University of Edinburgh

Claude Sammut

University of New South Wales

Abstract

Over the past fifteen years cognitive psychologists and AI scientists have been converging on mutually coherent models of complex decision skills. These models have now been applied to the implementation of real-time control systems. Machine learning has been introduced at the lower level of a 'blackboard' model. In this way rule-structured 'agents' were machine-synthesized from automatically logged samples of human behaviour. In flight-simulator tests synthetic autopilots have regularly flown complete missions without human intervention.

1 BEHAVIOURAL CLONES

In a new book, Collins (1992) puts as a criticism of artificial intelligence (AI) that intelligent behaviour in humans depends on higher-level processes that invoke and suspend automatized subcognitive routines according to context. The implication seems to be that AI workers are either not aware of, or are not making satisfactory progress towards, context-recognition capability. A rather different criticism of AI, from the connectionist camp, is that AI workers generally disregard lower-level control skills, concentrating only on conscious, higher-level components. The subcognitive lower levels, it is rightly stressed, should be built by learning from sensory data. This article discusses recent work which addresses both the criticisms of Collins and of the connectionists. We describe an AI program with a two-level design where the 'lower-level' agents are learned, while the upper-level context recognizer is hand crafted. Unlike the connectionists, we use symbolic learning.

Our extension of the multi-agent model is significant for two reasons.

- Human sub-cognitive skills are 'tacit' in the sense that the owner of such a skill is unaware of its mode of operation, except at the level of 'sub-goals' each of which is served by a separate procedure. Here we incorporate methods for making tacit skill explicit and thus offer, we believe for the first time, a tool for investigating the hidden logic of the sub-cognitive procedures themselves.

- Machine-executable forms of that logic can be used to simplify the construction of practical control systems by introducing 'multi-agent' architectures of the above form.

Each low-level agent may be regarded as an expert solver of a particular problem. The simplest, and earliest, 'committee-of-experts' model was proposed in AI by Allen Newell (1962). A chairman, who has global access to the problem-solving environment, selectively invokes members of a committee of specialists each of which has access to a different, very limited, part of the environment. More recently, related notions of distributed control have been elaborated in the 'blackboard model' of problem-solving (Nii 1986). A collection of routines, each with very specialized expertise, communicate by transmitting information to a shared memory, the 'blackboard', which also holds in-coming data. Each expert, or 'agent', only sees those parts of the blackboard that contain information directly relevant to its own task. A 'scheduler' is responsible for coordinating the responses of each expert, whose actions are triggered by the appearance of information in its own area of the blackboard. In cognitive psychology, Johnson-Laird (1988) has compared consciousness to a computer operating system, which acts as an executive, invoking and coordinating lower-level non-conscious processes. The blackboard model can be likened to a simplified operating system.

In the present work, specialist programs are likewise constructed to solve sub-tasks of a larger problem. A program that acts as 'chairman' invokes subsets of these specialists from time to time according to context. More importantly, the knowledge required to construct the chairman and the specialist problem solvers has been differently derived. The chairman embodies explicit knowledge that is easily articulated and therefore can be hand-crafted. The specialists implement low-level real-time control skills that, in a human, are not performed at a conscious level and therefore cannot be articulated. To create this kind of knowledge, each agent is separately derived by inductive learning of production rules from recorded human performance of the skilled task, a step which is an extension both of previous blackboard designs and of multi-agent AI systems in general.

The distinction between the 'chairman' and the 'committee of experts' has parallels in the psychology and cognitive science literature. In the study of attention within cognitive psychology, for example, a similar distinction is drawn between 'controlled' processes (i.e. those which demand conscious attention for their execution) and 'automatic' processes (tacit skills which operate without requiring conscious attention). In the context of perceptual learning, this particular distinction was first drawn by Shiffrin and Schneider (1977) and subsequently broadened by other researchers.

Complex control skills in humans, as implied above, are built of components which their possessors cannot explicitly communicate. But given sufficient sampling of subarticulate input–output, machine learning programs have been found capable of constructing rules which, when run as programs, deliver behaviours similar to those of the original exemplars (see Michie 1986 for the non-realtime case). These 'clones', i.e. exemplar-derived agents, are in effect symbolic representations of sub-symbolic behaviours. By a 'representation' we here mean no more than an operational specification.

After validating the methodology on simple pole-balancing tasks (Michie *et al.* 1990), I/O clones of constituents of a piloting skill have been successfully derived by machine learning in flight-simulator experiments. Additionally a flight plan is supplied which switches among logically concurrent sets of reactive behaviours. Such a set of clones can be thought of as a committee of autopilots, local to the given context, whose individual responsibilities are specialized for elevators, rollers, thrust, etc. They operate under a scheduler (the flight plan) that has been programmed to recognize the onsets of successive stages of the mission. In a more elaborately developed version, the scheduler's responsibilities would extend to reasoned revisions of the plan.

2 THE BASIC PROCEDURE

A flight simulation program is modified to log the actions taken by a human subject as he or she flies a simulated aircraft. The log file is used to create the inputs to an inductive learning program. The quality of the output from the induction program is tested by running the simulator in autopilot mode where the autopilot code is derived from the decision trees (equivalent to production rules) formed by induction. At the University of New South Wales (UNSW) source code to a flight simulator was made available by Silicon Graphics Inc., and the task was to fly a Cessna (Sammut *et al.* 1992). In confirmatory studies by Camacho at the Turing Institute,[1] the public-domain ACM flight simulator was used with the more difficult task posed by a simulated combat plane (Michie and Camacho 1994).

3 FLIGHT PLAN FOR SIMULATED CESSNA

1. Take off and fly to an altitude of 2000 ft.
2. Level out and fly to a distance of 32,000 ft from the starting point.
3. Turn right to a compass heading of approximately 330°.
4. At a North/South distance of 42,000 ft, turn left to head back towards the runway. The turn is considered complete when the azimuth is between 140° and 180°.

---

[1]Continued at the Oxford University Computing Laboratory, Wolfson Building, Oxford OX1 3QD, UK.

5. Line up on the runway. The aircraft is considered to be lined up when the aircraft's azimuth is less than 5° off the heading of the the runway and the twist is less than 10° from horizontal.

6. Descend to the runway keeping in line.

7. Land on the runway.

4 DATA LOGGING

The display update is modified so that when, and only when, the pilot performs a control action by moving the control stick or changing the thrust or flap settings, the immediately prior state of the simulation is written to a log file. This selective filter greatly reduces the bulk of the resultant file. In the UNSW work the logs finally used were derived from three subjects, who each 'flew' 30 times according to the preceding flight plan.

Referring to the performance of a control action as an 'event', with three pilots, and 30 flights each, the complete data set consisted of about 90,000 events. For each event the control adjustment was recorded to whichever of the following had been changed: rollers, elevator, thrust, or flaps. For the same event the values were recorded of 19 state variables measured at a moment selected 1–3 seconds earlier and inclusive of the then settings of the four control variables. The 'offset' makes approximate allowance for the pilot's delay in responding to complex stimuli.

The following are names of recorded variables: on-ground, g-limit, wing-stall, twist, elevation, azimuth, roll-speed, elevation-speed, azimuth-speed, airspeed, climbspeed, E/W distance, altitude, N/S distance, fuel, together with the settings of rollers, elevators thrust and flaps. It is the inclusion of these last four which enables individual agents to sample and take account of each other's decisions. They thereby achieve a collective co-ordination without need of input from the scheduler. The latter's inputs are currently restricted to signalling changes of context.

5 VALIDATION OF SYSTEM PERFORMANCE

Tests were made by substituting for the human pilot's input a program suite synthesized from one of the three trained subjects. The resulting autopilot system executed the entire flight plan with conspicuous competence, but with individual mannerisms characteristic of the flying styles of the human data source. Details are given by Sammut *et al.* (1992), whose more general statements extend to results obtained from the data of logs of the other pilots.

One of the notable features of the autopilot's behaviour is that it performs more consistently than the human pilot. A side-effect of the induction process is that behaviours which are not repeated in a consistent fashion are eliminated as 'noisy data'. This 'clean-up' effect is discussed by Michie and Camacho (1994) in greater detail.

6 DISCUSSION

From the viewpoints both of cognitive modelling and of technology, our scheme has a number of evident gaps. To be dependent entirely on learning from a human exemplar risks underspecifying what any given local autopilot is to do in unusual situations, i.e. those not adequately covered in the collection of sample behaviours. A trainee, for instance, may never have had a chance to see his/her instructor aborting a touch-down in a cross-wind. In the early stages of simulator training, and also later while 'learning on the job', the human learner plugs these gaps in his/her repertoire by trial-and-error learning. A recent simplification (Sammut 1994) of the BOXES algorithm (Michie and Chambers 1968; Sammut and Cribb 1990) for acquisition of control rules by pure trial and error has effected a large performance improvement. We are now studying it as a possible means of plugging the gaps.

In today's cognitive science, a picture is emerging in which high-level mental processes of deliberation use 'declarative' memory to set the goals and contexts for selective activation of numerous lower-level intuitive processes. Our architecture corresponds closely to Norman's (1981) activation–trigger–schema

(ATS) model. Activation is handled by the flight plan, state variables act as triggers and the rule sets which specify the different agents constitute the schemas.

According to Squire (1987), procedural skills are stored in separate 'procedural' memories. In Johnson-Laird's (1988) computational metaphor, they are coordinated by an operating system which 'sets goals for lower-level processors and monitors their performance. ... its instructions can specify a goal in explicitly symbolic terms, such as to get up and walk. It does not need to send detailed instructions about how to contract muscles'.

A primary aim of our research is to manufacture machine-executable descriptions of cognitive processes that are comprehensible. In human cognition, the upper-level processes are often explicitly symbolic and directly available to the investigator. But the lower levels are not, motivating our machine-aided reformulation of low-level procedures in symbolic form. To illustrate this point it is useful to draw a further analogy with the construction of computer programs. When one first sets out to write a computer program, one has in mind the desired behaviour of the program. This behaviour may be expressed using a specification language that gives a clear and precise characterization of the output expected for any given input. In the process of translating the specification into an operational program, clarity is typically sacrificed for efficiency. That is, while the implementation must correspond to the specification, the choice of algorithms and data structures obscures the program's logical content. Our approach to the machine-oriented study of subcognition is to 'reverse engineer' the mechanisms involved in performing skilled tasks. The aim is to yield executable specifications in symbolic forms perspicuous to the human mind and at the same time machine testable.

It is important to decide whether we wish to model such processes at the implementation level, i.e. understanding the details of how the nervous system performs a task, or at the specification level, i.e. what is the logical content of the neural activity. While much of the work undertaken by neuroscientists and neural net researchers is aimed at the former, our work is aimed at the latter.

7 LOOKING AHEAD

Our multi-agent hierarchy contains upper-level routines that have been explicitly programmed. These guide lower-level routines that have been derived inductively. A natural extension will replace parts of the upper levels themselves by inductive derivation from further experience, so that the high-level skills become, in part, tacit. Over 80 years ago such upward spread of automatization was noted by the mathematical philosopher A.N. Whitehead (1911) when he wrote:

It is a profoundly erroneous truism ... that we should cultivate the habit of thinking what we are doing. The precise opposite is the case. Civilisation advances by extending the number of important operations which we can perform without thinking about them.

REFERENCES

Collins, H. (1992). *Artificial Experts: Social Knowledge and Intelligent Machine*, Cambridge MA: MIT Press. Summary by the author in *New Scientist*, **134**, 20 June 1992.

Johnson-Laird, P.N. (1988). *The Computer and the Mind: An introduction to cognitive science*. Fontana, London.

Michie, D. (1986). The superarticulacy phenomenon in the context of software manufacture. *Proceedings of the Royal Society of London*, **A 405**, 185–212. Reproduced in D. Partridge and Y. Wilks (1992) *The Foundations of Artificial Intelligence*, Cambridge University Press, pp. 411–439.

Michie, D. and Camacho, R. (1994). Building symbolic representations of intuitive real-time skills from performance data. In *Machine Intelligence 13* (eds. K. Furukawa, S. Muggleton and D. Michie), The Clarendon Press, Oxford.

Michie, D. and Chambers, R. A. (1968). Boxes: An experiment in adaptive control. In *Machine Intelligence 2* (eds. E. Dale and D. Michie), Oliver and Boyd, Edinburgh.

Michie, D., Bain, M. and Hayes-Michie, J. (1990). Cognitive models from subcognitive skills. In *Knowledge-based Systems in Indus-*

trial Control (eds. M. Grimble, S. McGhee and P. Mowforth), Peter Peregrinus.

Newell, A. (1962). Some problems of basic organization in problem-solving programs. In *Conference on Self-organizing Systems* (eds. M. C. Yovits, G. T. Jacobi and G. D. Goldstein), Spartan Books, Washington, D. C.

Nii, P. (1986). Blackboard systems: The blackboard model of problem solving and the evolution of blackboard architectures. *AI Magazine* **7**(2), 38–53.

Norman, D.A. (1981). Categorization of action slips. *Psychological Review*, **88**, 1–15.

Sammut, C. (1994). Recent progress with BOXES. In *Machine Intelligence 14* (eds. K. Furukawa, S. Muggleton, and D. Michie), The Clarendon Press, Oxford.

Sammut, C. and Cribb, J. (1990). Is learning rate a good performance criterion for learning? In *Proceedings of the Seventh International Conference on Machine Learning* (ed. J.E. Laird), Morgan Kaufmann, San Mateo, CA.

Sammut, C., Hurst, S., Kedzier, D. and Michie, D. (1992). Learning to fly. In *Proceedings of the Ninth International Conference on Machine Learning* (ed. D.H. Sleeman). Morgan Kaufmann, San Mateo, CA.

Shiffrin, R.M. and Schneider, W. (1977). Controlled and automatic human information processing: II. Perceptual learning, automatic attending, and a general theory. *Psychological Review*, **84**, 127–190.

Squire, L.R. (1987). *Memory and Brain*, Clarendon Press, Oxford.

Whitehead, A.N. (1911). *An Introduction to Mathematics*, London: Williams and Norgate.

16

A Classification of Abduction: Abduction for Logic Programming

Kouichi Hirata

Kyushu University

Abstract

Abduction is a methodology of scientific inquiry. Peirce showed three types of abduction, and expressed them by one syllogism. In computer science, especially in the fields of automated reasoning and machine learning, various researches on abduction or abductive logic have been developed. In order to systematically understand such researches and to clearly discuss abduction, this paper classifies abduction into five types. This new classification is based on an interpretation of the syllogism in abduction and the definitions of hypotheses. We examine various researches on abduction so far developed and show that many researches on abduction can be placed in our classification. Furthermore, we discuss the most essential type of abduction in our classification for logic programming and default logic, and describe Prolog programs for abduction.

1 INTRODUCTION

In order to capture the nature of inference, the philosopher Peirce classified inference into three fundamental kinds: *deduction*, *induction*, and *abduction* (Peirce 1965; Ueyama 1978; Yonemori 1982). In this classification, which is based on the form of syllogisms, abduction is characterized as the inference of a case A from a rule $A \to C$ and a result C. Furthermore, he also placed these three kinds of inference at each stage of scientific inquiry. According to him (Peirce 1965; Ueyama 1978;

Yonemori 1982), every scientific inquiry begins with an observation of a *surprising fact*. The first stage, *abduction*, of scientific inquiry proposes a hypothesis to explain why the fact arises. The second stage, *deduction*, derives new conclusions from the hypothesis. The third stage, *induction*, tests empirically or corroborates the hypothesis and the conclusions. Hence, abduction is not only a kind of inference, but also a method of scientific discovery. The inference schema of abduction as the first stage of scientific inquiry is described in the following three steps (Peirce 1965; Ueyama 1978; Yonemori 1982):

1. A surprising fact C is observed.
2. If A were true, then C would be a matter of course.
3. Hence, there is reason to suspect that A is true.

In general, the above inference schema is depicted by a syllogism:

$$\frac{C \quad A \to C}{A}.$$

In philosophy of science, there has been much discussion of whether there could be a *logic of discovery*. Reichenbach (1938)—see also Brown (1977) and Thagard (1988)—proposed a sharp distinction between the *context of discovery* and the *context of justification*. He claimed that the philosophy of science should concern only questions of confirmation and acceptance that belong in the context of justification, and that the topic of discovery should be relegated to psychology and sociology. Furthermore, Popper (1959) also pointed out that the work of the scientist consists in putting forward and testing theories. He also distinguished sharply between the process of conceiving a new idea, and the methods and results of examining it logically. In the former, there is no such thing as a logical method of having new ideas, or logical reconstruction of this process. Every discovery contains an *irrational element*. In the later, the scientific knowledge is never verified, and it is only falsified. In other words, the work of the scientist consists of the context of discovery and the context of falsification. However, some philosophers, for example Hanson (1958), Kuhn (1970), and Brown (1977), have resisted this restriction. Brown (1977) claimed that, in scientific discovery, the context of justification is a part of the context of discovery, and we cannot draw a line between the context of discovery and one of justification. The relation between justification and discovery has remained unclear.

Peirce's philosophy of science is compatible with the above philosophy of Reichenbach or Popper. The first stage, abduction, of scientific inquiry is corresponding to the context of discovery. The second and the third stage, deduction and induction, also correspond to the context of justification or falsification. Note that the word 'logical' in the above assertion of Popper can be interpreted as universal validity in formal logic. Then, Popper's assertion can be considered that the context of discovery is not necessarily universally valid. Abduction is not valid, and is also likely to cause a *fallacy of affirming the consequent*. Hence, we can regard abduction as the context of discovery, that is, the method of scientific discovery. Hanson (1958) advanced the claim that abduction constitutes a logic of discovery.

In computer science, especially in computational logic and logic programming, many researchers have extensively studied abduction from various viewpoints.

Plotkin (1971) has studied abduction together with inductive generalization. There exist Shapiro's model inference system (1981) and inductive logic programming (Muggleton and Buntine 1988; Muggleton 1992) as the extensions of Plotkin.

Muggleton and Buntine (1988) have introduced the method of *inverting resolution* to construct logic programming from finite examples. Such a methodology is called *inductive logic programming*. Inductive logic programming has been developed by Muggleton (1992) and Ling (1989) has paid attention to the *constructive* method for inductive logic programming. These are also a kind of abduction, because they really propose hypotheses.

Genest *et al.* (1990) and Duval (1991) have suggested abduction for *explanation-based generalization*, which is an efficient technique for obtaining a general concept from examples and a background knowledge. Thagard (1988) has introduced *analogical abduction*, which is a kind of abduction combined with analogical reasoning.

Pople (1973)—see also Kunifuji (1987) and Inoue (1992)—has given one direction for the researches of abduction. There exist Poole's Theorist (1988), Kunifuji's hypothesis-based reasoning (1987), and abductive logic programming (Dung 1991; Eshghi and Kowalski 1989; Kakas and Mancarella 1990) as the extensions of Pople.

Poole (1988) discussed the relationship between Reiter's default logic (1980) and abduction, and showed that abduction can be viewed as a default logic. Kunifuji (1987) developed Poole's Theorist as a hypothesis-based reasoning system.

Eshghi and Kowalski (1989) discussed the relationship between negation as failure and abduction in logic programming. Kakas and Mancarella (1990) and Dung (1991) defined an abductive framework in nonmonotonic logic programming, and studied the semantics in that framework. Out of these studies there has emerged a new field of abductive logic programming.

There are researches of abduction in terms of a model of *belief*, which is a kind of modal logic, by Levesque (1989) and Selman and Levesque (1990). These are regarded as general extensions of Poole's logic (1988). Furthermore, they have claimed that different models of belief give rise to different forms of abductive reasoning, and have constructed a model of belief for abduction. They have also studied the relationship between the models of belief, default logic, and assumption-based truth-maintenance system.

Concerning expert systems, Cox and Pietrzykowski (1987) have investigated *diagnosis problems* by abductive inference. Pirri and Pizzuti (1990) have also combined the diagnosis problem with the stable model semantics which is one of the semantics of logic programming. Konolige (1992) has introduced a *causal theory*, and compared it with abduction. Bylander *et al.* (1991) has formulated abduction in order to analyse the computational complexity of abduction for propositional logic and for the diagnosis problem.

In computational linguistics, Hobbs *et al.* (1988) has introduced abduction in order to interpret natural language. Stickel (1991) has also investigated abduction deeply, and suggested a Prolog-like inference system to interpret natural language.

In order to systematically understand these various researches of abduction and clearly discuss abduction in the sense of Peirce, we classify abduction into five types. This new classification is based on an interpretation of a syllogism in Peirce's abduction and the definitions of hypotheses. We examine various researches on abduction so far developed and show that many researches on Peirce's abduction can be placed in our classification. Furthermore, we discuss the most essential type of abduction in our classification for logic programming and default logic, and describe Prolog programs for the abduction.

2 CLASSIFICATION OF ABDUCTION

The inference schema of abduction has been depicted by the following syllogism:

$$\frac{C \quad A \to C}{A}.$$

The following examples of A and C in the above inference schema are found in literature:

(a) C :'these beans are white',
   A :'these beans are from this bag' (Peirce 1965);

(b) C :'I heard somebody scream at midnight',
   A :'I thought she was attacked' (Ueyama 1978);

(c) C :'fossil shells are found, but far in the interior of the country',
   A :'the sea once washed over this land' (Peirce 1965);

(d) C :'the Atlantic coastline in Africa and America are similar',
   A :'the continental drift theory'
   (Ueyama 1978);

(e) C :'the fossil record',
   A :'the theory of natural selection in biology' (Ueyama 1978);

(f) C :'the data of observations of planets by Tycho Brahe',
   A :'an orbit of planets is an oval (Kepler's first law)' (Peirce 1965).

For the above examples, Peirce showed that there exist the following three types of *explanatory hypotheses*, which are proposed by abduction (Yonemori 1982). The first type is a hypothesis which can be confirmed, even if it is not confirmed at the abduction. The examples (a) and (b) belong to this type. The second type is a hypothesis which physically cannot be confirmed. The example (c) belongs to this type, because we cannot confirm that *there used to be a sea*. The third type is a hypothesis which in practice and in principle cannot be confirmed by our scientific knowledge. The examples (d), (e) and (f) belong to this type, because the hypotheses A could not be derived from the scientific knowledge they had at that time.

Various researches about abduction in computer science and computational logic are also related to at least one type of explanatory hypothesis. Hence, in this section, we introduce a classification which is based on three types of explanatory hypotheses. Note that, in the researches of abduction in computer science, a *background theory* is assumed in order to explain a surprising fact. First, by the definition of a background theory, we classify abduction in computer science into two types, abduction of a rule and of a theory. Here, a rule means an element of a background theory, while a theory means a background theory itself. Abduction of a rule is called *rule-based abduction*, and that of a theory *theory-based abduction*.

In rule-based abduction, a hypothesis A in a syllogism is a set of atoms. Then, for a surprising fact C and a hypothesis A, we denote rule-based abduction by $A \to C$ in a syllogism. On the other hand, in theory-based abduction, a hypothesis A in a syllogism is a theory. Then, for a surprising fact C and a hypothesis A, we denote theory-based abduction by $A \vdash C$ in a syllogism.

For rule-based abduction, it is our purpose to obtain a rule $A \to C$ and a hypothesis A to explain a surprising fact C. In order to capture the properties of rule-based abduction, we apply three types of explanatory hypotheses to rule-based abduction.

According to Peirce, abduction begins with an observation of a surprising fact (Peirce 1965; Ueyama 1978; Yonemori 1982). Hence, in rule-based abduction, a surprising fact must be *surprising* with respect to the background theory given in advance. Let P be a background theory, A be a set of atoms, and C be a surprising fact with respect to P.

(R1) The first type is an abduction that assumes existence of the rules in a given background theory. In this type, for a surprising fact C, we select a rule $A \to C$ in a background theory P, and propose a hypothesis A in P such that C is explained by the selected rule $A \to C$ and the hypothesis A. We call this type of abduction *rule-selecting abduction*.

(R2) The second type is an abduction that assumes existence of the rules in a background theory other than a given one. In this type, we assume that the set of background theories is given in advance. Then, for a surprising fact C, we find a rule $A \to C$ in a background theory P', possibly not P, and propose a hypothesis A. We call this type *rule-finding abduction*.

(R3) The third type is an abduction that cannot assume existence of the rules in any background theory. In this type, for a surprising fact C, we newly generate a rule $A \to C$ in a background theory P, and propose a hypothesis A in P such that C is explained by the generated rule $A \to C$ and the hypothesis A. We call this type *rule-generating abduction*.

If we apply the above three types to abduction for logic programming, then the syllogisms of rule-based abduction are illustrated as follows, where *sf* stands for a surprising fact. In rule-based abduction for logic programming, a surprising fact C with respect to a program P is regarded as a ground atom such that $P \nvdash C$. Note that, in the syllogisms of rule-selecting and rule-generating abduction, $P \cup A \vdash C$ holds for a proposed hypothesis A and a program P, by regarding A as the set $\{A\}$ of atoms.

(R1) rule-selecting	$\dfrac{C : sf\ wrt\ P \quad A \to C\ in\ P}{A\ (set\ of\ atoms)}$
(R2) rule-finding	$\dfrac{C : sf\ wrt\ P \quad A \to C\ in\ P'}{A\ (set\ of\ atoms)}$
(R3) rule-generating	$\dfrac{C : sf\ wrt\ P}{A \to C\ in\ P \quad A\ (set\ of\ atoms)}$

For theory-based abduction, it is our purpose to obtain a theory A to explain a surprising fact C. In order to capture the properties of theory-based abduction, we also apply three types of explanatory hypotheses to theory-based abduction.

(T1) The first type is an abduction that assumes existence of the theory in a given set of background theories. Note here that the set of background theories are given in advance. In this type, we can select and propose a theory A which makes the surprising fact C true. We call this type of abduction *theory-selecting abduction*. An inference schema of theory-selecting abduction is depicted by the following syllogism.

(T2) The second type of abduction which we could call *theory-finding abduction* is the same as the theory-selecting abduction above, because we must assume that there exists a set of background theories.

(T3) The third type is an abduction that cannot assume existence of the theory in the set of background theories. In this type, we generate and propose a theory A which makes the surprising fact C true. We call this type *rule-generating abduction*.

If we apply the above two types to abduction for logic programming, then the syllogisms of theory-based abduction are illustrated as follows. In theory-based abduction for logic programming, a surprising fact C with respect to a program B is also regarded as a ground atom such that $B \nvdash C$.

(T1) theory-selecting	$\dfrac{C : sf\ wrt\ B \quad A \vdash C}{A\ (theory)}$
(T3) theory-generating	$\dfrac{C : sf\ wrt\ B}{A \vdash C \quad A\ (theory)}$

Now we examine the various researches on abduction so far developed and show that all of them can be placed in our classification.

(R1) *Rule-selecting abduction*: Abductive logic programming (Dung 1991; Eshghi and Kowalski 1989; Kakas and Mancarella 1990) is a kind of rule-selecting abduction. It is different from Peirce's abduction in the following viewpoint: Peirce asserted that abduction begins with an observation of a surprising fact. (Peirce 1965; Ueyama 1978; Yonemori 1982). On the other hand, in their works on abductive logic programming,

Eshghi and Kowalski (1989), Kakas and Mancarella (1990), and Dung (1991) asserted that a hypothesis to explain the observed fact can be formed in the abductive framework. Kakas and Mancarella (1990) also asserted that the abductive framework is vacuous and ill-defined if there exist no models to explain the observation. Hence, an important problem for their work is to decide what explains a surprising fact rather than why the fact is surprising.

Abduction for explanation-based generalization by Genest *et al.* (1990) is a kind of rule-selecting abduction. However, what makes the surprising fact *surprising* depends on heuristics.

Abduction for natural language interpretation by Hobbs *et al.* (1988) and Stickel (1991) is a kind of rule-selecting abduction. In the formulation of Hobbs *et al.* (1988), they have dealt with first-order formulas with costs as the logical forms of abduction. On the other hand, Stickel (1991) has dealt with function-free definite programs as the logical forms of abduction.

Concerning expert systems, abduction for diagnosis problem by Cox and Pietrzykowski (1987) is a kind of rule-selecting abduction. They have introduced the concept of a *cause*, and dealt with resolutions for computing fundamental causes. Furthermore, the research of Pirri and Pizzuti (1990) can be regarded as the diagnosis problem in abductive logic programming.

(R2) *Rule-finding abduction*: Duval's abduction is a kind of rule-finding abduction. Duval (1991) dealt with the following abduction for explanation-based generalization: Let D be a domain theory, $A \leftarrow B \wedge C$ be a rule in D, and C be a surprising fact of D. Then, his system finds $C' \in D$ which is analogous to C, and adds a rule $A \leftarrow B \wedge C'$ to D. He called the addition of such a rule 'abduction'.

Thagard's *analogical abduction* (1988) is also a kind of rule-finding abduction.

(R3) *Rule-generating abduction*: The constructive operators such as V and W operators (Muggleton and Buntine 1988; Muggleton 1992; Ling 1989) in inductive logic programming are a kind of rule-generating abduction. Concretely, the constructive operators generate definite clauses from a finite set of surprising facts, called *examples*. Hence, examples are regarded as surprising facts in Peirce's sense.

(T1) *Theory-selecting abduction*: Poole's Theorist (1988) and Kunifuji's hypothesis-based reasoning (1987) are theory-selecting abduction, where the candidates of a hypothesis are given in advance. The main part of their researches is how to select a suitable hypothesis from the candidates.

As the extensions of Poole's research, there exists the research of abduction for a model of *belief* by Levesque (1989) and Selman and Levesque (1990). Their frameworks of abduction depend on a model of belief, which is a kind of modal logic. It is their purpose to construct a model of belief for abduction, not to find an explanation. However, we can regard their abduction as the extension of Poole's abduction (1988).

Konolige (1992) has investigated the relationship between abduction and the diagnosis problem by introducing a *causal theory*. We can regard it as the extension of Poole's abduction.

Bylander *et al.* (1991) have introduced another framed work of abduction for propositional logic. They have extended the symbol '$\rightarrow$' of logical implication to the causal relation, and analysed the computational complexity of abduction and the diagnosis problem. We can also regard it as the extension of Poole's abduction for propositional logic.

(T3) *Theory-generating abduction*: Shapiro's model inference system (1981) and inductive logic programming (Muggleton 1992) is a kind of theory-generating abduction. The model inference system and inductive logic programming *inductively* make definite programs. By the above systems, definite programs are constructed by surprising facts, if we regard examples as surprising facts.

3 RULE-SELECTING ABDUCTION FOR LOGIC PROGRAMMING

In order to know what abduction is and to apply it to machine discovery, we need to study each type of abduction more deeply. In the following sections, we study rule-selecting abduction, the most essential abduction for logic programming and default logic. First we deal with the class of logic programs for which rule-selecting abduction can be applied to propose hypotheses. We assume readers are familiar with the notions of logic programming (Lloyd 1987).

Let P be a definite program. Then we say that a ground atom α is a *surprising fact* of P if $P \nvdash \alpha$. Note here that P is given before α is given. For such an α, we propose a *hypothesis H* such that H is a set of atoms, $P \cup H \vdash \alpha$, and H is minimal with respect to set inclusion. We call the proposal of a hypothesis *abduction*. By regarding H as a conjunction of atoms and applying deduction theorem, if $P \cup H \vdash \alpha$ then $P \vdash H \to \alpha$. Hence it is a rule-selecting abduction in our classification.

Note that the above definition is the same as one in the abductive framework (Dung 1991; Eshghi and Kowalski 1989; Kakas and Mancarella 1990; Poole 1988). However, we are interested in how a hypothesis is proposed, but not in how semantics can be given in the abductive framework. The *rule-selecting abduction* for a definite program is a proposal of hypotheses.

Example 16.1 Let us consider a definite program P such that

$$P = \left\{ \begin{array}{l} p(f(X), f(Y)) \leftarrow p(X, Y), q(X), r(Y) \\ q(f(X)) \leftarrow q(X) \\ r(f(X)) \leftarrow r(X) \\ r(a) \end{array} \right\}.$$

The least Herbrand model $M(P)$ of P is $\{r(a), r(f(a)), \ldots\}$. There exists no atom α with the predicate p in $M(P)$. Suppose that a fact $p(f(a), f(f(b)))$ is given as a surprising fact with respect to P, i.e. $P \nvdash p(f(a), f(f(b)))$. Then, by rule-selecting abduction for P, we can select an H_i from $H_1 = \{p(f(a), f(f(b)))\}$, $H_2 = \{p(a, b), q(a), r(f(b))\}$, and $H_3 = \{p(a, b), q(a), r(b)\}$, and propose it as a hypothesis, for which it holds that $P \cup H_i \vdash p(f(a), f(f(b)))$.

The rule-selecting abduction can be realized in the following Prolog program `rs_abd`, which is a variant of partial evaluation in van Harmelen and Bundy (1988).

```
rs_abd(Goal,Leaves) :-
    clause(Goal,Clause),rs_abd(Clause,Leaves).
```

```
rs_abd((Goal1,Goal2),(Leaf1,Leaf2)) :-
   !,rs_abd(Goal1,Leaf1),rs_abd(Goal2,Leaf2).
rs_abd(Leaf,Leaf) :- !.
```

We can improve the program `rs_abd` using the idea of the *most specific abduction* in Stickel (1991) (see also Duval 1991; Inoue 1992) as follows.

```
msrs_abd(Goal,Leaves) :-
   clause(Goal,Clause),msrs_abd(Clause,Leaves).
msrs_abd((Goal1,Goal2),(Leaf1,Leaf2)) :-
   !,msrs_abd(Goal1,Leaf1),msrs_abd(Goal2,Leaf2).
msrs_abd(Leaf,Leaf) :-(not clause(Leaf,X) -> true).
```

The program `msrs_abd` returns all the leaves of SLD-trees as hypotheses, while the `rs_abd` program returns all the nodes.

By using the above `rs_abd` and `msrs_abd`, we can automatically propose some hypotheses if they terminate. Hence, we can find the class of logic programs for which the programs `rs_abd` and `msrs_abd` terminate. We call the clause whose predicate symbol of the head is p a *definition clause* of p.

Let P be a definite program and p be a predicate symbol. Then a *recursive definition* of p in P, denoted by $rec(P, p)$, is a definition clause of p defined by the following procedure:

1. Select a clause in P whose head predicate is p, and let it be $rec(P, p)$.

2. For $rec(P, p) = A \leftarrow B_1, \ldots, B_l, \ldots, B_n$, if there exists a clause $E \leftarrow F_1, \ldots, F_m$ such that $B_l\theta = E\theta$ for a substitution θ, and $pred(B_l)(= pred(E)) \neq p$, then eliminate the clause $E \leftarrow F_1, \ldots, F_m$ from P, and put

$$rec(P, p)= (A \leftarrow B_1, \ldots, B_{l-1}, F_1, \ldots, F_m, B_{l+1}, \ldots, B_n)\theta.$$

3. Repeat 2 until it cannot be applied.

A *recursive program* of p in P, denoted by $RP(P, p)$, is a program consisting of $rec(P, p)$ and clauses in P which is used in constructing $rec(P, p)$.

For a definite program P and a predicate symbol p, $rec(P, p)$ and $RP(P, p)$ are not unique in general.

Example 16.2 Let P_1, P_2 and P_3 be the following definite programs:

$$P_1 = \left\{ \begin{array}{l} p(f(X)) \leftarrow p(X), q(X,Y) \\ q(f(X), f(Y)) \leftarrow q(f(X), Y) \end{array} \right\},$$

$$P_2 = \left\{ \begin{array}{l} p(f(X)) \leftarrow p(X), q(X,Y) \\ q(f(X), f(Y)) \leftarrow q(X, f(Y)) \end{array} \right\},$$

$$P_3 = \left\{ \begin{array}{l} p(f(X)) \leftarrow p(f(f(X))), q(X,Y) \\ q(f(X), f(Y)) \leftarrow q(f(X), Y) \end{array} \right\}.$$

Then, $rec(P_i, p)$ and $RP(P_i, p)$ $(1 \leq i \leq 3)$ are:

$$rec(P_1, p) = p(f(f(X))) \leftarrow p(f(X)), q(f(X), Y)$$
$$rec(P_2, p) = p(f(f(X))) \leftarrow p(f(X)), q(X, f(Y))$$
$$rec(P_3, p) = p(f(f(X))) \leftarrow p(f(f(f(X)))), q(f(X), Y)$$

$$RP(P_1, p) = \left\{ \begin{array}{l} p(f(f(X))) \leftarrow p(f(X)), q(f(X), Y) \\ q(f(X), f(Y)) \leftarrow q(f(X), Y) \end{array} \right\},$$

$$RP(P_2, p) = \left\{ \begin{array}{l} p(f(f(X)) \leftarrow p(f(X)), q(X, f(Y)) \\ q(f(X), f(Y)) \leftarrow q(X, f(Y)) \end{array} \right\},$$

$$RP(P_3, p)$$
$$= \left\{ \begin{array}{l} p(f(f(X))) \leftarrow p(f(f(f(X)))), q(f(X), Y) \\ q(f(X), f(Y)) \leftarrow q(f(X), Y) \end{array} \right\}.$$

Let P_4 be the following definite program:

$$P_4 = \left\{ \begin{array}{l} p(f(X)) \leftarrow p(X), q(X,Y) \\ p(f(X)) \leftarrow p(f(f(X))), q(X,Y) \\ q(f(X), f(Y)) \leftarrow q(X, Y) \end{array} \right\}.$$

Then, there exist the following two $rec(P_4, p)$:

$$p(f(f(X))) \leftarrow p(f(X)), q(f(X), Y)$$
$$p(f(f(X))) \leftarrow p(f(f(f(X)))), q(f(X), Y).$$

Thus there also exist the following two $RP(P_4, p)$:

$$\left\{ \begin{array}{l} p(f(f(X))) \leftarrow p(f(X)), q(f(X), Y) \\ q(f(X), f(Y)) \leftarrow q(X, Y) \end{array} \right\},$$

$$\left\{ \begin{array}{l} p(f(f(X))) \leftarrow p(f(f(f(X)))), q(f(X), Y) \\ q(f(X), f(Y)) \leftarrow q(X, Y) \end{array} \right\}.$$

For a term t, $|t|$ denotes the length of t, that is, the number of all occurrences of symbols in t. For example, $|a|$ is 1 and $|f(f(a))|$ is 3. A clause $p(t_1, \ldots, t_n) \leftarrow B_1, \ldots, B_m$ is said to be *p-reducing with respect to the i-th argument*, if $|t_i\theta| > |s_i^l\theta|$ for any substitution θ and for any index l such that $pred(B_l) = p$, where s_i^l is the i-th term of B_l. A p-reducing clause with respect to some argument is called simply *p-reducing*. This definition is an extension of reducing and weakly reducing programs in Yamamoto (1992).

Example 16.3 In Example 16.2, the definition clause of p in P_1 and P_2 are p-reducing. $rec(P_1, p)$ and $rec(P_2, p)$ are also p-reducing. The definition clause of p in P_3 and $rec(P_3, p)$ is not p-reducing.

For p-reducing clause, the following lemma holds.

Lemma 16.4 Let $C = p(t_1, \ldots, t_n) \leftarrow B_1, \ldots, B_m$ be a p-reducing clause and $p(s_1, \ldots, s_n)$ be a ground atom. Then all the SLD-derivations of $\{C\} \cup \{\leftarrow p(s_1, \ldots, s_n)\}$ are finite.

Proof. Suppose C is p-reducing with respect to the i-th argument.

If $p(t_1, \ldots, t_n)$ and $p(s_1, \ldots, s_n)$ are not unifiable, then the derivation of $\{C\} \cup \{\leftarrow p(s_1, \ldots, s_n)\}$ is finitely failed.

Suppose $p(t_1, \ldots, t_n)$ and $p(s_1, \ldots, s_n)$ are unifiable. Since $p(s_1, \ldots, s_n)$ is ground, there exists a unifier θ for $p(t_1, \ldots, t_n)$ and $p(s_1, \ldots, s_n)$ such that $p(t_1, \ldots, t_n)\theta = p(s_1, \ldots, s_n)$. If $B_j\theta$ is the selected atom of the goal $\leftarrow B_1\theta, \ldots, B_m\theta$, and $B_j\theta$ and $p(t_1, \ldots, t_n)$ are not unifiable, then the derivation of $\{C\} \cup \{\leftarrow B_1\theta, \ldots, B_m\theta\}$ is finitely failed. Otherwise, suppose $B_l\theta$ is the selected atom of the goal $\leftarrow B_1\theta, \ldots, B_m\theta$. Suppose $B_l\theta$ and $p(t_1, \ldots, t_n)$ are unifiable. Note that $s_i^l\theta$ is ground, where s_i^l is the i-th argument in B_l. By the definition of p-reducing clause,

$$|s_i^l\theta| < |t_i\theta| = |s_i|.$$

Furthermore, if $p(t_1, \ldots, t_n)$ and $B_l\theta$ are unifiable, then, for the derivation of $\{C\} \cup \{\leftarrow B_l\theta\}$, there exists a unifier σ for $B_l\theta$ and $p(t_1, \ldots, t_n)$ such that $B_l\theta\sigma = p(t_1, \ldots, t_n)\sigma$. Then,

$$|s_i^l\sigma| < |t_i\sigma| = |s_i^l\theta\sigma| = |s_i^l\theta| < |s_i|.$$

Hence, the longest derivation of $\{C\} \cup \{\leftarrow B_1\theta, \ldots, B_m\theta\}$ is constructed in the following way.

Let G_1 be the initial goal $\leftarrow B_1\theta, \ldots, B_m\theta$. Then, by selecting each atom $B_l\theta$ in the derivation, we can obtain the following resolvent G_m of the derivation:

$$\leftarrow (B_1\theta_1, \ldots, B_m\theta_1), (B_1\theta_2, \ldots, B_m\theta_2), \ldots, (B_1\theta_m, \ldots, B_m\theta_m).$$

For any $B_l\theta_k(1 \leq l, k \leq m)$, $|s_i^l\theta_k| < |s_i|$. Furthermore, by selecting each atom $B_l\theta_k$ in the derivation, we can also obtain the following resolvent G_{m+m^2} of the derivation:

$$\leftarrow ((B_1\theta_1', \ldots, B_m\theta_1'), \ldots, (B_1\theta_m', \ldots, B_m\theta_m')),$$
$$\ldots, (\ldots, (B_1\theta_{m^2}', \ldots, B_m\theta_{m^2}')).$$

For any $B_l\theta_k'(1 \leq l \leq m, 1 \leq k \leq m^2)$, $|s_i^l\theta_k'| < |s_i| - 1$.

Hence, the length of the derivation of $\{C\}\cup\{\leftarrow B_1\theta, \ldots, B_m\theta\}$ is at most $\sum_{k=1}^{|s_i|} m^k$. The length of the derivation of $\{C\} \cup \{\leftarrow p(s_1, \ldots, s_n)\}$ is at most $1 + \sum_{k=1}^{|s_i|} m^k$.

The condition that `rs_abd` and `msrs_abd` programs terminate on P is characterized by the following head-reducing $RP(P, p)$.

Let $rec(P, p) = p(t_1, \ldots, t_n) \leftarrow B_1, \ldots, B_m$. Then, a recursive program $RP(P, p)$ is called *head-reducing* if it satisfies the following conditions:

1. If there exists a k such that $B_k = p(s_1^k, \ldots, s_n^k)$, then
(a) there exists a j such that $|t_j| > |s_j^k|$ for any k, and
(b) any B_l such that $B_l = q_l(u_1^l, \ldots, u_{n_l}^l)$ $(p \neq q_l)$ satisfies one of the conditions:
i. there exists a term u_i^l in B_l which is constructed by variables appearing in t_j, and the definition clause of q_l is q_l-reducing with respect to i-th argument, or
ii. the definition clause of q is not included in $RP(P, p)$.

2. Otherwise, any $B_l = q_l(u_1^l, \ldots, u_{n_l}^l)$ satisfies one of the following conditions:
i. there exists a term u_i^l in B_l which is constructed by variables appearing in $t_1, \ldots, t_n$, and the definition clause of q_l is q_l-reducing with respect to i-th argument, or
ii. the definition clause of q_l is not included in $RP(P, p)$.

Example 16.5 In Example 16.2, $RP(P_2, p)$ is head-reducing. On the other hand, $RP(P_1, p)$ is not head-reducing because it does not satisfy the condition 1 (b). $RP(P_3, p)$ is also not head-reducing because it does not satisfy the condition 1 (a). The first recursive program $RP(P_4, p)$ in Example 16.2 is head-reducing, but the second recursive program $RP(P_4, p)$ is not head-reducing. Furthermore, Prolog programs for defining a list, membership of a list and appending two lists are head-reducing.

For the termination of rule-selecting abduction, the following theorem holds.

Theorem 16.6 Let P be a definite program and p be a predicate symbol. If any $RP(P, p)$ is head-reducing, then all the SLD-derivations of $P \cup \{\leftarrow p(s_1, \ldots, s_n)\}$ are finite.

Proof. The result is proven by induction on the number of clauses in P. If the number is 1, then Lemma 16.4 implies the result.

Next suppose the result is true for $P = \{C_1, \ldots, C_k\}$, and let P' be $P \cup \{C_{k+1}\}$. Any $RP(P', p)$ is head-reducing by the induction hypothesis. Let C_{k+1} be the following clause:

$$p_{k+1}(t_1, \ldots, t_{n_{k+1}}) \leftarrow B_1, \ldots, B_l.$$

If the predicate symbol p_{k+1} does not occur in P, then all the input clauses of the derivation of $P \cup \{\leftarrow p(s_1, \ldots, s_n)\}$ do not include C_{k+1}. Thus the derivation of $P' \cup \{\leftarrow p(s_1, \ldots, s_n)\}$ is equal to that of $P \cup \{\leftarrow p(s_1, \ldots, s_n)\}$. Consequently, the derivation of $P' \cup \{\leftarrow p(s_1, \ldots, s_n)\}$ is finite by the induction hypothesis.

If the predicate symbol p_{k+1} occurs in the clause C_i of P, then there exists a clause C_i in P, and one of the following cases holds:

1. p_{k+1} occurs in the body of C_i.
2. p_{k+1} occurs in the head of C_i.

If any $RP(P, p)$ does not include C_i, then all the input clauses of the derivation of $P \cup \{\leftarrow p(s_1, \ldots, s_n)\}$ do not include C_i. Thus the derivation of $P' \cup \{\leftarrow p(s_1, \ldots, s_n)\}$ is equal to that of $P \cup \{\leftarrow p(s_1, \ldots, s_n)\}$. In both cases, the derivation of $P \cup \{\leftarrow p(s_1, \ldots, s_n)\}$ is finite by the induction hypothesis.

Thus suppose some $RP(P, p)$ includes C_i.

1. Suppose p_{k+1} occurs in the body of C_i. Let C_i be the following clause:

$$p_i(u_1, \ldots, u_{n_i}) \leftarrow D_1, \ldots, D_j, \ldots, D_m \quad (pred(D_j) = p_{k+1}).$$

By the induction hypothesis, if there exists an infinite derivation of $P' \cup \{\leftarrow p(s_1, \ldots, s_n)\}$, and $D_j\lambda$ and $p_{k+1}(t_1, \ldots, t_{n_{k+1}})$ are unifiable, where λ is a substitution, then the derivation of $P' \cup \{\leftarrow D_j\lambda\}$ is infinite. However, we can show that all the derivations of $P' \cup \{\leftarrow D_j\lambda\}$ are finite by the following discussion. If the derivation of $P' \cup \{\leftarrow D_j\lambda\}$ is infinite, then the derivation of $P' \cup \{\leftarrow B_1\sigma, \ldots, B_l\sigma\}$ is also infinite, where σ is a unifier of $D_j\lambda$ and $p_{k+1}(t_1, \ldots, t_{n_{k+1}})$. For any $B_i\sigma$, consider the predicate symbol $pred(B_i)$.

(a) Suppose that for any i, $pred(B_i)$ does not occur in P or $pred(B_i)$ is p_{k+1}. Then, all the input clauses of the derivation of $P' \cup \{\leftarrow D_j\lambda\}$ include only C_{k+1}. Since $RP(P, p)$ is head-reducing, $D_j\lambda$ has the argument which is a ground term, and C_{k+1} is p_{k+1}-reducing with respect to this argument by 1.(b) i. or 2. i. in the definition of head-reducing. Then, the derivation of $P' \cup \{\leftarrow D_j\lambda\}$ is finite by Lemma 16.4.

(b) Suppose there exists an i such that $pred(B_i)$ occurs in P and $pred(B_i) \neq p_{k+1}$. For such i, one of the following two cases holds.

i. Suppose there exists a clause C_j such that $pred(B_i) = pred(head(C_j))$ and some $RP(P, p)$ includes C_j. If $head(C_j)$ and B_i are not unifiable, then the derivation of $P' \cup \{\leftarrow B_i\sigma\}$ is finite, because all the input clauses of the derivation of $P' \cup \{\leftarrow B_i\sigma\}$ do not include C_j. Otherwise, suppose $head(C_j)$ and B_i are unifiable. Since any $RP(P', p)$ is head-reducing and includes C_j, C_j is $pred(B_i)$-reducing with respect to some argument. Note that this argument of $B_i\sigma$ is ground. By Lemma 16.4, the derivation of $P' \cup \{\leftarrow B_i\sigma\}$ is finite.

ii. Suppose there exists a clause C_j such that $pred(B_i) = pred(head(C_j))$ and any $RP(P, p)$ does not include C_j. Then all the input clauses of the derivation of $P' \cup \{\leftarrow B_i\sigma\}$ do not include any clause of any $RP(P, p)$. By the case (a), the SLD-derivation of $P' \cup \{\leftarrow B_i\sigma\}$ is finite.

By (a) and (b), there exists no infinite SLD-derivation of $P' \cup \{\leftarrow B_1\sigma, \ldots, B_m\sigma\}$.

2. Suppose p_{k+1} occurs in the head of C_i. Let C_i be the following clause:

$$A \leftarrow D_1, \ldots, D_m \quad (pred(A) = p_{k+1}).$$

Let $\leftarrow G_1\tau, \ldots, G_j\tau, \ldots, G_l\tau$ be the goal whose input clause is $A \leftarrow D_1, \ldots, D_m$ for the SLD-derivation of $P \cup \{\leftarrow p(s_1, \ldots, s_n)\}$. By the induction hypothesis, if there exists an infinite SLD-derivation of $P' \cup \{\leftarrow p(s_1, \ldots, s_n)\}$, and $G_j\tau$ and A are unifiable, then the SLD-derivation of $P' \cup \{\leftarrow G_j\tau\}$ is infinite. Then the SLD-derivation of $P' \cup \{\leftarrow B_1\sigma, \ldots, B_l\sigma\}$ is infinite, where σ is a unifier of $G_j\tau$ and A. By the same proof as the case 1, there exists no infinite SLD-derivation of $P' \cup \{\leftarrow B_1\sigma, \ldots, B_l\sigma\}$. Hence, all the SLD-derivations of $P' \cup \{\leftarrow p(s_1, \ldots, s_n)\}$ are finite.

Corollary 16.7 Let P be a definite program and p be a predicate symbol. If any $RP(P, p)$ is head-reducing, then, for any ground atom $p(s_1, \ldots, s_n)$, both of the following goals terminate:

```
:- rs_abd(p(s_1, ..., s_n),X)
:- msrs_abd(p(s_1, ..., s_n),X)
```

4 RULE-SELECTING ABDUCTION FOR DEFAULT LOGIC

In this section, we study rule-selecting abduction for default logic.

Poole (1988) (see also Inoue 1992) has defined an abductive framework and discussed its relationship to Reiter's default logic (1980). We can describe the relationship in term of our abduction for logic programming in the following way:

Theorem 16.8 (Poole 1988) Let $P \not\vdash \alpha$. Then there exists a hypothesis H such that $P \cup H \vdash \alpha$ if and only if there exists an extension E of default theory (D_H, P) such that $\alpha \in E$, where

$$D_H = \left\{ \frac{: w(X)}{w(X)} \,\middle|\, w(X) \in H \right\}.$$

The above theorem shows that there exists a belief including the explainable fact α, but it does not show how a hypothesis is constructed when a surprising fact is observed. Poole's abduction is *abduction for logic programming in terms of default logic*, but not *abduction for default logic*. Now we study abduction for default logic. Here we deal with *function-free closed normal default theories whose conclusions are positive atoms*, because it is known that there exists an extension for such a theory (Reiter 1980). Also we deal with definite programs and the *integrity constraint IC* as negative information, where $IC = \bigvee_{i=1}^{n}(\leftarrow G_i)$ and $G_i = G_1{}^i \wedge \ldots \wedge G_{n_i}{}^i$.

Lemma 16.9 Let P be a definite program and IC be an integrity constraint. If $P \cup IC$ is consistent then the least Herbrand model $M(P)$ of P is the model of $P \cup IC$ under the closed-world assumption (Lloyd 1987).

In logic programming, a surprising fact is an atom α such that $P \not\vdash \alpha$, and abduction is a proposal of a hypothesis H such that $P \cup H \vdash \alpha$. In default logic, a *surprising fact* is defined to be an atom α which is not included in any extension of the given default theory. For such an α, we propose a new default theory $(D, P \cup H)$, instead of the given default theory (D, P), such that some extension includes α. Hence, we regard such an H as a *hypothesis*.

We transform the given default rules

$$D = \left\{ \left. \frac{\alpha_i(\overline{X}) : w_i(\overline{X})}{w_i(\overline{X})} \; \right| \; 1 \leq i \leq l \right\} \; (\overline{X} : \text{tuple of variables}),$$

to a definite program

$$P_D = \left\{ w_i(\overline{X}) \leftarrow \alpha_i(\overline{X}) \; \left| \; \frac{\alpha_i(\overline{X}) : w_i(\overline{X})}{w_i(\overline{X})} \in D, 1 \leq i \leq l \right. \right\}.$$

For such P_D, the following lemma holds.

Lemma 16.10 Let (D, P) be a closed default theory, α be a ground atom. If $P \cup P_D \not\vdash \alpha$, then there exists no extension of (D, P) which includes α.

Proof. Let E be an extension of (D, P). By Reiter (1980), E is constructed in the following way:

$$E_0 = P$$
$$E_{i+1} = Th(E_i) \cup \left\{ w \;\middle|\; \frac{\beta : w}{w} \in D, \beta \in E_i, \neg w \notin E \right\}$$
$$E = \bigcup_{i \geq 0} E_i$$

Since $P_D = \left\{ w \leftarrow \beta \;\middle|\; \dfrac{\beta : w}{w} \in D \right\}$, $E_{i+1} \subseteq Th(E_i) \cup M(P_D)$ for any i. Then, $E \subseteq M(P \cup P_D)$. Hence, if $\alpha \notin M(P \cup P_D)$ then $\alpha \notin E$.

By the above lemma, we can regard a surprising fact in a default theory (D, P) as a fact α such that $P \cup P_D \nvdash \alpha$.

Let α be a surprising fact, $(D, P \cup IC)$ be a closed normal default theory, P be a definite program, and IC be an integrity constraint. Then, H is a *hypothesis* of the default theory $(D, P \cup IC)$ if it satisfies one of the conditions:

1. $P \cup H \vdash \alpha$ and $P \cup H \cup IC$ is consistent.
2. $P \cup H \nvdash \alpha$, $P \cup P_D \cup H \vdash \alpha$, and $P \cup P_D \cup H \cup IC$ is consistent.

Note that a hypothesis is assumed to be minimal with respect to set inclusion.

Example 16.11 Let (D, P) be a closed normal default theory:

$$D = \left\{ \frac{bird(X) : fly(X)}{fly(X)}, \frac{fish(X) : swim(X)}{swim(X)} \right\}$$
$$P = \left\{ \begin{array}{l} swim(X) \leftarrow penguin(X) \\ bird(X) \leftarrow penguin(X) \end{array} \right\}.$$

Then

$$P_D = \left\{ \begin{array}{l} fly(X) \leftarrow bird(X) \\ swim(X) \leftarrow fish(X) \end{array} \right\}.$$

Let IC_1 be $\leftarrow fly(X), swim(X)$.

1. If $P \cup P_D \nvdash fly(john)$, then candidates for hypotheses are

$$H_1 = \{fly(john)\}, \; H_2 = \{bird(john)\},$$
$$H_3 = \{penguin(john)\}.$$

H_1 satisfies the first condition, and H_2 satisfies the second condition. However, H_3 does not satisfy either, because $P \cup P_D \cup H_3 \cup IC_1$ is inconsistent. Hence, H_1 and H_2 are hypotheses.

2. If $P \cup P_D \not\vdash swim(john)$, then candidates for hypotheses are

$$H_4 = \{swim(john)\}, \ H_5 = \{fish(john)\},$$
$$H_6 = \{penguin(john)\}.$$

H_4 and H_6 satisfy the first condition, and H_5 satisfies the second condition. Hence, H_4, H_5 and H_6 are all hypotheses.

Let IC_2 be $\leftarrow bird(X), swim(X)$.

1. If $P \cup P_D \not\vdash fly(john)$, then candidates of hypotheses are

$$H_1 = \{fly(john)\}, \ H_2 = \{bird(john)\},$$
$$H_3 = \{penguin(john)\}.$$

H_1 satisfies the first condition, and H_2 satisfies the second condition. However, H_3 does not satisfy either, because $P \cup P_D \cup H_3 \cup IC_1$ is inconsistent. Hence, H_1 and H_2 are hypotheses.

2. If $P \cup P_D \not\vdash swim(john)$, then candidates of hypotheses are

$$H_4 = \{swim(john)\}, \ H_5 = \{fish(john)\},$$
$$H_6 = \{penguin(john)\}.$$

H_4 satisfies the first condition, and H_5 satisfies the second condition. However, H_6 does not satisfy either, because $P \cup H_6 \cup IC_2$ is inconsistent. Hence, H_4 and H_5 are hypotheses.

Lemma 16.12 $M(P \cup P_D)$ is an extension of (D, P).

Proof. Suppose E is constructed by the following way:

$$E_0 = \{f \mid f \leftarrow \in P\},$$
$$E_{i+1} = Th(E_i) \cup \left\{ w \ \middle| \ \frac{\alpha : w}{w} \in D, \alpha \in E_i \right\},$$
$$E = \bigcup_{i \geq 0} E_i.$$

Since $\dfrac{\alpha : w}{w} \in D$ is equivalent to $w \leftarrow \alpha \in P_D$, $M(P \cup P_D) = E$. By the closed-world assumption, $\neg w \notin E$ for any w. Then, E is an extension (Reiter 1980).

Lemma 16.13 If $P \cup P_D \vdash \alpha$, then $M(P \cup P_D)$ is an extension of (D, P) which includes α.

Proof. Since $P \cup P_D \vdash \alpha$, $\alpha \in M(P \cup P_D)$. By Lemma 16.12, $M(P \cup P_D)$ is an extension of (D, P).

Lemma 16.14 If $(D, P \cup IC)$ satisfies one of the following conditions, then $M(P \cup P_D)$ is a consistent extension of $(D, P \cup IC)$ which includes α.
1. $P \vdash \alpha$, and $P \cup IC$ is consistent.
2. $P \nvdash \alpha$, $P \cup P_D \vdash \alpha$, and $P \cup P_D \cup IC$ is consistent.

Proof. Suppose $(D, P \cup IC)$ satisfies the condition 1. By Lemma 16.9 and consistency of $P \cup IC$, $M(P)$ is the model of $P \cup IC$. Since $P \vdash \alpha$, $\alpha \in M(P)$. For any β, $P \vdash \beta$ if and only if $P \cup IC \vdash \beta$. Then, E is an extension of (D, P) if and only if E is an extension of $(D, P \cup IC)$. Since $M(P \cup P_D)$ is an extension of (D, P), $M(P \cup P_D)$ is an extension of $(D, P \cup IC)$.

Suppose $(D, P \cup IC)$ satisfies the condition 2. By Lemma 16.9 and consistency of $P \cup P_D \cup IC$, $M(P \cup P_D)$ is the model of $P \cup P_D \cup IC$. Since $P \cup P_D \vdash \alpha$, $\alpha \in M(P \cup P_D)$. If $P \cup IC$ is inconsistent, then $P \cup P_D \cup IC$ is also inconsistent, which contradicts the condition 2. Then, $P \cup IC$ is consistent. Hence, for any β, $P \vdash \beta$ if and only if $P \cup IC \vdash \beta$. Then, E is an extension of (D, P) if and only if E is an extension of $(D, P \cup IC)$. By Lemma 16.13, if $E = M(P \cup P_D)$ then $\alpha \in E$ and E is an extension of (D, P). Hence, $M(P \cup P_D)$ is an extension of $(D, P \cup IC)$.

According to Reiter (1980), if $P \cup IC$ is consistent, then an extension of $(D, P \cup IC)$ is also consistent. Hence, an extension of $(D, P \cup IC)$ which includes α is also consistent.

For a closed normal default theory (D, P), the following theorem asserts that if there exists a hypothesis H satisfying the definition, then there exists an extension of $(D, P \cup H)$. Hence, we can propose a default theory in which we believe a surprising fact when we observe it.

Theorem 16.15 Let (D, P) be a closed normal default theory and IC be an integrity constraint. Let $P \cup P_D \nvdash \alpha$. If there exists a hypothesis H satisfying the conditions of the definition of hypothesis, then $M(P \cup P_D \cup H)$ is a consistent extension of $(D, P \cup H \cup IC)$ which includes α.

Proof. By replacing P with $P \cup H$ in the proof of Lemma 16.14, we can obtain the result.

Example 16.16 Consider the default theory (D, P) in Example 16.11. In the case of IC_1, extensions E_i of $(D, P \cup H_i \cup IC_1)$ corresponding to the hypotheses H_i are:

$$E_1 = \{fly(john)\},\ E_2 = \{bird(john), fly(john)\},$$
$$E_4 = \{swim(john)\},\ E_5 = \{fish(john), swim(john)\},$$
$$E_6 = \{penguin(john), swim(john), bird(john)\}.$$

In the case of IC_2, extensions E_i of $(D, P \cup H_i \cup IC_2)$ corresponding to the hypotheses H_i are:

$$E_1 = \{fly(john)\},\ E_2 = \{bird(john), fly(john)\},$$
$$E_4 = \{swim(john)\},\ E_5 = \{fish(john), swim(john)\}.$$

5 PROLOG IMPLEMENTATION

We describe our realization of the rule-selecting abduction for default logic as a Prolog program. The main program is `hyp`, which checks consistency under an integrity constraint and outputs hypotheses. The integrity constraint is given as the third argument of `hyp` in a form of disjunctions (expressed by ';') of conjunctions (expressed by ',') of atoms. If there exists no refutation of a goal as conjunctions of the atoms in the integrity constraint, then the hypotheses are consistent with the given program and the integrity constraint.

The predicate `hyp` works as follows: The predicate `rs_abd` returns a hypothesis as its second argument for an input (ground goal) as its first argument. The predicate `rep_assert` adds a hypothesis given by `rs_abd` to the original program. The predicate `consistent` checks consistency for a hypothesis and an integrity constraint. The predicate `rep_retract` removes a hypothesis added by `rep_assert` from the original program. The predicate `ic` calls an integrity constraint given as the third argument of `hyp`, and returns 'true' (*resp.* 'fail') if the integrity constraint fails (*resp.* is 'true') on the original program.

```
hyp(Goal,Hyp,IC) :-
   rs_abd(Goal,Hyp),
   ((rep_assert(Hyp),consistent(Goal,Hyp,IC),
```

```
    rep_retract(Hyp))->true;!,fail).
consistent(Goal,Hyp,IC) :-
   (call(Goal)->
      (call(ic(IC))->(write(': consistent'),nl) ;
      (write(': inconsistent'),nl)) ;
   (write(': inconsistent'),nl)).
ic(IC) :- (call(IC)->fail;true).
rep_assert((Atom1,Atom2)) :-
   (atom(Atom1)->assert(Atom1);rep_assert(Atom1)),
   (atom(Atom2)->assert(Atom2);rep_assert(Atom2)).
rep_assert(Atom) :- assert(Atom).
rep_retract((Atom1,Atom2)) :-
   (atom(Atom1)->retract(Atom1);rep_retract(Atom1)),
   (atom(Atom2)->retract(Atom2);rep_retract(Atom2)).
rep_retract(Atom) :- retract(Atom).
```

The termination of the above Prolog program is guaranteed by the corollary of Theorem 16.7:

Corollary 16.17 Let P be a definite program, IC be an integrity constraint, and p be a predicate symbol. For any predicate q of IC, if any $RP(P,q)$ and $RP(P,p)$ are head-reducing, then the goal `:- hyp(`$p(s_1,\ldots,s_n)$`,X,IC)` terminates for any ground atom $p(s_1,\ldots,s_n)$.

When we deal with default logic in the above program, we transform the set of default rules D to a definite program P_D^+:

$$\left\{ w_i(\overline{X}) \leftarrow \alpha_i(\overline{X}), default\_w_i(\overline{X}) \;\middle|\; \frac{\alpha(\overline{X}) : w(\overline{X})}{w(\overline{X})} \in D, 1 \leq i \leq l \right\}$$

Thus, we interpret $default\_w_i(\overline{t})$ appearing in a hypothesis as $w_i(\overline{t})$.

Example 16.18 Consider $P \cup P_D^+$ which consists of the clauses:

```
fly(X)  :- bird(X),default_fly(X).     %%% default
swim(X) :- fish(X),default_swim(X).    %%% default
swim(X) :- penguin(X).                 %%% theory
bird(X) :- penguin(X).                 %%% theory
```

Since the above $P \cup P_D^+$ and the integrity constraint IC given in the third argument of **hyp** satisfy the conditions of Corollary

16.17, the `hyp` program terminates and outputs the following hypotheses:

```
?- hyp(fly(john),X,(fly(Y),swim(Y))).
penguin(john),default_fly(john): inconsistent
bird(john),default_fly(john): consistent
fly(john): consistent

?- hyp(swim(john),X,(fly(Y),swim(Y))).
fish(john),default_swim(john): consistent
penguin(john): consistent
swim(john): consistent

?- hyp(fly(john),X,(bird(Y),swim(Y))).
penguin(john),default_fly(john): inconsistent
bird(john),default_fly(john): consistent
fly(john): consistent

?- hyp(swim(john),X,(bird(Y),swim(Y))).
fish(john),default_swim(john): consistent
penguin(john): inconsistent
swim(john): consistent
```

6 CONCLUSION

We have classified abduction into five types based on an interpretation of a syllogism, examined various researches on abduction so far developed, and showed that all researches on abduction can be placed in our classification. Also we have studied the most essential type of abduction for logic programming and default logic in our classification, and have described Prolog programs for our abduction.

We can apply the `hyp` program to a domain theory of explanation-based generalization (Duval 1991; Genest *et al.* 1990). Thus, if the domain theory satisfies the condition of termination, then the candidates of training examples are derived by the `hyp` program.

We have left many important problems for future work. We will report elsewhere on the introduction of function symbols to default logic and its program, rule-finding abduction, and rule-generating abduction.

REFERENCES

Brown, H. I. (1977). *Perception, Theory and Commitment*. Precedent Publishing.

Bylander, T., Tanner, M. C., Allemang, D. and Josephson, J. R. (1991). The computational complexity of abduction. *Artificial Intelligence* **49**, 25–60.

Cox, P. T. and Pietrzykowski, T. (1987). General diagnosis by abductive inference. *Proceedings of 1987 Symposium on Logic Programming*, 183–189.

Dung, P. M. (1991). Negation as hypothesis: an abductive foundation for logic programming. *Proceedings of 8th International Conference on Logic Programming*, 3–17.

Duval, B. (1991). Abduction for explanation-based learning. *Proceedings of European Working Session on Learning (1991). Lecture Notes in Artificial Intelligence* **482**, 348–360.

Eshghi, K. and Kowalski, R. A. (1989). Abduction compared with negation by failure. *Proceedings of 6th International Conference on Logic Programming*, 234–254.

Genest, J., Matwin, S. and Plante, B. (1990). Explanation-based learning with incomplete theories: a three-step approach. *Proceedings of International Workshop on Machine Learning*, 286–294.

Hanson, N. R. (1958). *Patterns of Discovery*. Cambridge University Press, Cambridge.

Hobbs, J. R., Stickel, M., Martin, P. and Edwards, D. (1988). Interpretation as abduction. *Proceedings of 26th Annual Meeting of the Association for Computing Linguistics*, 95–103.

Inoue, K. (1992). Principles of abduction. *Journal of Japanese Society for Artificial Intelligence* **7**, 48–59 (in Japanese).

Kakas, A. C. and Mancarella, P. (1990). Generalized stable models: a semantics for abduction. *Proceedings of 9th European Conference on Artificial Intelligence*, 385–391.

Konolige, K. (1992). Abduction versus closure in causal theories. *Artificial Intelligence*, **53**, 255–272.

Kuhn, T. S. (1970). *The Structure of Scientific Revolutions*. University of Chicago Press, Chicago.

Kunifuji, S. (1987). Hypothesis-based reasoning. *Journal of Japanese Society for Artificial Intelligence* **2**, 22–87 (in Japanese).

Levesque, H. J. (1989). A knowledge-level account of abduction, *Proceedings of 11th International Joint Conference on Artificial Intelligence*, 1061–1067.

Ling, X. (1989). Learning and invention of Horn clause theories - a constructive method. *Methodologies for Intelligent Systems* **4**, 323–331.

Lloyd, J. W. (1987). *Foundation of Logic Programming* (2nd edn). Springer-Verlag, Berlin.

Muggleton, S. (ed). (1992). *Inductive Logic Programming.* Academic Press, New York.

Muggleton, S. and Buntine, W. (1988). Machine invention of first-order predicates by inverting resolution. *Proceedings of 5th International Conference on Machine Learning*, 339–352.

Peirce, C. S. (1965). *Collected papers of Charles Sanders Peirce (1839-1914).* Hartshone, C. S. and Weiss, P.(eds.). The Belknap Press.

Pirri, F. and Pizzuti, C. (1990). A stable model semantics for diagnostic hypothesis. *Proceedings of Pacific Rim International Conference on Artificial Intelligence '90*, 766–771.

Plotkin, G. D. (1971). A further note on inductive generalization. *Machine Intelligence* **6**.

Poole, D. (1988). A logical framework for default reasoning. *Artificial Intelligence* **36**, 27–47.

Pople, Jr. H. E. (1973). On the mechanization of abductive logic. *Proceedings of International Joint Conference on Artificial Intelligence*, 147–152.

Popper, K. R. (1959). *The Logic of Scientific Discovery.* Hutchinson, London.

Reichenbach, H. (1938). *Experience and Prediction.* University of Chicago Press, Chicago.

Reiter, R. (1980). A logic for default reasoning. *Artificial Intelligence* **13**, 81–132.

Selman, B. and Levesque, H. J. (1990). Abductive and default reasoning: a computational core, *Proceedings of 8th National Conference on Artificial Intelligence*, 343–348.

Shapiro, E. Y. (1981). *Inductive Inference of Theories from Facts.*

Research Report 192, Yale University.

Stickel, M. E. (1991). A Prolog-like inference system for computing minimum-cost abductive explanation in natural language interpretation. *Annals of Mathematics and Artificial Intelligence* 4, 89–106.

Thagard, P. (1988). *Computational Philosophy of Science*. MIT Press, Cambridge, MA.

Ueyama, S. (1978). The theory of abduction. *Jinbungakuhou* **43**, 103–155 (in Japanese).

van Harmelen, F. and Bundy, A. (1988). Explanation-based generalization = partial evaluation. *Artificial Intelligence* **36**, 401–412.

Yamamoto, A. (1992). Procedural semantics and negative information of elementary formal system. *Journal of Logic Programming* **13**, 89–97.

Yonemori, Y. (1982). *Peirce's Semiotics*. Keisou Syobou. (In Japanese).

COMPUTATIONAL LEARNING THEORY

17

Efficient Algorithms for Inductive Learning - an Application of Multi-Linear Functions to Inductive Learning

Hiroshi Tsukimoto and Chie Morita

Systems & Software Engineering Laboratory, Toshiba Corporation, 70, Yanagi-cho, Saiwai-ku, Kawasaki 210, Japan

Abstract

Although many algorithms have been presented for empirical inductive learning, there are few algorithms whose sample complexity and computational complexity have been theoretically analysed. Moreover, although many algorithms have been presented in computational learning theory, few algorithms can be applied to empirical inductive learning problems. Our final target is to present efficient algorithms for attribute-based inductive learning, whose sample complexity and computational complexity lend themselves to theoretical analysis. This paper presents efficient algorithms for attribute-based inductive learning. The algorithm can deal with $\{0,1\}$ attributes, multi-valued attributes and $[0,1]$ attributes simultaneously in the same way. The algorithms differ from the families of ID3 and AQ11. The algorithms rely on the space of multi-linear functions presented by the author. The space of multi-linear functions is a Euclidean space and includes Boolean functions. One feature of the space is that both $\{0,1\}$ attributes and $[0,1]$ attributes can be dealt with in the same way. Two algorithms are presented. One is based on multiple regression analysis and the other is based on spectral techniques. The first algorithm predicts values by multiple regression analysis using a multi-linear function. Sample complexity is discussed based on the results of Linial and Haussler. The hypotheses are generated based on the approximation of the multi-linear function by a Boolean function. The computational complexity is not polynomial, but it can be reduced to polynomial if the multi-linear function is limited to linear. The second algorithm is an extension of Linial's algorithm to [0,1]. Only a prediction algorithm is presented.

1 INTRODUCTION

In empirical learning, many algorithms for attribute-based inductive learning have been presented. However, there are few algorithms whose sample complexity and computational complexity have been theoretically analysed. One of the reasons is that the algorithms must deal with several kinds of data together, so the analyses are difficult.

On the other hand, in computational learning theory, many algorithms have been presented and studied. However, few algorithms can be applied to the problems dealt with in empirical inductive learning. One of the reasons is that data are almost always limited to $\{0,1\}$ in order to make the theoretical analyses possible.

A gap exists between between empirical learning and theoretical learning. It is important to narrow that gap. Our final target is to present efficient algorithms for empirical attribute-based inductive learning, whose sample complexity and computational complexity lend themselves to theoretical analysis.

This paper presents efficient algorithms for attribute-based inductive learning. (Hereinafter, we use inductive learning for attribute-based inductive learning.) The algorithms can deal with $\{0,1\}$ attributes, multi-valued attributes and [0,1] attributes in the same way at the same time. The algorithms differ from the families of ID3 (Quinlan 1986) and AQ11 (Michalski and McCormick 1971).

The algorithms rely on the space of multi-linear functions presented by the author (Tsukimoto 1990,1994). For example, multi-linear functions of two variables are represented as $axy+$

$bx + cy + d$, where a, b, c and d are real and x and y are $\{0,1\}$ or $[0,1]$. There are two important points. One is that the space of multi-linear functions is a model for logics, which includes the space of Boolean functions. The other is that the space of the multi-linear functions can be made into a Euclidean space by introducing an inner product. Therefore, multi-linear functions can be approximated by Boolean functions. One feature of the space is that both $\{0,1\}$ attributes and $[0,1]$ attributes can be dealt with in basically the same way, the only exception being in the definition of the inner product. Since multi-valued attributes can be reduced to $\{0,1\}$ by introducing dummy attributes, attributes used in empirical inductive learning can be dealt with in the space.

Two algorithms are presented. One algorithm follows: The values are predicted by multiple regression analysis using a multi-linear function, which is an easy extension of usual multiple regression using linear functions. Sample complexity is discussed based on the results of (Linial *et al.* 1993) and (Haussler 1992). We experimentally confirm that the algorithm works well with a few examples. The hypotheses are generated based on the approximation of the multi-linear function obtained by a Boolean function. The approximation can be regarded as a pseudo maximum likelihood method using the principle of indifference (Keynes 1921). The computational complexity is not polynomial, but it can be reduced to polynomial if the multi-linear function is limited to linear.

The second algorithm is based on spectral techniques (Hurst *et al.* 1985). A prediction algorithm using Fourier transform was presented in Linial (1993). We extend the algorithm to $[0,1]$. Only a prediction algorithm is presented. Hypothesis generation and error analysis will be included in future work.

The space of multi-linear functions, which is an extended model for logics, is outlined in Section 2. The algorithm based on multiple regression analysis is presented and is discussed in Section 3 and 4. In Section 5, the algorithm based on spectral techniques is briefly explained.

2 MULTI-LINEAR FUNCTIONS—AN EXTENDED MODEL FOR LOGICS

Tsukimoto (1990, 1994) presented an extended model for logics where logical functions including non-classical logical functions are represented as points (vectors) in a Euclidean space.

Hereinafter, let $F, G, \ldots$ stand for propositions, $f, g, \ldots$ stand for functions, $X, Y, \ldots$ stand for propositional variables and $x, y,$ $\ldots$ stand for variables.

2.1 Intuitive explanation

We explain why a logical function is represented as a vector. It is worth noticing that classical logic has properties similar to a vector space. These properties are seen in Boolean algebra with atoms, and this is a model for classical logic. Atoms in Boolean algebra have the following properties:

1. $a_i \cdot a_i = a_i$ (unitarity);
2. $a_i \cdot a_j = 0$ $(i \neq j)$ (orthogonality);
3. $\Sigma a_i = 1$ (completeness).

For example, for the proposition $\overline{X} \vee Y = XY \vee \overline{X}Y \vee \overline{XY}$, $\overline{X} \vee Y$ is represented as $(1, 0, 1, 1)$, where $XY = (1, 0, 0, 0)$, $X\overline{Y} = (0, 1, 0, 0)$, $\overline{X}Y = (0, 0, 1, 0)$, $\overline{XY} = (0, 0, 0, 1)$. Atoms in Boolean algebra correspond to unit vectors. In other words, atoms in Boolean algebra are similar to the orthonormal functions in a Hilbert space. This paper shows that the space of logical functions actually becomes a Euclidean space. The progression from Boolean algebra to Euclidean space is divided into three stages.

1. Represent Boolean algebra by elementary algebra. In other words, present an elementary algebra model for classical logic.
2. Expand the model to the space of multi-linear functions.
3. Introduce an inner product to the above space and construct a Euclidean space where logical functions are represented as vectors.

2.2 An elementary algebra model for classical logic

2.2.1   *Definitions*

Definition 17.1 Let $f(x)$ be a real polynomial function. Consider the following formula:

$$f(x) = p(x)(x - x^2) + q(x),$$

where $f : \{0, 1\} \to R$ and $q(x) = ax + b$, where a and b are real. τ_x is defined as follows:

$$\tau_x : f(x) \to q(x).$$

The above definition implies the following property:

$$\tau_x(f(x^n)) = f(x).$$

Definition 17.2 In the case of n variables, τ is defined as follows:

$$\tau = \prod_{i=1}^{n} \tau_{x_i}.$$

Example 17.3 $\tau(x^2 + y + 1) = x + y + 1.$

Definition 17.4 Let L be the set of all functions satisfying $\tau(f) = f$. Then $L = \{f : \tau(f) = f\}$. In the case of two variables, $L = \{axy + bx + cy + d | a, b, c, d \in \mathbf{R}\}$.

Definition 17.5 L_1 is inductively defined as follows:

1. Variables are in L_1.
2. If f and g are in L_1, then $\tau(f \cdot g), \tau(f + g - f \cdot g)$ and $\tau(1 - f)$ are in L_1. (We call these three calculations τ *calculation.*)
3. L_1 consists of all functions finitely generated by the (repeated) use of 1. and 2.

2.2.2   *A new model for classical logic*

Theorem 17.6 Let the correspondence between Boolean algebra and τ calculation be as follows:

1. $F \wedge G \Leftrightarrow \tau(fg);$

2. $F \vee G \Leftrightarrow \tau(f + g - fg)$;

3. $\overline{F} \Leftrightarrow \tau(1 - f)$.

Then $(L_1, \tau$ calculation$)$ is a model for classical logic; that is, L_1 and τ calculation satisfy the axioms for Boolean algebra (Tsukimoto 1990, 1994).

Example 17.7 $(X \vee Y) \wedge (X \vee Y) = X \vee Y$ is calculated as follows:

$$\begin{aligned}
\tau((x + y - xy)(x + y - xy)) &= \tau(x^2 + y^2 + x^2 y^2 + 2xy - 2x^2 y - 2xy^2) \\
&= x + y + xy + 2xy - 2xy - 2xy \\
&= x + y - xy.
\end{aligned}$$

2.3 Extension of the model

The model is extended from L_1 to L which was defined in Section 2.2.1. $f : \{0,1\}^n \to \mathbf{R}$. L obviously includes Boolean functions and linear functions (see Fig. 17.1).

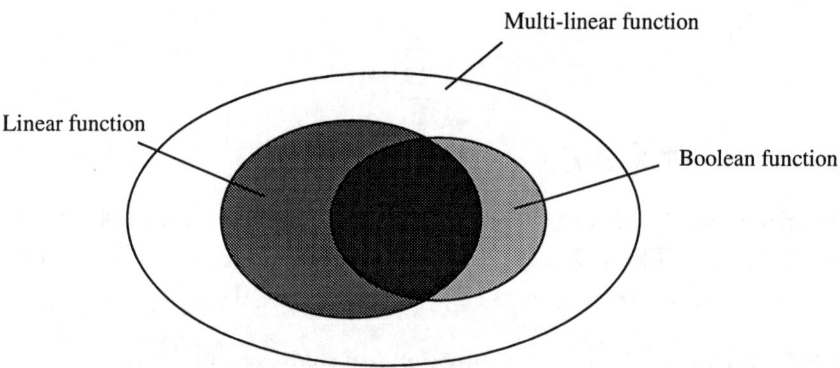

Figure 17.1. Multi-linear function

The domain is also extended to [0,1]. $f : [0,1]^n \to \mathbf{R}$. L is called the set of multi-linear functions. Hereinafter, L will be made into a Euclidean space (a finite-dimensional inner product space).

2.4 Euclidean space

2.4.1 *Inner product and norm*

Definition 17.8 In the case of [0,1], an inner product is defined as follows:

$$< f, g >= 2^n \int_0^1 \tau(fg)\,dx,$$

where f and g are in L, and the integral is generally a multiple integral.

In the case of $\{0,1\}$, an inner product is defined as

$$< f, g >= \sum \tau(fg),$$

where this sum spans the whole domain.

Example 17.9 In the case of two variables, let $f = f(x,y)$ and $g = g(x,y)$, then $< f, g >= (\tau(fg))(1,1) + (\tau(fg))(1,0) + (\tau(fg))(0,1) + (\tau(fg))(0,0)$, where $(\tau(fg))(1,1)$ is the value of $\tau(fg)$ at $x = 1$ and $y = 1$.

Definition 17.10 A norm is defined as

$$\| f \|= \sqrt{< f, f >}.$$

L becomes an inner product space with the above norm. The dimension of this space is finite, because L consists of the multi-linear functions of n variables, where n is finite. Therefore, L becomes a finite dimensional inner product space, namely a Euclidean space.

2.4.2 *Orthonormal system*

The orthonormal system is as follows:

$$\phi_i = \prod_{j=1}^{n} e(x_j) \ (i = 1, ..., 2^n, j = 1, ..., n),$$

where $e(x_j) = 1 - x_j$ or x_j. It is easily understood that these orthonormal functions are the expansion of atoms in Boolean algebra.

Theorem 17.11

$$< \phi_i, \phi_j >= \begin{cases} 0(i \neq j), \\ 1(i = j), \end{cases}$$

$$f = \sum_{i=1}^{2^n} <f, \phi_i> \phi_i.$$

it can easily be verified that the orthonormal system satisfies the following properties:

Example 17.12 The representation by orthonormal functions of $x + y - xy$ of two variables (dimension 4) is as follows:

$$f = 1 \cdot xy + 1 \cdot x(1 - y) + 1 \cdot (1 - x)y + 0 \cdot (1 - x)(1 - y)$$

and the vector representation is $(1, 1, 1, 0)$, where the bases are $xy = (1, 0, 0, 0), x(1 - y) = (0, 1, 0, 0), (1 - x)y = (0, 0, 1, 0)$ and $(1 - x)(1 - y) = (0, 0, 0, 1)$.

The space of the functions of n variables is 2^n-dimensional. The vector representation of Boolean functions is the same as the representation expanded by atoms in Boolean algebra. This Euclidean space is an expansion of the Hasse diagram of classical logic. The vector representation of a multi-linear function is called a logical vector. The vector representation of a Boolean function is called a Boolean vector.

3 THE ALGORITHM BASED ON MULTIPLE REGRESSION ANALYSIS: PREDICTION

From the above discussion, the space of multi-linear functions can deal with $\{0,1\}$ attributes and $[0,1]$ attributes. In inductive learning, we have to deal with multi-valued attributes. Multi-value can be reduced to $\{0,1\}$ by introducing dummy attributes.

3.1 Reduction of multi-value to $\{0,1\}$

In inductive learning, each example is given as the conjunction of attribute values. Let a_i be an attribute and n_i be the number of the attribute values. For example, let a_1 be colour and the attribute values be $\{red, blue, yellow\}$, and let a_2 be age and the attribute values be $\{old, new\}$, then an example is given as $red \wedge new$ (We are now neglecting the class).

We introduce dummy attributes, each of which corresponds to a single attribute value. For example, in the above case, we introduce five dummy attributes $\{red, blue, yellow, old, new\}$, whose attribute values are binary, that is, 1 and 0. For example, $(color = red) \wedge (age = new)$ is represented as $red \wedge \overline{blue} \wedge \overline{yellow} \wedge \overline{old} \wedge new$. The number of dummy attributes is $\sum n_i$, and each attribute is binary. Thus, multi-valued attributes can be reduced to $\{0,1\}$ attributes. Class can also be reduced to binary by introducing dummy attributes.

3.2 Multiple regression analysis

We introduced dummy attributes to reduce multi-valued attributes to $\{0,1\}$ attributes. We can normalize continuously valued attributes to $[0,1]$ attributes. In addition, since $\{0,1\}$ can be regarded as real, multiple regression analysis can be applied to the data of $\{0,1\}$ attributes, $[0,1]$ attributes and multi-valued attributes simultaneously in the same way.

Linear functions are usually used for multiple regression analysis, while multi-linear functions are generally used in inductive learning.

3.3 Experiments

We present two experiments by using Chess End-Game and Mushroom. Linear functions are used in the experiments. Data consist of $\{0,1\}$ attributes and multi-valued attributes.

1. *Chess End-Game—KPa7KR*: Classes are *win* and *not win*. The number of attributes is 36 and the number of examples is 3196.

2. *Mushroom Database*: Classes are *edible* and *poisonous*. The number of attributes is 22 and the number of examples is 8124.

Training examples are randomly chosen from the above data. Test examples are randomly chosen from the rest and the accuracy is calculated.

Table 17.1 shows the results.

The values are the accuracy and the values in parenthesis are the numbers of training examples. Our algorithm's results are good. Our algorithm's result in *Chess End-Game* is a little worse than that of ID3. However, our algorithm's result can

Table 17.1. Experimental results.

	Chess End-Game	*Mushroom*
Our algorithm	93.0% (400)	99.9% (300)
ID3	96.4% (400)	99.9% (2708)
	(Buntine 1989)	(Wirth and Catlett 1988)

be said to be good because our algorithm's computational complexity is polynomial. On the other hand, our algorithm can learn *Mushroom* with less training examples than ID3, which shows that our algorithm's sample complexity is good. Figure 17.2 shows the accuracy with respect to the number of training examples. The data is *Chess End-Game*. More experiments will be included in future work.

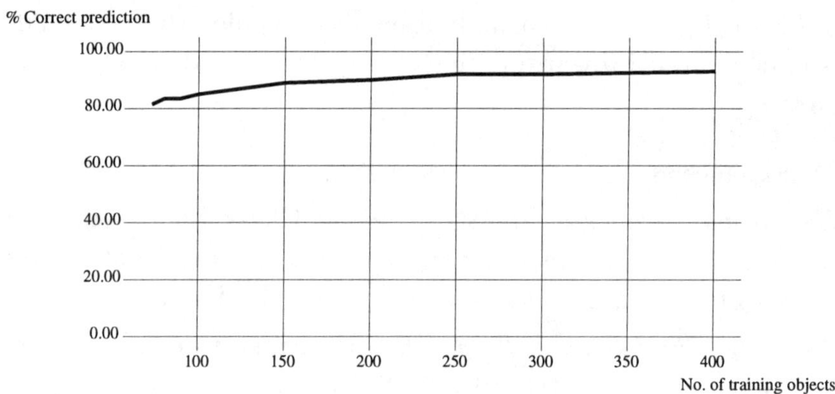

Figure 17.2. Chess End-Game.

3.4 Sample complexity

The sample complexity of the algorithm is briefly explained in the case of $\{0,1\}$ attributes (and multi-valued attributes). Let kth-order terms stand for terms containing k variables, for example, xyz is a 3rd-order term. We call multi-linear functions consisting of up to kth-order terms k-multi-linear functions.

First, the sample complexity is evaluated by the pseudo dimension (Haussler 1992). The VC dimension is defined on the sets of $\{0,1\}$ valued functions (Blumer *et al.* 1989). Haussler (1992) extended the VC dimension to the pseudo dimension which is defined on the sets of real-valued functions.

Theorem 17.13 (Haussler *et al.* 1992) Let d be the pseudo dimension of the hypothesis space. Let h_t and h_e be the optimal hypothesis and the empirical hypothesis, respectively. Let m be the sample number. Let $|\cdot|$ be the norm. Let ϵ and δ be real numbers. If the range of multi-linear functions used for regression is $[0,1]$, for any probability distribution,

$$\text{Probability}(|t - h| \geq \epsilon) \leq \delta \text{ if } m \geq \tfrac{a}{\epsilon^2}(2\ d\log_2 \tfrac{b}{\epsilon} + \log_2 \tfrac{c}{\delta}),$$

where a, b and c are coefficients.

In the case of n variables, a k-multi-linear function, the pseudo dimension of the space is polynomial (Dudley 1978). Therefore, the sample complexity is polynomial of n, $\frac{1}{\epsilon}$ and $\frac{1}{\delta}$.

The above discussion is concerned with the error in the hypothesis space. The error between target functions and the optimal hypothesis is evaluated as follows:

Theorem 17.14 (Linial *et al.* 1993) Assume that the probability distribution is the uniform distribution. Let f be a Boolean function, there exists a k-multi-linear function g such that $\| f - g \| < \epsilon$, where k is at most $O(log(n/\epsilon)^2)$.

Error analysis has been briefly explained with some conditions. More detailed study will be included in future work.

4 THE ALGORITHM BASED ON MULTIPLE REGRESSION ANALYSIS: HYPOTHESIS GENERATION

4.1 Approximating a multi-linear function by the nearest Boolean function

Theorem 17.15 Consider that a logical vector is approximated by the nearest Boolean vector. Let (f_i) be a logical vector. Let $(g_i)(g_i = 0$ or $1)$ be a Boolean vector. The approximation method is as follows:

$$g_i = \begin{cases} 1(f_i \geq 0.5), \\ 0(f_i < 0.5). \end{cases}$$

Proof. The nearest Boolean vector minimizes $\sum(f_i - g_i)^2$. Each term can be minimized independently and $g_i = 1$ or 0. Therefore, the above approximation method is obtained.$\square$

Example 17.16 Let $z = 0.6x - 1.1y + 0.3$ be obtained by multiple regression analysis. The function is transformed to

$$z = -0.2xy + 0.9x(1-y) - 0.8(1-x)y + 0.3(1-x)(1-y),$$

that is, the logical vector is $(-0.2, 0.9, -0.8, 0.3)$. By the above method, the logical vector is approximated to $(0, 1, 0, 0)$, which represents $x(1-y)$. Thus, $0.6x - 1.1y + 0.3$ is approximated to $x(1-y)$, that is, $X \wedge \overline{Y}$.

The approximation can be regarded as a pseudo-maximum likelihood method using the principle of indifference (Keynes 1921). The proof, which is based on (Tsukimoto and Morita 1994), was given in (Tsukimoto 1994). This approximation method can be regarded as an extension of the method developed in threshold logic.

4.2 Approximating a linear function by the nearest Boolean function

We introduced dummy attributes for multi-valued attributes in 3.1. Therefore, negative literals can be represented by other positive literals, as in the example in Section 3.1, $\overline{red} = blue \vee yellow$. We also introduce dummy attributes into $\{0,1\}$ attributes so that negative literals can be represented by other positive literals. As a result, if the attributes are limited to $\{0,1\}$ or multi-valued, the hypotheses can be limited to monotone disjunctive normal form (DNF) formulas (We also call them DNF formulas in the case of multi-valued attributes.)

The computational complexity of the algorithm for hypothesis generation is not polynomial. But if the functions for regression are linear and the attributes are $\{0,1\}$ or multi-valued, the computational complexity can be reduced, as explained below.

4.2.1 *Relation between the linear function obtained by multiple regression analysis and the representation by orthonormal functions*

Let $p_1x_1 + \cdots + p_nx_n$ stand for the linear function obtained by multiple regression analysis. Let

$$a_1 x_1 \cdots x_n + a_2 x_1 \cdots x_{n-1}(1-x_n) + \cdots + a_{2^{n-1}} x_1 (1-x_2) \cdots (1 - x_n) + \cdots + a_{2^n-1}(1-x_1) \cdots (1-x_{n-1})x_n + a_{2^n}(1-x_1) \cdots (1-x_n)$$

stand for the representation by orthonormal functions, where the orthonormal functions are placed lexicographically. Then,

$$p_1 x_1 + \cdots + p_n x_n = a_1 x_1 \cdots x_n + a_2 x_1 \cdots x_{n-1}(1 - x_n) + \cdots + a_{2^{n-1}} x_1 (1 - x_2) \cdots (1 - x_n) + \cdots + a_{2^n-1}(1 - x_1) \cdots (1 - x_{n-1})x_n + a_{2^n}(1 - x_1) \cdots (1 - x_n).$$

Each a_i can be easily calculated as follows. For example, let $x_1 = x_2 = \cdots = x_n = 1$. Then the right-hand side of the above formula is a_1 and the left-hand side is $p_1 + \cdots + p_n$. Thus, $a_1 = p_1 + \cdots + p_n$ is obtained. Similarly, let $x_1 = x_2 = \cdots = x_{n-1} = 1$ and $x_n = 0$, then $a_2 = p_1 + \cdots + p_{n-1}$ is obtained. The others can be calculated in the same manner. Thus, the a_i's are as follows:

$$a_1 = p_1 + \cdots + p_n,$$
$$a_2 = p_1 + \cdots + p_{n-1},$$
$$\cdots$$
$$a_{2^{n-1}} = p_1,$$
$$a_{2^{n-1}+1} = p_2 + p_3 + \cdots + p_{n-1} + p_n,$$
$$\cdots$$
$$a_{2^n-1} = p_n,$$
$$a_{2^n} = 0$$

4.2.2 *The condition that x_i exists in the Boolean function after approximation.*

Theorem 17.17 The existence condition for $x_{i_1} \cdots x_{i_k}$ is as follows:

$$\sum_{i_1}^{i_k} p_{i_j} + \sum_{1 \leq j \leq n, j \neq i_1, \ldots, i_k, p_j < 0} p_j \geq 0.5.$$

Proof. Consider the existence condition of x_1 in the Boolean function after approximation. (For simplification, this condition is called the existence condition.) Because $x_1 = x_1 x_2 \cdots x_n \vee x_1 x_2 \cdots (1 - x_n) \ldots \vee x_1(1 - x_2) \cdots (1 - x_n)$, the existence of x_1 equals the existence of the following terms:

$$x_1 x_2 \cdots x_n ,$$
$$x_1 x_2 \cdots (1 - x_n),$$
$$\ldots$$
$$x_1(1 - x_2) \cdots (1 - x_n).$$

The existence of the above terms means that all coefficients of these terms $a_1, a_2, ..., a_{2^{n-1}}$ are greater than or equal to 0.5 (See 4.1). That is, $MIN\{a_i\} \geq 0.5 (1 \leq i \leq 2^{n-1})$, which will be denoted by $MINa_i$ for simplification.

Because the a_i's $(1 \leq i \leq 2^{n-1})$ are

$$a_1 = p_1 + \cdots + p_n,$$
$$a_2 = p_1 + \cdots + p_{n-1},$$
$$\ldots$$
$$a_{2^{n-1}} = p_1,$$

each $a_i(1 \leq i \leq 2^{n-1})$ contains p_1. If each p_j is non-negative, $a_{2^{n-1}}(= p_1)$ is the minimum because the other a_i's contain other p_j's, therefore the other a_i's are greater than or equal $a_{2^{n-1}}(= p_1)$. Generally, since each p_j is not necessarily non-negative, $MINa_i$ is the a_i which contains all negative p_j. That is, $MINa_i = p_1 + \sum_{1 \leq j \leq n, j \neq 1, p_j < 0} p_j$, which necessarily exists in $a_i(1 \leq i \leq 2^{n-1})$, because $a_i(1 \leq i \leq 2^{n-1})$ is $p_1 +$ (arbitrary sum of $p_j(2 \leq j \leq n)$). Therefore, $MINa_i = p_1 + \sum_{1 \leq j \leq n, j \neq 1, p_j < 0} p_j$. From the above arguments, the existence condition of x_1, $MINa_i \geq 0.5$, is as follows:

$$p_1 + \sum_{1 \leq j \leq n, j \neq 1, p_j < 0} p_j \geq 0.5.$$

Since $p_1 x_1 + \cdots + p_n x_n$ is symmetric for x_i, the above formula holds for other variables; that is, the existence condition of x_i is $p_i + \sum_{1 \leq j \leq n, j \neq i, p_j < 0} p_j \geq 0.5$. Similar discussions hold for higher order terms such as $x_1 x_2$. As a result, the existence condition of $x_{i_1} \cdots x_{i_k}$ is as follows:

$$\sum_{i_1}^{i_k} p_{i_j} + \sum_{1 \leq j \leq n, j \neq i_1, ..., i_k, p_j < 0} p_j \geq 0.5.$$

4.2.3 *Generation of monotone DNF formulas*

The algorithm generates terms using the above formula from terms of the lowest order up to a certain order. A monotone DNF formula can be generated by taking the disjunction of the terms generated by the above formula. A term whose existence has been confirmed does not need to be re-checked in higher-order terms. For example, if the existence of x is confirmed, then it also implies the existence of xy, xz ,..., because $x = x \vee xy \vee xz$; hence, it is unnecessary to check the existence of xy, xz,.... As can be seen from the above discussion, the generation method of monotone DNF formulas includes reductions such as $xy \vee xz = x$.

Example 17.18 Let $y = 0.65x_1 + 0.23x_2 + 0.15x_3 + 0.20x_4 + 0.02x_5$ be the linear function obtained by multiple regression analysis. The existence condition of $x_{i_1} \cdots x_{i_k}$ is

$$\sum_{i_1}^{i_k} p_{i_j} + \sum_{1 \leq j \leq n, j \neq i_1,...,i_k, p_j < 0} p_j \geq 0.5.$$

In this case, each p_i is positive; therefore the above formula can be simplified to $\sum_{i_1}^{i_k} p_{i_j} \geq 0.5$. For x_i, the existence condition is $p_i \geq 0.5$. For $i = 1, 2, 3, 4, 5$, $p_1 \geq 0.5$, therefore x_1 exists. For $x_i x_j$, the existence condition is $p_i + p_j \geq 0.5$. For $i, j = 2, 3, 4, 5$, $p_i + p_j < 0.5$, therefore no $x_i x_j$ exists. For $x_i x_j x_k$, the existence condition is $p_i + p_j + p_k \geq 0.5$. For $i, j, k = 2, 3, 4, 5$, $p_2 + p_3 + p_4 \geq 0.5$, therefore $x_2 x_3 x_4$ exists. Because higher-order terms cannot be generated from x_5, the algorithm stops. Therefore, x_1 and $x_2 x_3 x_4$ exist and the monotone DNF formula is the disjunction of these terms, that is, $x_1 \vee x_2 x_3 x_4$.

4.2.4 *Summary of the efficient algorithm*

Let attributes be $\{0,1\}$ and multi-valued. The algorithm is as follows:

1. Execute multiple regression analysis using linear functions.
2. Let $\sum p_i x_i$ be one of the linear functions.
   Using $\sum_{i_1}^{i_k} p_{i_j} + \sum_{1 \leq j \leq n, j \neq i_1,...,i_k, p_j < 0} p_j \geq 0.5$, generate terms $(x_i,\ x_j,$ etc$)$ from terms of the lowest-order (x_i) up to a certain order. If $p_{i_1}, ..., p_{i_k}$ satisfy the above formula, they will not be used again.

3. Generate a monotone DNF formula by taking the disjunction of the generated terms.

4. Repeat 2. and 3. for all the linear functions.

4.2.5 *Transformation of monotone DNF formulas to multiple-valued logical functions*

The monotone DNF formulas can be easily transformed to multiple-valued logical functions by replacing each variable by the corresponding attribute value. For example, let $\{x_1, x_2, x_3, x_4, x_5\}$ correspond to $\{red, blue, yellow, old, new\}$ and we have a monotone DNF formula, $x_1 x_4 \lor x_2$, as a result. Then we have a multiple-valued logical function $(red \land old) \lor blue$. If there are parts such as $red \lor blue \lor yellow$ in the multiple-valued logical function, such parts can be transformed to 1. Some readers may think that impossible terms such as $red \land blue \land yellow$ would appear, but such terms never appear in principle because examples are never given as the conjunction of attribute values of an attribute, for example, examples are given as $red \land \overline{blue} \land \overline{yellow}$ and never given as $red \land blue \land yellow$. However, if impossible terms should appear in the multiple-valued logical functions, the terms are deleted.

4.2.6 *An example for generating hypotheses*

Let X and Y be attributes. Let X's and Y's attribute values be $\{x_1, x_2, x_3\}$ and $\{y_1, y_2\}$. Let C_1 and C_2 be classes with $C_1 = x_1 \lor x_3 y_1$ and $C_2 = x_2 \lor x_3 y_2$. Table 17.2 shows examples. On the bottom are shown the representations of the examples shown on the top using dummy attributes. These tables are used for multiple regression analysis.

For C_1, the linear function obtained by multiple regression analysis is $0.83x_1 - 0.16x_2 + 0.33x_3 + 0.33y_1 + 0.0y_2$. By step 2 in the algorithm in Section 4.2.5, x_1 and $x_3 y_1$ exit. Therefore, $x_1 \lor x_3 y_1$ is obtained. For C_2, the linear function obtained by multiple regression analysis is $-0.16x_1 + 0.83x_2 + 0.33x_3 + 0.0y_1 + 0.33y_2$. By step 2 in the algorithm in Section 4.2.5, x_2 and $x_3 y_2$ exit. Therefore, $x_2 \lor x_3 y_2$ is obtained. Thus, we have $C_1 = x_1 \lor x_3 y_1$ and $C_2 = x_2 \lor x_3 y_2$, which are correct results.

Table 17.2. Examples represented by dummy attributes.

X	Y	class
x_1	y_1	C_1
x_1	y_2	C_1
x_2	y_1	C_2
x_2	y_2	C_2
x_3	y_1	C_1
x_3	y_2	C_2

X			Y		
x_1	x_2	x_3	y_1	y_2	C_1
1	0	0	1	0	1
1	0	0	0	1	1
0	1	0	1	0	0
0	1	0	0	1	0
0	0	1	1	0	1
0	0	1	0	1	0

X			Y		
x_1	x_2	x_3	y_1	y_2	C_2
1	0	0	1	0	0
1	0	0	0	1	0
0	1	0	1	0	1
0	1	0	0	1	1
0	0	1	1	0	0
0	0	1	0	1	1

4.3 Computational complexity of the algorithm

The computational complexity of the multiple regression analysis is polynomial of the number of variables (n).

The number of the mth-order terms $(x_{i_1}...x_{i_m})$ is $\binom{n}{m}$. Therefore, the computational complexity of generating the mth-order terms is polynomial of $\binom{n}{m}$, that is, polynomial of n. Thus, the computational complexity of generating up to the kth-order terms is $\sum_{m=1}^{m=k} \binom{n}{m}$, which is polynomial of n. Therefore, the computational complexity of generating monotone DNF formulas from the linear functions is polynomial of n. However, the sum of the number of up to the highest-order $(=n\text{th})$ terms is $\sum_{m=1}^{m=n} \binom{n}{m} = 2^n$; therefore, the computational complexity of generating up to the highest order terms is exponential.

However, Linial *et al.* (1993) showed that

$$\sum_{|S|>k} \hat{f}(S)^2 \leq 2M2^{-k^{1/2}/20},$$

where f is a Boolean function, S is a term, $|S|$ is the order of S, k is any integer, $\hat{f}(S)$ denotes the Fourier transform of f at S and M is the size of the function for the circuit (see Section 5).

The above formula shows the high-order terms have very little power; that is, low-order terms are informative. Therefore, a good approximation can be obtained by generating terms up to a certain order; that is, the computational complexity can be reduced to polynomial by adding small errors. A detailed theoretical analysis of the error will be included in future work.

5 THE ALGORITHM BASED ON SPECTRAL TECHNIQUES

We present another prediction algorithm, which is an extension of the algorithm in Linial *et al.* (1993) to [0,1].

5.1 Spectral techniques and a prediction algorithm

This subsection is devoted to the brief explanation of (Linial *et al.* 1993). Spectral techniques are usually used in signal processing, but spectral techniques have also been developed in digital logic (Hurst *et al.* 1985). (Linial *et al.* 1993) presented a prediction algorithm using spectral techniques.

The function space is the space of multi-linear functions, whose domain is $\{0,1\}$ and whose codomain is $\mathbf{R}$. The inner product is the same as in 2.4, ignoring weight parameters. The norm is also the same as in 2.4. The orthonormal functions are as follows:

$$\chi_S(x_1, ..., x_n) = \begin{cases} +1 & \text{if } \sum_{i \in S} x_i \text{ is even,} \\ -1 & \text{if } \sum_{i \in S} x_i \text{ is odd,} \end{cases}$$

where S is the subset of variables' suffixes $\{1, ..., n\}$. Boolean functions of n variables are $f : \{0, 1\}^n \to \{-1, 1\}$.

For a given distribution D, an algorithm is called an (ϵ, δ, D) prediction algorithm if

$$\Pr_D[\hat{f} \text{ disagrees with } f \text{ on more than an } \epsilon \text{ fraction of the inputs}] \leq \delta,$$

where $\hat{f}$ stands for a prediction for f.

Theorem 17.19 (Linial *et al.* 1993) The algorithm below is an (ϵ, δ, U) algorithm for learning circuits of depth d and size

M, where U is the uniform distribution. For every fixed d, the algorithm runs in quasi-polynomial time in ϵ, δ, and M

Learning phase. The algorithm observes f on m randomly chosen, sample points $x_1, ..., x_m$, where $m = 4(2n^k/\epsilon)\log(2n^k/\delta)$ and $k = (20\log(2m/\epsilon))^d$. Its approximation for the Sth coefficient of F is

$$\alpha_S = \frac{\sum_{i=1}^m f(x_i)\chi_S(x_i)}{m}$$

For all $|S| \leq k$, and $\alpha_S = 0$, for all $|S| > k$.

Prediction phase. The predicted value of f on input x is

$$\hat{f} = \text{sign}\left(\sum_{|S|\leq k} \alpha_S\chi_S(x)\right).$$

5.2 Extension to [0,1]

First, we rewrite the orthonormal functions using an elementary algebra model (see Section 2.2). The orthonormal functions are represented as follows:

$$\chi_S = \prod_{i\in S}(1 - 2x_i)$$

The above functions are easily confirmed to be the same as defined in (Linial *et al.* 1993). These orthonormal functions can be extended to [0,1], that is, the following properties hold:

$$\langle \chi_i, \chi_j \rangle = \left\{ \begin{array}{l} 0(i \neq j), \\ 1(i = j), \end{array} \right.$$

where the inner product is as follows:

$$\langle f, g \rangle = \int_0^1 \tau(fg)dx.$$

Therefore, the prediction algorithm in Linial *et al.* (1993) is effective on [0,1], that is, the real domain. Note that, in our model, Boolean functions of n variables are $f : \{0,1\}^n \rightarrow$

$\{0,1\}$, while, in Linial *et al.* (1993), Boolean functions are $f : \{0,1\}^n \to \{-1,1\}$. Therefore some modification of weight parameters is necessary. It remains to be checked whether the prediction algorithm in Linial *et al.* (1993) is an (ϵ, δ, U) algorithm on [0,1], and this will be included in future work. Hypothesis generation using spectral techniques will also be included in future work.

6 CONCLUSIONS

This paper has presented efficient algorithms for attribute-based inductive learning. The algorithm can deal with $\{0,1\}$ attributes, multi-valued attributes, and [0,1] attributes simultaneously in the same way.

The algorithms rely on the space of multi-linear functions presented by the author. The space of multi-linear functions is a Euclidean space which includes Boolean functions. One feature of the space is that both $\{0,1\}$ attributes and [0,1] attributes can be dealt with in the same way.

Two algorithms have been presented. The first one predicts values by multiple regression analysis using a multi-linear function. Sample complexity was discussed based on the results of Linial and Haussler. The hypotheses are generated based on the approximation of the multi-linear function by a Boolean function. In general, the computational complexity is not polynomial, but it can be reduced to polynomial when the multi-linear function is linear and attributes are limited to $\{0,1\}$ or multi-valued. The other algorithm was an extension of Linial's algorithm to [0,1]. Only a prediction algorithm has been presented. Table 17.3 shows a summary.

There are several open problems to be solved.

1. The algorithm based on multiple regression analysis:
    (a) more detailed error analysis;
    (b) error analysis with [0,1] attributes;
    (c) efficient algorithms for hypothesis generation in the case of k-multi-linear functions;
    (d) efficient algorithms for hypothesis generation with [0,1] attributes.

Table 17.3. Summary.

Regression				
	functions	data	error analysis	computational complexity
Prediction	multi-linear	{0,1}, multi, [0,1]		polynomial
	multi-linear	{0,1}, multi	(Linial *et al.* 1993) (uniform distribution) (Haussler *et al.* 1992) (sample complexity: polynomial, distribution-free)	polynomial
Hypothesis	multi-linear	{0,1}, multi	pseudo maximum likelihood	exponential
	linear	{0,1}, multi	(Linial *et al.* 1993) (uniform distribution)	polynomial $(\leq k)$

Spectral				
	functions	data	error analysis	computational complexity
Prediction	multi-linear	{0,1}, multi, [0,1]		polynomial
	multi-linear	{0,1}, multi	(Linial *et al.* 1993) (sample complexity: quasi-polynomial, uniform distribution)	polynomial
Hypothesis	multi-linear			

2. The algorithm based on spectral techniques;
   (a) error analysis in the case of [0,1] attributes;
   (b) hypothesis generation.

Multi-linear functions are effective not only for inductive learning but also for other purposes such as structural analysis of neural networks, a kind of nonlinear regression analysis and so on.

REFERENCES

Blumer, A., Ehrenfeucht, A., Haussler, D. and Warmuth, M. K. (1989). Learnability and the Vapnik–Chervonenkis dimension *J. ACM*, **36**(4), 929–965.

Buntine, W. (1989). Learning classification rules using Bayes, *Proceedings of the 6th International Workshop on Machine Learning*, pp. 94–98.

Dudley, R. M. (1978). Central limit theorems for empirical measures, *Ann. Prob.*, **6** (6), 899–929.

Haussler, D. (1992). Decision theoretic generalization of the PAC Model for neural net and other learning applications , *Information and computation*, 78–150.

Hurst, S.L., Miller, D.M. and J.C. Muzio (1985). *Spectral Techniques in Digital Logic*, Academic Press, New York.

Keynes, J.M. (1921). *A Treatise on Probability*, Macmillan, London.

Linial, N., Mansour, Y. and Nisan, N. (1993). Constant depth circuits, Fourier transform, and learnability, *Journal of the ACM*, **40**(3), 607–620.

Michalski, R.S. and McCormick, B.H. (1971). Interval Generalization of Switching Theory, *Report No.442*, Dept. of Computer Science, University of Illinois, Urbana.

Quinlan, J.R. (1986). Induction of decision tree, *Machine Learning* **1**, 81–106.

Tsukimoto, H. (1990). A topological model for propositional logics, *Transactions of Information Processing Society of Japan* **31**, 783–791 (in Japanese).

Tsukimoto, H. (1994). The discovery of logical propositions in numerical data, *AAAI'94 Workshop on Knowledge Discovery in Databases*, pp.205–216.

Tsukimoto, H. and Morita, C.(1994). The discovery of propositions in noisy data, *Machine Intelligence 13*, pp.143-167, Oxford University Press, Oxford.

Wirth, J. and Catlett, J. (1988). Experiments on the costs and benefits of windowing in ID3, *Proceedings of the Fifth International Conference on Machine Learning*, pp.87–99.

INDEX

Figures are indicated by *italic page numbers*, tables by **bold page numbers**, and footnotes by suffix 'n'.